D1590632

King Arthur's Last Battle

KING ARTHUR'S LAST BATTLE

Arthur's Death in America

Robert MacCann

IMPERATOR

IMPERATOR PRESS
Sydney Australia

www.kingarthursvoyagetoamerica.com

First published in Australia in 2023.

 A catalogue record for this
book is available from the
National Library of Australia

ISBN: 978-0-9945102-5-9

Book cover map by Sarah Dunning Park.

CONTENTS

PART I   ARTHUR IN BRITAIN

1	Arthurian Texts	1
2	Gildas	23
3	Arthur	45
4	Arthur's Father	85
5	Arthur's Bard	105
6	Catastrophe in Scotland	127

PART II   THE VOYAGE AND AFTERMATH

7	Disastrous Voyage to America	141
8	The Killing of Arthur	175
9	Decline in Arthur's Kingdom	197

PART III   AMERICAN CLAIMS

10	Madoc	215
11	Inscriptions on Stone	257
12	Pre-Columbian white people in America	277
13	Irishman in West Virginia, AD 710	293
14	Ancient Roman coins in America	301
15	Arthur in America	311

Notes	327
Bibliography	353
Index	377

LIST OF FIGURES

2.1	Vortipor Stone	25
2.2	Statue of Gildas in Brittany	32
3.1	Dinarth Hillfort	52
3.2	Stone on which Huail was said to be beheaded	53
3.3	Bwrdd Arthur hillfort	54
3.4	Great and Little Ormes at the Morfa Rhianedd	55
3.5	Arthurian sites in north Wales and Galloway	61
3.6	Loch Ryan (Arthur's Rheon) in Galloway	62
3.7	Pictish Symbols at Trusty's Hill	62
4.1	People linked to Einion Yrth and Uthr	100
4.2	Arthur as Einion's Son	101
7.1	Arthur's probable route to America	158
7.2	The 'brindled ox' (buffalo)	163
7.3	Hopewell Carving of a River Otter	163
7.4	The Mound City Enclosure	167
8.1	St Edmund shot by Danes	194
8.2	Arthur shot by Native Americans	165
11.1	Inscriptions at Luther Elkins site	261
11.2	Bat Creek Stone and Macoy's Hebrew	273

1
THE ARTHURIAN TEXTS

NEW EVIDENCE FOR ARTHUR'S EXISTENCE

Did there exist a sixth-century historical King Arthur on whom the legendary accounts were based? Although answers to this question have fluctuated over the centuries, from around the 1970s the trend in academia has shifted to the negative. As the usual texts that support Arthur as a historical figure have not changed, the current academic pessimism has been a result of a more critical or sceptical appraisal of these texts. Evidence that was considered to be convincing in earlier times is now rejected as insufficient. This evidence will be critically reviewed in this chapter.

But what if new evidence became available? This book argues that important evidence for Arthur's existence and details about his life is given in three Welsh poems – *Spoils of Annwfyn*, *Battle of the Trees* and *Chair of the Sovereign*. They appear in the Book of Taliesin whose manuscript, Peniarth 2, is in the National Library of Wales and dates to the early 1300s. They are well known to specialists in the Welsh language but have rarely, if at all, been used in scholarly historical research on Arthur's life. They are introduced below and arguments are outlined which suggest that they are very early. A major problem with the poems is they were initially thought to be baffling and nearly impossible to translate. Early attempts at translations were primitive including the brave attempts of the Reverend Robert Williams which appear in Skene (1868). The mystery created by these translations was a factor in allowing the poorly-argued beliefs to take hold that Arthur and his men were mythological figures or Celtic gods or 'gods of sun and storm' (e.g. Squire, 1905; Loomis, 1927).[1]

From the 1980s, great progress has been made in translating them. In 1984 Marged Haycock and John Bollard independently published modern scholarly translations of *Spoils of Annwfyn* and Haycock later translated all three poems in her *Legendary Poems from the Book of Taliesin*. Other scholarly translations by John Koch and Sarah Higley have also shone new light on *Spoils of Annwfyn* while Patrick Ford had translated the very difficult *Battle of the Trees* in 1977. However the poems are usually classified as 'legendary' and are thought to be worthless for providing historical data. I argue here that this is a huge mistake and that the poems are sixth century, the earliest of them composed not long after Arthur's death. These poems are in the 'voice' of Arthur's bard and it is argued here that they were in fact composed by Arthur's bard. If this claim is true, then they provide priceless information on Arthur.[2]

ARTHUR'S VOYAGE TO AMERICA

An astonishing feature of these poems is that two of them mention a long sea voyage by Arthur to a place the bard calls Annwfyn. One of the poems, *Spoils of Annwfyn*, is entirely about this visit and describes the voyage as a disaster where the expedition was decimated after enduring woeful conflict. The poem builds to a climax where near the end the bard reveals that Arthur too was killed. *Battle of the Trees* has a section on Annwfyn which mentions the inhabitants gathering for battle by means of the streams which was followed by torrid fighting. The third poem, *Chair of the Sovereign*, describes the conditions in Britain after Arthur's death. It begins with a eulogy to Arthur but the distressed bard understandably does not mention Annwfyn. However the bard does mention that three stewards were appointed to mind the country in Arthur's absence which implies that Arthur was expected to be away from Britain for a considerable time. There are a number of features of the poems, discussed in Chapter 7, which strongly imply that Annwfyn was sixth-century America.

This surprising view of Arthur sailing to America and dying there is far removed from the conventional imagery of Arthur on a large horse in heavy armour hacking his way through his opponents with a huge sword, his enemies being the Saxons or Mordred's traitorous army. However much of this modern imagery is false, deriving from the *Historia Brittonum*, Geoffrey of Monmouth, the French Romances and Malory. The poetry suggests that his main enemies were the Irish and Picts. While the idea that Arthur reached America may shock readers who are conditioned with this false imagery, I am not the first to suggest it, as shown below.

The following authors either suggest or directly state that Arthur was thought to have explored overseas.

1138: Geoffrey of Monmouth's Avalon

Geoffrey's pseudo-history, *Historia Regum Britanniae* (History of the Kings of Britain), henceforth *HRB*, gave Arthur a prominent role. He did not write it *ex nihilo* but had knowledge of a wide range of sources and weaves them into a vivid story, like a historical novel, inventing scenes, dialogue and sometimes changing historical facts to improve his story. He also wrote a poem *Vita Merlini* (Life of Merlin) which extended his *HRB* account of the death of Arthur.[3]

When it came to Arthur's death Geoffrey was faced with a problem. He knew two versions, at vastly different locations. One was from the *Welsh Annals*, AD 537, which states that Arthur and Medrawd were killed in the battle of Camlan. Camlan was naturally thought to be in Britain and he located it at the River Camblam (River Camel) in Cornwall. Another suggested site is Camboglanna, a fort on Hadrian's Wall. There are also several Camlan names in the River Dyfi valley. Camlan means 'crooked river bank' or 'crooked enclosure', with the former being more plausible for a battle site. Geoffrey should have ended Arthur's life at Camlan, as in the *Welsh Annals*.[4]

The second location was at a distant undiscovered land overseas. Geoffrey coined the name 'Avalon' for this new land, from the Welsh *afal* (apple). He was thus linking it to the Promised Land of the Saints, visited by St Brendan in his *Navigatio*, where there was not a tree without fruit. Several scholars have identified it with America.[5]

To his credit, Geoffrey did not ignore this second extraordinary option but combined the two to create a clumsy hybrid. Thus he wrote that Arthur was only wounded at Camlan. He was then taken to his ship for a long voyage to Avalon for his wounds to be healed, which required a navigator 'to whom the seas and the stars of heaven were well known' (Parry, 1925). Geoffrey made Barinthus the navigator of Arthur's ship as Barinthus had sailed to the Promised Land of the Saints before Brendan and had told Brendan about it. Thus in 1138, over 350 years before America was discovered, Geoffrey thought that Arthur had sailed to the same place as Brendan.[6]

1191 Gerald of Wales

Gerald of Wales in *Education of a Prince* refers to the bogus discovery of Arthur's grave at Glastonbury in 1191. Although a grave was dug up, the contents were faked by the monks to draw attention to their holy place, so that funds could be raised to rebuild. However Gerald did not know this, believing the grave was authentic and he comments on the disparity between this find and the Arthurian legends known to the public (Thorpe, 1978).

> In our own lifetime Arthur's body was discovered at Glastonbury, although legends had always encouraged us to believe that there was something otherworldly about his ending, that he had resisted death and had been spirited away to some far-distant spot.

Gerald was a harsh critic of Geoffrey's work and told an amusing story of how demons were attracted to the *HRB* book when it was placed on the bosom of the prophet, Meilyr. His reference to legends would not have been based on Geoffrey's unreliable work.[7]

1569 Mercator's wall map

Mercator was one of the leading intellectuals of Europe and in 1569 succeeded in projecting a map of the world onto a flat surface in such a way as to be valuable to sailors. This projection was untenable at the poles, so he created a circular inset of the lands around the North Pole. Attached to this inset he added a box of Latin text stating that King Arthur of Britain had sent his people to inhabit these northern lands. He had obtained this detail from Jacob Cnoyen, from Holland, who was said to have explored the northern regions (Taylor, 1956).[8]

1578 John Dee's case to Queen Elizabeth

Dee was a brilliant scholar who excelled in numerous fields, especially mathematics, navigation and astronomy. When he gave his lectures in Paris on Euclid's geometry, it caused a sensation. His own natural philosophy set down in *Propaedeumata* in several ways anticipates Newton's *Principia Mathematica* by over a century (Woolley, 2001). He also thought that in a vacuum all bodies would fall with the same acceleration, a scientific law later studied by Galileo and attributed to him. In Dee's time, mathematics was often viewed suspiciously – he was once charged with 'calculating', 'conjuring' and 'witchcraft' after drawing up a horoscope for Queen Mary. He sought knowledge in all areas and to him the occult was another way to understand the mind of God, not clearly delineated from science as it is today.[9]

On becoming aware of the circular inset in Mercator's wall map, Dee asked him for his source and received a long letter giving Cnoyen's account which contained excerpts from the *Gestae Arthuri* (Deeds of Arthur), a work that is now lost. This outlined two voyages of Arthur into the northwest Atlantic via Iceland to a place called Grocland. This is shown as an island near the position of Baffin Island, Canada in the maps of Mercator, Ortelius and in Dee's 1580 map.

Dee also obtained a long list of Scandinavian lands said to be under Arthur's control which appears in a number of sources. As discussed in Chapter 7, this lands list is associated with a political text that was written in the reign of William I, probably circa 1070-75. In order for this political text to have credibility, it would require a widespread public belief well before this that Arthur had at least explored the north in order to justify the northern lands being under his control. Although Geoffrey of Monmouth includes six northern conquests of Arthur in his *HRB*, it is argued later that he obtained all except one of these from the earlier Scandinavian lands list. From these details, and other European legends, Dee argued that Arthur had sailed to north America and in August 1578 presented this case to Queen Elizabeth I (MacMillan, 2004). Dee appears to have made this deduction without any knowledge of *Spoils of Annwfyn*.[10]

Further support for Arthur's northern forays appears in the Welsh tale, *Culhwch and Olwen*, which states that Arthur had taken twelve hostages from *Llychlyn* (Norway). Dating estimates for this tale have a wide variance but it shows no influence from Geoffrey and contains archaic language much older than the Mabinogi stories.

It is possible that the ultimate source underlying the above beliefs that Arthur sailed to a distant land is *Spoils of Annwfyn*. Yet none of these secondary sources mention it. Geoffrey would hardly acknowledge sources as he wanted to present the definitive history. His claim that he didn't write it himself but merely translated an old Welsh history into Latin is not credible. He is often indifferent to historical accuracy. For example, he uses Gildas' history but selects four of the five kings that reign simultaneously and makes them reign successively, ending with Maglocunus. It takes chutzpah to mangle a crucial historical text like this and pretend that he is just translating an old book.

THE TRADITIONAL ARTHURIAN EVIDENCE

There are a small number of Arthurian texts that are generally used in researching the historical Arthur. These have been thoroughly studied and the current consensus is that they do not provide enough evidence to justify a historical Arthur. Charles-Edwards (1991) sums up: 'there may well have been an historical Arthur ... the historian can as yet say nothing of value about him'. When the new poetic evidence is used it will be shown that a good deal may be said about Arthur.[11]

Y Gododdin (The Gododdin), AD 550

It is argued in Chapter 3 that the excessive pessimism about this text is misplaced, it being valuable early evidence for Arthur. It comprises a series of poetic stanzas on the heroism of about 300 Gododdin men who left their stronghold in Edinburgh to fight the Angles at Catraeth, probably modern Catterick. Most of the stanzas concern this, but some refer to other locations, and others are obvious late additions. The Gododdin were a British tribe whose large territory ranged from about the River Tees northward to Edinburgh.

Although they were decisively defeated at Catraeth, the stanzas commemorate them. Many of the stanzas were probably composed in Edinburgh not long after the battle, about AD 550. One of the stanzas lavishly praises a hero, Gorddur, but despite his valour in battle it notes in a negative aside 'though he was not Arthur'. If this reference was part of the original stanza and the stanza dated to about AD 550, then it would be strong evidence for Arthur's existence and that he was viewed as a great warrior at that early date. However some scholars have challenged the very early dating of this stanza, and whether the Arthurian clause was actually in the original stanza, or was instead a late interpolation; e.g. Jarman (1988).[12]

In Chapter 3 it is argued that this stanza was early (perhaps about 550) and that a late interpolation was unlikely. The Gorddur stanza is compared with a second stanza that contains similar poetic features, including another negative aside, which suggests that both stanzas were composed by the same poet. The second stanza is then analyzed for its historical content which shows that it had to be composed at an early date, before the *obsesio Etin* of AD 638 in the Annals of Ulster. This records the siege of Edinburgh which soon after fell to the Angles. If the same poet composed both stanzas then the Arthurian stanza also must have been composed around this early date.

Marwnad Cynddylan (Deathsong of Cynddylan)

Arthur also appears in an elegy for the British leader, Cynddylan. He was allied with Penda the king of Mercia, a Saxon kingdom in central England. In 655 Penda, and probably Cynddylan, were killed by Oswiu of Northumbria in the battle of Winwaed. Jenny Rowland (1990) argues that this elegy relates to Cynddylan's death in the battle.[13]

In line 45, the poet refers to the British warriors as his brothers-in-arms. In line 46, they are called whelps (*canawon*) of Arthur, his descendants in that they were equally valorous, e.g. Koch, 2006:

> 46 *canawon artir wras, dinas degyn*
> the whelps of great Arthur, the mighty citadel

The word *artir* is taken by most experts to be *artur*, allowing the line to make sense but Rowland emends *artir wras* to *arddyrnfras* giving 'strong-handed' whelps, a major change. This is unlikely. The 'whelps' then don't have a heroic ancestor named in the poem, whereas Arthur is a natural fit for this role. It also creates a puzzle as to how men who were badly defeated could be described as 'the mighty citadel' or in her more general rendering, 'a resolute protection'.[14]

The earliest manuscript dates to 1631-34, but Bromwich (1975-6) maintains that it is an authentic 600s poem similar in phraseology, metre and style to *Y Gododdin*. It was possibly composed soon after the battle, probably in what is now Shropshire (Green, 2007). If this c. 655 date is correct, it would have been about 118 years after the death of Arthur, when he was viewed as a warrior hero of the past, but before the fables about him had developed.[15]

This mention is similar to the *Y Gododdin* stanza but no one has argued it is an interpolation. In both, Arthur was not at the battle but served as the epitome of heroism. Both are mere mentions, comparing fallen warriors in the eulogies with the heroism of Arthur and his men. They are valuable evidence for Arthur's historicity.

Geraint son of Erbin Poem

A third reference to Arthur appears in an elegy to Geraint the son of Erbin (*Gereint fab Erbin*). The poem is in the Red Book of Hergest, the Black Book of Carmarthen and in a fragment from the White Book of Rhydderch, but with differing stanzas and stanza orders. Rowland (1990) gives a composite reconstruction, based on the fuller Red Book order and she notes the variants from the other texts. Stanza 15 of the Red Book refers to Arthur as follows.

> In Llongborth were slain to Arthur
> brave men who hewed with steel
> emperor, director of the toil (of battle).

This stanza has Arthur's brave men being slain, as Arthur directs the battle. As the battle leader of combined armies, he is called 'emperor'. However Stanza 8 of the Black Book version differs in the first line where the poet 'saw (belonging) to Arthur' brave men who hewed with steel, a quite different meaning. Sims-Williams (1991) argues that the Red Book version where Arthur's brave men were being slain is the more probable. It agrees with the Geraint stanza where his brave men were also being slain. This poem is different from the others as Arthur is portrayed as fighting in a battle rather than being a heroic exemplar from the past. Both Arthur's army and Geraint's were taking heavy losses, which is not the usual view of Arthur's invincibility.[16]

Llongborth means 'ship harbour' or 'sea port' indicating that the battle was near the coast. An interesting suggestion that associates the names Geraint, Llongborth, and a real battle site is the harbour at Penbryn Beach in Ceredigion, in the west of Wales. Bartrum (2009) refers to the belief of Theophilus Evans in 1740 that Llongborth was Llanborth in the parish of Penbryn. Over the centuries, the 'Llong' part of Llongborth may have been displaced by 'Llan' (village). Evans refers to a battle site there whose old name meant 'Field of the Killing' or 'Field of Massacre'. A few miles inland from the beach is a site called *Bedd Geraint* – the grave of Geraint. This location suggests that the enemy was probably the Irish.[17]

The poet calls Arthur *amherawdyr* or *ameraudur* (emperor) in the Red and Black Book versions, consistent with its use by Adomnán in his *Life of Columba,* written in the late 690s. Adomnán calls Oswald *imperator* (emperor) after he defeated the British king, Cadwallon (Sharpe, 1995). Rowland (1990) dates the poem from about 850 to the late 800s but Koch (1994) suggests it could have its beginnings in the 700s. The unusual emphasis on the slaying of Arthur's men could also suggest a 700s dating, a time before Arthur was portrayed as virtually invincible in the *Historia Brittonum*. This reference to Arthur is less valuable than *Y Gododdin* and *Marwnad Cynddylan* as it is further away from Arthur's time, perhaps 200 years, but is valuable in that Arthur has not yet accrued any legendary features, with his men being slain in what appears to have been a bloody battle.[18]

Four Men named after Arthur (about 560-610)
In the approximate period AD 560-610, four men were born who were named 'Arthur', a name that was earlier 'practically unknown' according to Chadwick and Chadwick (1932). This sudden cluster of naming men 'Arthur' in a short time period is difficult to account for unless there was a hero of this name who had lived earlier in the late fifth century or sixth century. About two decades after Arthur's death (in 537), the first man named after Arthur was born around 560, Artur the son of Aedán of Dalriada. The others were Artuir the son of Bicoir, Artur the grandfather of Feradach and Arthur the son of Petr. Three of them were linked to southwest Scotland and the son of Petr had an Irish pedigree. These namings and the Arthur stanza in *Y Gododdin* imply that Arthur had made a huge impression in the north.[19]

Historia Brittonum (History of the Britons), 829-30
The *Historia* is a Latin work compiled in AD 829-830 from earlier sources. There are eight recensions, each one comprising a family of related manuscripts. The most complete recension is the Harleian of

which the main manuscript is Harley MS 3859, held in the British Library. In the first half of the 20th century it was used as a prime source for historical research on early medieval British history but it is now viewed sceptically after the work of David Dumville (1972-4a; 1972-4b; 1975-6; 1976-7; 1977; 1986; 1994) and his progressive editing of the *Historia* recensions. It seems to be a disjointed patchwork of material assembled from disparate sources but he describes it as a synchronizing history, a type of work where the author attempts to combine all the material (no matter how contradictory) into a slick and coherent whole. He also argues that it was written in a uniform latinity and that it is of little historical value for events from the fifth to the seventh centuries. Wendy Davies (1982) views it differently as 'an ill-synthesized and ill-digested work' and concludes that it is not possible to generalize about its value. It must be used with caution but it may contain items of useful information which should be related to other material, if possible, to assess their validity.[20]

It lists twelve Arthurian battles, including Badon. Most scholars agree that the battle names derive from a Welsh battle-list poem but the validity of this poem is disputed. John Lloyd (1911) thinks that the terrible British defeat at Chester in 615 was used for the location of Arthur's Chester battle and that Arthur's other battle locations were taken from various battles fought by others and then credited to him. Rachel Bromwich (1975-6) also thinks that Arthur's battle list was based on other famous battles. If this is true, it suggests the poem was composed late, beyond the memories of Arthur's people and that the poet was probably not from north Wales. Peter Field (2008) disagrees with Lloyd and Bromwich and exposes the weaknesses in their case. However although their evidence is weak, the inclusion of battles that Arthur did not fight could be true in some cases.[21]

Welsh Annals, about AD 950

Arthur also receives two mentions in the *Welsh Annals*. The first entry for the year AD 516 refers to his victory at Badon Hill:[22]

> Battle of Badon in which Arthur carried the cross of Our Lord Jesus Christ *on his shoulders* for three days and three nights and the Britons were victors.

This Badon entry shares an unusual feature concerning 'shoulders' with Arthur's *Historia Brittonum* battle at Guinnion which suggests the Annals Badon entry was not independent of the *Historia*:[23]

> The eighth battle was on the castle Guinnion, wherein Arthur bore the image of St Mary, the ever-virgin *upon his shoulders*, and the pagans were turned to flight on that day, and there was a great slaughter of them by virtue of our Lord Jesus Christ and by virtue of St Mary the Virgin his mother.

It is doubtful that Arthur carried items on his shoulders into battle, in one case a cross and the other, an image of Mary. Stephens (1849) suggests that *scuid* (shoulder) became confused with *scuit* (shield). As the entries share this confusion it suggests they are not independent. The Annals entry was probably influenced by the battle-list poem as the *Historia* has a battle at *Tribruit* (rhyming with *scuit*) suggesting that it referred to a shield. Perhaps Arthur bore a cross on his shield at Guinnion in the original poem but this was misread by a scribe as carrying a cross on his shoulders. The author of the Annals entry may have seen this variation of the battle-list poem and it influenced his wording of the Badon entry. He possibly also knew the story of Oswald setting up a cross on the battle field in his victory over Cadwallon. The final *Historia* version may be due to a monk changing carrying the cross to carrying an image of the Virgin Mary.[24]

The second Annals entry for AD 537 refers to Arthur's death at the battle of Camlan:[25]

> The strife of Camlan in which Arthur and Medraut perished. And there was plague in Britain and Ireland.

It is argued from the Camlan meaning of 'crooked river bank' that the battle took place near a river in America. In contrast to popular belief, the bards portray Medrawd as good natured: Meilyr Brydydd and Gwalchmai ap Meilyr praise their kings lavishly: they have the 'nature of Medrawd' and 'Arthur's strength, the good nature of Medrawd' (Lloyd, 2017). The mystery of his role may never be resolved. Perhaps an affair with Gwenhwyfar began after Arthur sailed to Annwfyn and the tradition of this affair became attached to Camlan, centuries later, where it was naturally thought that they fought each other. The c. 950 Annals entry containing Medrawd may simply be based on this belief. Geoffrey of Monmouth placed the affair when Arthur was overseas. While the tradition of his Camlan death is strong, the late material stating the affair was the cause of the battle is hardly plausible and the bards high praise of Medrawd throws doubt on the annal entry.[26]

Assessment of the Traditional Evidence

This evidence suggests a historical Arthur, renowned for his prowess in battle, whose fame had spread widely across Britain. If an early reference to him in *Y Gododdin* is correct he was seen as the epitome of valour just a few decades after his death. The *Marwnad Cynddylan* poem and the naming of men 'Arthur' in a short interval, after the name had been almost unknown, also indicates his huge impact. But some traditional details are insecure or wrong. The *Annals* Badon entry was probably influenced by a version of the battle-list poem and was written centuries after the battle. Its battle date of AD 516 is also wrong, as argued in Chapter 2. The Camlan entry also seems to have been influenced by late legendary material on Medrawd.

It will be argued later that the poem underlying the *Historia* battle list was not composed by Arthur's bard but by a later poet. This greatly weakens the authority of the list although some of the locations given in the list are quite plausible, in particular the four battles in Lindsey and the battle at Chester.

A key text not discussed until Chapter 2 is *De Excidio Britanniae* (On the Ruin of Britain) by Gildas, a British cleric. It is often said that Gildas did not mention Arthur but it is argued here that he was the 'Bear' of *Dineirth* and the Pharaoh in the *De Excidio*, an overking above the five kings berated by Gildas. This would locate Arthur in north Wales, a location that is supported by the Welsh texts.

THE THREE CRUCIAL WELSH POEMS

The three important Welsh poems are now introduced, outlining their content and reasons for believing that they are genuine sixth-century poems. The historical poet Taliesin did not compose them as his style was quite different. Their authorship is discussed in Chapter 5.

Spoils of Annwfyn (*Preideu Annwfyn*)

The poem's Welsh title is pronounced *Pry-thee Ahn-oo-vin* where 'd' functions as the Welsh 'dd' with the 'th' sound. The 'w' is here a vowel, like the 'oo' sound in 'soon', and the 'f' is pronounced like English 'v'. It relates a disastrous voyage by Arthur to a land called Annwfyn. They entered by a 'strong door' river and made their way inland. Annwfyn is often equated with an imaginary Welsh/Irish Otherworld which is reached by sea voyages in the early tales. It is not a place souls go after death but a paradise which living people can visit (Loomis, 1956). In contrast to Arthur's ordeal, the Otherworld in the *Voyage of Bran son of Febal* and *Connlae's Adventure* is a place where the people live in harmony with no death, decay or sin. However in *Spoils of Annwfyn* the voyage is a catastrophe described as a 'woeful conflict'. The bard mournfully remarks at the end of each of the first six stanzas that only a small number of Britons survived. It is possible that darker versions of the Otherworld such as *Dún Scáith* ('fortress of shadow') emerged from a knowledge of *Spoils of Annwfyn*. From the features identified in the poem it is evident that Annwfyn was sixth-century America. The content also indicates that Arthur was killed there and his body and grave were lost – he was unable to be brought back to Britain.[27]

Battle of the Trees (*Kat Godeu*)

This is a long difficult poem where many lines are opaque. The poet laments that he is now an old man but was once a warrior-bard and had sung his poems before the 'Lord of Britain'. The latter is Arthur, who is referred to by name later in the poem. Despite its difficulty, it has a valuable 16-line section on Annwfyn which mentions torrid fighting and the death of a lord in a concealed place. The poet calls him the 'boar'. Fierce animals were often used as epithets for warriors. As Annwfyn is uniquely associated with Arthur and his men, it is argued that the lord is Arthur and the bard is describing his death. This poem is closely linked to *Spoils of Annwfyn*, but the two poems are very different. *Spoils of Annwfyn* is a masterpiece, having complex lines with clever internal rhyme, which skilfully creates an atmosphere of dread. *Battle of the Trees* has much shorter lines with disparate sections that reflect a loss of skill due to the bard's old age.

Chair of the Sovereign (*Kadeir Teÿrnon*)

This poem is set in Britain after Arthur's death in Annwfyn. It refers to a ceremony for Arthur where he is blessed by a wise man and presumably where prayers were said for his soul. The tribute gives important details about Arthur. He is brave, authoritative and wise. Several lines mention his military prowess, in one of which he is surprisingly likened to Aladur, an obscure Celtic god who was equated with Mars (the Roman god of war) by the romanized Britons. Despite his warlike nature, a line states that he respected the scriptures, which is consistent with the later sources that he was a Christian king. The 'Chair' (*kadeir*) in the title is Arthur's throne and the theme of the poem is that Arthur has been killed and now the throne is vacant. This poem gives his location in Britain, the great esteem his men held for him, a northern region where he restored order, and contemporary detail on the troubles in Britain after his death.

The language of the Britons in Arthur's youth was *British*, a language similar to Latin. By the very early 6th century the language had lost its final syllables, case endings and medial vowels and had evolved into *Brittonic*, which eventually evolved into Old Welsh. Could the three poems have been composed in the 6th century? While there is no easy answer to this question there are indications that it was possible. Koch (2006) states that a language similar enough to Welsh existed in the 6th century to enable poetry composed then to survive the language modernization into Old and Middle Welsh.[28] The evidence for the antiquity of the poems derives from three classes of argument:

1. the remnants of archaic language in the poems,
2. content in other better-dated ancient texts derives from content in the three Welsh poems, showing that the latter were earlier,
3. the content coherently fits the historical situation.

None of these arguments are conclusive when critiqued individually but the case becomes stronger when they are considered as a whole. Oddly enough it is *Spoils of Annwfyn*, the poem thought to describe a visit to the Celtic Otherworld, for which the evidence is the strongest. Space only allows for a brief discussion here.

SPOILS OF ANNWFYN: SIGNS OF AN EARLY DATE

Archaic Language Remnants

Koch (1985-6; 1988; 1996; 2006) draws attention to archaic language remnants in *Spoils of Annwfyn*. He notes three instances of archaic third person plural deponent verbs, which were inherited from the early Proto-Celtic. One of these verbs written *glywanawr* needs an 'or' ending to rhyme with the following lines and this 'or' ending occurred in older forms of the verb. Koch concludes from this that an earlier manuscript of the poem was written in the 700s.[29]

Early works that copied Spoils of Annwfyn

This poem has content that has been copied and elaborated, or copied and misunderstood, in other early texts. One instance that supports Koch's conclusion is the 'iceberg' incident in the *Historia Brittonum* where Irish sailors observe a 'glass tower in the middle of the sea' (*turrim vitream in medio mari*). They see people standing on the glass tower and question them but can get no reply, an incident so inane that it suggests it was misunderstood from another source.

It was indeed copied from *Spoils of Annwfyn* where Arthur's men met the Annwfyn people, who were standing on a wall, but could not understand them as the languages were different. In the previous line the poem relates that they had earlier sailed past a 'glass fortress', a metaphor for a large iceberg. In the *Navigatio* of Brendan, an iceberg is called a 'crystal pillar' in the sea. Jackson (1959b), Sims-Williams (1991) and Haycock (2007) all note the close relationship between the *Historia* tale and the above events in lines 30-32 of *Spoils of Annwfyn*. The *Historia* story was probably in a written form in the 700s and was compiled into the *Historia* in 829-30.[30]

A similar incident occurs in the *Voyage of Bran* where Bran's crew approach an Otherworld island where the people do not answer them, not because the two groups have different languages but as a 'magical' property of the island itself. When one of the crew goes onto the island he becomes like this himself, being then unable to communicate with his shipmates. This poem is dated from the 600s (Meyer, 1895; Thrall, 1917; Carney, 1976) to a date range of late 600s-early 700s (Carney, 1983; Mac Mathúna, 1985; McCone, 2000).[31]

A second link with *Voyage of Bran* is the four *banneu* (peaks) from *Spoils of Annwfyn* which have a natural explanation as four geological peaks near the Britons' camp. In *Bran* the peaks are elaborated – they are four pillars of white bronze on which the Otherworld island sits, like stilts, holding up the island above the sea: 'four pillars uphold it'; 'Pillars of white bronze under it'. This imagery is also in the late poem *I Petition God* where Haycock (2007) translates *banneu* as 'turrets' in 'around its turrets are the wellsprings of the sea'. *Spoils of Annwfyn* is again being copied and elaborated in *Bran*.[32]

Another link is in *Connlae's Adventure*, a very early Irish work. The 'glass fortress' in *Spoils of Annwfyn* inspired later authors to include glass objects in the Otherworld. In Connlae's case, he left with the fairy woman in a glass boat. In *Voyage of Mael Duin* (800s) an island has a glass bridge. While the 'glass fortress' is a metaphor about a natural object (iceberg), the glass boat and glass bridge are not.[33]

Mael Duin also has a 'revolving fort' which was derived (wrongly) from line 12 in *Spoils of Annwfyn* at some point in the distant past. Instead of an absurd 'turning fort', it is the bard who is turning to view the four peaks. It also borrows 'door of Hell's gate' from line 20 and creates an island with a fiery, revolving rampart containing a door, the fiery nature representing the flames of Hell. The Irish work *Bricriu's Feast* (700s) also employs the revolving fort.[34]

Spoils of Annwfyn is also linked to the *Dún Scáith* stanzas in the *Phantom Chariot of Cú Chulainn* while three stanzas are in the *Tragic Death of Cú Roí*. Sims-Williams (1982) dates *Cú Roí* to the 700s, as do Cross and Slover (1936). It seems to copy 'the strong door' from *Spoils of Annwfyn* where the 'door' is the river entry point to Annwfyn and the 'strong' refers to the currents. This 'door' is misunderstood in *Dún Scáith* where Cú Chulainn sails to an Otherworld island fort that literally had strong doors, being made of iron.[35]

Dún Scáith also copies the 'gate of Hell' from *Spoils of Annwfyn*, a metaphor for the disasters of Annwfyn. But the Irish poem treats the fort literally as Hell, a place of shadow (*scáith*) with a pit like the biblical Hell (Revelations 9: 2-10) from which serpents emerge to attack the hero. The above copyings and elaborations from *Spoils of Annwfyn* suggest that it was composed in the 600s or earlier.[36]

The poem reflects the historical situation

Spoils of Annwfyn is consistent with the content of the *De Excidio* and was composed shortly after it. Gildas mentions a north Wales hillfort, translating its name *Dineirth* as *receptaculum ursi*, in English, the 'Bear's fort'. In Modern Welsh it became Dinarth. It is very unlikely that animal bears were there when Einion Yrth subdued north Wales. Even if they were, the bears would have been removed as it was highly valuable because of its defensive advantages and elevated location. In the Brittonic language *arth* means 'bear'. It is argued here that Arthur took over the fort when Maglocunus resigned the throne and that the fort then became informally known as the Bear's fort. Arthur's military strength and leadership eventually gained him the support of the five kings. He was the Pharaoh noted in the *De Excidio*.[37]

Spoils of Annwfyn places Arthur in north Wales. His bard refers to the *Devwy* meadows (from *Deva*) the meadows along the Dee, which runs through Chester. The *Chair of the Sovereign* refers to Arthur wearing the lorica of Lleon (i.e. Chester). Arthur also had a mistress, Garwen, who was buried on the *morfa rhianedd*, the long beach at Llandudno not far from *Dineirth*. Garwen's father, Hennin Henben, was buried at Dinorben, a hillfort a few miles to the east.[38]

The content of *Spoils of Annwfyn* indicates that it was composed not long after the *De Excidio*. Gildas expected an angry reaction and so wrote it anonymously. Yet no such response is noted in the usual sources as they were far too late. But *Spoils of Annwfyn* does reply to the *De Excidio* where Arthur's bard savagely attacks the monks in the last five of the eight stanzas. This suggests it was composed at the time the *De Excidio* was being heatedly discussed, about AD 540.[39]

BATTLE OF THE TREES: SIGNS OF AN EARLY DATE
Archaic Language Remnants

John Koch (1991) gives an important example of archaic language in *Battle of the Trees* and it is interesting that it appears in the Annwfyn section in lines 201-2: *Ef gwrith, ef datwrith, ef gwrith ieithoed*. 'He (God) made, He remade, He made peoples (again)'. *Gwrith* is archaic, being derived from the inferred word in Brittonic, *wrichto-. It also appears in lines 4 and 146 of the poem.[40]

Further, Marged Haycock (2007) refers to the very high frequency of archaic absolute verbal forms in the poem – *eithyt, gwneithyt, seinyssit, gwiscyssit, bernissit, ffynyessit, glessyssit* and *gorthoryssit* which appear in the battle of the treetops section in lines 83, 85, 91, 93, 106, 111, 112 and 117 respectively. In Haycock (1990), she earlier remarked on the archaic syntax, the 'subject+verb' word order: e.g. *ffuonwyd eithyt* (line 83), *auanwyd gwneithyt* (line 85) and *onn goreu ardyrched* (line 100), rarely used elsewhere.[41]

An Early Work that copied from Battle of the Trees

An event in *Battle of the Trees* was copied and misunderstood in *Dún Scáith*. It concerns a battle between a dragon and an army of trees that is called the 'battle of the treetops' within the Welsh poem. It is argued in Chapter 6 that while the event is presented as a fantasy, with many humorous touches involving the small plants in the battle, it was based on a terrifying real event decades earlier which the bard thought was a forerunner to Judgement Day. It involved a heavy bombardment from cometary debris that produced massive bloodshed.

The dragon is described just before the battle in lines 30-40, in similar terms to the earlier accounts of Typhon in Hesiod's *Theogony* and the *Dionysiaca* of Nonnos of Panopolis. Both accounts describe Typhon's battles with Zeus. Typhon the beast is a complex mixture of fearsome creatures. Both accounts use 'dragon' to describe aspects of him and both give him 100 heads. Nonnos elaborates on the earlier account of Hesiod, giving Typhon a tangled army of snakes, a battalion of hands, 'snaky throats' that spat poison, many necks, legions of arms, and bristles on his head that emitted poison. His serpents were described as 'speckled'. Hesiod implies snakes without stating it explicitly by describing Typhon's 'flickering dusky tongues'. Although the beast was complex, and varied with the imagination of the author, it was regarded as a single entity.[42]

The dragon in *Battle of the Trees* shared many of these features. He was huge, scaly, and had 100 heads. He had a battalion under the root of each tongue and battalions in the napes of his necks. He was like a black forked toad and a speckled crested snake. Sinful human souls were being tormented in his skin. It is clear that the bard was describing a single entity but the author of *Dún Scáith* misunderstood this and mistook new features of the beast as separate creatures. He thought the beast was a dragon, but was accompanied by a toad and a snake. He was taking this from *Battle of the Trees* as neither Hesiod nor Nonnos give any descriptors of a toad. The bard states that he pierced a great scaly beast (line 30), but doesn't say that he pierced a great scaly beast, and a toad, and a snake.[43]

In *Dún Scáith* Cú Chulainn vanquished three waves of attackers. He first was attacked by snakes and, after destroying them, was then attacked by toads and fought them off. Finally he was attacked by dragon-like monsters and killed them. It is hard to believe the bard of *Battle of the Trees* was constructing a story in which the trees were attacked by snakes, then toads and then a dragon. It is clear that the author of *Dún Scáith* was familiar with the earlier *Battle of the Trees* and misunderstood it or created a variation based on it.[44]

The archaic language and the evidence that the very early *Dún Scáith* copied from *Battle of the Trees* suggests the latter could date to the 600s or earlier. There are also features shared by *Battle of the Trees* and *Spoils of Annwfyn* suggesting a common bard.

CHAIR OF THE SOVEREIGN: SIGNS OF AN EARLY DATE
Archaic Language Remnants

This work has an archaic language feature identified by Koch (1985-6; 1997), the Brittonic word *rechtur*, which occurs in a rhyming sequence that includes the words *rechtur* (line 6), *rwyfyadur* (line 7) and *uur* (line 10). The semi-Latin word *rechtur* is the equivalent of the Latin word *rector* for 'governor' and refers to Arthur's maintaining order over southwest Scotland. Surprisingly, these same three words appear together in the same order in *Y Gododdin* stanza B2.36, on the hero Tudfwlch, and also in an equivalent line in stanza B1.14. Koch (1997) regards *rechtur* as a valid sixth-century Brittonic word, the Britons' language at the time of Arthur. He classifies the Tudfwlch stanza as archaic, before the fall of Edinburgh in AD 638.[45]

My view is that *Chair of the Sovereign* and many of the *Y Gododdin* stanzas are sixth-century but the repetition of the three words in two different works suggests they were useful as rhyming words and hence their use in poetry may have continued well after the sixth century. Thus the appearance of *rechtur* in *Chair of the Sovereign* by itself is not sufficient to show that the poem was early.

Close relationships to the other two poems

Despite the above, *Chair of the Sovereign* has strong links to the other poems suggesting that it was also a sixth-century poem. Compare it with *Spoils of Annwfyn*, which puts Arthur in north Wales by naming the River Dee as part of his domain. *Chair of the Sovereign* also places Arthur in north Wales but does not do this through copying. When mourning Arthur's death it states that he wore the lorica (breastplate) of Lleon, which refers to *Caer Lleon* (Chester) or northeast Wales in general. It also describes Arthur's death with the same expression *diua* ('annihilation') as *Spoils of Annwfyn*.

It also shares the unusual mix of Christian beliefs and the gaining of poetic inspiration from the cauldron. While it does not mention Annwfyn explicitly, it does say that stewards were appointed to mind the country, implying that Arthur was away from Britain. It also shares the trademark use of questions in the poem and the use of the number 3 and its multiples.

Chair of the Sovereign also has strong links to *Battle of the Trees*. Both poems refer to Arthur as being in the Galloway region of south Scotland. In *Battle of the Trees* Arthur is at the fort *Caer Nefenhyr* in the territory of the ancient Novantae tribe. *Chair of the Sovereign* does not copy this but gives the place as *Rheon*, the area around Loch Ryan. Both places are highly valued in Welsh tradition – *Nefenhyr* is mentioned by Arthur's gatekeeper in *Culhwch and Olwen* and *Pen Rhionydd* (Rheon) is given as Arthur's northern court in the very first Welsh Triad.

A second commonality is the bard's unusual integration of beliefs, both in Christianity and the transmigration of the soul. In *Battle of the Trees* he relates an appeal to God to save the Britons and claims that Christ's crucifixion was one of the three greatest cataclysms in the history of the world. His belief in transmigration is shown throughout the poem. In *Chair of the Sovereign* he shows his Christian beliefs in his approval of Arthur's reverence for scripture and in his praise for the 'True One' (God) and God's pronouncements. His belief in the transmigration of the soul is shown in lines 37-8 where he refers to a previous incarnation as a nobleman.

It may be useful to revisit the above dating discussion after becoming familiar with material presented later in the book. Another coverage of arguments for an early dating of the poems is given in MacCann (2016). In the chapters to come the traditional material is combined with data from the three Welsh poems, the *Welsh Triads, Stanzas of the Graves* and other Welsh sources to give a more complete picture of Arthur's life and his disastrous expedition to America.[46]

First, however, the important historical text of Gildas will be discussed. Although he wrote more of a complaint than a history, his work has a historical section which is more accurate for the years of his own lifetime but is vague and of uncertain validity for much of the fifth-century. His vivid account of the lives of five contemporary kings is riveting and conveys a rare and authentic picture of what life was like in early sixth-century Britain. This was the time of Arthur.

2
GILDAS

THE RUIN OF BRITAIN

In about AD 537, a British cleric named Gildas wrote an inflammatory 'history' that criticized the kings, their bards, the military and clergy of Britain. In the *De Excidio Britanniae* he paints a vivid picture of southwest Britain just after the time of Arthur. He excoriates five kings about whom he was very well informed, revealing their murders, their plundering, and their sordid sex lives. In 731 when the Saxon priest, Bede, published his *Ecclesiastical History* he was able to use Gildas' work to justify the Saxon takeover of Britain. 'Saxon' is here used in a general sense to include the Saxons, Angles and Jutes.

Gildas outlines the events up to the Britons' current state. After the Romans left in 410 the Irish and Picts renewed their raids, prompting the king, Vortigern, to hire Saxon warriors to fight them. After some time, the Saxons rebelled against the Britons and took control of large parts of eastern Britain. Under Ambrosius, the Britons won an initial victory over the Saxons but after that the battle results were mixed. Finally a British victory at Badon Hill brought peace in the west up to the time of writing, but internal fighting among the Britons was rife. Arthur, an older contemporary of Gildas, is the Badon commander in later sources. I argue here that he was the overking that Gildas refers to as *Pharaoh* (using a biblical metaphor), the five kings being part of his retinue. Gildas' criticisms of these kings are given below.

Constantine

Gildas calls him the 'tyrant whelp of the filthy lioness of Damnonia'. By 'Damnonia', Gildas is making a pun on Dumnonia, the peninsula comprising modern Devon and Cornwall. The 'filthy lioness' probably means his mother. Constantine had made an oath that he would not harm his people, however at the holy altar of a church he ambushed two unsuspecting young princes. Dressed in the habit of a holy abbot, he tore at their sides with sword and spear, killing them and their two guardians. This outrage followed his earlier frequent adulteries until he finally he put his wife away, and turned to sodomy.[1]

Aurelius 'Caninus'

Gildas calls the next king Aurelius 'Caninus', the latter word meaning 'doglike'. He is making a pun on another name of the king which was probably Cynan. Large hounds were admired in those days for their hunting and fighting qualities and the word for hound appears in the names of Cuneglasus and Maglocunus, but here Gildas mocks the king with the insulting 'doglike'. It is possible that Aurelius was one of the degenerate grandchildren of Ambrosius Aurelianus (Lloyd, 1911). He had also committed similar adulteries, fornications and parricides to Constantine. Gildas accuses him of an unjust thirst for civil war and constant plunder. His fathers and brothers were apparently also like this and had died youthful deaths. As a result he was now left alone 'like a solitary tree, withering in the middle of the field'.[2]

Vortipor

Gildas calls Vortipor the 'tyrant of the Demetae', his kingdom being in the southwest Wales region of Dyfed. His rule had featured numerous murders and adulteries. Gildas berates him as 'the bad son of a good king', his father being the Christian king, Aircol, the Welsh form of the Latin Agricola. Gildas remarks that his head was already whitening and that the end of his life is gradually drawing near. His wretched soul is now heavily burdened by the rape of his shameless daughter after the removal and honourable death of his wife.[3]

Cuneglasus

Gildas calls Cuneglasus 'red butcher' distorting his name's meaning. The *glas* part means blue/green/grey while the *cun* part means hound. Jackson (1982) claims that Gildas uses a rare meaning of 'tawny' for *glas*, and interprets the hound part as a dog that tears flesh, hence 'red butcher'. Cuneglasus had been rolling in the filth of his wickedness since his youth. Gildas calls him '(you) bear' in the second person, and driver of the chariot of the Bear's Fortress in the third person, an odd change. He wages war against men and God. Against men, he uses 'arms special to himself' implying expertise in warfare. Against God, he continually provokes and injures the holy men who are present by his side. Gildas accuses him of anger and rage and of rejecting his wife to take up with her villainous sister, who had promised herself to God. Cuneglasus was a first cousin to Maglocunus, the fifth king.[4]

Figure 2.1. This stone, discovered in 1895 in Dyfed, commemorates Vortipor, one of the five kings berated by Gildas. His great grandson was named after Arthur. Note the Irish Ogam on the left edge of the stone. (Photo: R. MacCann).

Maglocunus

He was the son of Cadwallon Lawhir who reigned in Anglesey. As a youth he probably killed his paternal uncle, Owain Danwyn, for his throne in Rhôs. As Gildas used *avunculus*, strictly the maternal uncle, some argue he meant the unknown brother of Maglocunus' mother (Lloyd, 1911). If this were true, both the maternal and paternal uncles were kings and a relatively small region had three kings, Cadwallon, Owain and the other uncle. Others think that Gildas used the term more generally. Winterbottom (1978) translates it as 'uncle', Morris (1978) and Miller (1975-6) thought he was Owain, Dumville (1984a) wasn't dissuaded by *avunculus* in considering whether Owain was meant and Bartrum (2009) says that it was possibly Owain. A similar issue arises in the *Historia* where *atavus* is used to describe Cunedda as the ancestor of Maglocunus which strictly means the fifth ancestor, the great-great-great-grandfather, but the pedigrees have Cunedda as the third ancestor. Gruffydd (1989-90) takes it to mean just 'ancestor' and notes other instances of kinship terms used more loosely.[5]

Maglocunus found his reign unsatisfying and eventually resigned the throne to become a monk. However, he could not stay the course as a monk and returned to his former way of life, like a sick hound returning to his 'disgusting vomit'. On his return he spurned his first wife and killed both her and his nephew (his brother's son), which allowed him to marry his nephew's wife. She had colluded with him and encouraged him in these two murders according to Gildas. The wedding was a public one and its legitimacy was proclaimed by the lying tongues of his 'parasites', the latter being his bards.[6]

Ridiculing the Bards

The bards were a key part of a king's retinue whose main purpose was to compose praise poetry, creating imagery that put the king in a favourable light. They were also repositories of knowledge about the king's forebears and the noble and generous acts of the king. Gildas ignores this necessity and ridicules Maglocunus' bards:[7]

> Your excited ears hear not the praises of God ... but empty praises of yourself from the mouths of criminals who grate on the hearing like raving hucksters – mouths stuffed with lies and liable to bedew bystanders with their foaming phlegm.

The reality was that the essence of the bard's job necessitated praising the king and ignoring his faults. Any bard that departed from this line would not be tolerated and would endanger his life.

The Soldiers are Cowards

Gildas spews forth his worst ridicule and denigration for the British military. Early in the *De Excidio*, he portrays the Britons as cowards who meekly surrender without a fight:[8]

> The British offered their backs instead of shields to their pursuers, their necks to the sword. A cold shudder ran through their bones; like women they stretched out their hands for fetters. In fact, it became a mocking proverb far and wide that the British are cowardly in war and faithless in peace.

Yet when the British had previously fought back against the Romans, as Boudicca did, she is called a 'treacherous lioness' who 'butchered the governors', with all his sympathy given to the Romans.

Later, when describing the British soldiers stationed at Hadrian's Wall to contain the raids of the Irish and Picts, Gildas continues the denigration of the British warriors:[9]

> ... there was stationed on the height of the stronghold, an army, slow to fight, unwieldy for flight, incompetent by reason of its cowardice of heart, which languished day and night in its foolish watch.

Gildas, of course, was not present at any of the conflicts above that he so vividly describes. They were well before his time. Yet like Geoffrey of Monmouth, he was skilful in inventing specific details to portray the British military as cowards and incompetents. In the section just before his account of the five kings, Gildas has more harsh words for the military. He refers to the current kings who were exalting their military companions:[10]

> ... their military companions, bloody, proud and murderous men, adulterers and enemies of God – if chance, as they say, so allows: men who should have been rooted out vigorously, name and all.

Gildas is saying that, if the opportunity arises, the military men should be obliterated and their names should be erased from history. In his *Ecclesiastical History*, Bede used Gildas extensively and approved of this principle of erasure, as shown by his remark on evil kings:

> ... the name and memory of those apostates ought to be utterly blotted out from the list of Christian kings and that no year should be assigned to their reign.

Bede actually put this principle into practice when he obliterated the British king, Cadwallon, from the king list of Northumbria, assigning the year of his reign to the following English king, Oswald.[11]

WHERE WAS THE DE EXCIDIO WRITTEN?

Gildas knew that his work would arouse controversy and could put his life in danger. In Chapter 37, in referring to his history, he mentions 'the rain showers of the hostile that will compete to beat upon it'. In Chapter 65, he states:

> ... my two sides are protected by the victorious shields of the saints; my back is safe at the walls of truth; my head as its helmet has the help of the Lord for its sure covering. So let the rocks of my truthful vituperations fly their constant flights.

The potential physical danger to Gildas has influenced many scholars to believe he could not have written in Wales, but perhaps in the north of Britain, Dorset, Ireland, or Brittany. Gildas notes that the Picts were in the north of Britain and that they were in the 'far end' of the island which implies that he was in the south. Given the Saxon dominance in the east, it suggests Gildas was in the southwest. It implies that Wales is a very plausible option, considering his intimate knowledge of the Welsh kings, especially Maglocunus and Cuneglasus.[12]

The Monastery at Bangor-on-Dee

John Koch (2013) plausibly suggests that Gildas was writing from the huge monastery at Bangor-on-Dee, a few miles south of Chester. He argues that after the Roman withdrawal in 410, a secular ruler over Chester may have endowed a large area of land (previously used by the

Roman soldiers) to the church. This gift would have prevented lawless or unauthorized settlers on vacant land and was probably the setting for the monastery at Bangor-on-Dee.[13]

For AD 601, the *Welsh Annals* give 'Sinodis Urbis Legion' (Synod of Chester) which refers to Augustine meeting the British clergy near Chester. Bede describes this event which he placed at Augustine's Oak. It involved Augustine's attempt to resolve their differences in religious customs. Bede also describes a second meeting in 603 between the two groups. He states that most of the British at the meeting came from 'their most famous monastery' called *Bancornaburg* and that the monastery abbot was *Dinoot*. Koch observes that these are both Old English names, which implies an Old English source.[14]

Bede also describes the battle of Chester (about 615) where a large group of monks were praying for a British victory against the Saxon army of Aethelfrith. The monks were guarded by an old former king, Brocmail, and his men (see Chapter 5). Most of the monks were from the monastery of *Bancor*. Aethelfrith first slaughtered about 1200 of the monks after Brocmail and his men had fled and then won the main battle which took place at Heronbridge (Tolley, 2016), 14 miles north of the monastery. Koch states that three names in Bede's account were Brittonic: *Carlegion*, *Bancor* and *Brocmail*. This required a British written source which almost certainly came from the monastery as the murdered monks were from there.[15]

Bede included details about the Bangor-on-Dee monastery in his account of the battle. He writes that it was so large that when it was divided into seven parts with superiors over each, no part had less than 300 men, and that all these men were accustomed to live by the labour of their hands. The monastery is also noted in the *Welsh Triads* (Triad 90) – it had 2400 men and, of these, 100 served God in prayer and worship for each hour, being relieved by another 100 for the next hour, and so on. Thus the prayer and worship was continuous for the 24 hours in the day, and for the days thereafter.[16]

Two British manuscripts
The Saxon priest Bede, in Jarrow, obtained two British manuscripts that originated in southwest Britain. One gave an account of the Battle of Chester and came from Bangor-on-Dee. The second was the *De Excidio*. If Gildas did write the *De Excidio* there it would explain his

intimate knowledge of the Welsh kings, Maglocunus in particular. Bangor-on-Dee would have been the probable place for Maglocunus to begin his journey to become a monk after deposing his uncle Owain from the throne in nearby Rhôs. Gildas also knew that Owain's son, Cuneglasus, had holy men who were 'present in the flesh' by his side. So the brutal Cuneglasus was a nominal Christian who was advised by holy men. The latter could have supplied intimate details to Gildas on Cuneglasus, and also Maglocunus after he had left the monastery.

If the *De Excidio* was written at Bangor-on-Dee then a copy of it and a copy of the battle at Chester may have travelled together in their journey which ended with Bede at Jarrow. The early manuscripts of the *De Excidio* would have been anonymous to protect Gildas but Bede somehow knew that he was the author. The copy he received may have named Gildas, this being inserted by the monks at Bangor-on-Dee.

In this scenario, Gildas was the 'needle in the haystack', using the immense size of the monastery to remain anonymous. As mentioned earlier, previous scholars thought that Gildas could not have written in Wales as he would have been killed by the kings had his authorship been discovered.

THE TIME OF WRITING

If the time of writing the *De Excidio* were known, then the date of the battle of Badon would be known. Gildas states he was born in the year of this battle and one month of the 44th year since the battle had passed. This implies he was writing in February.[17]

The traditional date for the *De Excidio* is around AD 540; e.g. John Morris (1978). David Dumville (1984b) estimates a range of 525 to 550. Robert MacCann (2016) argues for an upper limit of 540, as tree-ring dating implies an environmental disaster from 540 to 550 which Gildas would have noted as God's punishment for the Britons, had it already occurred. He suggests the late 530s. Clare Stancliffe (2018) sensibly argues that as Gildas was an authority in the Irish and British churches, his death at 570 in the 'Chronicle of Ireland' would be close to the true date. Alex Woolf (2018) has a similar view to Stancliffe. This constrains making the estimate of the writing date too early, as it would make Gildas too old at death in 570. Stancliffe estimates about 535 for the writing.[18]

The Mystery Cloud of 536-7

David Woods, writing in the *Journal of Theological Studies* in 2010, may have pinned down a more precise date for the *De Excidio*. He links an unusual statement from Gildas in Chapter 93.3 to a mystery cloud that had dimmed the sun and darkened the moon in 536-7. This phenomenon was seen by Cassiodorus in Italy, Zachariah of Mitylene, John of Ephesus, Procopius, and John Lydus in Constantinople. It was caused by the dust veil from several simultaneous volcanic eruptions from the west coast of America/Canada (see the Chapter 9 account). The statement of Gildas in 93.3 is:[19]

> Rather does a dense cloud and black night of their sin so loom over
> the whole island that it diverts almost all men from the straight way...

Is this just a Gildas metaphor which pictures sin as a dense cloud, or does a real dense cloud inspire the metaphor? The elements of the sentence suggest the latter interpretation, although as Woods says, firm proof is not possible. The cloud in the quotation is dense in the daytime and thus dims the sun. If this is all that was said, then one would just conclude that Gildas is picturing sin as a dense cloud. But the 'black night' allusion implies the moon was being greatly dimmed, as in the Cassiodorus description. Why should Gildas bother with this aspect? The first daytime imagery is sufficient to depict sin. Then the cloud looms over the whole island, a most unusual metaphor. Gildas does point out that there are good people in the island of Britain, yet the cloud covers the whole island. Following the logic of the metaphor, the parts of Britain where the people are living Godly lives should be bathed in glorious sunlight.

I am inclined to believe that Gildas was seeing the 536-7 cloud and that it inspired the 'cloud as sin' metaphor. Woods takes his argument further. He notes that Gildas had started his book ten years earlier but lacking confidence, he deferred finishing and publishing it. Woods argues that, to Gildas, the cloud may have heralded the 'last days' and this prompted him to throw off his fears and speak out against the sins of the Britons, as God would expect him to do. If we take 536-7 as the time the cloud appeared in Britain, Gildas was probably writing in the February of 537. Counting back 44 years from this would give 493 as the year for the battle of Badon.

Figure 2.2. The statue of Gildas in Morbihan, Brittany. © Romary / Wikimedia Commons.

SPECULATIVE TIMELINE

A speculative timeline for key events from AD 410 to the time of Gildas is now given, a hazardous task. However it does allow a close study to be made so that weaknesses can be more easily seen (HB is *Historia Brittonum* and DEB is *De Excidio Britanniae*).

410 Romans leave Britain. Irish and Picts resume their attacks.

415 Estimated birth year of Ambrosius Aurelianus.

425 Vortigern comes to power (HB: sect. 66).

428 Vortigern invites Saxons to fight Irish and Picts (HB: sect. 66).

429+ Saxons increase in numbers.

435+ Vortigern lives in fear of Ambrosius (HB: sect. 31).

437 Ambrosius, aged about 22, fights Vitalinus at Wallop (HB: sect. 66).

441 Saxons revolt and control much of eastern Britain (*Gallic Chronicles*).

446-7 Appeal to Aetius (three times consul) for help against Saxons.

450 Ambrosius aged about 35 wins initial British victory in the west.

450+ Mixed battle results against Saxons (roughly AD 450-93).

470 Estimated birth year of Arthur.

480 Estimated birth year of Maglocunus.

493 Siege of Badon Hill; Gildas is born; Ambrosius is about 78, if alive.

537 Gildas aged 44 writes DEB; Arthur is killed.

547 Maglocunus dies of Yellow Pestilence, aged about 67.

570 Gildas dies aged 77 (from 'Chronicle of Ireland').

Others have created timelines like this under the assumption that Gildas is reasonably accurate in his interpretation and his sequence of events. This timeline is based on the belief that Gildas is wrong in thinking that the appeal to Aetius was for aid against the Picts and Irish. It takes the position of Stevens (1941) that the barbarians were the Saxons. It also assumes that the 441 Saxon control of east Britain, reported in the *Gallic Chronicles*, is essentially correct. The 'anchor points' for this timeline are thus 410 for the Romans leaving, 441 for the Saxon revolt, about 447 for the appeal to Aetius, 493 for Badon, 537 for the year of Gildas writing, and about 570 for the death of Gildas. The other dates are fitted into this framework. Rather than use date ranges here, point estimates are used. Apart from the appeal to Aetius, most date ranges are hard to estimate and could be misleading in implying a greater precision than is actually possible.[20]

Even if Woods' argument on the dense cloud is not accepted, the year of writing the *De Excidio* cannot be too far away from the 537 date if it is accepted that Gildas died around 570. Thus Badon was fought in 493 or close to it. This is quite different from the 516/18 date in the *Welsh Annals*. It seems that the latter date is the result of an incorrect calculation and not a date that was recorded at the time.

Gallic Chronicles

An important anchor point is given by the two *Gallic Chronicles*, the chronicle to AD 452, and to 511, which give similar entries implying an early Saxon domination in east Britain. Miller (1978), Muhlberger (1983), Jones and Casey (1988) and Burgess (1990) have studied them. Miller and Burgess are sceptical but scholars are now inclined to accept the chronicles' validity for the AD 441 date. Higham (2018) gives a literal translation of the 441 entry from the 452 chronicle:

> The Britains [i.e. the British provinces] even at this time have been reduced by various catastrophes and events over a wide area into the rule of the Saxons.

Higham concludes that it is reasonable to believe that a well-informed author in southern Gaul in 452 thought that a Saxon conquest of much of Britain had occurred about 10 years earlier (around 441) and that this should be given some weight. He points out that it accords well with the Saxon cremation cemeteries found in east Britain, north of the Thames, in the period c. 425–450.[21]

This early 441 date is also consistent with the *Historia Brittonum* entries which give 425 for the first year of Vortigern's reign and 428 for the year he invited the Saxons to Britain as mercenaries to fight the Irish and Picts. From the time they purportedly arrived c. 428 it would give them 13 years to consolidate their power in eastern Britain until they were dominant. If the *Historia* information is ignored entirely, estimates of their time of arrival would give similar values.[22]

The 441 date also has implications for Arthur's role. If he was born circa 470 then the Saxons had another 30 years to consolidate their dominance before he was even born. Their numbers would have been too large to drive them from the greater part of Britain and subject them to servitude, as stated in the Breton *Legend of St Goeznovius*, such statements being gross exaggerations.[23]

The Problem of Dating Ambrosius

In Chapters 31 and 66 the *Historia* may preserve ancient knowledge of Vortigern and Ambrosius. In 31, Vortigern was said to be fearful of Ambrosius, an unexpected comment. In 66, for the early date of 437, two Britons with Roman names, Ambrosius and Vitalinus, fought each other at Wallop in Hampshire. The battle between two British armies suggests that the Saxons were not yet a threat there and is consistent with this early date. If Ambrosius led an army to battle in 437 he can hardly have been born much later than 415. It implies he was about 78 when Badon was fought, if still alive. To overcome this timing problem Morris (1973) invents another Ambrosius Aurelianus, the father of the Ambrosius whom he thought was fighting in the 460s. This gives two people named Ambrosius Aurelianus, both of whom happened to be generals who led their armies to battle. It allows Ambrosius 1 to have fought at Wallop and Ambrosius 2 to have fought in the 460s.[24]

If we reject this ad hoc 'fix' and accept the *Gallic Chronicles'* 441 date for Saxon control and the 493 date for Badon, then Ambrosius could not have been the victor at Badon. The gap of 52 years between 441 and 493 means that if Ambrosius led a fightback a few years after 441, then he was too old to fight at Badon. This does not depend on accepting the early 437 *Historia* date. Padel (1994) and Wood (1999) argue that removing a paragraph break to agree with the tenth century manuscript implies that Ambrosius won Badon. This is hardly credible as the manuscript is 400 years after Gildas wrote and tells us nothing about the original format. Further, no Welsh tradition links Badon to Ambrosius and Gildas attributes future victories to 'our countrymen', not Ambrosius. If he thought Ambrosius had won Badon he would have emphasized it and added to his earlier praise. After all, it would have been the victory of a *Roman* Briton, in stark contrast to the incompetent and cowardly Britons he had ridiculed.[25]

The timeline assumes that the appeal to Aetius happened in one of the two earliest years of the possible date range, leaving about 5-6 years from the Saxon revolt before the shattered Britons could form a coherent strategy. When this appeal failed, a military strategy under Ambrosius may then have been conceived. While this is logical, there is no certainty, and it may not have happened this way. The initial victory could have occurred before the appeal, or even after 450, with the main constraint on its date being Ambrosius' age.

35

If Arthur was born in 470 he would have been 23 when Badon was fought so it's possible that he was the commander. But it is shown later that his bard doesn't mention Badon as one of his achievements which weakens the argument that he was the victor there. Maglocunus' birth year estimate of 480 is based on the fact that he had a younger brother whose son had reached adulthood and had married. An additional period of time probably passed between Maglocunus' killing of this nephew and his marrying the nephew's wife, as Gildas remarks that he wanted the marriage to be seen as legitimate.[26]

Gildas thought the grandsons of Ambrosius were 'greatly inferior' to his excellence. Using 30 years to a generation gives a grandson age of 60 in 535 but there would have been younger ones if Ambrosius or his sons had fathered children when older than 30. Gildas may have formed a judgement on them over the period AD 520-537.

ARTHUR IN THE DE EXCIDIO

Arthur is not directly named in the *De Excidio*, which has led some scholars to conclude that he did not exist as a historical figure. This does not take into account Gildas' tendency to hide the names of kings through puns, or substitute names that depict the king unfavourably. The fifth-century king, Vortigern, was heavily criticized for inviting the Saxons into Britain as mercenaries to fight the Picts and the Irish. Gildas remarks: 'How desperate and crass the stupidity!' Surprisingly, Gildas does not call him Vortigern (meaning 'overlord') but puns on his name in calling him 'arrogant tyrant'. Later he calls him 'Pharaoh' and a third time calls him 'ill-fated tyrant'. Perhaps this was a case in which Gildas decided to erase the king's name from history.

A greater king than Maglocunus

Gildas regarded Maglocunus as the strongest of the five kings, as he had driven many other kings from their lands, killing some. Given this, it comes as a shock when he hints that there was a more powerful king than Maglocunus. In Chapter 33, he describes Maglocunus as:[27]

1) mightier than many both in power and malice (33.1)

2) superior to almost all the kings of Britain, both in kingdom and in the form of thy stature (33.2)

So a very small number of kings (perhaps only one) were mightier in power and superior in their kingdoms to Maglocunus. Kenneth Dark (2000a) summarizes this situation:[28]

> Gildas describes the sins of contemporary kings, naming five such rulers and implying the existence of a 'greater' king in Britain.

To Gildas, the Saxons were unworthy barbarians and he wouldn't have included their kings. He does not name any other current British king outside the five. While their sins are horrendous to us, the kings of the Franks, described by Gregory of Tours, were just as bad. Gregory was not selecting the worst kings, but reporting factually on what he knew. This suggests that the five British kings that Gildas described were no worse overall than the other British kings. It would be a statistical anomaly if the five worst British kings all happened to be concentrated in southwest Britain. How then did Gildas select them? It appears that he selected them because they were powerful kings in the land where he lived and because he had a great deal of information on their lives. The statements in 33.1 and 33.2 suggest that Gildas knew of a powerful king in the same land, probably Wales, who was even more powerful than the great Maglocunus.

Arthur as 'the Bear'

Another hint of an overking comes from Gildas calling Cuneglasus '(you) bear' and 'driver of the chariot of the Bear's Stronghold' (32.1). There have been several interpretations of 'Bear's Stronghold', but none as plausible as that of Winterbottom (1978) who disregards the unlikely theories that Gildas was referring to the star constellation, Ursa Major, or that the stronghold was named after animal bears.[29]

Winterbottom accurately translates *receptaculum ursi* (genitive singular) to get 'Bear's Stronghold' implying one Bear who owned the fort. If Cuneglasus had owned it, Gildas would have avoided the third person and used 'your fort' or an expression like this. It implies that Cuneglasus was subordinate to the Bear. As will be shown below, there is only one person who fits the role of overking at this very time and whose name was perfect for the epithet of 'the Bear' (*arth* in the Brittonic language) – Arthur. If Arthur was 'the Bear' then it is likely that he was the king who was more powerful than Maglocunus.

Arthur as the sixth-century 'Pharaoh'

In Chapter 23.2 Gildas refers to the fifth-century overking, Vortigern, as Pharaoh. In 37.2, he refers to a sixth-century overking, stating that the five kings were subject to Pharaoh. This imagery is from the story of the Exodus, where the Israelites, led by Moses, escaped from Egypt and the Pharaoh's army of chariot drivers were drowned in the Red Sea. Gildas is referring to this event in stating that the five mad and debauched kings are part of the retinue of a Pharaoh:[30]

> ... these five mad and debauched horses from the retinue of Pharaoh which actively lure his army to its ruin in the Red Sea ...

The obvious candidate for the overking is Arthur. He is the overlord of Cuneglasus and as the latter is subordinate to Pharaoh it suggests that Arthur is the overlord of the other kings. He is placed in the overking role in the *Historia Brittonum* where he led a coalition of the subkings' armies as the *dux bellorum*. The three Welsh poems use five different terms to refer to Arthur as a king – *wledic, pendeuic, ri, rechtur* and *teÿrnon* as discussed in Chapter 3.

The Five Kings control Pharaoh's Army

Gildas significantly changes the details from the biblical account. In the Exodus, the chariot drivers were part of the Pharaoh's retinue but here the five kings are included as horses. Furthermore, the Pharaoh's soldiers would have controlled their horses in following the Israelites, but here the dominance is transferred to the horses. The five mad and debauched kings are now the chariot horses, taking control of the Pharaoh's soldiers and pulling them to their ruin.

Why has Gildas changed these details? He refers to the Pharaoh's army in the clause 'which actively lure his army to its ruin' and seems to be implying that in Britain, the Pharaoh was no longer in control of his army. Instead, the five kings were effectively in control and were recklessly bringing these soldiers to their ruin, possibly through the destructive internal wars that Gildas condemns. The use of 'lure' in Gildas' statement suggests that the soldiers were being enticed to plunder through the influence of the five kings. Gildas refers to the plundering of Maglocunus in 33.5 as follows:[31]

> What retribution would you expect for this alone from the just judge, even if it had not been followed by the sort of thing that did follow: for again he said through his prophet: 'Woe to you who plunder – will you not yourself be plundered?'

Gildas doesn't say the Pharaoh was dead, but in the Pharaoh's absence or inactivity, the five kings now have no constraints on them. This fits a situation where Arthur was in Annwfyn and the survivors had not yet returned to Britain. Arthur's death was not yet known. Cuneglasus is subject to both the Bear and Pharaoh. Rather than have him being subject to two overkings, an improbable event, this suggests that the Bear and the Pharaoh were the same overking, Arthur, known by the epithet 'the Bear'. Gildas' treatment of Arthur is thus similar to how he treated the fifth century Vortigern. He punned on 'Vortigern' to get 'arrogant tyrant' and also called him 'Pharaoh'.

A Rebuttal of Higham's Argument

To avoid interrupting the above argument, certain issues have been set aside which will be dealt with here. A leading proponent of the view that Arthur was not historical, Nicholas Higham (2018), interprets the text of Gildas differently. As Higham's views are influential, his arguments will now be examined in detail.

Gildas likens each king to an animal – a dragon, bear, leopard and a lion (twice). Higham rightly states that Gildas was using a metaphor based on the composite beast from Revelation 13: 2. A similar 'beast' with different details is given in Daniel 7: 1-8. I agree that Gildas had this imagery in mind as I noted in MacCann (2016). If this was all the information available, then the likening of Cuneglasus to a bear would be of little consequence. However the issue is more complex.[32]

A key point concerns Gildas referring to Cuneglasus as the chariot driver of the 'Bear's Stronghold'. This refers to a fort in Rhôs (Jackson, 1982) a region linked to Einion Yrth, his son Owain and grandson Cuneglasus. Higham (2018) refers to forts named *Dineirth* in both Ceredigion and Rhôs but doesn't state that the small Ceredigion one he mentions first is hardly suitable. British archaeologist Kenneth Dark (1994) rightly remarks that this fort is 'not a good contender for identification with Gildas's *receptaculi ursi*'.[33]

Higham claims Gildas made a play on *Dineirth* to render it in Latin as *receptaculum ursi*. This is true but it does not justify his false and unsupported claim: 'This has absolutely nothing to do with Arthur'.[34] On the contrary, a detailed analysis points directly to Arthur as shown below. There are two translations to consider – (1) the critical one of Gildas translating *Dineirth* from *British* to Latin and (2) the routine one made by modern scholars from Latin to English:

Dineirth	→	*receptaculum ursi*	(1)
receptaculum ursi	→	Bear's Fortress	(2)

Dineirth contains two parts, *din* meaning 'fort' and *eirth*, the genitive singular of *arth* (bear) in *British*. Jackson (1982) and Sims-Williams (1990) both state that Gildas made a direct translation of *Dineirth* into Latin where *Din* gives *receptaculum* and *eirth* gives *ursi*. The play that Gildas made was to use *receptaculum* (refuge, den) rather than a Latin equivalent of the more commonly used 'fort' as the fort was owned by a person known as 'the Bear'. His play on words is trivial.[35]

It is obvious that the *Dineirth* fort and the Biblical 'beast' are independent. The *Dineirth* fort existed whether or not the 'beast' made of animals was put into the Bible. Gildas knew what *Dineirth* meant in *British* and translated it to Latin to show the fort was owned by 'the Bear'. The latter cannot be explained away, despite Higham's claims. Importantly, the fort's name was created when *British* case endings were being used in speech, here, the genitive singular. Jackson (1953) thought that *British* had evolved into *Brittonic* around the middle 500s with the loss of case and final syllables but this timing is too late. Sims-Williams (1990) thinks that it occurred early in the first half of the sixth century. Such old names could survive in a fossilized form as people accepted them as names. Jackson (1982) notes that *Dineirth* survived to the 1200s as a town name in Llandrillo-yn-Rhôs.[36]

The above suggests the *Dineirth* name originated in the late fifth or early sixth century as an informal descriptor to denote the owner of the fort, a person whose name was suitable for the epithet, the Bear. This fits perfectly with the conjecture that Arthur took over the fort when Maglocunus resigned the throne. If the latter was born c. 480 and was about 15 when he killed Owain, he began his reign c. 495. His reign was troubled and he may have resigned after 5 years or less which would put Arthur's accession to around 500. This hypothesis is hardly forced, as Arthur's name only differs from the *Brittonic* word for 'bear' by two letters. This is not saying that Arthur's name derived from 'bear'. It may have derived from 'Artorius' which would become 'Arthur' when used in Welsh.

Cuneglasus wasn't the bear who owned the fort as Gildas' language implies two bears. He refers to Cuneglasus in the second person with '(you) bear' and uses the third person in calling him 'chariot driver of the Bear's Stronghold'. This distinction would usually be a signal that two bears are meant and that Cuneglasus was only being called '(you) bear' as he was part of the retinue of the Bear who owned the fort. This is consistent with the fact that Cuneglasus' name is related to 'dog', not 'bear' (as Gildas knew) and with the fact that Gildas mentioned a Pharaoh above the five kings who were part of his retinue.

Higham appears to imply that Gildas took 'bear' from the biblical beast and applied it to Cuneglasus, thus naming his abode 'the bear's fort'. But this cannot explain the name *Dineirth*. In AD 537 people would not have used this old genitive case ending. The *Dineirth* name did not originate from Gildas but from the fort's naming about 40 years earlier. Higham has the causal direction the wrong way round. Gildas used the pre-existing *Dineirth*, based on Arthur, to choose 'bear' for Cuneglasus from the four animals.

A RESPONSE TO GILDAS – SPOILS OF ANNWFYN

Gildas knew that his work would be attacked, but there is nothing in the traditional sources that does this. They are too late and occur after Bede in 731 had enhanced Gildas' reputation as the historian of the Britons. Time had moved on and the recipients of the Gildas insults and their immediate descendants were long gone. However there is one early source that did respond angrily to Gildas, although this has not been recognized – the *Spoils of Annwfyn* poem. This poem aptly fits the context of the *De Excidio*. The poem comprises eight stanzas in which the first three differ significantly from the last five. The former stanzas deal with details of the journey and lament that only a few survived, but they do not mention the monks.

In contrast, the last five stanzas fiercely attack the monks. Further, every opening line of the last five stanzas denigrates the monks. This is extraordinary for a poem that scholars have dated centuries after the *De Excidio* and which is widely interpreted as a fictional visit to a Celtic Otherworld, where all is peace and harmony. The sustained attacks on the monks should have no place in such a poem.

Three times the bard begins the stanzas with 'I set no value on little men'. By 'little' he may mean of little accomplishment, of little value, or little physically compared to the warriors. As a soldier himself he would have resented the denigration of the military from weaklings who had contributed nothing to defending the country. He explicitly identifies the 'little men' with the monks in Stanza 4, Line 29 where he implies that their only use is scripture learning.

29   I set no value on little men – (merely) concerned with scripture.

In Stanza 5, Line 35 the bard responds to the statements of Gildas that the British military men were cowards by mocking the monks with 'loose their shield straps'. This is a statement of the obvious, that the monks were not defending the country, with the added implication that *they* were the cowards.

35   I set no value on little men – loose their shield straps.

In Stanza 6, Line 43 the bard again attacks the monks. The bard, now back in Britain was one of the few survivors of Annwfyn. He had been through hell in Annwfyn, an experience which had thoroughly tested him physically and mentally. He sees the monks as not only being physically weak but also mentally weak, living their soft and regulated lives, free of danger, not having to face testing or harsh conditions.

43   I set no value on little men – weak their resolve.

The bard's main denigration of the monks, however, concerns their ignorance of Annwfyn. They did not see things and they did not know things that happened there. He begins with 'Beyond the glass fortress they [the monks] did not see the valour of Arthur', an implication that Arthur fought valiantly there before being killed. This theme of the monks' ignorance continues throughout all of the last five stanzas. Of the 32 lines that comprise the last five stanzas, 21 are concerned with denigrating the monks, about 66%.

Why were the monks being attacked when the author was Gildas? Arthur's bard would not have known who the author was, but the monks' views were probably well known. In Chapter 16, Gildas implies that the monks shared his views, as their devout prayers spurred him on to write his complaint on the sins of the Britons. The many biblical references in his work indicate an author who had devoted his life to studying the Bible. On his return from Annwfyn Arthur's devastated bard would have been enraged by the slanders of the kings, bards and military by the anonymous author and concluded that he had to be one of the monks. The *Spoils of Annwfyn* emphasizes the hostility between the lords and monks in the last two stanzas, where he depicts the two groups clashing over an issue. Stanza 7 begins:

49   Monks draw together, like a pack of dogs,

50   from a clash with lords who know.

Stanza 8 begins:

53   Monks draw into a pack, like wolves,

54   from a clash with lords who know.

The Welsh word for 'clash' is *cyfranc* and Marged Haycock (2007) notes its primary meaning as 'clash' or 'contention'. So the lords are in contention with the monks, and the monks are shrinking back in fear. In each case, the monks are denigrated, being compared to dogs and wolves. This was probably a payback by the bard. Recall that Gildas denigrated both Aurelius 'Caninus' (Cynan) and Maglocunus by insultingly comparing them with dogs.[37]

It seems that the contentious issue was the savage criticism of the Britons from the *De Excidio* and the lords may have been pressuring the monks to give up the anonymous author. There is also a second issue. From Lines 50 and 54, there was something the lords knew that the monks didn't know, in keeping with their ignorance of all the other things mocked by the bard throughout the last five stanzas. The secret of what the lords knew was devastating and would have shocked the monks: that Arthur had been killed in Annwfyn and now there was no Pharaoh in charge of the five kings whom they had ridiculed.

3
ARTHUR

DINARTH: ARTHUR'S STRONGHOLD

It is argued that Arthur was 'the Bear' whose fort was being protected by Cuneglasus. This fort is located centrally in north Wales, consistent with several texts that place Arthur there. Jackson (1982) states that the *receptaculum ursi* of Gildas is a direct translation of *Din Eirth*, the fort's ancient name. It translates to 'the Bear's fort'. He also notes that in the 1200s the village at Llandrillo-yn-Rhôs was still called *Dineirth*, which eventually became Dinarth in Modern Welsh. There is a hillfort which had that name in Rhôs-on-Sea, on the north Wales coast, and there is a Dinerth Road on its western side. It was called Dinarth up to about 1875, when its name was changed to *Bryn Euryn* according to Longley and Laing (1997). The *Camelot* name is a fiction created by the 12th-century French poet, Chrétien de Troyes.[1]

As Gildas probably wrote from Bangor-on-Dee he would have been well aware of this hillfort and who occupied it as it was only 45 miles away. It is well positioned to give an advance warning of approaching enemies and has spectacular views along the north Wales coast and to the west where Anglesey and Puffin Island can be seen. To the south there are woodland views, a region where Arthur's forest retreat of Kelliwic in Kernyw was probably located. The *kernyw* name may have derived from the Great Orme and Little Orme headlands jutting out into the Irish Sea where each resembles a 'horn' of an animal (Welsh: *corn*). See the photos in Figure 3.4. Watson (1926) argues that the Cornovii tribes were called this because they lived on or near 'horns' of land. About 9 miles south of Dinarth the *kernyw* name survives in the village of Llangernyw (enclosure of Kernyw).[2]

The hillfort would have been difficult to attack. Before seaborne raiders could even reach the fort, they would have to cross long flat stretches where they would be visible. The hill itself sloped steeply on its north and northwestern flanks where attackers would be met by volleys of spears, thrown from above. On the south and southwest flanks, the slope was very steep and broken by precipitous scarps, making an attack there very difficult and unlikely to succeed.

The hillfort was investigated by Longley and Laing (1997) who thought that the site comprised a strong citadel on the summit and dependent outwork. There may have been an enclosed terrace below the summit. Trial excavations on the summit revealed an impressive rampart that was 3.7 metres wide and faced at the front with a single width of large high-quality limestone blocks. The back of the rampart originally was also faced with these blocks. Between these two sets of facing blocks was a random concentration of large limestone blocks and small limestone rubble which constituted the core of the rampart. The front face of the rampart was about 14 degrees off the vertical. Longley and Laing comment that 'the summit defences must once have been substantial and impressive'. While it doesn't resemble Iron Age hillforts in the area, it does resemble Garn Boduan on the Llŷn Peninsula and Scottish hillforts such as Dunadd in Argyll, Dundurn in Perth and Kinross, and Dumbarton Rock in Strathclyde.[3]

Although Dinarth was at one of the best locations for a defensive fort in north Wales, Arthur probably did not stay there permanently. He would have moved around the various *maerdrefi* (the royal estate centres) of north Wales being visibly supported by the people in his home territory and reinforcing his relationships with them. In times of unrest he probably returned to Dinarth and could call upon military support from across his north Wales domain.

MORE EVIDENCE FOR ARTHUR IN NORTH WALES

The evidence from Gildas on the Bear's Stronghold is vitally important in placing Arthur in Gwynedd (north Wales). As Gildas was probably based only 45 miles away from Dinarth and was a contemporary of Arthur, his evidence provides a test for the validity of the three Welsh poems, which are attributed in this book to Arthur's bard. Two of these poems place Arthur in north Wales and several other Welsh texts also place him there, as shown in the places named below.

River Dee: Spoils of Annwfyn

In Stanza 5 of *Spoils of Annwfyn* the bard is mocking the ignorance of the monks on what happened in Annwfyn. He is thinking about the origins of the Annwfyn people (Native Americans) and whether they were part of God's creation on the Sixth Day and he remarks at the end of this topic that they 'did not go to the Devwy meadows' (line 38).

Devwy probably refers to the river Dee that runs through Chester (Roman name *Deva*). This name seems to be a compound of *Deva* and *gwy*, the latter meaning 'water' or 'liquid' and is a component of river names. Another nearby example is the river Conwy, which some argue is a compound of *Cyn* (first) and *gwy* (river). *Devwy* also appears in another poem, the *Spoils of Taliesin*, a poem in which Koch and Carey (2003) tentatively translate *Devwy* as 'Dee'. This mention of the Dee implies that it was an important location in the bard's home territory. It could suggest that Arthur's expedition actually departed from the mouth of the Dee. The bard appears to be saying, in effect, that while Arthur's crew visited Annwfn the Annwfyn people don't ever visit the River Dee, from where the Britons sailed.[4]

After the Romans left, Chester retained some of its population and its port remained in use (Snyder, 1998; Koch, 2013). The presence of a synod near Chester in AD 601 and Bede's lavish praise for Britain's 'most famous monastery' at Bangor-on-Dee, a few miles to the south, suggest that Chester held its importance in the sixth century.[5]

Chester: Chair of the Sovereign

Chair of the Sovereign reflects life in Britain after Arthur's death. The bard sadly notes that the warriors are bereft from the annihilation of the prince with the fiery nature and the 'lorica of *Lleon*' (line 67). This prince was Arthur and the mention of *Lleon* directly associates him with Chester. *Caer Lleon* (the fort of the Legion) is Chester and the lorica is Arthur's battle vest. Marged Haycock (2007) notes that Lleon could also mean northeast Wales in general. The *Historia Brittonum* also lists an Arthurian battle at Chester.[6]

Dinarth and Dinorben: Stanzas of the Graves

The *Stanzas of the Graves* appear in the Black Book of Carmarthen and record the burial places of prominent people in early medieval Britain. They are translated and discussed by eminent Welsh scholar, Thomas Jones (1967). Two people of interest are Garwen, one of Arthur's mistresses, and her father, Hennin Henben, the latter epithet meaning 'old chief' or 'old head'. In Stanza 70, Garwen is said to be buried on the *morfa* (beach). Jones explains that this is the *Morfa Rhianedd* (Beach of the Maidens) and identifies it with the long beach at Llandudno which stretches between the Great and Little Ormes, only a very short distance from Dinarth. Moreover, Triad 57 of the *Welsh Triads* lists Garwen, the daughter of Hennin, as one of Arthur's mistresses (Bromwich, 2006). So Gildas places 'the Bear' at Dinarth and an independent source, *Stanzas of the Graves*, places Garwen's burial a short distance away. Further, in Stanza 71 Hennin is said to be buried at Dinorben, only 9 miles to the east of Dinarth. These two burials fit perfectly with Arthur being the Bear of Dinarth.[7]

Arfon: Lineage of the Heroes

The Lineage of the Heroes (*Bonedd y Arwyr*) tells us that Arthur had a son, Cydfan, with Eleirch the daughter of Iaen (Bartrum, 1966). It appears that Arthur did not marry Eleirch, so Cydfan was probably illegitimate. The *Culhwch and Olwen* story tells us that the sons of Iaen were men of Caer Dathl. Fortunately the location of Caer Dathl is given in the Mabinogi story, *Math son of Mathonwy*, where it says that there was a court at Caer Dathl in Arfon (Ford, 1977). This is important because Arfon ('facing Môn') was in north Wales, but on the western side where its territory faced Anglesey, whose ancient name was Môn. Eleirch is not listed as one of his mistresses in the Welsh Triads but it appears that Iaen's family were proud of this link with Arthur for these obscure details to survive and be recorded. The sources are consistent in locating Arthur in north Wales, ranging from Arfon in the west, to Dinarth in the middle, and Chester in the east.[8]

Dinas Brân near Llangollen: Arthur and Brân

An important hillfort in north Wales is called Dinas Brân (Brân's fort), where Brân is a mythological figure modelled on Arthur. He appears in *Branwen daughter of Llŷr*, a Mabinogi story where the incidents closely resemble those in *Spoils of Annwfyn*. *Branwen* was written centuries later around 1120-30. It substitutes Ireland for Annwfyn and Brân for Arthur.

Thomas Jones (1964) suggests that it is a rationalized form of an earlier story told in *Spoils of Annwfyn*. *Branwen* not only copies from this poem, but also copies from *Chair of the Sovereign* and other material on Arthur, including the *Gestae Arthuri* (Deeds of Arthur). In using all this Arthurian material the author of *Branwen* makes it evident that he thought that Brân and Arthur were equivalent. These similarities are listed below.[9]

1   Both men took their warriors overseas: Arthur to Annwfyn and Brân to Ireland. The author of Branwen substituted a well-known overseas location rather than Annwfyn.

2   Stewards were needed to mind the country in their absence: for Arthur in *Chair of the Sovereign* and Brân in *Branwen daughter of Llŷr* and Triad 13 (Haycock, 2007; Ford, 1977, Bromwich, 2006). As Brân only went to Ireland, a short travel distance, the need for seven stewards to mind the country in his case is an absurdity.

3   Both men fought a disastrous battle while overseas.

4   Both men were associated with a cauldron while fighting overseas.

5   Both men were killed in their battle.

6   Seven men survived Arthur's battle in Annwfyn and seven men survived Brân's battle in Ireland.

7   Three men thought to have sailed to Annwfyn with Arthur were Taliesin, Pryderi and Manawydan (the latter in the poem *I Petition God*, Pryderi in *Spoils of Annwfyn* and Taliesin, as Arthur's supposed bard who lived to compose the poem). These same three went to Ireland with Brân and were among the seven survivors of Brân's battle.

8   Both Arthur and Brân were called 'Blessed', Arthur in *Chair of the Sovereign* and Brân in *Branwen daughter of Llŷr*.

9   In the *Gestae Arthuri*, Arthur was warned about the magnetic rocks under the water that could attract ships containing iron and wreck them. In Brân's story, the Irish thought that magnetic rocks under the water would stop his progress across the River Shannon (Taylor, 1956; Ford, 1977).

10 Brân means 'crow'. In folklore, Arthur's soul exists in the form of a crow, as noted in Cervantes' *Don Quixote*. In Cornish folklore, Arthur's soul lives in the chough, the red-legged crow (Chambers, 1927).

Why did the author replace Arthur with Brân and replace Annwfyn with Ireland in his strange tale? In brief, the killing of Arthur in the mysterious Annwfyn was followed by a series of disasters in Arthur's north Wales domain that led to the view that Arthur was ill-fated. One theory is that a superstition developed against the direct use of his name and Brân was one figure who replaced Arthur. This theory will be later discussed. Thus the hillfort Dinas Brân is of interest. It is on the north of the Dee near Llangollen. Dark (1994) states that a strong fort with two banks and ditches preceded the medieval castle and that some structures terraced into the hill seem to be linked to the fort. He thinks that it could have had a sixth-century occupation.[10]

This area is linked to Arthur. Three miles north of Dinas Brân is a tall cliff called *Craig Arthur* and at the top is a rock formation called *Cadair Arthur* (Arthur's Chair). There are also two springs called *Ffynnon Arthur* south of the Dee whose co-ordinates are given by the RCAHMW (1914). They are mentioned by Edward Lhuyd in his 1698 *Parochialia*. Other links involve Gwenhwyfar and her father, Gogfran Gawr. Lhuyd noted *Kroes Gwenhwyvar*, a stone cross near the Dee. W. T. Simpson in his 1827 *Guide to Llangollen* said that the cross had been removed 'only a few years' but its base remained. It was located at 52°58'15"N, 3°9'4"W by the RCAHMW. A local tradition recorded by Pennant (1883) puts Gogfran's fort in Old Oswestry, 10 miles away. Whether Gwenhwyvar was a real person is uncertain. Her name is the Welsh version of Irish *Findabar* ('white fairy') but this doesn't imply she should be seen as such, any more than girl named Fay is seen as a fairy. Her Irish-derived name is in line with the Irish being in north Wales. She first appears in *Culhwch and Olwen* as Arthur's wife but having no association with Medrawd. The cross would not date to her time but perhaps to c. 1200, after Geoffrey's pseudo-history.[11]

There is no record of a king called Brân who lived at Dinas Brân and no associations with him in the area, unlike Arthur where there are many. Although they are not strong enough to constitute evidence, they show that people believed that Arthur was prominent there. If Brân was a mythical figure based on Arthur as argued here then Arthur may have been the real owner of the fort.

The Stone of Huail (Gildas' brother)

In Ruthin, north Wales, there is a boulder on which Arthur was said to have beheaded Huail. The Rhuys *Life of Gildas* says that Gildas and Huail were sons of Caunus (Caw) from *arecluta* ('on the Clut'). This was thought to be Strathclyde but seems suspect for the reasons below. Gildas refers to the north, where the Picts were, as the 'far end' of the island, an odd remark if he grew up there. Secondly, he gives vivid details of Welsh kings but nothing on northern kings. Thirdly, he gives an inaccurate history of the Antonine wall which is near this *arecluta*.

If he were born there, one would expect him to mention his birth place when discussing this nearby wall, as he did with Badon and his birth year, but he didn't. It is also odd that many of his siblings are linked to Wales, not *arecluta*: e.g. Celyn, Gallgo, Gofan, Eugrad, Gwrddelw, Gwrhai, Meilig and Peithien. Did they all migrate to Wales as Gildas supposedly did? Did his father, Caw, also migrate, as he is linked to *Edeirnion* in north Wales near the Dee (Bartrum, 2009).[12]

The *Life of Cadoc*, by Lifris of Llancarfan, places Caw in Scotland and has Caw tell Cadoc that he had reigned for many years beyond mons Bannauc. Given the above doubts, it is possible that the river *Clut* is not the Clyde in Scotland but the Clwyd in north Wales and that mons Bannauc is Bron Bannog, close to the Clwyd which runs through Ruthin. The RCAHMW says that this peak appears in Lhuyd (1699), *Parochialia*, Vol. II. A second *Life of Gildas* by Caradoc of Llancarfan says that Huail would often 'swoop down from Scotland' and carry off spoils from Arthur which is far-fetched if he were in Strathclyde and Arthur in Wales. It further says that Arthur captured Huail on the Isle of Man and killed him. However if the stone is genuine it seems that Huail was taken to Ruthin for the beheading.[13]

Gerald of Wales, following his tour of Wales in 1188, explains the bitterness of Gildas as follows (Thorpe, 1978):

> The Britons maintain that, when Gildas criticized his own people so bitterly, he wrote as he did because he was so infuriated by the fact that King Arthur had killed his own brother [Gildas' brother Huail].

Gildas hated the British military, calling them 'enemies of God ... who ought, together with *their very name*, to be assiduously destroyed'. It could explain why he did not directly name Arthur. It's even possible he went to his brother's execution, an anonymous figure in the crowd, as the Bangor-on-Dee monastery is only 18 miles from Ruthin.[14]

Bwrdd Arthur

In addition to Dinarth and Dinas Brân, there are other north Wales hillforts linked to Arthur. *Bwrdd Arthur* (Arthur's board or table) is a flat-topped hillfort on the north coast of Anglesey and like Dinarth it looks out over the Irish Sea. It is a huge 13 acres and has excellent views of Red Wharf Bay and across to the Great Orme. Kenneth Dark (2000a) classifies it as a probable abode of an elite family.[15]

Figure 3.1. Dinarth hillfort: looking northwest towards the Little Orme, with the Irish Sea in the background. (Photo: R. MacCann).

Figure 3.2. The limestone boulder on which the brother of Gildas, Huail, was thought to be beheaded by Arthur, on display in the town of Ruthin, north Wales. (Photo: R. MacCann).

Figure 3.3. Bwrdd Arthur (Arthur's Table) in northeast Anglesey, looking towards Puffin Island, with the Great Orme visible in the far background. (Photo: R. MacCann).

Figure 3.4. The Morfa Rhianedd at Llandudno (Thomas Jones, 1967) where Arthur's mistress, Garwen, was buried. Top: the Great Orme. Bottom: the Little Orme. (Photos: R. MacCann).

Moel Arthur and Moel Fenlli

Both these are linked to Arthur. Moel Arthur is 5 miles from Ruthin
and gives spectacular views over the surrounding countryside. From
its summit, the Irish Sea is visible in the distance to the north.

Moel Fenlli is 2 miles from Ruthin and is linked to Arthur through
a bard in the 1200s, Bleddyn Fardd, who used Arthur as an exemplar
of valour. He was praising Dafydd ap Llewelyn's might in battle and
compared him to Arthur when Arthur fought at Caer Fenlli.[16]

Fort of Cai, in north Wales

Cai (Sir Kay) from Caius was one of Arthur's battle horsemen. Welsh
tradition puts him at Caer Gai, earlier a Roman fort, near Bala Lake.
The RCAHMW (1921) locates it at 52°52'7"N, 3°40'3"W and states that
the tradition was known in the late 1500s and may be much older. It
was also called Caer Gynyr after Cai's father (Roberts, 1941-4).[17]

ARTHUR'S BATTLES

Twelve battles are attributed to Arthur in the *Historia Brittonum*, a
Latin work of 829-830. It was thought that the author was a Briton
called Nennius from north Wales. However David Dumville (1972-4a)
shows that it was late (1164-66) that the prologue, with the name spelt
Ninnius, was copied into the Corpus Christi 139 manuscript. It was a
late and secondary development over 330 years from the writing date.
If its author did not write the *Historia* then his implication from the
prologue that it was compiled from a 'heap' of mostly unchanged raw
material is invalidated. Dumville is critical of the *Historia* and believes
that it is is of no historical value for the period 400-600. Other scholars,
knowing its limitations, treat it with caution but are more optimistic
that it may preserve useful information.[18]

The battle list derives from a Welsh poem, as suggested by Hector
and Nora Chadwick (1932) and Jones (1964) suggests that the battle
names could form part of the rhyming scheme. Jackson (1949; 1959a)
also argued that the awkward Latin phrasing implied that the Welsh
phrases were being translated literally into Latin. The theory that the
list was based on a Welsh poem has been endorsed by leading scholars.
As Welsh poems about other kings were composed in the 500s, one

which listed Arthur's battles could in theory provide valuable evidence for his existence. Before the list, an introduction to the Saxons is given (not reproduced here) referring to Hengist and Octha and the Saxon kings of Kent. It is the author's attempt to fit Arthur into the battles against the Saxons. Whether he fought in Kent is doubtful and shows the problems of taking the author's statements as facts. He had limited knowledge that he was attempting to fit into a coherent scheme.[19]

The battles at Guinnion and Badon have unrealistic elaborations which almost certainly were not in the original poem.

> Then Arthur fought against them in those days, along with the kings of the Britons, although he was the leader in battle.

- The first battle was at the mouth of the river which is called *Glein*.
- The second, and third, and fourth, and fifth were on another river which is called Dubglas, and is in the region of *Linnuis*.
- The sixth battle was on the river which is called *Bassas*.
- The seventh battle was in the forest of *Celidon* (Latin: *silva celidonis*), that is *Cat Coit Celidon* (in Welsh).
- The eighth battle was at the fortress of *Guinnion*, in which Arthur carried the image of Saint Mary, perpetual virgin, on his shoulders, and the pagans were put to flight on that day, and there a was great slaughter of them through the power of our Lord Jesus Christ and the power of the holy Virgin Mary, his mother.
- The ninth battle was fought in the *City of the Legion*.
- The tenth battle was fought on the bank of the river which is called *Tribruit*.
- The eleventh battle occurred on the mount which is called *Agned*.
- The twelfth battle was on mount *Badon*, where in one day there fell 960 men to one assault of Arthur; and no one felled them except he alone, and in all the battles he was the victor.

The battles given here are from the *Harleian* family of manuscripts. In another manuscript family, the *Vatican*, the battle at Agned is replaced by one at Bregion. Geoffrey of Monmouth identifies Agned with Edinburgh but his basis for this is unknown and scholars have not given any support for this identification.[20]

Unfortunately, despite the many popular works claiming to be able to identify the battle sites, perhaps only four have been accurately identified as shown below.

City of the Legion	$\longrightarrow$	Chester
Coit Celidon	$\longrightarrow$	Forest in southwest Scotland
Linnuis	$\longrightarrow$	Lindsey (Lincoln)
Bregion	$\longrightarrow$	High Rochester, Northumberland

The above equivalences only identify the probable sites. It is a separate issue as to whether Arthur actually fought there. As noted earlier some scholars have thought that battles fought by others were credited to Arthur, including Urien's battle at Bregion. An extreme claim is that the 615 battle of Chester, where the Angles killed 1200 British monks, was rebadged as Arthur's *victory*. It is hard to see how this well-known disaster, reinforced by Bede's account, could be forgotten. As Arthur wore the lorica of 'Lleon' (Chester) it is probable that he was defending it against a raid, perhaps from the Irish.

Linnuis (Lindsey) is the most convincing battle site. It's not too far from Chester and the Angles were settled there before Arthur's time. The fact that the *Historia* places four battles at such a credible site is significant. These would have been aggressive strikes into Anglian territory and it is a very plausible region for Arthur to have fought. It's unlikely to have been a battle name borrowed from elsewhere. It is linked to a river *Dubglas* ('blue-black') and Bachrach (1990) suggests the Humber as a possibility, noting that it was called *Umbri maris* in Chapter 61 of the *Historia*. It is possible that the author of the poem referred to the Humber by the Welsh *Dubglas* (with its black element) due to the Latin *umbra* (shadow, darkness).[21]

The battle of Celidon wood could be a real battle as Arthur was in Galloway but there is another option. It may refer to the 'battle of the treetops' (Chapter 6), a barrage from cometary debris that the bard thought heralded Judgement Day. This disaster is in the *Battle of the Trees* poem. The bard of the poem underlying the *Historia* battles may have obtained the battle from the tree-battle poem and made it one of Arthur's battles (Williams, 1968). If true, this gives another reason for believing *Battle of the Trees* is a very early poem.[22]

The battle at *Tribruit* (*Tryfrwyd*) was not borrowed as it appears in an Arthurian poem, *Pa Gur*. Here Manawydan, another man linked to Arthur, brought back shattered shields. Of the other battles, *Glein* means 'pure or clear' (water) and may survive as the 'Glen'. There is a river Glen in Lincolnshire which is a possibility. *Bassas* is obscure although the Welsh *bas* means 'shallow' (water), while the fortress of *Guinnion* appears to mean the 'stronghold of the white people' (Jackson, 1945). This seems to be a non-specific name for a battle site with the fair-skinned Angles.[23]

Arthur probably fought on horseback armed with shield, sword and spear. Rowland (1995) cites poetry and other sources to discuss battle tactics. Arthur's warband probably had horses who were tractable and courageous, being able to charge into foot soldiers to allow the riders to launch spears at close range or to use thrusting spears. When these were lost or used up they would slash with swords. The horse itself was a weapon, knocking down warriors, sometimes trampling them. Such riding skill would only come from prolonged practice.[24]

The Siege of Badon Hill

Geoffrey locates Badon at Bath, as do Leeds (1933), Tolstoy (1960-2) and Burkitt and Burkitt (1990). Jackson (1953-8) suggests one of the Badbury hills near Swindon, Faringdon or Blandford but Field (2008) favours the Welsh border area. Breeze (2015) argues for the Ringsbury hillfort near Braydon forest. There is currently no consensus.

ARTHUR IN GALLOWAY, SCOTLAND

Rheon

Chair of the Sovereign locates Arthur primarily in north Wales but gives him a major role in Galloway, where he made a huge impression. Line 6 refers to his governing of Rheon, using the semi-Latin *rechtur* for governor, a word that John Koch (1997) argues was archaic. *Rheon* still survives as *Ryan* and refers to the area around Loch Ryan which is bordered in the west by the Rhinns. This location is given by Watson (1926), Crawford (1935), McCarthy (2004) and Haycock (2007).

Rheon also appears in the very first Welsh Triad as the location of Arthur's northern court where it is called *Pen Rhionydd*, the use of *pen* being apt for a headland (Bromwich, 2006; Haycock (2007).[25]

The British Novantae Tribe

In c. 150 Ptolemy in distant Alexandria wrote about the *Novantarum promontory*, shaped like a hammerhead, now called the Rhinns of Galloway. In the time of the Romans, the area was controlled by the Novantae tribe. *Battle of the Trees* places Arthur at *Caer Nefenhyr*, a fort of a king of the Novantae, so the tribe still held sway in Arthur's time. *Culhwch and Olwen* also places Arthur at Caer Nefenhyr.[26]

His Novantae association may look to be anachronistic but there is early evidence for the Novantae name in Arthur's time. *Y Gododdin* stanza B2.39 praises a Cynon, who was from Aeron (Ayrshire) and was associated with *Nouant*, Ptolemy's Novantae (Koch, 1997). Men like Cynon, who fought for Gododdin, would know of Arthur's fame in the west and tell of his glory in Gododdin, as in B2.38. Arthur's link to the Novantae is also evidence for the antiquity of the poems. It is hard to imagine an 11th century bard composing a fiction which links him to an obscure tribe from the Roman era. This is far removed from the imagery of Geoffrey and seems to be accessing ancient knowledge. *Coit Celidon* also places Arthur in Galloway. Jackson (1945) argues that this forest was not far from both Glasgow and Carlisle, putting it in Galloway. Thus five texts link Arthur to Galloway.[27]

- Chair of the Sovereign: Rheon
- Triad 1:   Pen Rhionydd
- Battle of the Trees: Caer Nefenhyr
- Culhwch and Olwen: Caer Nefenhyr
- Historia Brittonum: Coit Celidon

Gwalchmai (also Walwen, later Sir Gawain)

Arthur's battle horseman, Gwalchmai, is also linked to Galloway. In his history, William of Malmesbury (1125) said that Gwalchmai's grave was found in the reign of William I (1066-87). Our interest is not in the grave itself, which is probably bogus, but in the detail that he came from Walweitha (Galloway) and that his mother was Arthur's sister:[28]

> At this time was found in the province of Wales called Ros the tomb of Walwen, who was the not degenerate nephew of Arthur by his sister. He reigned in that part of Britain which is still called Walweitha [Galloway]...The tomb...was found in the time of King William upon the sea shore, fourteen feet in length.

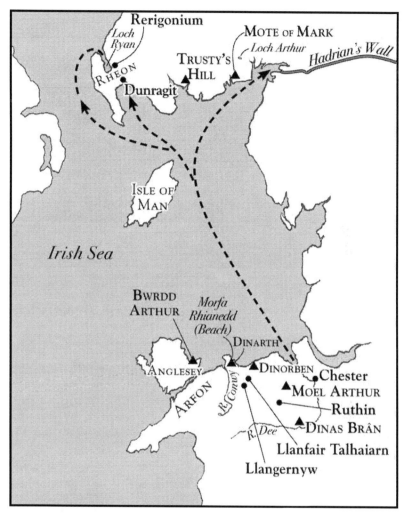

Figure 3.5. Arthur's north Wales domain and the Galloway region which he protected. (Map adapted from Sarah Dunning Park).

Figure 3.6. Loch Ryan (Arthur's Rheon) in Galloway, Scotland. On the east side of the loch looking north. (Photo: R. MacCann).

Figure 3.7. Pictish Symbols at Trusty's Hill. (Photo: R. MacCann).

There are places called Rhôs in north Wales and Dyfed but *Stanzas of the Graves* gives a different site. In Stanza 8 it states: 'The grave of Gwalchmai is in Peryddon as a reproach to men' (Thomas Jones, 1967). Peryddon has been used as another name for the Dee and near its mouth are three places called Walwen, not far from each other. One is near the shore east of Holywell, another is just west of Halkyn, and the third is near Whitford. As the tomb was on the sea shore, the site near Holywell is favoured if the north Wales site was intended.[29]

Was Arthur's family from the North?
In an early triad, Triad 4, Gwalchmai is one of three men of the isle of Britain who are fit to rule. The other two men are Llachau, the son of Arthur, and Rhiwallawn. Rachel Bromwich (2006) interprets the triad as 'qualified by descent to rule'. William of Malmesbury's statement that Gwalchmai's mother was Arthur's sister and that he reigned in Galloway is very interesting.[30]

This information is pre-Galfridian as William published 13 years before Geoffrey. If Gwalchmai reigned in Galloway it would usually imply that Arthur's sister lived there and raised him there until he came to power. This could explain why Arthur took his soldiers to Rheon to defend it and to restore order. If his sister was from Galloway was Arthur also originally from the north? In Chapter 4 it is shown that there are some indications that Arthur's father and his father's brothers, or warband, were from the north in the region of Manau Gododdin and later came south to conquer the Irish in north Wales and settle there, partitioning the lands amongst themselves.

Speculation on Arthur's Role in Galloway
Chair of the Sovereign places Arthur in both *Caer Legion* (Chester) and Galloway. At the time Gildas wrote, Arthur seems to have been established as a powerful Pharaoh who controlled north Wales. He may have had ships berthed in the mouth of the Dee at Chester. From there, it would not have taken long to sail to Loch Ryan, passing the Isle of Man on the way. It is possible that the kings of Galloway asked him for help to repel invaders. This is too far west for these to be Saxons so the possible invaders would be the Irish and Picts, both of

whom had terrified the Britons by their bloodthirsty raids according to Gildas (*De Excidio*, 14-16, 19). Portpatrick on the west coast of the Rhinns is only about 20 miles from Ireland, just across from the major port at Belfast.

Lloyd Laing and David Longley (2006) comment on the dense line of defensive forts located along the west coast of the Rhinns. Given the proximity to Ireland, the most likely invaders were the Irish, but raids by the Picts were also possible. The Trusty's Hill hillfort in Galloway has a rocky outcrop near its entrance inscribed with Pictish symbols (Forsyth and Thickpenny, 2016; Cessford, 1994) which could imply a successful raid from the Picts.[31]

ARTHUR'S FAME IN SCOTLAND – Y GODODDIN

Arthur in Stanza B2.38

Stanza B2.38 of *Y Gododdin* praises the hero *Gorddur* for his valour, noble qualities, and generosity. It states that he enticed down black crows in front of the fortress wall, meaning that crows feasted on his opponents' bodies. In an aside, the bard then states *'though he was not Arthur'*. This was not an insult – the very fact that Gorddur could be compared to Arthur was an honour to him. It is clear that Arthur served as the epitome of a warrior's might and courage. This used to be considered strong evidence for Arthur's historicity, but doubts about an early dating have been expressed. It is argued here that B2.38 shares many features with Stanza B2.28, suggesting that the same bard composed both. Furthermore, it is argued that B2.28 has internal content implying that it was composed very early, perhaps about AD 550. This would imply that B2.38 was also early.[32]

An Early Dating for Stanza B2.28

B2.28 praises the hero *Yrfai* for his swift horsemanship, his eagerness for battle and his valour. He is called Golistan's son. John Koch (1997) has convincingly shown that Golistan is the equivalent of Wolstan (variants Wulfstan, Ulfstan), an Anglo-Saxon name. It explains the following surprising aside: *'though his father was no prince'*. The fact that Yrfai had a Saxon father is astonishing for a man who was praised profusely and had a high rank in the fort of Eidin (now Edinburgh), being called a 'lord of Eidin'. This strongly implies an early date for the stanza, well before the Saxons were threatening the Britons in the north and around Eidin. It appears that Yrfai had proved himself in previous battles and was a man of fine judgement whose word 'was heeded', as it says in the stanza.[33]

Composed when few Angles in Bernicia

Further evidence that B2.28 was composed at an early date is based on the poet naming the enemy as the Deira, probably Angles who had settled in the east, south of the river Tees (Dumville, 1988a). They had not yet moved north into British Bernicia in any significant numbers. The battle site Catraeth, probably Catterick, also suggests this. If the site wasn't Catterick, it may have been another site in Deira. The fact that the Gododdin men rode down to Catraeth (about 150 miles) to fight the Angles implies there were few Angles in Bernicia.

In the decades after Catraeth, the Angles were settling north in British Bernicia. Dumville plausibly states: '... once the Anglo-Saxon kingdom of Bernicia began, there would have had to be a fight to the finish between it and the Gododdin.' Such battles are reported in the *Historia Brittonum* where Urien and other kings fought against them. This fighting is also in the Book of Taliesin poems on Urien and Owain. Finally in AD 638 Edinburgh fell in a siege. It is unlikely that B.28 would have heavily praised a man with a Saxon father after the Britons had lost Edinburgh and Bernicia to the hated Saxons. Given the above, a stanza date of 550-60 is defensible.[34]

Stanzas B2.38 and B2.28 composed by the Same Bard

The B2 stanzas are of interest as they contain many more pre-Middle Welsh features than the A and B1 stanzas. Although certainty is not possible, it seems likely that the two stanzas had a common author, due to their unique sharing of four important features:

1. Negative comparison in an aside
2. Enjambment – where further words, after the end rhyme, are needed to complete the line
3. Same expression to start successive lines
4. Name emphasized at end of stanza.

Consider the following examples:

1. Negative Comparison in an Aside

B2.28   'though his father was no prince'.

B2.38   'though he was not Arthur'.

2. Enjambment

B2.28   Gnaut mab Golistan cen nei *bei* | guledic i tat.

B2.38   Go Chore brein du ar *uur* | caer.

The rhyming words for B2.28 and B2.38 are italicized, but the line continues after the vertical bar to complete the meaning.

3. Same Expression to Start Successive Lines

B2.28   Line 4:   Gnaut...   (It was usual for...)
         Line 5:   Gnaut...   (It was usual for...)

B2.38   Line 4:   Go dolei...   (He used to give...)
         Line 5:   Go chore...   (He used to entice...)

4. Name Emphasized at End of Stanza

B2.28   bloodied before the lord of Eidin – Yrfai.

B2.38   before the barrier of alder wood – Gorddur.

While 2, 3 and 4 occur separately in other stanzas, the occurrence of all three in another B stanza is non-existent and no other stanzas have the negative aside. If the same poet composed both, then the Arthur aside could be as early as AD 550, just over a decade after his death when his fame would be fresh in the minds of the people.

The Chadwicks (1932) say that the name Arthur was 'practically unknown' earlier but now fathers began to name their sons after him: Artur, son of Aedan, Artuir, son of Bicoir the Briton, and Artur, the grandfather of Feradach. A fourth case appears in the Irish *Expulsion of the Déisi* and a Dyfed pedigree. This Arthur was a great grandson of Vortipor. Arthur's great deeds in Novantae territory had two effects, the naming of babies after him in the west and his huge reputation with the Gododdin in the east. Men like Cynon, associated with the Novantae, but who fought for Gododdin in the east, would have spread his fame. This is a far more satisfactory explanation of his appearance in stanza B2.38 than arbitrarily assuming a late interpolation.[35]

WAS ARTHUR THE COMMANDER AT BADON?

Apart from the underlying *Historia* battle-list poem, the absence of Badon from other Welsh poetry leads to doubt about Arthur and Badon. *Chair of the Sovereign* is the main problem. It begins by giving a eulogy to Arthur, listing his great deeds and ending in a ceremony where his soul is blessed. In line 6, the bard thinks that Arthur's main military achievement was his governing of Rheon in Galloway. He does not mention Badon. However, the importance of this battle may have been overrated. It was not a battle to expel the Saxons from Britain as they had firm control over the east. It was probably fought in the southwest and was more a battle to stop the Saxons moving further westward. It is possible that Arthur was the commander at Badon, but his bard may not have known about it.

If Arthur were at Badon there are two conditions that must be met for his bard to be ignorant of it. Both are highly probable in my view. One is that the battle was little known publicly around 537 and only later developed its fame as a result of its mention in Gildas, Bede, the *Historia* and *Welsh Annals*. The battle's importance greatly increased in the public mind when in 731 Bede virtually copied Gildas's account of Badon, having no other knowledge of this battle.

In 537, the battle had taken place 44 years earlier and few people were probably aware of it. The limited schooling available at the time is unlikely to have taught it. No early source except Gildas mentions it, the Welsh Triads ignore it and the Welsh bards show no interest in it. It is possible that it was far less important at that time than it later became as a result of Gildas, Bede, and its association with Arthur in the *Historia Brittonum* and *Welsh Annals*. Consider the grandiose statement of John Morris (1973) for one modern view:[36]

> Badon was the 'final victory of the fatherland'... The British had beaten back the barbarians. They stood alone in Europe, the only remaining corner of the western Roman world where a native power withstood the all-conquering Germans.

This could be compared to what Gildas actually said, from Michael Winterbottom's (1978) translation:[37]

> From then on victory went now to our countrymen, now to their enemies ... This lasted right up to the siege of Badon Hill, pretty well the last defeat of the villains, and certainly not the least.

Gildas' language is muted. He implies that there were some skirmishes after Badon and his remark that the Saxon defeat was certainly *not the least* suggests that, although the siege was decisive, there had been greater British victories. It gives the sense that it was the accumulation of battles that eventually stopped the Saxon raids, rather than a single massive victory. If it were not for his birthday occurring in the same year, one wonders whether Gildas would even have mentioned it.

The second condition required for the bard's ignorance of Badon is that he was not at the siege. In *Battle of the Trees* he says that he had sung from a young age and in the next line that he had sung before the lord of Britain, Arthur. He was probably much younger than Arthur and, as he believed that Virgil's golden age had began, he apparently outlived the cold temperature period in Britain that lasted until about 550 (see Chapter 9). He composed *Spoils of Annwfyn* and *Chair of the Sovereign* around 540 and a few decades later when he was an old man he composed *Battle of the Trees*, perhaps around 560-65. When he composed this poem he was old with limited mobility and relied on people to visit him. He laments that he had only one visitor named Goronwy. If he did compose *Battle of the Trees* about 560-65 he may have been too young to have been at Badon Hill in 493.[38]

Arthur's Bard did not compose the Historia poem

If Badon was little known c. 537 then the underlying *Historia* poem was probably composed after Gildas or Bede had made it famous. A second issue is that the *Coit Celidon* battle may have been taken from *Battle of the Trees*, composed around 560-65. Arthur's bard did not compose the underlying *Historia* poem as he did not mention Badon as Arthur's victory in his other poems. Another bard must have composed it using whatever sources he could find and he probably obtained Badon from either Gildas or Bede and the other battles from British traditions. It strongly weakens any inference made from the *Historia* battle list that Arthur won the battle at Badon Hill.

HOW DID ARTHUR BECOME KING OF RHOS?

It is argued that Arthur was the 'Bear' whose main fort was Dinarth in Rhôs. The Harleian recension states: 'Arthur fought against them in those days, along with the kings of the Britons, although he was the leader in battle.' The Vatican recension adds: 'though there were many more noble than him.' Therefore some infer that Arthur wasn't a king. However a scholarly analysis by Snyder (2005) draws the conclusion: we must 'abandon the notion that the Historia proves that Arthur was no king.' Although the Vatican note may be true of Arthur, a strong leader could take the throne with popular or military support.[39]

If Arthur was born c. 470 when he reached his late teens he would have been involved in the battles to overcome the Irish in north Wales and the Saxon encroachments on lands originally held by the Britons. Here he evidently showed the skills and leadership that eventually made him the paragon to which other warriors could be compared. Rachel Bromwich (1975-6) thinks that Arthur was probably a hero in Strathclyde or another northern realm but his pacifying of Rheon probably came after he became the overlord in north Wales.[40]

When a young Maglocunus killed his uncle Owain who was king of Rhôs he would have killed off other royal rivals. He probably reigned for a short period before resigning to become a monk. In the Harleian pedigrees, Cuneglasus was Owain's son. If he were old enough to be a threat, he should have been killed in the coup. Yet when Gildas was writing, this coup was around 40 years in the past, Cuneglasus was still alive, and 'the Bear' now owned Dinarth with Cuneglasus as his general. It seems that Arthur had replaced Maglocunus. It appears that Arthur's strong leadership and Christian beliefs had gained him the support of Maglocunus. Cuneglasus may have been a baby at the time of the coup and was spared by Maglocunus.

The late pedigree, *Bonedd yr Arwyr*, shows Arthur as the great grandson of Cunedda through his mother, Eigyr, but it is difficult to trust this and it is now very unlikely that Cunedda was ever involved in the conquest of north Wales. In the next chapter, an argument is given that ties Arthur more precisely to the royal lines, making him a relative of Maglocunus and Owain Danwyn and giving greater clarity on how he was able to take the throne of Rhôs.[41]

Arthur as King in the Poems

Gildas' use of Pharaoh in the *De Excidio* implies that Arthur had power over other local kings and thus was a king himself. *Spoils of Annwfyn* applies three titles to Arthur in praising him after his death. These are *wledic, pendeuic* and *ri. Battle of the Trees* also uses *wledic* to refer to Arthur, an ancient title. *Chair of the Sovereign* uses both *ri* and *pendeuic*, and two new terms, *rechtur* and *teÿrnon*, to refer to Arthur. The semi-Latin *rechtur* is equivalent to the Latin, rector, meaning 'governor'. In practice, any one of these five terms would indicate a king. In *Chair of the Sovereign* the main theme is Arthur's Throne and who will replace him. In lines 11-12 it refers to Arthur's 'commensurate chair amongst the lordly retinue'.

Why wasn't Arthur in the Rhôs Genealogy as King?

There is a distinction between a king list and a genealogy. Arthur may have been seen as an interloper who interrupted the royal succession from Owain to Cuneglasus. Neither Maglocunus nor Arthur appear in the lineage although they both held the throne of Rhôs. In addition, scholars have argued that a superstition arose in Wales against using Arthur's name, as will be discussed in Chapter 9.

CLAIMS THAT ARTHUR WAS A KNOWN FIGURE

Some try to establish Arthur's existence by claiming that Arthur was a historical figure, X. This allows various features of X, including his location, to be attributed to Arthur, falsely fleshing out the shadowy figure of Arthur. However there is no need to argue that Arthur was another person. Neither Alcock (1971) nor Morris (1973) did this in their major books on Arthur. The six figures below, each claimed to be King Arthur, will now be briefly discussed:

1. Artur, son of Aedan of Dalriada
2. Ambrosius Aurelianus
3. Owain Danwyn
4. Cuneglasus
5. Athrwys son of Meurig
6. Riothamus.

Artur son of Aedan

Artur (Arturius) has the advantage of having a name equivalent to Arthur. He was a prince, the obscure son of King Aedan of Dalriada, and died relatively young at the battle of Miathi in about 590-96. Nora Chadwick (1953) suggests that he could be the original Arthur. The best paper on this is by Michelle Ziegler (1999) who provides a detailed account of the northern historical affairs and identifies the problems of equating Artur with Arthur. She states: 'Like many candidates for the historical "King Arthur", there is only slightly more evidence than his name'. The eminent scholar, Rachel Bromwich (1975-6), points out that Aedan was called in Welsh tradition the 'wily' or 'treacherous', as shown by his derogatory mention in Triad 54. Given this she argues that it would be improbable that his obscure son became the hero of the Britons. Artur lived too late to be Arthur, was probably born about 20-30 years after Arthur's death, and did not have a reputation as a warrior. He was probably named after the real Arthur.[42]

Ambrosius Aurelianus

Ambrosius was a Romano-Briton whose 'parents had worn the purple' which probably refers to their aristocratic Roman heritage. According to Gildas he was the first to lead the Britons in their fightback against the Saxon onslaught and win an initial victory. This establishes him as a historical leader and a general which on the surface would make him a good fit for Arthur.

However, there are three major problems. Both 'Ambrosius' and 'Arthur' are names. They are not titles. So Ambrosius was not called Arthur. Secondly, the Welsh were familiar with Ambrosius and clearly distinguished him from Arthur. Both men appear in the *Historia Brittonum* in different roles. By this time Ambrosius had developed legendary features (as Arthur had) and there appears as a boy wizard, born of a virgin mother, who prophesied the future to Vortigern. His identity with the general of Gildas comes from his name and his claim that his father was a Roman consul. Arthur appears in the battle list discussed earlier. Thirdly, Ambrosius was probably born at least 50 years earlier than Arthur. If the Welsh distinguish between them it is unlikely that they were the same person.[43]

Owain Danwyn

Owain appears in a Harleian pedigree as the father of Cuneglasus and 'Danwyn' is an epithet meaning the 'white-toothed'. Unfortunately, nothing else about him is known. Given that his name 'Owain' is not 'Arthur', he is not King Arthur.

Cuneglasus is called the chariot driver of the Bear's Stronghold. This use of the third person implies that Cuneglasus was not the Bear but had an important role in defending the Bear's fort. One could infer (wrongly) that Owain, his father, owned the fort and thus conclude that Owain must be the Bear. However at the time the *De Excidio* was written Owain was long dead, killed by Maglocunus around 40 years earlier when the latter was in the 'first years' of his youth, about 15. It is doubtful that Gildas would still ascribe the ownership of the fort to Owain this long after his death. Furthermore, the name 'Owain' has nothing to do with 'bear'. The latter almost certainly derives from the current owner of the fort at the time of Gildas writing, Arthur, whose name was perfect for the 'the Bear' epithet.[44]

Cuneglasus

Cuneglasus is a far more likely candidate for Arthur. His name would usually translate to 'blue or grey hound' which could be an epithet. It seems doubtful that his parents named him 'blue hound', although not impossible as there are heroic references to blue-grey armour in poetry (Williams, 1987; Haycock, 2007) and 'hound' can be an epithet for warrior. If 'Cuneglasus' is an epithet, his real name could have been 'Arthur'. The fact that he fought with 'arms special to himself' could be indicative of Arthur's military prowess. Secondly, the fact that he was involved with two sisters, abandoning his wife to take up with her villainous sister, could perhaps suggest Gwenhwyfar and her sister Gwenhwyfach who are depicted in conflict in late traditions. However, none of this material is very strong.[45]

The wording of Gildas implies that Cuneglasus does not own the Bear's Stronghold and that he is only called '(you) bear' because he is part of the Bear's retinue. He also seems to be less powerful than his cousin, Maglocunus, and all five kings are part of the retinue of a powerful Pharaoh who is more likely to be Arthur.

Athrwys son of Meurig

Much more is known concerning Athrwys, so a close comparison with Arthur is possible. This material comes from the Book of Llandaff (*Liber Landavensis*), written in Latin and translated into English by William Rees (1840). The manuscript, 17110E, is held in the National Library of Wales and has been studied expertly and comprehensively by Wendy Davies (1979).

The name of Athrwys is spelt differently in each pedigree list that mentions him. These spellings with the manuscripts in parentheses are: *Atroys* (Harley MS 3859.28), *Adroes* (Jesus College MS 20.9), *Athrawes* (ABT 15) and *Athrwys* (Book of Llandaff). Note that in all these cases there is no 'r' following the initial 'A'. Arthur is both spelt and pronounced differently to each variation of Athrwys. In the old poem *Y Gododdin*, both the names 'Arthur' and 'Athrwys' appear, where the latter is a different Athrwys to Meurig's son (Koch, 1997) and the poem treats them as separate names. They are clearly not the same name.[46]

Arthur and Athrwys differ considerably in their dates. Arthur died in 537/9 whereas the Book of Llandaff states that Athrwys did not become king until after the Yellow Pestilence (Rees, 1840) which had killed Maglocunus in 547/9. So Athrwys became king about AD 550, about ten years after Arthur had died. However Wendy Davies (1979) dates Athrwys to about 605–655, putting him much later than Arthur. She also argues that Athrwys probably died before Meurig and thus did not become king.[47]

As can be seen from the abundant evidence given earlier, Arthur was based in north Wales. Athrwys, however, lived in southeast Wales in Gwent and Glywysing.

Arthur is given twelve battles in the *Historia Brittonum* and a further battle at Longborth, probably at Penbryn beach in Llanborth, from the poem *Geraint son of Erbin*, and he was killed at Camlan. In the Book of Llandaff there is no record of Athrwys fighting any battle, but his grandfather Tewdrig was killed aiding his son Meurig in battle against the Saxons near Tintern ford (Rees, 1840). Thus the Book of Llandaff recorded a battle for Tewdrig and Meurig but no battles for Athrwys. Not a single source associates Athrwys with Camlan.[48]

Arthur's father was Uthr (with the Pendragon epithet, meaning 'chief of warriors'), but the father of Athrwys was Meurig (Rees, 1840). Uthr can be used as both a name, as in the Book of Taliesin poem on Madoc, or the adjective 'terrible' (causing 'terror'). Nowhere in the Book of Llandaff is Meurig called Uthr or Pendragon.[49]

Arthur's mother was Eigyr from *Bonedd yr Arwyr*, Pedigree 31, but the mother of Athrwys was Onbrawst (Rees, 1840). Arthur had two brothers, Madoc and Gormant, the latter being his half-brother (Bartrum, 2009). Athrwys also had two brothers, but with completely different names, Frioc and Idnerth (Rees, 1840).[50]

Arthur had three sons, Llacheu, Gwydre, Cydfan and a daughter, Archfedd. His 'son' Amr in the *Mirabilia* was probably not historical. Athrwys had two sons, Morgan and Ithael. Arthur's wife was probably Gwenhwyfar, from a strong tradition, whereas Athrwys seems to have married Cenedlon, according to Bartrum (2009). These differences are clearly seen from the table below.[51]

	Arthur	**Athrwys**
Name	Arthur	Atroys, Adroes, Athrawes, Athrwys
Dating	Badon 493; died 537/9	Became king after 550
Location	North Wales	Gwent and Glywysing, Southeast Wales
Battles	14 battles	No battles
Father	Uthr	Meurig
Mother	Eigyr	Onbrawst
Brothers	Madoc, Gormant	Frioc, Idnerth
Children	Llacheu, Gwydre, Cydfan, Archfedd	Morgan, Ithael
Wife	Gwenhwyfar?	Cenedlon?

This table shows that the two men differ in every detail and it seems extraordinary that some have argued that two such different figures could really be the same person. The incisive historian Sharon Turner (1852) was well aware of this theory and wisely states that Athrwys was too petty a personage to be Arthur.[52]

One reason why the 'Athrwys was Arthur' equation took hold was that it was promulgated by notorious forger, Iolo Morganwg ('Ned of Glamorgan'), his real name being Edward Williams. He was a talented man and a persuasive one who was an industrious collector of old manuscripts from all over Wales, and a very proud south Welshman. However he was driven to create a brilliant past for south Wales to negate the beliefs that north Wales, about which he held a fierce resentment, contained the purest survival of Welsh traditions (Gwyn Williams, 1979). His creation of the *Gorsedd* rituals was accepted into the Eisteddfod and its pageantry is now a highlight.[53]

A less successful creation of the past was his invention of a fake language, *Coelbren y Beirdd*, an alphabet that he falsely claimed was handed down from the ancient bards. This was denounced in 1893 by the learned scholar, J. Romilly Allen, as a 'gigantic fraud'. There are no examples of the alphabet before Iolo's time.[54]

His skilful literary forgeries, which were exposed by the dedicated scholarship of G. J. Williams, have meant that anything associated with him is tainted. The great Welsh scholar, Sir Ifor Williams, sums up the problems associated with Iolo's writings:[55]

... the greatest forger of Welsh documents that Wales has ever known ... if any one should persist in using Iolo's faked MSS to support any theory or thesis, he does so at his own risk and peril.

In his *Iolo Manuscripts*, his south Wales bias is extreme. Against all reason, he locates Urien, Taliesin and Talhaearn in south Wales, and wanted a south Wales Arthur. He found him in Athrwys and, knowing that Morgan was Athrwys' son, he slyly altered a pedigree (Morganwg, 1848) to make it say:[56]

Morgan, the son of Arthur had the cantrev of Gwent ...

Riothamus

Ashe (1981; 1995) believes that a late fifth century king, Riothamus, could be the historical Arthur. The historical situation in Gaul is given by Jordanes in his *Gothic History*, AD 551. The translation below comes from Mierow (1915).[57]

> Now Eurich, king of the Visigoths, perceived the frequent change of Roman Emperors and strove to hold Gaul by his own right. The Emperor Anthemius heard of it and asked the Brittones for aid. Their King Riotimus came with twelve thousand men into the state of the Bituriges by the way of Ocean, and was received as he disembarked from his ships. Eurich, king of the Visigoths, came against them with an innumerable army, and after a long fight he routed Riotimus, king of the Brittones, before the Romans could join him. So when he had lost a great part of his army, he fled with all the men he could gather together, and came to the Burgundians a neighboring tribe then allied to the Romans.

Ashe thinks that this Riotimus [Riothamus] could be Arthur which would put his battle in Gaul at the early date of about 470. A key point of disputation is the interpretation of the word *Brittones* in the above quote. Ashe thinks it means Britons and in giving the above passage he replaces Brittones with Britons. However, as Ashe is aware, most scholars think that Brittones means the Bretons from western Gaul. Gregory of Tours briefly mentions the defeat as follows:[58]

> The Bretons were expelled from Bourges by the Goths and many were killed at Bourg-de-Déols.

This translation by Lewis Thorpe (1974) takes the *Britanni* of the Latin text to be the Bretons. Ashe argues that the coming by 'way of Ocean' implies it had to be the Britons, as the Bretons were already there in Gaul and could travel to the Bituriges by land, but Higham (2018) argues that the Bretons probably sailed west by ocean from Brittany around the headlands to enter the Loire River. The 12,000 men seems like an exaggeration of the army size for either scenario.[59]

Further information on Riothamus comes from a letter written by Sidonius Apollinaris to Riothamus. Sidonius was writing on behalf of an obscure person whose grievance was that 'the Bretons are secretly enticing his slaves away' to join their army. Dalton (1915) translates the people in the army as Bretons. This obscure person was delivering the letter himself and Sidonius was concerned that he may not get a fair hearing. He asks Riothamus to confront the parties and decide the matter on its merits. The letter shows that Sidonius knew Riothamus well as shown by his remembering examples of the latter's honour:[60]

> Yet I do my best to remember the burdensome and delicate sense
> of honour which makes you so ready to blush for others' faults.

This wording implies that Sidonius knew Riothamus over an extended period. It suggests that Riothamus lived in Gaul as a Breton and thus was unlikely to have been Arthur of Britain.

A second problem with the identification of Arthur with Riothamus is the difference of names. Ashe (1995) argues that Riothamus is a title meaning 'most kingly' and was applied to a man whose real name could have been Arthur. While Riothamus may have originally been a title it seems that it became used so often that it supplanted the king's name. Arthur is either called 'Arthur' or an obvious warrior epithet such as 'the Bear' or the 'boar'. Higham argues that Jordanes treats Riothamus as a name in calling him 'King Riothamus'. If it were a title it would be 'King most kingly', an absurdity. The only record of a battle fought by Riothamus is one he lost and he did not die in battle but fled with the remainder of his men to the Burgundians.[61]

A major problem with identifying Arthur with Riothamus is that there is no connection with the British material. *Spoils of Annwfyn* states that Arthur sailed across the shores of the world to get to Annwfyn. Geoffrey of Monmouth has the ship guided by a navigator to whom the stars and seas were well known to imply the journey was long and hazardous. He replaces Annwfyn with Avalon (from *afal*, 'apple') to link it with legends of a distant land in the west where the trees were abundant with fruit. Ashe tries to capitalize on this by noting there is an Avallon about 87 miles east of Bourges to which Arthur could have fled. But places named after apple orchards are to be expected and a short land-based journey has nothing to do with a long sea voyage. The Arthur of the Welsh sources is connected to the early sixth century through the *Welsh Annals* and to his connections to people who lived in this period. Riothamus was not Arthur but it is possible that Geoffrey of Monmouth was influenced by Riothamus' battle in Gaul in constructing his fictional Arthur.[62]

WAS ARTHUR A MYTHICAL FIGURE?

From the late 1800s to the mid twentieth century the study of Welsh linguistics was making sound progress which accelerated throughout that century. In contrast, the study of Welsh literature gave rise to weird theories which are still held by some. Instead of tight reasoning with due attention to the nature of the sources, these theories were formed by making loose associations. For example, John Rhŷs (1891) thought that Gwalchmai was a compound of *gwalch* (hawk or falcon) and *mai* (month of May). Rhŷs notes that Malory (1485) states that Gwalchmai had a solar peculiarity that in battle his strength grew until midday and then wanes afterwards. As May heralds the summer, Rhŷs concludes that Gwalchmai was a Solar Hero. It is more likely that *mai* means 'plain' or 'plains' so that Gwalchmai means hawk of the plains, a heroic name for a warrior. Here we see a pre-conceived model of the Solar Hero and loose associations derived from a late and unhistorical text. Squire (1905) regarded Arthur and his knights as Celtic gods and Loomis (1927) thought they could be 'gods of sun and storm'.

John Lloyd was sceptical about the validity of Arthur's battles in the *Historia* but argued that there were 'many circumstances which tend to establish his real historical existence'. He wryly remarks that if our only knowledge of Maglocunus had been derived solely from Welsh tradition (i.e. the Maelgwn Gwynedd tales) then[63]

> ... he would, without a doubt, have been treated like Arthur, as a purely mythical figure and perhaps would have been refined into a solar deity. But in the pages of the *De Excidio* he is unmistakeable flesh and blood.

The solar deity fad has died out but the idea of Arthur as a myth who came to be regarded as historical has been re-argued. In his John Rhŷs Memorial Lecture, Van Hamel (1934) argues that Arthur was mythical but became 'historicized' just like the mythical Irish hero,

Finn. Later works such as Padel (1994) and Green (2007) elaborate on this theme. They all focus on the *Mirabilia* (Marvels), a probable 9th century document in the same manuscript as the *Historia*.

The Mirabilia

These are 'marvels' associated with sites in Britain. They include a hot pool that adjusts its temperature to that which the bather desires; a log linked to a well that returns to the well when removed, and so on. By the early 800s, the marvels about Arthur had started to develop. Two appear in the *Mirabilia*. One involves Arthur killing his son Amr and burying him. The marvel is that when men measure the grave it is sometimes six feet, or nine feet, or twelve feet or fifteen feet. When you measure it at one time, the next time it will be a different length. Van Hamel, Padel and Green use this marvel to argue that Arthur moved in a world of magic.[64]

Secondly Arthur's dog, Cabal, meaning 'horse', leaves a footprint mark on a stone when Arthur was hunting a giant boar. The marvel is that when the stone is removed from on top of a pile, it reappears there the next day. The boar is used to claim that Arthur moved in a world of magical animals. However, the boar is not uniquely associated with Arthur. The boar, called Twrch Trwyth, appears in the poem *Gorchan Cynfelyn* from the Book of Aneirin, where 'the prowess of the hero is compared to that of the boar' (Jarman, 1989-90). It is significant that Arthur is not mentioned at all in this poem. Jarman thinks that it may date to the 7th century and Koch (1987) thinks it unlikely that it was composed in the 6th century.[65]

The theme of heroes hunting a great boar is ancient, told centuries before Christ in Greece, where the tale is a prelude to the story of the Trojan War. A giant boar was sent by Artemis to destroy the Calydon region in Aetolia. A later account appears in *Metamorphoses* by the Roman poet Ovid, who lived at the time of Christ (Miller, 1916). The boar hunt tales later came to Britain to appear in *Gorchan Cynfelyn* (without Arthur), then the *Mirabilia*, and later *Culhwch and Olwen*. If Jarman is right, Arthur's link to the boar started about 200 years after *Gorchan Cynfelyn*. It seems that Arthur's fame was now so great that human enemies were no longer formidable enough or interesting enough, so the giant boar was used as an adversary.[66]

Green thinks that texts portraying Arthur fighting exotic creatures imply that the Britons saw Arthur as a supernatural protector against such threats. Green lists them: 'Arthur protected the Britons from – dog-heads, cat-monsters, giants, dragons, witches, shape-shifters and divine boars'. Now credulous people surely existed in the 6th century and others may have jested about such creatures (as they do today) but there is nothing to indicate the Britons were worried about such creatures. Gildas in his *De Excidio* discusses the threats to the Britons but there is no mention of the above threats. To Gildas the threats were raids from the Irish, Picts and Saxons and disasters and famines. Similarly, the exotic creatures of Green have no place in the daily lives of the contemporary Franks, as related by Gregory of Tours.[67]

Apart from the *Mirabilia*, the texts she uses are 1100s or later and tell us nothing about how the Britons saw Arthur in c. 500, being 600 years after his time. The 'evidence' from these texts is worthless.

Padel and Green rely on 12th century texts

Padel relies on much the same texts as Green and also uses the *Lives* of St Cadog and St Carannog. Jackson (1959a) suggests that the monks saw them as little better than 'worthless fairy-tales' to show the saints' superiority over Arthur. However Padel uses these tales to claim that Arthur was associated with magic. Yet all the magic actually comes from Cadog and Carannog in besting Arthur. He is just presented as a man with no such powers which makes Padel's claim look contrived. Padel would never accept a 12th century source that implied Arthur was historical yet fills his paper with 12th century sources that he uses to argue that Arthur was a myth. He gives the latest possible date for Arthur's mention in *Y Gododdin* (10th century) to try to discredit it as an Arthurian source yet seems oblivious to the irony that it is still two centuries earlier than the sources on which he relies. The very late 'evidence' he provides is worthless.[68]

They omit evidence against the mythological view

Both Padel and Green focus on Arthur appearing in Chapter 73 of the *Mirabilia* but fail to point out that two historical people, Illtud and Meurig, are also in the *Mirabilia* just before Arthur in Chapters 71 and 72 and are both associated with equally miraculous events. Higham

(2018) takes an uncritical approach to the mythological view and also does not mention the marvel linked to Meurig. As historical people are appearing in the *Mirabilia* then Arthur's appearances there can hardly imply that he was mythical.[69]

Ambrosius developed legendary features

Padel and Green also fail to mention the telling example of a real battle leader who by the time of the *Historia* had accrued legendary features, as Arthur had. In the *De Excidio* Ambrosius is a man of Roman stock who led the first British victory against the Saxons. But in the *Historia* he appears as a wizard, with powers of prophecy, born of a virgin, but whose father was a Roman consul ('worn the purple' in Gildas). He repeatedly confounds Vortigern's *magi* by his supernatural knowledge of the magical events occurring in the foundations of the fort.[70]

Ambrosius and his lords associated with the exotic creatures

They also fail to mention that the lords of Ambrosius ('Emrys') are in *Pa Gur,* along with Arthur, and thus are also associated with Green's exotic creatures. Jackson (1959b) states that if he was the Ambrosius of Gildas (which seems certain) then 'he is in strange company here'. See the *Pa Gur* translation of Koch and Carey (2003) for the Emrys and Ambrosius equivalence.[71]

Features of the landscape

Padel and Green focus on features of the landscape named after Arthur but the dates when Arthur's name is linked to the landforms are very late. In an attempt to link Arthur closely to Finn, Padel makes the totally unsupported statements 'these wild and rocky landscapes are Arthur's natural environment' and 'Arthur's domain is where other people do not live'. Not a single source can be found to justify these. On the contrary, Arthur is presented as a king living at his illustrious court (*Culhwch and Olwen*, *Life of Illtud*) and is always interacting with people. Padel's claim of Arthur living outside society is based on the model that he is like Finn and the fact that landscape features are named after him. It causes Padel to make distortions in his claims. The landscape features provide zero evidence on how people saw Arthur in the 500s. Their naming after Arthur, where known, is very much later than the 500s and so this 'evidence' is again worthless.[72]

Comments on the mythological model

There is no sixth-century evidence for this model. It fails to explain Arthur's fame. It fails to explain when the 'mythical Arthur' appeared and how and when the 'mythical Arthur' came to be regarded as a man. The model is a false one. In contrast, the Welsh texts show when and where Arthur lived and how his fame developed.

Spoils of Annwfyn gives an unrelenting attack on the monks which is most convincingly explained as a reply to the *De Excidio*. The places the poem c. 540 and Arthur's death just before this which makes him a contemporary of Gildas. This dating is confirmed by *Chair of the Sovereign* which describes severe flooding in north Wales not long after Arthur's death. Tree ring dating in nearby Ireland indicates huge flooding there at a date around 540.

Arthur can be shown to have interacted with real people though credible sources. Triad 57 gives him a mistress, Garwen, whose father is named as Hennin. *Stanzas of the Graves*, no. 70, says that she was buried on the *morfa*, the beach at Llandudno, quite close to Dineirth. Stanza 71 says that Hennin was buried at Dinorben, several miles to the east of Dineirth, where a cromlech thought to be his burial site was noted in an archaeological study.

An impressive hillfort named *Dineirth* is located in north Wales. Gildas didn't coin its name as the genitive case endings were gone by his time, but translated its existing name as the Bear's fort. Its origin fits a time c. 500 when the case endings were used in speech and when Maglocunus resigned the Rhôs throne to become a monk. Arthur is the most likely candidate for the 'Bear' who had replaced Maglocunus. His interactions with the nearby Garwen and Hennin add weight to this. Another independent source, *Lineage of the Heroes*, gives Arthur a son Cydfan with Eleirch, Iaen's daughter, who lived at Caer Dathl in Arfon, another north Wales location. To add to these, the poems place Arthur in north Wales through the river Dee and his wearing the lorica of Lleon (Chester). These sources give a convincing scenario for Arthur as a strong *gwledig* in north Wales. Other secondary sources reinforce the evidence that Arthur was based there. There are hillforts with his name or associated with him in tradition. Unlike the mythical model, this Welsh material gives plausible and coherent details for Arthur that are free of legendary matter.

SUMMARY OF ARTHUR

Gildas translates the name of a major hillfort in Rhôs (*Dineirth*) as *receptaculum ursi* (the Bear's Fort). Arthur's name is perfect for the epithet of 'the Bear', differing from the Brittonic for bear (*arth*) by only two letters. This sets a stringent test for my claim that the three Welsh poems are authentic poems by his bard. If they place Arthur in any other location such as Cornwall, Somerset, South Wales etc. then their variance from Gildas would refute their authenticity. But they refer to the Dee and Caer Lleon, key features of north Wales. Arthur's wooded retreat of Kelliwic in the region of *Kernyw* also survives in the placename, *Llangernyw*, about nine miles south of Dineirth.

One poem praises Arthur's governing of *Rheon* as a major exploit. Rheon refers to Loch Ryan in Galloway and the very first Welsh Triad gives Arthur a northern court in *Pen Rhionydd*. He may have been motivated to intervene there if his nephew Gwalchmai (his sister's son) was a king in Galloway, as mentioned in the history of William of Malmesbury. To go from north Wales to Galloway would only be a few days sailing. His authoritative governing of Galloway gave him such fame that men in the west began naming their sons after him. This fame spread across Scotland to the Gododdin capital at Edinburgh in the east where he was regarded as the epitome of valour.

As Arthur's bard doesn't mention Badon in his other poems, the poem underlying the *Historia* battles wasn't composed by him which severely weakens any inference from this list that Arthur won Badon. While much of his fighting may have been against the Irish and Picts, his battles in Lindsey against the Angles look to be authentic and do not appear to be a borrowing from other battles. It would also be rash to discount some other battles which could derive from tradition. It is argued that Badon's fame as a decisive battle has been overrated and may have largely developed after it was mentioned by Gildas and Bede and later associated with Arthur.

In the next chapter, the mystery of where Arthur's father, Uthr Pendragon, fits into the British kings is unraveled. It is shown that Uthr is the same epithet as Yrth and that Uthr Pendragon is the king Einion Yrth who was the founder of the Gwynedd dynasty.

4
ARTHUR'S FATHER

Earlier it was argued that Arthur replaced Maglocunus as king of Rhôs after the latter resigned to become a monk. This was based on Gildas' reference to the *Dineirth* fort, which at that time was being guarded by Cuneglasus. In order for Arthur to have gained this throne it is probable that he had some relationship to the royal family whose members included Owain Danwyn, Maglocunus and Cuneglasus. In this chapter a speculative argument is given that connects Arthur more precisely to this royal family. Arthur's father is popularly known as Uthr Pendragon, where *pendragon* is an epithet meaning 'chief of warriors' and Uthr is taken to be a name. It is argued here that he was a known historical figure. This king is Einion Yrth.

UTHR PENDRAGON

Early evidence that Uthr Pendragon was thought to be Arthur's father comes from a Book of Taliesin poem which has the title written in red *marwnat vthyr pen*. In the margin of the script a later hand has added *mar. vthyr... dragon* so the poem is now called *Marwnat Vthyr Pendragon* (Haycock, 2007; Koch (2006). The poem is in the 'voice' of Uthr although Uthr's name does not appear in the poem. The word *marwnat* means 'deathsong' and applies where a bard commemorates the death of his king, but obviously Uthr cannot be composing it after his own death. The poem's attitude is that Uthr was old and nearing death as implied by lines near the end of this poem and was composing his own epitaph. In line 31 he mentions that he was also a bard. If early, the poem most likely did not have a title and *marwnat vthyr pen* would have been created for it by a later scribe.[1]

Dating the Poem

The poem is difficult to date but one line (line 3) suggests that it is pre-Galfridian (before Geoffrey of Monmouth). This line refers to Uthr wearing blue/grey armour:

3   **Neu vi a ewir gorlassar**
      It is I who's called 'Armed in Blue'

Geoffrey calls him Uther and infers from line 3 that he was also called 'gorlassar'. He creates a fantasy where Merlin magically changes Uther into the shape of Gorlois, the husband of Igerna (Eigr) in the fantasy. As Uther now looks like Gorlois he is able to enter Igerna's Tintagel Castle and lie with her, from which Arthur is born. Gorlois is later killed by Uther's men when escaping from a siege, leaving Uther free to marry Igerna. So it seems that the poem existed before Geoffrey's *HRB* as he used it as a source for Arthur's birth fantasy.[2]

Line 38 of the poem could mention Mary, the mother of Christ, as translated by Haycock but she thinks this translation is uncertain. Mary is prominent in Arthur's battle list in the *Historia* so Mary was important in Britain in AD 830. Geoffrey Ashe (1982) argues that the *De Excidio* (in Chapter 28.1) could imply a British interest in Mary in the sixth century. When two princes were murdered by Constantine in a church in Dumnonia they had placed their trust in Constantine's oath not to harm them and in the Mother (*genetrix*). Ashe states that in Christian Latin up to AD 600, *genetrix* was used for Mary, Mother of God while *mater* was used for Mother Church. In Latin, *genero* means 'give birth'. If Ashe is correct then a mention of Mary in the poem would not imply that the poem was necessarily late.[3]

Another Welsh poem *Pa Gur* is pre-Galfridian, dating from the 900s (Roberts, 1991) to c. 1100 (Sims-Williams, 1991). It mentions a Uthir Pendragon but doesn't say he was Arthur's father, although this was probably understood as common knowledge.[4]

Uthr's connection to Arthur

There are four references in *Marwnat Uthr Pendragon* that connect Uthr to Arthur, two of which are specific to a north Wales Arthur.

1. In line 12 Uthr says he gave 'vigorous swordstrokes against the sons of Cawrnur'. In Chair of the Sovereign (lines 13-14) Arthur killed Cawrnur's horsemen and in Caradoc's Life of Gildas, Arthur fought and killed Caw's son, Huail.

2. In line 14, Uthr says that he had a ninth share of Arthur's valour, nine being a sacred number. While he was not Arthur's equal, he was comparable to Arthur, an honour. This is similar to the line in *Y Gododdin* where another warrior is compared to Arthur.

3. In line 24 Uthr says there would not be life (for the Britons) if not for his offspring, implying that his son, or sons, were renowned for defending the Britons. This, combined with his comparing himself to Arthur, and that they both fought Cawrnur's sons, is the basis for the belief that Arthur was his son.

4. In lines 19-20, Uthr states 'It was I who gave Henben swords of great protective power'. Henben was Hennin Henben, the father of Garwen, Arthur's mistress. She was buried on the *Morfa Rhianedd* near Dineirth. Hennin was buried at Dinorben to the east.[5]

In the poems, Uthr and Arthur fought Cawrnur's sons and in another source, Arthur fought Caw's son, Huail. Caw and Cawrnur appear to be the same person. Caw's name varies across the sources – *Caunus* in the Rhuys *Life*, *Nau* in the Caradoc *Life*, and Caw in *Life of Cadoc* and *Culhwch and Olwen*.

Cawrnur is a compound epithet of *cawr* (giant or hero) and *nur* (lord), indicating a lord of large stature, a feature his bard would have praised. In the *Life of Cadoc*, Caw is portrayed as a giant. Caw and his sons probably lived in north Wales, as argued earlier, so this places Uthr and Arthur there and in point 4, they are also linked to north Wales through Henben and his daughter Garwen.

EINION YRTH

It is argued below that Einion Yrth was the founder of Gwynedd, the first member of two notable pedigree lines, one line descending from his son Cadwallon Lawhir, through Maglocunus (Maelgwn Gwynedd) to the great Cadwallon (in the seventh generation) who briefly took back much of Northumbria from the Saxons. The other line descended from his other son Owain Danwyn, through Cuneglasus.

North Wales Foundation Legend

Einion appears in the foundation legend of north Wales where he is said to be one of the sons of Cunedda who purportedly expelled the Irish from north Wales. As will be discussed below, there is now a great doubt as to whether Cunedda actually came to Wales at all and indications that it was Einion Yrth who was the dominant force in the conquest of the Irish in north Wales.

The *Historia Brittonum* outlines the legend, given below.[6]

> Maelgwn, the great king, was reigning among the Britons in the region
> of Gwynedd, for his ancestor, Cunedag, with his sons, whose number
> was eight, had come previously from the northern part, that is from
> the region which is called Manau Gododdin, one hundred and forty-
> six years before Maelgwn reigned. And with great slaughter they
> drove out from those regions the Scotti [Irish] who never returned
> again to inhabit them.

Chadwick (1958) and Dumville (1977) were sceptical about the legend,
while Gruffydd (1989-90) defended it, but not its details. Chadwick
later abandoned her scepticism. Lloyd (1911) thought that the Irish
were not greatly displaced but that they ceded control and he noted
that the Irish language still existed there in the sixth century.[7]

After the Harleian genealogies, detail is given on the sons and the
boundaries of their lands.[8]

> These are the names of Cunedda's sons, who were nine in number:
>
> Tybion the first-born who died in the region called Manau Gododdin
> and did not come with his father and brothers mentioned before.
> Meirion, his son, divided the possessions among [Tybion's] brothers.
> 2. Ysfael, 3. Rhufon, 4. Dunod, 5. Ceredig, 6. Afloeg, 7. Einion Yrth,
> 8. Dogfael, 9. Edern.
>
> This is their boundary: from the river which is called Dyfrdwy [Dee],
> to another river, the Teifi. And they held very many districts in the
> western part of Britain.

These men had kingdoms named after them: Meirion (Meirionydd),
Ysfael (Ysfeilion), Rhufon (Rhufoniog), Dunod (Dunoding), Ceredig
(Ceredigion), Afloeg (Afloegion), Dogfael (Dogfeiling) and Edern
(Edeirnion). The only son who did not have a kingdom named after
him was Einion Yrth who apparently was important in himself - he did
not need an eponymous function. Einion is thought to be associated
with the kingdom of Rhôs (Bartrum, 2009).[9]

Cunedda Poem contradicts the Legend

The Book of Taliesin contains a poem on Cunedda called *Marwnad
Cunedda* (Deathsong of Cunedda) that appears to contradict the north
Wales foundation legend. It has been translated by Haycock (2007)

and Koch (2013) who take different positions on the authenticity of the poem, Koch suggesting that it could be early. Gruffydd (1989-90) takes a similar view to Koch, as follows.[10]

> There is nothing in the poem, as far as I can see, to suggest that it was composed in the ninth century for some political end. It reads in fact like a North British poem composed soon after Cunedda's death: there is no reference at all in it to his exploits in North Wales.

The Foundation Legend has Cunedda coming from *Manau Gododdin*, around modern Stirling, whereas the poem seems to refer to his men as 'men of Bryneich' (Bernicia). Koch takes this as referring to British Bernicia, the northeast region that was taken over by the Angles in the late sixth century, leading to their capture of Edinburgh in 638.

The enemy in the Foundation Legend were the Irish in north Wales but the enemy in the poem were the Coeling, British warriors who were descendants of Coel. The most illustrious descendant of Coel was Urien of Rheged who fought the Angles in the late 600s. Two forts are named in the poem: Carlisle and *Kaer Weir*, the latter a fort on the River Wear, for which Koch suggests Binchester or Chester-le-Street but other possibilities are Durham or Wearmouth. Clashes between the men of Bryneich and the Coeling in the poem occurred at these two forts. There is no mention of the Irish or the Saxons or of Wales. At the poem's end in line 42, the bard announces that Cunedda is dead, destroyed by the Coeling.[11]

Dating Marwnad Cunedda
The authority of the poem depends on whether it has an early date. As noted above, Gruffydd writing in 1989, thought it an authentic poem but could not consider it fifth century due to the linguistic work of Jackson (1953) in his *Language and History in Early Britain*. He thought it may have been a reworking of a fifth-century poem by a later north Wales poet before the ninth century. The objections of Ifor Williams are sensibly countered by Gruffydd. He remarks that the formulaic Taliesin introduction may be dismissed as a late addition and that the older form of Cunedda's name, Cunedag (pre AD 750), was modernized to the false form, Cunedaf, which would generically rhyme with the same words as Cunedag. Koch (2013) also considers it

to be authentic and thinks that it has its origins in the fifth century. He argues that the pre-Old Welsh form of Cunedda's name (Cunedag) is the best linguistic fit for the poem and discusses the other pre-Old Welsh archaisms in it. He sums up as follows.[12]

> So the text we have is Bernician propaganda – pre-Anglo Saxon, pre-Christian Bernician propaganda, and it seems very hard to avoid putting an early date on such a thing, at least as a coherent and well-preserved tradition.

Who led the conquest of the Irish in north Wales?

If *Marwnad Cunedda* is indeed early then it is doubtful that Cunedda ever came to Wales and fought the Irish there. Koch (2006) raises the possibility that the 'sons' who divided up Gwynedd (north Wales) may not have been Cunedda's real sons and that Cunedda may not have been the head from which the pedigree lines of Gwynedd descended. In Koch (2013) he refers to a 'linguistic splice' that differentiates two segments of a pedigree line. The first is that from Cunedda back to his ancestors. This sequence has pre-Old Welsh features. The second is from Einion Yrth to his descendants and this sequence is in Old Welsh. He suggests that a written pedigree from the north (Cunedda back to his ancestors) was grafted onto a Welsh pedigree that had once begun with Einion. Thus it was probably Einion Yrth who was the true head of the first dynasty of Gwynedd. This suggests that it was Einion Yrth who came to north Wales with other men (who were not necessarily his brothers) and conquered the Irish. There is other early evidence to show that Einion was held in the highest esteem. So great was his fame that one of the greatest Welsh heroes, Cadwallon, was compared to him. We will now look at Cadwallon's valour to show how highly a poet around AD 632 regarded the earlier Einion.[13]

CADWALLON – 'ANOTHER EINION'

The great Cadwallon was seven generations later than Einion. He was celebrated as a leader of the Britons who, after his fortunes in battle had reached a nadir, fought back to recover much of Northumbria from the English, aided by the able Mercian king, Penda. Cadwallon's domination of Northumbria is extensively covered by Bede.

Early Saxon aggression into Gwynedd came from Aethelfrith who had united the two Anglian kingdoms of Bernicia and Deira. In about AD 615 he travelled all the way from Northumbria to Chester where he defeated the British army, killing its king, Selyf (Solomon). Before this bloody battle he committed the atrocity of murdering 1200 unarmed monks who were away from the battle site praying for the Britons. The Saxon priest Bede sums up Aethelfrith:[14]

> He ravaged the Britons more extensively than any other English ruler.
> … For no ruler or king had subjected more land to the English race or settled it, having first either exterminated or conquered the natives.

Aethelfrith was killed in battle by Raedwald around 616 and thus did not have enough time to consolidate his hold on north Wales. In 616 Edwin took over as king of Deira and Bernicia and Aethelfrith's sons Eanfrith, Oswald and Oswui went into exile. Edwin then continued the aggressive Saxon expansion. His home was at Yeavering in distant Bernicia in the Cheviots (Kirby, 2000) but this was no obstacle for his relentless drive southwest into British lands.[15]

After the conquest of the Irish in the 400s the home of Cadwallon's Gwynedd ancestors was the large island of Anglesey separated from the north Wales coast by the Menai Strait. Cadwallon probably resided at Aberffraw on Anglesey like his ancestors. This whole region came under attack from Edwin who began threatening the west of Britain. The *Historia Brittonum* (in Chapter 63) records that Edwin annexed the British kingdom of Elmet and expelled its king, Certic (Koch and Carey, 2003). This may have helped him to gain access to the Irish Sea and according to Bede he conquered the Menavian Islands, both the Isle of Man and the home of Cadwallon, Anglesey.[16]

The Battle of Long Mountain

The order and details of Cadwallon's struggles against Edwin are not clear but an attempt will be made here to present a possible ordered sequence, influenced by the work of Koch (2013). Cadwallon's exploits are celebrated in two Welsh poems, both edited by Geraint Gruffydd (1978). One poem *Marwnad Cadwallon* from the *Red Book of Hergest* lists 14 battles that he supposedly fought. This poem is in the Englyn metre comprising stanzas of three lines. It was probably composed in the 800-900 period (Koch, 2006) and the battle list is not dissimilar to Arthur's, with some perhaps not fought by him added to genuine battles. One that seems genuine because it made a huge impression on the Welsh is that at Mount *Digoll*, better known as Long Mountain. It is on the opposite (east) side of the River Severn from Welshpool, in a region called Meigen. See Bromwich (2006) for Stanza 4 below and the following translation of Triad 69.[17]

> The camp of famous Cadwallon,
> on the summit of Digoll mountain;
> seven months and seven battles each day.

The third line gives a not uncommon bardic exaggeration using the sacred number 7, presumably to indicate the intensity of Cadwallon's battles with the English. The battle also appears in the *Welsh Triads* in Triad 69, 'Three Defilements of the Severn' which gives more detail:

> Cadwallawn when he went to the Contest of Digoll, and the forces of Cymry with him; and Edwin on the other side, and the forces of the Loegr [the English] with him. And then the Severn was defiled from its source to its mouth; ...

This triad names Edwin, leader of the English, as the adversary. It does not say that Cadwallon won this battle and seems to imply that the Severn was defiled by the excessive blood that was shed from the battle. According to Peter Bartrum (2009) the battle appears to be referred to in the *Welsh Annals* for the year AD 632 where the Latin text is *Strages Sabrinae* ('the slaughter of the Severn').[18]

Meigen

In Stanza 5 of *Marwnad Cadwallon* Cadwallon was camped by the River Severn in Meigen. As noted above, Meigen was the territory that encompassed Long Mountain. The fact that this stanza immediately follows the Long Mountain one indicates that the author is placing Cadwallon in the same area and not some other place in Britain named Meigen. One then wonders whether this is the same battle as the Long Mountain one or a separate engagement in the same area. Bromwich (2006) translates Stanza 5 as follows.

The camp of Cadwallon on the Severn,
and from the far side of Dygen,
almost burning Meigen.

Bromwich (2006) points out that Dygen Freidden is the old name for
the Breiddin Hills in Montgomeryshire which are close to the River
Severn on the western side. Meigen is also noted in Triad 55 where
Cadwallon appears in the first part with what appears to be a horse
Myngan (white mane) who is involved in sending a message. Edwin is
mentioned in the second part. Unfortunately the meanings of these
parts are obscure.[19]

Cadwallon was rightly perceived as a great hero by the British and
Bromwich interprets the Long Mountain and Meigen battles as being
distinct and significant victories. However the language of Triad 69
makes no mention of a victory to Cadwallon, instead describing it as a
'Contest'. The defilement of the Severn by the blood of the fallen could
imply that much of the blood was British. Had it been viewed as mostly
English blood then the triad's author would surely have celebrated a
victory for Cadwallon. The battle could have been a stalemate or even
a gallant loss of Cadwallon's. A second issue is that Meigen was British
territory and the 'almost burning Meigen' of Stanza 5 could suggest
that the English had gained the upper hand. It is possible that this was
Cadwallon's first courageous attempt to stop Edwin from progressing
into Gwynedd.

The Loss of Anglesey and Exile
Bede reports that Edwin had conquered Cadwallon's ancestral home,
Anglesey. Information from the British side implies that Cadwallon
was nearly captured. For a date given as 629 the *Welsh Annals* say that
he was besieged on *insula Glannauc*, now Puffin Island, a tiny island
off Anglesey (Koch, 2006). This island appears in the *Bwrdd Arthur*
photo in Figure 3.3. To survive, Cadwallon had to exile in Ireland.
Welsh Triad 29 refers to his war-band staying with him in Ireland and
not asking for any support lest they be forced to leave him. They were
thus called one of 'The Three Faithful War Bands of the Island of
Britain' (Bromwich, 2006). The fact that Cadwallon was well received
in Ireland suggests that the Irish were concerned about the expansion
of Edwin's power.[20]

Cadwallon's Resurgence

In Ireland Cadwallon may have consolidated his position by adding to his faithful warband. Kirby (2000) suggests that he could have been gathering reinforcements there. The Saxon onslaught now gave them dominance of the Irish Sea which may have led to considerable Irish support for Cadwallon. Koch (2013) refers to a Book of Taliesin poem called 'May God raise up the British Nation' which seems to have a line on Cadwallon establishing a base in Ireland.[21]

> When Cadwallon came over the Irish Sea, he re-established his court in Ardd Nefon.

Koch states that *Ardd Nefon* looks like an Irish place name. Further information on Cadwallon comes from the poem *Moliant Cadwallon* which has translations into English by Breeze (2001), Koch and Carey (2003) and Koch (2013). Although no ancient manuscripts survive it appears to have been composed by a poet familiar with Cadwallon's campaign not long before his conquest of Northumbria. Ifor Williams (1951) thought it was composed around 632 when Cadwallon set out for the north. Its authenticity is accepted by Williams (1951), Parry (1955), Gruffydd (1978), Breeze (2001) and Koch (2013).[22]

Breeze remarks on the value of the poem.[23]

> The value of the poem to Cadwallon for historians of Northumbria should need no underlining. Yet it also provides a lesson in historical judgement. Dumville [1988a] has remarked casually of this poem that it 'probably cannot' be taken as contemporary. For both historical and linguistic reasons it is hard to accept this view. Every test we can apply to the poem suggests it was written on the eve of the invasion of Northumbria.

The following interpretation is based on Koch's (2013) translation. There are a number of lines referring to Cadwallon's sea voyage which imply that his route back from Ireland was not a direct one. Four lines are of particular interest, lines 14-15: 'May God grant protection to his bold high hosts, so that the wind and waves do not exhaust them' and lines 34-35: 'In the warband's encampment, the bright lodgings for mounted warriors: deliverance from the exhaustion of the ship in an enclosure of swords'. Thus the voyage appears to be an arduous one and this is confirmed by the mention of *Porth Ysgewin* in line 43, 'on the estuary where borders meet'. This place is modern Portskewett near the Severn estuary in southeast Wales, a very unlikely place to be if liberating Anglesey.[24]

Koch argues that when in Ireland Cadwallon and his men may have moved south out of Edwin's reach and sailed from the south of Ireland, around the south of Wales and into the Severn estuary to eventually meet with Penda, the Saxon king of Mercia. A few years earlier Penda had defeated Cynegils and Cwichelm in a battle at Cirencester which resulted in a treaty whereby Mercia now controlled the region along the Severn valley (*Anglo-Saxon Chronicle A*, for AD 628). The poem also mentions Cadwallon giving hospitality at Caer Caradog, which Breeze (2001) identifies with Caradog in Herefordshire, citing Ekwall (1960) who noted its 1292 recording of *Cayrcrado*c. This is about 28 miles north of Portskewett. At a convenient point, Penda's Mercian forces joined the heterogeneous forces assembled by Cadwallon to provide a formidable army.[25]

While Cadwallon was progressing on his indirect route a British uprising had erupted on Anglesey, either planned or spontaneous, perhaps inspired by news of Cadwallon's return. At some stage on their route north Cadwallon heard a report on the fighting occurring on Anglesey as shown by lines 16-17 from Koch (2013).[26]

> An oral report has come to me from Gwynedd's expanse:
> their men killed in the lethal combat of fighters who would not submit.

By 'their men' is meant the English fighters. The Britons were in the process of liberating Anglesey.

Cadwallon's Victory

Bede provides the most detailed report of Cadwallon's establishing his imperium over Northumbria albeit in an extraordinarily biased and Anglo-centric coverage. He writes that a fierce battle was fought at *Haethfelth*, which is Hatfield Chase near Doncaster. Cadwallon was victorious, Edwin was killed and his whole army was either slain or scattered. Bede gives the date as 12 October 633. One of Edwin's sons,

Osfrith, was also killed while his other son, Eadfrith, deserted to Penda who kept him at his court and afterwards killed him. Bede viewed Osric, a son of an uncle of Edwin, as the new king of Deira and in the following summer Osric besieged Cadwallon in a fortified town, possibly York. However Cadwallon took him by surprise when he suddenly broke out of the town with all his forces and killed Osric and destroyed his army. Bernicia's new king was a son of Aethelfrith, Eanfrith, who had returned from exile. In the face of Cadwallon's dominance, Eanfrith was in a weak position and he unadvisedly came to Cadwallon with twelve thegns to beg for peace. Cadwallon would have none of it and so killed Eanfrith as well. He aggressively ruled Northumbria for a year before being killed in battle at Heavenfield (near Hexham) by Oswald, a younger brother of Eanfrith.[27]

Frank Stenton (1971) said of Cadwallon: 'These events changed the course of British as well as English history. Cadwallon was the only British king of historic times who overthrew an English dynasty, and the British people never found an equal leader.' Cadwallon's ally, Penda, who was not at Heavenfield, later killed Oswald in battle in about 642 at *Maes Cogwy* (traditionally thought to be Old Oswestry) when Oswald was aggressively attacking in British territory. Penda had Oswald's body dismembered.[28]

Cadwallon compared to Einion Yrth

The poem *Moliant Cadwallon* is profuse in its praise for Cadwallon on the eve of his successful attack on Edwin. Koch (2013) translates lines 47-50 as follows.[29]

> Standing before a giant, one may fail to comprehend
> what could be higher than you, generous diademed lord,
> except the treetops, sky and stars:
> Cadwallon, *another Einion*: the imperium.

Cadwallon is praised as another Einion, a huge shock as Cunedda was thought to be his illustrious ancestor, the founder of Gwynedd, but no mention is made of him. It implies that it was Einion who conquered the north Wales Irish, not Cunedda. If the bard composed the poem c. 632 it's not unlikely that he had accurate knowledge of Cadwallon's forebears. This knowledge may have been earlier than the tradition that grafted Cunedda onto the pedigree.

CONNECTION BETWEEN UTHR AND EINION YRTH

It is well known that Uthr can be used as both a name and an epithet. As an epithet Uthr means 'terrible', 'dreadful', 'awful' etc., not in the modern sense of being bad at something or of bad character, but in the sense of inspiring awe, terror or dread in one's enemies. John Koch (2006) points out that in two manuscripts of the *Historia Brittonum* Arthur is referred to as *mab uter*, which can be translated as 'awful son' or 'son of Uthr'. Rachel Bromwich (2006) also discusses this issue of the name or the epithet.[30]

Uthr as an epithet

The Welsh historical dictionary *Geiriadur Prifysgol Cymru* (GPC) is the result of an ongoing research project that is proving invaluable to modern scholars. The GPC gives the following range of meanings for 'Uthr':

Fearful, dreadful, awful, terrible, tremendous, mighty, overbearing, cruel, wonderful, wondrous, astonishing, excellent.

The tenor of early Welsh poetry, including *Marwnat Uthr Pendragon*, was that the king needed to emphasize his might and power to create fear and dread in his enemies so that his kingdom remained safe. A strong king who was successful and feared may have attracted an epithet to his name to reflect these qualities. Thus the king would be known by both his real name and the epithet. In everyday speech the epithet may have been often used.

Kings whose names may be epithets

Two kings whose names appear to be the result of epithets are the well-known Vortigern and Cuneglasus. As John Morris (1973) states, Vortigern means 'overlord' and it appears doubtful that his parents named him this as a baby. Morris speculates that his real name may have been Vitalinus and that Vortigern was the Vitalinus mentioned in the *Historia Brittonum* who fought Ambrosius at Wallop in AD 437. Unfortunately this equivalence cannot be established as there is not enough information but it does seem a good example where an epithet took over and the king whose real name became obscured was known as Vortigern to future generations.[31]

Cuneglasus also has an unusual name in which the most obvious translation is 'blue hound'. Again it is doubtful that his parents would have called him this. In Gildas' *De Excidio* he is portrayed as waging war with 'arms special to yourself'. Recall line 3 in Uthr's poem at the beginning of this chapter where Uthr is called 'armed in blue'. The 'blue' part of Cuneglasus could refer to blue/grey armour. The 'hound' part can refer to warriors. It is possible that his real name is unknown and his martial qualities are being shown by an epithet.

Marwnat Vthyr Pendragon heavily emphasizes the warrior aspect of Uthr. For example consider the following consecutive lines from Marged Haycock's translation.[32]

> It was I who stormed a hundred citadels.
> It was I who slew a hundred stewards.
> It was I who shared out a hundred mantles.
> It was I who cut off a hundred heads.
> It was I who gave Henben
> swords of great protective power.

While Uthr at some point became used as a name it is likely that it began as an epithet attached to the king's name indicating that the king was feared, this imagery being promoted by his bard.

The Meaning of Yrth

Yrth is definitely an epithet attached to the name Einion. What does it mean? When the GPC is consulted, Yrth is equated to Gyrth and a mention of the usage Enniaun Girt (Einion Yrth) c. 1100 is given. A range of meanings for Yrth/Gyrth in Welsh is given:

garw, caled, aruthr, ffyrnig, cryf ...

Of these, *garw* means rough or rugged and *caled* means hard as in Arthur's sword *caledfwlch* (hard cleft), *ffyrnig* means fierce, while *cryf* means strong or powerful. The third item *aruthr* is shown in the GPC as the compound adjective formed by 'ar' + 'uthr' where *ar* often means 'on', but another alternative, 'concerning', may be meant here. The GPC sections for 'aruthr' and 'uthr' show that they have the same meaning. This demonstrates that there is a very close relationship between *uthr* and *yrth* where the former's meaning is actually part of the meaning of the latter.

The following English words obtained from the Welsh words in the Uthr and Yrth GPC sections show the range of characteristics that could be attributed to the kings.

Uthr	Yrth
dreadful	dreadful
awful	awful
terrible, terrifying	terrible
fearful, frightening	frightful, frightening
fierce	fierce
cruel	cruel
harsh	harsh
merciless	merciless
strong, powerful	strong, powerful
tyrannical, oppressive	savage, angry
wonderful, wondrous	wonderful
astonishing	astonishing
strange	strange

Are there features of Yrth that don't appear in Uthr? There are words relating to beating, ramming and pushing or thrusting but these don't seem to be relevant to a king's epithet. The word *caled* (hard) does not appear under Uthr but this could be subsumed under cruel, harsh, merciless or strong. Also *garw* (rough, rugged) doesn't appear under Uthr but this can also be subsumed under correlated characteristics such as strong, powerful, mighty and so on.

Lloyd in 1911, without the aid of modern linguistics, rendered Yrth as 'impetuous', placing a question mark after it. He based this on Dafydd ap Gwilym's mention of another king with the Yrth epithet, Brychan Yrth, where the Welsh word used for Yrth was *nerthawg*. In the GPC, the *nerth* core occurs in the primary descriptors for the Uthr meaning, not the Yrth meaning, showing how closely these epithets are related. It means 'mighty, strong'. *Uthr* and *Yrth* mean the same thing in practice, a strong, ruthless king who caused fear and dread in his enemies. It looks like a separate Arthurian tradition arose in which *Yrth* became the name *Uthr* under the influence of the name 'Arthur' and later another epithet, '*pendragon*', was added.[33]

Einion Yrth and Uthr lived in the same region

There are other reasons to believe that Uthr was Einion Yrth. The first is location. Einion is associated with Rhôs by Bartrum (1966) in the ABT section (*Achau Brehinoedd a Thywysogion Cymru*). Uthr is also linked to Rhôs as argued earlier from the protection he gave Henben, the location of Dineirth, and Arthur's relationship with Garwen.

Einion Yrth and Uthr lived in the same time period

The second reason concerns the time when they lived which is best considered diagrammatically as shown in Figure 4.1.

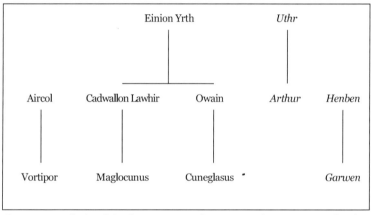

Figure 4.1 Relationships between people connected to Einion and Uthr

On the right hand side Uthr, Arthur, Garwen and Henben are in italics and are connected to each other. They form a distinct group that must be related in time to Einion's group. Another group is on the left hand side where Vortipor is the son of Aircol (the Welsh form of Agricola). As Vortipor is a contempory of Maglocunus in the *De Excidio* then his father Aircol is a contemporary of Cadwallon Lawhir.

Both Aircol and Henben appear in no. 71 of *Stanzas of the Graves* where it says that Henben's grave is in Dinorben and Aircol's grave is in Dyfed. As Dinorben (northeast Wales) and Dyfed (southwest Wales) are at the extreme opposite ends of Wales why did the stanza's author pick out these two, from many possible names, to put together in the stanza? It seems that he thought the two lived in the same time period although their graves were distant. If this is tentatively accepted then it links Hennin Henben to Einion's group. He is a contemporary of Cadwallon Lawhir and Owain Danwyn.[34]

This is supported by the late story, the *Tale of Taliesin* (Ford, 1977) which names the senior bard at Maglocunus' court as Heinin Fardd. Haycock (2007) thinks it possible that he could be Hennin Henben. The tale may be implying that he is older than the king by making him the elder bard. This is not to imply that the real Henben was a bard of Maglocunus (although it is not impossible) but only that the author of the tale thought that Henben lived at the same time as this king.[35]

As Arthur had a mistress, Garwen, it suggests he was older than her, so he is placed in Henben's generation but was probably younger than the others. If Arthur was the Pharaoh over the five kings then one would expect him to be older than Maglocunus and the other kings but not too old as to be unable to assert his authority. This would put Uthr at around the same time period as Einion. As Uthr protected Henben it also suggests that he was older than Henben, having long experience in military matters. Arthur may have assisted his father in protecting Henben against the Irish and thus came to know Garwen.

Hypothesized relationship of Arthur to Einion

The *Historia* Vatican recension says that many were more royal than Arthur which suggests he was probably the result of Einion's liaison with a mistress as in Figure 4.2. Owain may have had other sons before Cuneglasus who were killed by Maglocunus in the coup.

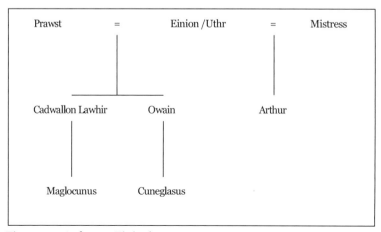

Figure 4.2 Arthur as Einion's son

Prawst was probably Cadwallon Lawhir's mother (Bartrum, 2009), and probably also Owain Danwyn's. Here Arthur is shown to be a half brother to Owain. This gives a convincing scenario of why Arthur was able to take the Rhôs throne. When Maglocunus killed Owain he was in the 'first years' of his youth, about 15. He grew into one of the tallest men in Britain and no doubt was tall and strong in his youth. Gildas doesn't state how long he ruled, only that his rule was not to his liking, which could imply some opposition to his reign. When he resigned to become a monk, he may have agreed for Owain's half brother, Arthur, to take over, the latter a Christian with a huge military reputation who could provide stability. Given that Arthur was the paternal half uncle of Maglocunus, they would have known each other. Arthur was also the paternal half uncle of Cuneglasus who may have been only a young boy at this time and too young to rule.[36]

Conquering the North Wales Irish

Lloyd (1911) thinks that the conquest of north Wales took place in two stages. The first led by Einion captured the north coast and part of the west, but not Anglesey and Arfon and it was his son Cadwallon Lawhir who finally conquered these regions. In Triad 62 Cadwallon fought the Irish at *Cerryg y Gwyddyl* (rocks of the Irish) in Anglesey (Bromwich, 2006). Einion's fame came from these successes. Ceredig, who fought in these battles, named his son Einion (Gruffydd, 1989-90).[37]

We may compare Einion and Uthr as follows. Einion fought in Rhôs against the Irish while Cadwallon was fighting the Irish west of the Conwy. Uthr was fighting in Rhôs at Dinorben to protect Henben who was a contemporary of Cadwallon (Figure 4.1). This suggests that Uthr was Einion and that the 'swords of protection' he gave Henben were against the Irish.[38]

Given that Arthur was a half brother to Cadwallon Lawhir, though probably younger, it would not be implausible if he was involved in the final stages of conquering the Irish. There is a line in the *Marwnat* that could support this. Below are two translations of line 24, the first by Haycock (2007) and the second by Coe and Young (1995).[39]

> There would not be life were it not for my progeny.

> The world would not exist were it not for my offspring.

This line has been taken to refer to Arthur, as Uthr had earlier stated that he had a ninth share of Arthur's valour. However the use of the term *eissillyd*, 'progeny' or 'offspring', rather than 'son' suggests that more than one son was involved in protecting the Britons. If Uthr was Einion Yrth then these two sons may have been Arthur and Cadwallon Lawhir and Uthr may have been thinking about the battles against the Irish. Arthur probably also fought the Irish in defending Rheon in Galloway as the Rheon peninsula (the Rhinns) was just over 20 miles across the Irish Sea from Ireland. He possibly also fought the Irish with Geraint near Penbryn beach if *Bedd Geraint*, a few miles inland, is genuinely Geraint's grave.

SUMMARY: WHY UTHR WAS EINION YRTH

Arguments for equating Uthr with Einion Yrth are given below:

- Einion Yrth was a much more significant figure than he appears in history books. The work of Lloyd (1911), Gruffydd (1989-90) and Koch (2013) point to his importance as the probable founder of the Gwynedd dynasty by wresting control from the Irish.

- Einion was located in Rhôs, as were Uthr and Arthur through their links to Hennin Henben and Garwen, and also Arthur's association with Dineirth.

- Einion Yrth and Uthr lived in the same time period which places Arthur as an older contemporary of Maglocunus and the other four kings in the *De Excidio*.

- The meanings of Yrth and Uthr are for all practical purposes identical.

- The argument that Arthur was Einion's son and half brother to Owain explains how he was able to obtain the Rhôs throne after Maglocunus resigned it and how and when the Bear's Fortress in Rhôs obtained its name.

5
ARTHUR'S BARD

INTRODUCTION

Who was the author of the Welsh poems *Spoils of Annwfyn, Chair of the Sovereign* and *Battle of the Trees*? In the public perception the non-warrior figure most commonly associated with Arthur is Merlin, the name Geoffrey of Monmouth adapted from the original Myrddin. In medieval and modern imagery he is portrayed as a wizard assisting the king but there are a number of Welsh poems said to be composed by him. A late Welsh triad, Triad 87, is about the bards at Arthur's court (Bromwich, 2006).[1]

> Three Skilful bards were at Arthur's Court:
> Myrddin son of Morfryn,
> Myrddin Emrys,
> and Taliesin.

Two Merlins are listed, one a son of Morfryn based in Scotland, and a Myrddin Emrys associated with Carmarthen in southwest Wales. This reflects the two separate traditions about Merlin figures that Geoffrey tried unsuccessfully to merge into one figure. As will be shown below, the Scottish Merlin was likely based on a real person named Llallawg. The third bard in the triad, Taliesin, was a sixth-century historical bard whose poems appear in the *Book of Taliesin*. On the surface, he would seem a strong contender for Arthur's bard. Both Merlin and Taliesin will now be discussed.

MERLIN

The Historia Brittonum Legend

One strand of the Myrddin Emrys figure derives from a legend in the *Historia Brittonum* in Chapters 39-42. The story features Vortigern, the fifth-century king called Pharaoh by Gildas. He was the king who allowed Saxon mercenaries into Britain to fight the Irish and Picts and was later despised by generations of Britons. The story relates that Vortigern took his own daughter as his wife and had a son by her and was condemned by St Germanus. Vortigern asks his *magi* (wizards) for advice and they tell him to find a fortified stronghold so he can defend himself. He eventually finds a place to build in the mountains of Snowdonia but is repeatedly thwarted when the building materials of wood and stone mysteriously disappear each night.

He asks his *magi* what to do and they tell him to find a fatherless boy, kill him and sprinkle his blood on the building site. After a search they find a fatherless boy in Glywysing (Glamorgan), southeast Wales. His mother states she didn't know how he was conceived in her womb as she had never known a man. The boy is presented to Vortigern and in a series of incidents concerning the foundations of the building site he consistently gets the better of the king's *magi*. This culminates in them finding two sleeping dragons (also called worms or snakes) in the foundations who fight each other. Although the red one was at first weaker he eventually drives the white dragon away. The boy explains that the red dragon represents the British people and the white one, the English invaders, who would eventually be driven away across the sea. The boy tells Vortigern that he cannot build there and to search widely to seek another site, while he would remain there.[2]

Ambrosius with legendary features

When the king asks the boy his name the boy replies 'Ambrosius' and the story narrator remarks that he was shown to be *Embreis Guletic* (Ambrosius the sovereign). The king then asks him from what family was he was descended and the boy replies that his father was a Roman consul, which identifies him with the Ambrosius Aurelianus from the *De Excidio*, the gentleman who began the British fightback and whose parents 'wore the purple', a sign of high rank.

This story weaves two historical figures, Vortigern and Ambrosius, into a fictional tale so poorly constructed that the 'fatherless boy' had a royal Roman father. Had Gildas in his *De Excidio* not mentioned them both, Ambrosius by his name, and Vortigern by an obvious pun on his name, they would have been dismissed as mythical. In this *Historia* tale the boy wizard *is not called Merlin*, but Ambrosius, and is associated with Glamorgan in southeast Wales. However, Geoffrey of Monmouth in his *HRB* later merged this southeast Ambrosius with Myrddin, a legendary prophet from Carmarthen in southwest Wales to create Merlin Emrys.

Geoffrey's HRB creation of Merlin Ambrosius (Emrys)

Carmarthen was originally called *Moridunon* ('sea fort') where *mor* means 'sea' and *dun*, 'fort'. After a long time, the name contracted to *Myrddin* or Merddin and the embedded 'fort' meaning was forgotten. Then a redundant prefix *caer* (fort) was added, giving *Caermyrddin* and the 'm' finally softened to 'f' to get *Caerfyrddin*, its Welsh name. However early incorrect speculation on how the town got its name had given Caerfyrddin = Caer (fort) + Myrddin and it was wrongly thought to be named after person named Myrddin. But there was no Myrddin behind the town name. Thus a Myrddin figure was created who was a shell without substance, but the bards filled this gap to create stories about him to give him a legendary existence as a prophet.[3]

Geoffrey's conversion of 'Myrddin' to Latin would give a name like *Merdinus* similar to the Latin, *merda* ('dung') which explains why he used *Merlin*. In his *HRB* he adapts the *Historia* story about the boy wizard Ambrosius, but now calls him Merlin and places him in Kaermerdin instead of Glamorgan. Twice 'Ambrosius' is attached to Merlin's name. His mother is now made the daughter of the Demetia king. Geoffrey interrupts his own *HRB* story to insert his *Prophecies of Merlin*, of dubious worth, some being his own creations. He also has Merlin work to bring the huge stones from Ireland to Stonehenge and has him predict the king's death from a comet's advent. Merlin is also used to change the shape of Uthr so that he can sleep with Igerna to beget Arthur. This Merlin was the Merlin Emrys figure, Emrys being the Welsh for Ambrosius.[4]

Scottish Myrddin (Llallawg or Lailoken, son of Morfryn)

When he wrote *HRB* Geoffrey was apparently unaware of tales from Scotland about a crazed prophet and wild man of the woods. From the 700s and onwards this material had come down to Wales in varied forms that was expressed in verse by unknown Welsh poets. The man's real name was Llallawg or Llallogan (also Lailoken) but the Welsh identified him with Myrddin and he absorbed the characteristics of the Scottish figure while retaining the Myrddin name. These Welsh poems were then thought to have been composed by Myrddin. Llallawg was probably historical and fought in the battle of Arfderydd about 8 miles north of Carlisle. The name Arfderydd survives in the parish name, Arthuret. It was a real battle that was fought about AD 573.

There is no single account of Llallawg's life. It must be constructed from scraps in the Welsh 'Myrddin' poems and Scottish tales where he is called Lailoken. Of the Welsh poems (attributed to the non-existent Carmarthen Myrddin) the most important are:

(i)   Apple Trees
(ii)   Greetings, Little Pig
(iii)   The Dialogue of Myrddin and Taliesin
(iv)   The Conversation of Myrddin and his sister Gwenddydd

Poems (i)-(iii) appear in the *Black Book of Carmarthen*, c. 1250, and (iv) in the *Red Book of Hergest*, c. 1400, but they contain detail that is much older. In (iv), Myrddin's sister, Gwenddydd, calls him Llallawg and also Llallogan, a diminutive of Llallawg, a term of endearment. This poem also refers to him as the son of Morfryn. In the Scottish material below he will be called Lailoken. He appears in the Scottish story *Lailoken and Kentigern* where the latter is the Scottish saint also known by the pet name, Mungo. He lived in the late 500s, around the same time as Lailoken and his sphere of influence was in the same general region. Lailoken was probably transplanted into the story about Kentigern to allow the story to show the saint's compassion to a poor unfortunate man. In reality they probably never met, but it had the fortuitous effect of preserving features of the Lailoken legend as Kentigern was an important figure in the church.[5]

Lailoken and the Battle of Arfderydd

The battle and the combatants appear in the *Welsh Annals* for the date AD 573 as follows:

> The battle of Armterid (between the sons of Elifer and Guendoleu son of Keidiau, in which battle Guendoleu fell: Merlin went mad.)

The battle name, Armterid, is just an older form of Arfderydd which suggests that the annalist was accessing older material than that in the 'Myrddin' poems. The original form of the entry was simply 'The battle of Armterid' (*bellum armterid*). The mention of the 'Merlin' name is obviously a late addition that postdates Geoffrey's *HRB*. In *Bonedd Gwŷr y Gogledd* (Descent of the men of the North) the sons of Eliffer are given as Gwrgi and Peredur. If the above Annals entry is correct then the battle was an internecine one as the genealogy shows that Gwrgi and Peredur were first cousins to Gwenddolau, Eliffer being the brother of Ceidio, Gwenddolau's father. The fort of Gwenddolau was almost certainly at the site of modern Carwinley, deriving from Caer Wenddolau as argued by William Skene (1865).[6]

From poems (i)-(iv) the following picture emerges. Lailoken's lord was Gwenddolau who was 'chief of the kings of the North, greatest in generosity'. Lailoken was honoured at the court, and gained prestige as a warrior, being able to wear a golden torc into battle. The battle was a disaster for Gwenddolau, a bloody defeat in which he was killed. The *Lailoken and Kentigern* story states that the battle took place on the plain between Lidel and Carwannok, a corruption of an early form of Carwinley. Lidel must be the Liddel Water which runs into the River Esk about a mile northwest of Carwinley which means the battle was virtually on Gwenddolau's doorstep. It was an attack on the heart of his kingdom in which his fort must have been captured. It devastated Lailoken who was traumatized by the slaughter. The story relates the terrible vision in the sky that he experienced.[7]

> In that fight the sky began to split above me, and I heard a tremendous din, a voice from the sky saying to me, 'Lailochen, Lailochen, because you alone are responsible for the blood of all these dead men, you alone will bear the punishment for the misdeeds of all. For you will be given over to the angels of Satan, and until the day of your death you will have communion with the creatures of the wood'. But when I directed my gaze towards the voice I heard, I saw a brightness too great for human senses to endure. I saw, too, numberless martial battalions in the heaven like flashing lightning, holding in their hands fiery lances and glittering spears which they shook most fiercely at me.

Lailoken descended into madness and fled into the Caledonian forest where he lived like an animal for many years. The Annals entry, the above pedigree and a further triad, Triad 44, imply that Gwrgi and Peredur led the attack but some scholars think that Rhydderch Hael was the leader. The poems show Lailoken hiding in the forest in fear of Rhydderch and his dogs. Rhydderch was the king of Alt Clut, based at Dumbarton Rock. He was a historical king, appearing in *Adomnán's Life of Columba* written c. 700, and also in the *Historia Brittonum* where he was fighting against the Angles of Northumbria.[8]

Lailoken the Prophet and his Triple Death

The Scottish story *Vita Merlini Silvestris* comprises two parts. The first is *Lailoken and Kentigern* as noted above. The second is *Lailoken and Meldred* where King Meldred imprisons Lailoken to get him to prophesy. Instead he poses riddles which reveal the queen's adultery in the king's garden. He also foretells his own death, a threefold death. The queen uses this apparent nonsense to discredit him as a liar who cannot die three times. She later hires shepherds to kill him.

The details are in *Lailoken and Kentigern*. He foretells his triple death, initially saying that he will die from being crushed by stones and cudgels but Kentigern doesn't believe it. When asked again about the death, Lailoken says he will die by being pierced by a sharp wooden stake. When asked a third time, he says he will die by drowning. No one believes him, but he died that day when stoned and beaten by shepherds hired by Meldred's queen. While being beaten he fell into a river onto a sharp stake and his head fell underwater, fulfilling the threefold death and thus proving himself a true prophet.[9]

Geoffrey's Merlin in his Vita Merlini poem

When Geoffrey composed *Vita Merlini* in c. 1150 he used the Scottish material to create a different Merlin to that in his *HRB* but he modified the Scottish details to remove material inappropriate for a wizard of Arthur. A feature of the Scottish material was the guilt that Lailoken felt in the heavenly vision and in *The Apple Trees* where he caused the death of his sister's son and daughter and was thus estranged from her. As a result of this guilt he became a babbling madman.

Geoffrey greatly downplayed the insanity of Merlin and removed any personal guilt. Instead, Merlin flees to the forest as a sensitive soul grieving for the dead. He is more like the Christian saints who sought solitary places to meditate. Further, Merlin could not be on the losing side so he is made an ally of King Rhydderch, his feared enemy in the Scottish material. Gwenddydd, Merlin's sister, is surprisingly made the adulterous queen, but of Rhydderch instead of Meldred. As in the *HRB*, Merlin is from southwest Wales but is now a king who fights in the distant Old North. His beloved lord, Gwenddolau, is now the bitter enemy; Peredur of the Old North is now made a king of Gwynedd. Gwrgi is left out. To Geoffrey, the characters in his sources are merely pawns to be moved into any role to suit his desired narrative.[10]

Geoffrey relates the threefold death prophecy but doesn't apply it to Merlin but to a boy who appears three times, disguised differently each time by the queen, his sister, Gwenddydd (now called Ganieda). Each time he predicts a different death for the boy and the king thinks he is wrong about the queen's infidelity. Later when the boy was a man his death included all three elements of Merlin's prediction.[11]

Poem (iii) gives a dialogue between Myrddin and Taliesin. Geoffrey follows suit in his *Vita Merlini* where he brings Taliesin (who has returned from Brittany) to meet Merlin. Taliesin then gives a long monologue about features of the natural world which mentions the isle of apples (Avalon) and the nine sisters there, led by Morgen, who practise the healing arts and other magical feats. After the battle of Camlan, Merlin and Taliesin take the wounded Arthur to Avalon by ship so that his wounds can be healed by Morgen.[12]

There are huge problems with Geoffrey's portrayal of Merlin. It fractures the Scottish relationships and is chronologically impossible. Geoffrey was aware of the latter, and to reinforce that the Merlins of the *HRB* and the *Vita* were the same, he has Merlin say at the end of a long series of prophecies: 'All these things I formerly predicted more at length to Vortigern in explaining to him the mystic war of the two dragons...'. As a ballpark estimate, say Merlin met Vortigern c. 450 when he was about ten, and thus was born around 440. The battle of Arfderydd was in 573 and he lived 50 years in the forest (Poems (i) and (ii)). This would give him a lifespan of about 180 years. Gerald of Wales in his *Itinerarium Cambriae* could see that the two Merlins were obviously distinct as follows.[13]

There were two Merlins, the one called Ambrosius, who thus had two names, prophesied when Vortigern was king ... The second Merlin came from Scotland. He is called Celidonius, because he prophesied in the Calidonian Forest.

The Merlin (Llallawg) based on the Scottish material is the Merlin son of Morfryn. Geoffrey's *Vita Merlini* Merlin is an unsuccessful blend of this Scottish Merlin and his earlier Merlin Emrys in his *HRB*. Of these, the latter didn't exist, being created by a false etymology. The Llallawg Merlin probably existed (his life being enhanced by fantasy) but had no connection with Arthur, being born after Arthur's death.

111

TALIESIN

While the southwest Wales Merlin did not exist as a historical person and there is some doubt about the existence of the Scottish Merlin, there is no doubt at all about the existence of Taliesin. He is mentioned as one of the group of five famous sixth-century bards in the *Historia Brittonum*. His poems and other poems attributed to him are in the *Book of Taliesin*, held in the National Library of Wales at Aberystwyth (MS Peniarth 2). Daniel Huws (2000) dates this manuscript to about 1300-1350. The book comprises quite a diverse collection of about 60 poems, all ostensibly by Taliesin but the number of poems actually composed by him is thought to be twelve or less. The vast majority are not by Taliesin but were composed much later, at different times by different authors. The three Arthurian poems that are argued here to be the work of Arthur's bard are also in this book but as will be argued below cannot have been composed by Taliesin.[14]

Twelve Poems possibly by the Real Taliesin

Ifor Williams(1968) identified twelve poems from the *Book of Taliesin* which he thought were composed by the real sixth-century Taliesin:

1. Praise of Kynan Garwyn
2. Battle of Gwen Ystrat
3. Urien of Erechwydd
4. At home with Rheged's Folk
5. What if Urien were slain?
6. Battle of Argoet Llwyfein (against 'Flame-bearer')
7. Rheged Arise
8. Spoils of Taliesin
9. The Appeasement of Urien
10. Elegy to Owain
11. Battles of Gwallawg
12. Praise of Gwallawg

Poem 1 praises Kynan Garwyn, the son of Brochfael (Brocmail), who was king in Powys in the late sixth-century. Kynan's young son, Selyf (Solomon), was killed at the battle of Chester, c. 615 (*Welsh Annals*).

Poems 2 to 9 address the great hero of the northern regions, Urien Rheged. Poem 10 is an elegy to Urien's son, Owain, who is credited with killing the Anglian chieftain with the epithet 'Flame-bearer' and defeating his army. Poems 11 and 12 are addressed to Gwallawg, a king based at Elmet (Leeds) who is Urien's ally in the *Historia* account of the Britons' battles against the Angles.[15]

Praise of Kynan Garwyn

This poem is treated at length as Taliesin probably didn't compose it. If he wasn't the author then there is no reason to place him in Powys. Koch (2006) viewed it sceptically and said that it lacked a Christian outlook and that its archaic spelling set it apart from the other poems, while Saunders Lewis (1968) thought it improbable that the poem was by Taliesin. Koch (2013) later changed his views and argued it was a Taliesin poem, in line with Ifor Williams, who argued it was composed by Taliesin when he was Kynan's bard in Powys. He thought that the poet later left Powys and moved north to Rheged to became Urien's bard. Williams remarks that Urien was fighting the Angles in the years 572-592, having obtained these dates from the Moore Memoranda. However this conjectured move of Taliesin from Powys to Rheged is not compatible with the circumstances of the Chester battle. Kynan's son, Selyf, was killed in the battle and Bede adds that a Brochfael was guarding the monks, away from the battle site. The Welsh poem says that Brochfael was Kynan's father. Instead of condemning the Saxon chief who murdered the monks, Bede maligns old Brochfael:[16]

> They had a guard named Brocmail, whose duty was to protect them against the barbarians' swords while they were praying ... Brocmail and his men at the first enemy attack turned their backs on those whom they should have defended, leaving them unarmed and helpless before the swords of their foes.

The argument below requires that this Brochfael was Kynan's father, the former king, and not another Brochfael. Chadwick (1963) argues that he was Kynan's father and it would be natural for the former king to assist in the defence. It was earlier argued that the written source for the battle came from a monk who survived it and saw the death of half of his fellow monks. If Brochfael was a nonentity it is unlikely the monk would have mentioned him but the ex-king was recognizable by his distinctive teeth. The monk may have been enraged that the former king, praised by his bards for his valour, had fled and abandoned the monks to be slaughtered. The embittered monk may have added this to his account to let the truth be known.[17]

Dating Kynan's Battles

As Selyf fought at Chester his grandfather Brochfael was very old when guarding the monks which could explain his flight when the Angles attacked. This allows an estimate of his age and the floruit of Kynan. Given a shorter life span then, it is hard to imagine that Brochfael was much older than 60 at the battle, so assume he was 60 in 615 and born in 555. If Kynan was born when Brochfael was 20, and Selyf was born when Kynan was 20, then Selyf was about 20 at the battle. These rough estimates are not unreasonable and show that it was possible for both Brochfael and Selyf to be at the battle, but if they are accepted, then *Kynan was only about 25 in 600.*

If Brochfael's age is set younger than 60 in 615, say 50, then Kynan becomes 10 years younger in 600, only 15, and Selyf is only 10 at the battle, which is untenable. The point here is to show that, as Kynan was young in 600, many of his battles would have occurred after this date. The situation is improved if we make Brochfael older, say 65, at the battle, which makes Kynan about 30 in 600, but it is unrealistic to make Brochfael any older than this.

Kynan's bard praised him for his plundering battles fought all over Wales. If he was 25 - 30 in 600, these probably took place around the 600-610 period. Such aggressive campaigning would create enemies and could explain why he wasn't at Chester. He was probably killed in battle beforehand. If Kynan was fighting c. 600-610 then it was after Urien's battles had finished (c. 572–592). Kynan's bard was still in Wales when Urien fought and later composed his poem to Kynan when Urien's battles were already over. Taliesin could not have composed the poem to Kynan and then moved north to compose the poems to Urien. My view is that the poem to Kynan is early, around 600-610, but that the bard was not Taliesin.

The Battle of Gwen Ystrat (Gwen Valley)

Urien's men are called 'Men of Catraeth' implying he held sway over the famous battle site. Koch (1997) gives an innovative argument that the poem is referring to the Gododdin defeat at Catraeth from the view of the victor, Urien Rheged. He argues that Urien and Gwallawg led a coalition of the Coeling and an ethnically mixed Deiran army to defeat the Gododdin attackers. Both leaders were Coeling, the descendants of Coel Hen. He also argues that the Gododdin were aided by the Picts. In *gwyr prydein* ('men of Britain'), he emends *prydein* to *pryden* which denotes the Picts and translates line 6 as 'The Picts advancing towards combat in hosts'. However Pennar (1988) and Ford (1999) do not emend it. Pennar translates it, 'the scourge of the men of Britain in their battle lines' and Ford translates it, 'Britain knows widespread destruction!' If the battle of Gwen Valley is viewed as the Gododdin defeat at Catraeth then some potential problems follow:[18]

- The poem does not refer to the Gododdin.
- Urien's foes are pale-faced (*garanwynyon*) as the Angles were.
- The battle site is at Llech Wen, not Catraeth.
- *gwyr prydein* may just refer to Urien's plundering of the Britons.
- The Gododdin B verses do not name the Coeling as the enemy.
- The B verses instead name the enemy as Saessons (Saxons) in B1.7, Deira in B2.28, B1.14 and Lloegr in B1.19.

It is worth reading Koch's views in Sections III and IV of his Historical Introduction. A major issue concerns the poem's dating. Graham Isaac (1998) analyzes the number of syllables in the three parts of each line which generally gives a 3 3 3 pattern, 9 syllables per line. He argues that if the poem was early then the prosthetic vowels would not be there (e.g. the 'y' in *ystrat*). Removing them reduces line 7 to only 7 syllables from an original of 9. Lines 15 and 30 are also affected. He concludes that the poem post-dates the development of the prosthetic vowel and thus gives it the surprisingly late date of 1050-1150.[19]

Koch (2013) replies that the poem's metre is best understood as patterns of accented phrases, rather than syllable counts, and that it is hard to conceive how a system of counting syllables could arise when the syllabic structure of the language was in flux. Koch's discussion of this issue undercuts the foundations of Isaac's precise argument. The question of the poem's date is still open. The content of the poem is consistent with the other Urien poems and suggests that it could be a genuine poem of Taliesin.[20]

Urien, Gwallawg and Catraeth

Poem 12 calls Gwallawg 'magistrate of Elfed [Elmet]', probably the area around Leeds. In Harley 3859 he is Lleënawg's son and descends from Coel Hen, like Urien. The *Historia Brittonum* states he was one of four kings who fought the Angles, the others being Urien, Morgan and Rhydderch. In *Moliant Cadwallon*, discussed earlier as a poem composed c. 632, Gwallawg appears in lines 30-31.[21]

> 30 Fierce Gwallawg caused
> 31 the greatly renowned death toll at Catraeth

This suggests that he joined forces with Urien to take Catraeth. If Koch (1997) is wrong in thinking that Catraeth and Gwen Ystrat were the same battle, and Urien and Gwallawg did take Catraeth, then was it before or after the Gododdin battle? Catraeth is mentioned in two Urien poems: 'men of Catraeth' in *Battle of Gwen Ystrat* and 'ruler of Catraeth' in *Spoils of Taliesin*. In both, it is the first place mentioned. These suggest that great prestige was obtained from conquering Catraeth – that they had won glory in avenging the earlier Gododdin defeat there. The latter probably occurred around 550 and its retaking by Urien and Gwallawg around 570-80. The retaking may only mean that they had won an initial battle, giving temporary glory and spoils, before it was later taken again by the Angles.

Both kings were not far from Catraeth. Gwallawg was at Elmet, 45 miles to the south. The Urien poems name *Erechwydd*, meaning a place of 'fresh' water, implying many rivers or lakes. Other locations are *Idon* (river Eden) and *Llwyfenydd*, the river Lyvennet (Hogg, 1946) which meets the Eden at Temple Sowerby and the *Eirch* which seems to be the Arkle Beck, a stream that runs into the Swale near Catterick. All these are not far from Catterick (Catraeth).[22]

The Validity of the Poems

It is uncertain how many of the 11 or so poems will survive a future critical analysis but there are incidents in some of them that strongly suggest an early date. One riveting poem is the *Appeasement of Urien* which describes dissent within Urien's family. Meirion Pennar (1988) discusses the situation where Urien is getting old and his sons treat him disrespectfully – 'the throwing of twigs at an old man'. Pennar notes the age-old Welsh tradition of throwing twigs of hazel wood at a person to ridicule them, this custom appearing in the poetry of Dafydd ap Gwilym and the story, *Peredur*. Taliesin defends Urien and says that he'll not go to Urien's progeny, the kings of the north, but he is also careful not to offend Urien's sons. He skilfully transforms the twigs into hurtling spears.[23]

> Your regal sons, the most generous of men:
> from now on their twigs will be whistling
> towards the land of their enemy.

Given that Urien was a great hero of the Welsh, it's hard to imagine a bard of the 1100s composing a poem like this containing unflattering intimate details of conflict in the family.

Another poem that seems genuine is *Rheged Arise*. The bard states that originally he was 'not one of yours' indicating that he grew up in another region. Later he comments on a battle at Mathrau, stating that the men of Rheged fought badly around the king. He can't sugarcoat the disaster and says that it would not be good to lie about it. These remarks would hardly be expected from a 1100s bard composing a heroic poem.[24]

Themes of the Poems

For the purposes of this discussion Poems 2 to 12 are assumed to have been composed by Taliesin. These poems are well constructed ones concerned with the practical matters that characterize a good king. He is profusely praised for defending his kingdom, keeping his people safe, and for his generosity to his warriors, bard and subjects. The bard is completely dependent on the king for his subsistence and thus has the incentive to compose positive imagery. Conversely, a disaffected bard who is removed could satirize a king, a scenario that the king would want to avoid.

In the poems to Urien and Owain, Taliesin's praise of the king seems genuine as noted in the conflict between Urien and his sons. In Poem 5 *What if Urien were slain*? Taliesin confronts the possibility that Urien may be slain and pictures him being brought back on a bier, his white hair washed with blood. When Urien returns in triumph, Taliesin's relief and joy is palpable.[25]

Urien's defending his people is shown in Poem 6, *Battle of Argoed Llwyfein*. Here the Anglian chief, Fflamddwyn (the flame-bearer), is demanding hostages as a sign of submission to his overlordship but Owain defiantly yells back that no whelp of Coel would pay anybody a hostage. While this is taking place, Urien and his army are hidden behind the crest of a hill. They take the Angles by surprise in a great victory where Fflamddwyn is killed by Owain according to his elegy in Poem 10. The English enemy are called by terms such as *eigyl* (Angles) or the men of *lloegyr*, the eastern part of Britain now taken over by the English. Poem 3, *Urien of Erechwydd*, refers to Urien pillaging their homesteads and burning their settlements.

Other battles against fellow Britons occur where the aim appears to be plunder and some of these seem to be quite distant from Urien's homeland. There are battles against Manau (the western Gododdin), Aeron (Ayrshire in western Scotland), Powys to the south, and Alclud (Alt Clut), the rock of Dumbarton. Certainly the spoils of these raids are appreciated by the bard. They include horses, calves, cows, oxen, ornaments and garments. Taliesin's attitude is that a good king shares out the hard-won spoils to his people which then enhances his status and fosters loyalty.

Why Taliesin could not have been Arthur's Bard

The poetry above, while skilful, is conventional praise poetry. The bard praises the king for defending his kingdom, his valour in battle, gathering spoils, his imperious character (like his famous ancestors) and his generosity in giving to his people. He doesn't wonder why things in the world are like they are or express philosophical views or act like a teacher in conveying information. Any personal views of this type, if they exist, are hidden. His expressed knowledge concerns only the king and his actions. His poems are very different to the Arthurian poems whose author was a sage interested in esoteric matters, how the world worked and the role of God.

As argued earlier, Ifor Williams' belief that Taliesin composed first to Kynan in Powys and then moved north to be Urien's bard seems improbable. In addition, the poem to Kynan expresses a much harsher attitude than the other poems: 'Wretched chieftains, you quake before Kynan' and 'They are slaves to Kynan'. Eight of the twelve 'Taliesin' poems show evidence of a Christian outlook but this poem is one of the four that doesn't. If this poem is not one of Taliesin's then there is no reason to place Taliesin initially in Powys. He was a bard of the north and too late in time to have been Arthur's bard.[26]

The late cartoonish material in *Tale of Taliesin* which puts Taliesin in Maelgwn's north Wales court is implausible. It is hardly feasible for him to have been Maelgwn's bard in the period c. 510-545 and later go north to compose poems to Urien and Gwallawg about their valour in battles fought in the period 572–592.

Taliesin's association with Arthur appears to derive from the false belief that he composed the Arthurian poems. Geoffrey apparently believed this and his *Vita Merlini* portrays Taliesin as Arthur's bard, who with Merlin took the dying Arthur to Avalon. After this, the public perception of Taliesin as Arthur's bard became well established.

TALHAEARN – ARTHUR'S BARD

There was a renowned poet who is a good fit for Arthur's bard. He appears to have been regarded as the leading bard of the sixth century. It will be shown below that this bard lived at the same time and in the same area as Arthur – his name was Talhaearn. In Chapter 61, the *Historia Brittonum* of AD 829-30 lists five famous British bards from the sixth-century.[27]

Then Talhaearn 'Father of Inspiration' achieved renown in poetry; and Neirin, and Taliesin, and Bluchbard, and Cian, who is called 'Wheat of Song', were at the same time famous in Brittonic poetry.

This statement treats Talhaearn differently to the other four bards. He is named first and is given the most prestigious title of 'Father of Inspiration' (*Tad Awen*) which seems to imply that he was the most eminent poet. Geraint Gruffydd (1989-90) comments on the title of Talhaearn and his unusual name.[28]

> Of the five ... Talhaearn Tad Awen is in some ways the most intriguing, not only because his epithet implies some kind of primacy, but also because his name – an extremely rare one – occurs in place-name elements not far from Dinorben ...

As poetic inspiration was crucial to the bards, his epithet certainly does imply some kind of primacy. Secondly he is treated separately to the other four, who are then considered as a group. He is also given his own accolade of achieving 'renown in poetry', another prestigious tribute unique to him, whereas the other bards were 'famous in poetry' at the same time.

The latter point also implies he was of a different time period to the other four. As Taliesin was the bard to Urien whose floruit was in the second half of the sixth century, it suggests that Talhaearn was earlier than the other bards, in the first half of the sixth century. This conclusion was also reached by John Morris-Jones who stated that Talhaearn was the earliest Welsh poet (in Williams, 1980). It is argued below that Talhaearn was probably Arthur's bard.[29]

Gruffydd points out that the name, Talhaearn, is an 'extremely rare one' and identifies four sites in north Wales not far from Dinorben which surprisingly contain the name. The main one is Tre Talhaearn (the town of Talhaearn), which is now called Llanfair Talhaiarn, the addition of 'Llanfair' to acknowledge the St Mary's Church there. This village is very close to Dinarth, only about 9 miles or a 3 hour walk. Gruffydd speculates as to whether Talhaearn may have been a bard of Maglocunus or his forebears, placing him at exactly the right time for Arthur. Given his closeness to Dinarth, and this time period, he must be a prime candidate for Arthur's bard. The name Talhaearn is formed from *tal* meaning 'brow' or 'forehead' and *haearn* meaning 'iron', that is 'iron brow', quite suitable for a warrior bard.[30]

The Arthurian poems

Of the five bards mentioned in the *Historia*, only two have surviving poetry attributed to their names, Taliesin and Aneirin, the latter to whom the stanzas of *Y Gododdin* are ascribed although there are some he obviously did not compose. Nothing apparently survives from the leading poet, Talhaearn. However, it is argued below that his poetry does survive in the three Arthurian poems in the Book of Taliesin: *Spoils of Annwfyn, Chair of the Sovereign* and *Battle of the Trees*.

Ifor Williams places the poems in the Book of Taliesin into various categories, one being 'Poems of the Legendary Taliesin' which has 15 poems. He states that this legendary Taliesin 'combines the powers of a magician, a sorcerer, and a prophet'. He places two of the Arthurian poems there: *Battle of the Trees* and *Chair of the Sovereign*. It is easy to see why the former has been placed there with its long sections on reincarnation and its animated trees battling a mysterious enemy. This poem is discussed in the next chapter.[31]

However Williams' fine judgement deserts him concerning *Chair of the Sovereign*, which contains many sober facts about Arthur, the devastation of his men from the Annwfyn disaster, and the conditions in north Wales after Arthur's death. Williams was probably reacting in disgust to the mention of an Elphin at the poem's end, who he equated with the Elphin in the cartoonish *Tale of Taliesin*. With this Elphin in mind he remarks: 'Every poem which mentions Elphin should be rejected without hesitation...'. However, Elphin was a sixth-century name. In *Y Gododdin*, stanza A.37, an Elphin is mentioned who was a paragon of valour – 'valour in attack like that of Elphin'. The warrior Eithinyn, 'bull of combat', is praised because he was like Elphin (Koch, 1997), a far cry from the foolish Elphin of *Tale of Taliesin*.[32]

The compiler of the Book of Taliesin had placed *Spoils of Annwfyn* just before the eight poems to Urien and Williams does not put *Spoils of Annwfyn* in the legendary category, placing it with the historical poems to Urien. In a letter to Roger Loomis he compares its language to that of *Armes Prydein*, c. 900, and says 'How much earlier, I cannot say yet' (Loomis, 1941). John Koch (1985-6; 1996) thinks that it cannot be later than the 700s. The early features he identifies are consistent with a sixth-century dating.[33]

Arthur's Bard

The creation of the two categories, 'historical Taliesin' and 'legendary Taliesin' is an oversimplification. Arthur's bard has some features of the legendary Taliesin but the latter exaggerates these. The Arthurian poems reveal an intellectual outlook with Christian beliefs which have been integrated with the old beliefs of the transmigration of the soul. Arthur's bard composes many lines describing his previous earthly states in both animate and inanimate matter.

Strabo remarks that the Gauls honoured three classes of learned men, the *bards*, the *vates* and the *druids*. The bards were poets, the vates were diviners and the druids were philosophers. Arthur's bard combined the first and third functions. He delights in mysteries and often expresses information indirectly which must have left some of his audience wondering what he meant. His style is to ask questions to emphasize his own authority, and to draw attention to important points. He boasts of incidents or events he has seen of which the monks were totally ignorant. However, these boasts are not about isolated pieces of book learning but things he has seen in Annwfyn. He also ridicules the monks through the use of implied questions about events in Annwfyn that are important to him.[34]

He was a devout Christian but was also a warrior bard who fought in Annwfyn. In *Battle of the Trees* he recalls, as a young man, riding his horse Melyngan who was 'swift as a seagull'. This gives a sharp contrast with Taliesin, who didn't go into battle with Urien but stayed home at the settlement deeply worried about whether Urien would be brought home dead on a bier.[35]

Inclusion of Talhaearn's poems under Taliesin's name

When the *Historia* was compiled in 829-30, Taliesin didn't have the huge reputation that later developed. Talhaearn was the pre-eminent poet and Taliesin was just one of the four who were famous poets. The process of how Taliesin's fame grew is lost to us, but once an initial set of poems thought to be his was created it may have served as a useful repository for other poems. To address the problem of poems difficult to classify, other poems were included under his name, including high quality anonymous poems. This probably led to popular poems having their features and phrasing imitated in the composition of new poems.

A process like this would have inflated his reputation and led to the creation of late stories like the *Tale of Taliesin* where he repeatedly gets the better of Maelgwn and his bards.

It is suggested here that the three Talhaearn poems, after a period of oral transmission, were written into a single manuscript. At some point their authorship may have been lost in manuscript damage or in the copying and they were placed with the Taliesin poems. Perhaps the 'Tal' part was preserved with the rest of the name indecipherable, the scribe assuming that they were Taliesin's. Some such process could have caused the poems to be placed into the Taliesin group.

'Father of Inspiration'

A prominent theme in the Arthurian poems is 'poetic inspiration' which may have led to the 'father of inspiration' title for Talhaearn. In *Spoils of Annwfyn*, the bard is boasting about the quality of his poetry. In Line 11, he is being showered with praise after singing his poetry. Two lines later he says:

13   My poetry, from the cauldron it was spoken.
14   By the breath of nine maidens it was kindled.

Who were these nine maidens who kindled the fire? Stories about nine maidens who practised magic had existed for centuries, as is shown from the work of Pomponius Mela in AD 43-44. In his *Chorographia* (Description of the World) he mentions nine priestesses who reside on the island of Sena (off Gaul) and who practise the arts of magic. Among their powers were the ability to heal the incurable, control the weather, predict the future and change their shape. It is likely that tales of this type were well known at the time of Arthur in order for the bard's audience to understand the reference.[36]

Geoffrey of Monmouth was also familiar with them but in his typical fashion elaborates them with the details that are familiar to us today. In his *Life of Merlin* Geoffrey locates them in Arthur's Avalon instead of the isle of Sena. He makes them sisters, and creates names for each one, with Morgen the leader being more beautiful and more skilled in healing than the others. Morgen later became known as 'Morgan le Fay' (the fairy) in the later Arthurian romances.[37]

What did the bard mean by saying that his poetry came from the cauldron? One option is that his poetry was so inspired that it was seemingly produced by magic. A second option is that he actually mixed potions to enhance his poetic inspiration. While this may seem less likely, given his esoteric interests it is not impossible.

In *Chair of the Sovereign*, the poem is about Arthur and the sad aftermath of the sea voyage. He begins the poem by stating that this poem is one of his most inspired:

1   The proclaiming of a clear poem,

2   of inspiration beyond measure

Later in the poem the bard delivers a series of lines where he expresses thanks for various things. They usually begin 'it is fine when...'. In Lines 35 and 36 he states:

35   (it is) fine when came from the cauldron

36   the three-part inspiration.

It appears that the three-part inspiration is an acknowledgement of the triune nature of God and, to the bard, God is the ultimate source of poetic inspiration.

The Greatest Sage

The only information available on Talhaearn appears in a long poem in the Book of Taliesin called *Angar Kyfundawt*. In lines 165-6 it says that 'Talhaearn is the greatest sage'. This is a perfect fit for the author of the three Arthurian poems. The bard is interested in philosophical matters such as the transmigration of the soul, the nature of poetic inspiration, prophecy, the origins of people, the workings of God, all combined with a devout belief in Christianity.

He was apparently familiar with Virgil's *Eclogue* 4, as he knew of the golden age to come foreseen by Virgil, whom he mentions by name at the end of *Battle of the Trees*. He used imagery from the *Dionysiaca* of Nonnos of Panopolis in his account of the battle against the 'dragon' in *Battle of the Trees*, to be discussed in the next chapter. He also liked to ask questions to emphasize his role as a sage.

God is the True Judge

In lines 70-2 of *Angar Kyfundawt* the poet says that, according to the utterance of Talhaearn, God was the true judge of the worth of the world. This is reminiscent of Lines 33-4 in *Chair of the Sovereign*:

33   It is fine when the True One shines;

34   even finer when He speaks.

SUMMARY OF THE CASE FOR TALHAEARN

The arguments for identifying Talhaearn with Arthur's bard are presented below:

- Taliesin could not have been Arthur's bard because of the vastly different styles between the historical and Arthurian poems.

- Taliesin lived at too late a time to be Arthur's bard.

- Talisesin was a bard of the north, distant from north Wales.

- Talhaearn was a devout Christian, as was Arthur's bard.

- Talhaearn was called the 'greatest sage', a role perfectly fitting Arthur's bard.

- Talhaearn lived close to Dinarth, only 9 miles away.

- Talhaearn lived in the first half of the sixth century, as did Arthur's bard.

- Talhaearn was the 'father of poetic inspiration', a theme heavily emphasized in the Arthurian poems.

6
CATASTROPHE IN SCOTLAND

ENCOUNTER WITH A DRAGON

In Galloway, Scotland, Arthur experienced a disaster that is presented in *Battle of the Trees*. This poem has been of interest to Celtic scholars for many years and its interpretation is difficult. On a superficial level its main theme concerns an army of trees who have been animated by a magician, after God answered the Britons' prayers for help. The bard describes the carnage: 'the blood of men up to our thighs'. The trees then fight a mysterious enemy. Although not the main theme of this book, an explanation is attempted which if true could provide a date when Arthur was in Galloway. It was composed when the bard was an old man, when the Scotland disaster that he is about to describe and Arthur's Annwfyn voyage were in the distant past.

The poem has a number of 'sections', with the tree battle being the longest. It is called 'the battle of the tree tops' in line 26, while the whole poem is known by the title 'Battle of the Trees'. The poem opens with a section on the transmigration of the soul. In the first 23 lines, the bard recalls some of the states of existence of his soul before he was 'unfettered' – before he became a human. For example, he had once been a mottled sword, a droplet in the air, in the radiance of the stars, a word in writing, a bridge, a bubble in a drink, a string in a harp, a tree in a fire, etc. He believed in the transmigration of the soul, as the Druids did, but also believed that God was in charge of everything and he was a devoted Christian who believed that Christ's crucifixion was one of the three greatest cataclysms in history (in lines 73 and 244). The poem also has a section on the fighting in Annwfyn and the death of Arthur which will be discussed in Chapter 8.

In Line 24, he states that he was a bard who had sung from infancy and then introduces the 'battle of the tree tops' section.[1]

> 26 I sang in the battle of the tree tops
> 27 before the lord of Britain.

Who was this lord of Britain? In lines 189-204, the bard describes his fighting under Arthur in Annwfyn, implying that he was Arthur's bard.

Thus the lord of Britain whom he sang before was Arthur, the only king named in the poem. After introducing this battle of the tree tops but before his vivid account of the battle, he introduces the enemy – a dragon-like creature, as translated by Coe and Young (1995).[2]

30 I pierced a great scaly beast,
31 on him were a hundred heads
32 and an army (for harshness)
33 under the root of his tongue,
34 and another army which was
35 on his necks.
36 A black, forked toad,
37 on him a hundred claws.
38 A speckled, crested serpent,
39 a hundred souls through sin
40 are tormented in its skin.

Dragons

This imagery resembles the giant beast, Typhon, who fought the Greek god, Zeus, in Hesiod's *Theogany*, composed c. 700 BC, and translated by Most (2018). An elaborated account is given in the *Dionysiaca*, by Nonnos of Panopolis, composed about AD 400-450 (Rouse, 1940). Both use 'dragon' as one descriptor for the complex beast. It has a hundred heads, many necks, a serpent-like nature, speckled skin, an army of snakes, and shooting poison of the tongues. It seems that the bard was familiar with this imagery, possibly from Nonnos. Although Typhon was a beast of the Earth, he was so large that he reached into the heavens to create havoc there. After he wrecked the heavens he 'shifted to the rocks, leaving the air, to flog the seas'.[3]

The Christianized Britons were familiar with the dragon. In the Book of Revelation in the Bible a huge fiery red dragon (Satan), with seven heads and ten horns, casts down to earth one third of the stars with its tail. This account was written about AD 81-96. The Britons were also familiar with the use of the *draco* military standard used by the Romans from about the third century. It consisted of a hollow cast-metal head mounted on a tall pole and a trailing coloured cloth, about 1.5 metres long that formed a tube that tapered towards the end. As the wind passed through it, it whistled and howled, which was intended to evoke a feeling of dread in the opposing army. Gildas around AD 537 used *draco* in describing Maglocunus as the 'dragon of the island' (probably the island of Anglesey) to indicate his military strength. The *Historia Brittonum* of 829-30 relates an incident where the young wizard, Ambrosius, describes a fight between a red and a white dragon reflecting the struggle between the Britons and Saxons. Another reference to the dragon occurs in the ancient Welsh poem, *Gwarchan Maeldderw*, where the poet refers to the 'the Pharaoh's red dragon' in line 21, as translated by Graham Isaac (2002).[4]

Meteors and Comets as Dragons

Pliny the Elder in his *Natural History*, c. AD 77, gave an impressively detailed description of the types of comets known, including one called Typhon as shown below (Rackham, 1938).[5]

> A terrible comet was seen by the people of Ethiopia and Egypt, to which Typhon the king of that period gave his name; it had a fiery appearance and was twisted like a coil, and it was very grim to behold: it was not really a star so much as what might be called a ball of fire.

Victor Clube and William Napier (1990) theorize that the stories of Hesiod and Nonnos derive from a powerful fireball swarm hitting the Earth which the Greeks interpreted as a cosmic battle. They think that the debris striking the earth came from a comet, probably from the constellation Taurus. While sophisticated writers like Pliny thought comets to be natural objects like stars, others thought of them as more malevolent objects that foreshadowed disaster.[6]

There is ample evidence that fireball storms from the debris of comets were thought to be fiery dragons by many. McBeath (2003), Warner (2003) and Avilin (2007) discuss the folktales of people in eastern Europe and Russia where there were widespread beliefs that meteor showers were dragons. Baillie (1999) also discusses ancient Chinese records to point out that the meteoric fireballs were thought to be dragons. It is very likely that the rarer comets were also believed to be dragons. There are also two early references to dragons in the Irish *Annals of Ulster* and one in the *Anglo-Saxon Chronicle*, as shown for the years 735, 746 and 793.

Annals of Ulster

735   A huge dragon (draco) was seen, with great thunder after it, at the end of autumn.

746   Dragons (dracones) were seen in the sky.

Anglo-Saxon Chronicle

793   Here were dreadful forewarnings come over the land of Northumbria and woefully terrified the people: these were amazing sheets of lightning and whirlwinds, and fiery dragons were seen flying in the sky.

Battle of the Tree Tops

Was there a real disaster behind the bard's account of the magically animated trees fighting a dragon? It is argued below that the account was based on a fireball storm from the debris associated with comet Halley which appeared in AD 530. The poem was composed decades after a terrible event which the bard then thought was the beginning of the horrors leading to Judgement Day.

Now the event was long past and the bard is taking comfort in the prophecy of Virgil of the golden age to come. As the horror was past, the bard placed the event in a magical setting. The magician, Gwydion, appealed to God and Christ to deliver the Britons from the dragon's attack. Through God's help, Gwydion was able to fashion an army of trees to impede the dragon. The bard envisaged the dragon attacking from above as he called it the 'battle of the tree tops' and also refers to the tree tops in Lines 145-7 as follows.[7]

145   The top of the birch put forth leaves for us,
146   [its] vigour reinforced us;
147   The top of the oak ensnared [the enemy] for us.

The bard, as well as later bards making additions, created humorous lines by bringing small, insignificant vegetation as warriors into the battle. Bracken, broom, gorse, heather and clover all join the battle. Clover's contribution is praised as follows: 'A terrifying array was the surging clover'. While these lines are cleverly done, and would have created great entertainment, there are other lines implying a terrifying reality. The Britons were being massacred, as shown in Line 68, and the bard was witnessing this as shown by his use of 'our'. This is followed by his calling this disaster the greatest of the three cataclysms in the history of the world.[8]

> 68 The blood of men up to our thighs.
>
> 69 The greatest of the Three Cataclysms
>
> 70 which came to pass in the world:
>
> 71 and one came about
>
> 72 as a result of the story of the Flood,
>
> 73 and [the second was] Christ's Crucifixion
>
> 74 and [the third is] The Day of Judgement to come.

Some scholars believe that the poem is just an imaginative fantasy but the bard is a staunch Christian whose distress seems real in relating the call to Christ to save them. All three cataclysms are from the Bible and the bard initially thought that the current cataclysm heralded the Day of Judgement. The Welsh words translated 'to come' are *rac llaw*, which literally means 'before the hand', that is 'at hand'. So the coming Judgement is not in the distant future, but for the bard it appeared to be starting now. For a Christian bard to create a tree-battle fantasy purely to entertain and place it in the same category as the Crucifixion and Judgement Day lacks credibility – it would trivialize and demean the importance of those events. He repeats these cataclysms near the end of the poem to emphasize their importance.

COMET HALLEY

In AD 530, Halley's comet made another return visit to the inner solar system where it loops around the Sun in a thin ellipse of higher than average eccentricity. When it is closest to the Sun its position is known as the perihelion. At the other extreme, when furthest from the Sun out beyond Neptune, its position is called the aphelion. It was seen by Chinese astronomers who described it as a 'broom star', that is, a comet with a tail. The tail was pure white and about 9 degrees long. Distances within the solar system are measured by the astronomical unit (au), conceived as the average distance of the Earth from the Sun but now defined as a constant, 149,597,871 km. In 530, Halley's comet was 0.28 au away at its closest approach to the Earth.[9]

Halley completes its circuit around the Sun in about 76 years but the gravitational effects of other planets, mainly Jupiter, modify this period. Viewed from above the Sun's north pole, the Earth and other planets orbit anti-clockwise around the Sun. The Earth's orbit defines a plane, the *ecliptic plane*, and the other planets' orbits are close to this plane, except for Mercury which inclines to it by 7°. In contrast to the planets, Halley orbits clockwise around the Sun and its orbital plane inclines at 18° to the ecliptic. The comet is usually south of the ecliptic, about 10 au below it at aphelion, but on its return journey it rises above it before descending below it again. The point where it reaches the ecliptic plane on its ascent is the *ascending node* and the point where it reaches the ecliptic on its descent is the *descending node*. The former node is associated with the Orionid meteor showers and the latter node with the Eta Aquariid meteor showers.

Components of the Comet

Halley's comet has a core described as a 'dirty snowball' that is roughly the shape of a peanut. It was found to be unexpectedly black from the 1986 appearance, a black crust of dust and rock that conceals much of the ice which also comprises the core. This ice is mostly frozen water but also includes frozen material such as ammonia, carbon dioxide, methane, and carbon monoxide. For most of its orbit the comet is 'inactive' but when within 6 au of the Sun it develops a coma around the core comprising gas and dust. Then two months before perihelion it develops a tail which points away from the Sun. This tail persists until five months after the perihelion visit (Hughes, 1987). The Sun's heat vaporizes the icy substances, releasing gas and dust particles to form the coma. The dusty tail is formed as the Sun's radiation pushes dust particles away from the coma. A second ion tail might also form as the Sun's solar wind converts the comet's gases into ions (charged particles) that also stream away from the coma.[10]

Meteoroid Stream

These tails differ from the larger-particle meteoroid stream formed by the comet decaying each time it nears the Sun. Over countless orbits of the comet the meteoroids have dispersed all the way around the elliptical path into a wide stream distributed around the path. Every year the Earth passes twice through this stream, even though Halley may be well away from the Earth. In April/early May the Earth meets this stream and the meteoroids enter the Earth's atmosphere, burning up to give the Eta Aquariid meteor showers. The Earth then continues anti-clockwise, leaving the meteoroid stream, until it meets it again in October to give the Orionid meteor showers.

ETA AQUARIID OUTBURSTS

Egal et al. (2020) discuss meteor shower outbursts where the Orionids and the Eta Aquariids display two to four times their usual activity level. They note that the Eta Aquariids are of concern for spacecraft safety, citing their long duration, high flux, occasional outbursts and their high velocity (about 66 km/second). They also list Eta Aquariid outbursts from ancient Chinese observations in 74 BC, AD 401, 443, 466, 530, 839, 905, 927 and 934. The AD 530 year is of considerable interest as comet Halley also completed a perihelion visit that year on September 27 after the April/May outburst.[11]

Minimum orbit intersection distance (MOID)

An important measure is the MOID between the orbits of Halley and the Earth close to Halley's ascending and descending nodes. Egal et al. graph them showing how they have varied over the centuries. In 1000 BC, the MOID near the ascending node was very small while the MOID near the descending node was large. However in our year of interest, AD 530, the MOID near the descending node was very small while the MOID near the ascending node was notably larger. Estimating from their graph, the 530 descending node MOID was only about 0.009 au, which looks close to the lowest estimated MOID value over the 4000 year period they graph. Currently, in 2023 this MOID value near the descending node is about 0.065 au.[12]

It will be shown that an unusual convergence of conditions was occurring when Halley approached perihelion in 27 September 530 and was discharging additional meteoroids close to the Earth's orbit which the Earth would later plough through in April and May 531 for the Eta Aquariids. Egal et al. make the salient inference.[13]

> The proximity of the comet around AD 500 might explain the existence of strong Eta Aquariids outbursts reported in ancient Chinese observations.

Cometary Dust after 530

Dallas Abbott et al. (2014a; 2014b) argue that Halley's comet was a significant source of atmospheric dust in 530. Her data comes from the ice cores drilled from Greenland (72.6°N, 38.5°W) as part of the Greenland Ice Sheet Project 2 (GISP2). From the ice brought up from the drilling, each year can be identified, and even parts of the year. This runs in parallel with dendrochronology (tree ring dating), both giving data on what conditions were like in ancient times. In tree ring dating, the rings' lack of growth, or limited growth, or frost damage can provide information on the climate the trees experienced.

In ice core studies, the material found in the ice provides the data. In this case, the core samples were from 360.51 to 361.80 metres in depth, which they identify with the years AD 540 to 533. In Abbott et al. (2014a) they investigate the presence of Nickel-rich fragments and iron-oxide cosmic spherules and argue that these probably imply an extraterrestrial source for the dust. In Abbott et al. (2014b) they investigate Tin-rich and Nickel-rich particles and cosmic spherules all found together in their samples and infer from these that the source was probably a comet.[14]

Atmospheric dust at this time may also be inferred from Zachariah of Mitylene (Hamilton and Brooks, 1899).[15]

> And the stars in the sky had appeared dancing in a strange manner, and it was the summer of the year eleven [533]. And it lasted about six or seven years, until the year three [540].

The 'dancing stars' would indicate a dust loading in the atmosphere according to Baillie (1999). Abbott et al. (2014b) argue that Halley's comet on its 530 perihelion visit was the source of the cometary dust as it was most concentrated around the April/May period in their ice samples, the time of the Eta Aquariids.[16]

They provide a graph showing that cometary dust falls off sharply from 533 to 536, and continues to fall to 540. So cometary dust cannot explain the severe environmental downturns in 536 and 540, which it will be shown involve dust from volcanic eruptions. This issue will be taken up in Chapter 9, where the extreme long-lasting downturn after Arthur's death was a factor in the some of the Britons developing a superstition against the direct use of his name.[17]

HALLEY'S IMPACT IN AD 530-31

A battle lasting 30 days

The poem's 'battle of the treetops' section in line 62 states that the battle's duration was 30 days. This is hardly feasible for a conventional battle between two armies, so the bard must have been thinking of a different circumstance.

> 61 (Warriors) were cast down around the battlefields
> 62 for thirty days of battle.

However if the opponent were the dragon, mentioned just before the battle, then the 30 days makes sense. When Halley's comet appeared in AD 530, it was first seen on the 29 August and was last seen on the 27 September, the latter when it was at perihelion position (Yeomans et al., 1986; Tsu, 1934). That is, it was seen for 3 days in August and 27 days in September, 30 days in all. This supports the idea that the bard was seeing Halley's comet and was identifying it with the dragon he had described in lines 30-40.[18]

Halley's Comet and Mean Motion Resonances

In 530, Halley's Comet again made a perihelion visit, but after the Eta Aquariids outburst for this year. This visit was rather unusual. Instead of returning to perihelion around the average 76 years, the comet took 79.3 years (Yeomans and Kiang, 1981).[19]

This is the longest orbital period ever recorded for comet Halley. In this case the delay was caused by Halley itself being trapped in a gravitational 'sweet spot' by Jupiter, known by the term *mean motion resonances* (MMR). This has been recently studied with remarkable results in which ancient meteoroid debris trapped by Jupiter can create meteor shower outbursts in modern times. Two main MMR of comet Halley with Jupiter may be noted. From 1404 BC to 690 BC, Halley was in a 1:6 MMR with Jupiter, where Halley completed one orbit for every six orbits of Jupiter.

In the second, from 240 BC to AD 1700, Halley was in a 2:13 MMR where Halley completed two orbits to Jupiter's thirteen. The 3.3 year delay in Halley arriving in AD 530 can be attributed to the 2:13 MMR according to David Hughes (1987).

MMR and Meteoroid Clumping

What is the effect of Halley undergoing a 2:13 MMR for 770 years from 240 BC to AD 530? Sekhar and Asher (2014) state that Halley's meteoroids would not be uniformly distributed along the orbital path but form 13 clumps that are spaced around the entire orbit.[20]

> we can visualize ... 13 resonant zones spaced in mean anomaly along the whole orbit, each zone consisting of individual librating particles.

If the Earth's orbit passes through one of these 13 clumps or zones it creates a much more powerful meteor shower than usual, an outburst. Sekhar and Asher state that when the comet itself is resonant (as distinct from its ejected meteoroids) it remains in a single resonant zone. When the comet goes out of resonance it would keep moving between zones and hence populate each zone gradually with its ejected meteoroids. Of course if the Earth's orbit misses one of these clusters then there is no outburst, but the poem implies a dire scenario which could be explained if in 530 the Earth did meet one of these clumps with the descending node MOID being at, or very close to, its smallest value over the last 3000 years.[21]

A Strong Outburst in 530

In 1958, Imoto and Hasegawa's catalog of historical records of meteor showers was translated from Japanese to English and published. Then Chinese records compiled by Zhuang Tian-shan (1966; 1977) and the Beijing Observatory (1988) were added. Hasegawa (1993) used these lists to create a more comprehensive catalog. Her first sixth-century record is an Eta Aquariids outburst in 530, described as follows.[22]

> More than 1,000 stars to the northwest.

By 'stars' the ancient observer means shooting stars, or meteors. The hypothesis here is that the Earth passed through one of these dense clumps in April 530, as part of the Eta Aquariids, creating the heavy meteor shower above. This was well before the approaching Halley was actually visible to the observers on Earth. It first became visible on 29 August and swept through perihelion on 27 September 530, discharging the material that would enrich its meteoroid stream for the Earth to meet again in April 531.

A Notable Outburst in 531

Dall'Olmo (1978) lists meteor showers, meteorites and meteors from European sources. In Arthur's time, only two events are given, a single meteor in 518 and a huge event in 531, described as follows.[23]

> A great meteor shower regarded as an omen.

This is a very strong contender for the battle of the treetops as the poem relates that Arthur regarded the catastrophe as an omen that needed an interpretation from his *magi*.

What would the bard see from the earth?

In April 530 the bard would have witnessed an intense Eta Aquariids meteor shower. Then on 29 August he would have seen the dragon appear and watched it for 30 days until it left on 27 September. In about three weeks, the Earth's orbit would again meet comet Halley's meteoroid stream causing the Orionid showers which wouldn't have been as spectacular as the 530 Eta Aquariids. Finally in April 531 the Earth would again meet the Eta Aquariids meteoroid stream under the likely conditions (for an outburst) of the very small minimum orbital intersection distance. It seems that this was such a severe outburst that people wondered what it meant for the future.

The Dall'Olmo listing only gave the year, not the month, so we can't be sure that the 531 event was the Eta Aquariids but it does seems likely. Sekhar and Asher say that each of the 13 clumps may give up to 2 years of outburst possibilities so it is possible the Earth did again encounter one of these clumps. It is also seems to be the case that the 530 incoming Halley would have enriched whatever clump it met by populating it with new material from its nucleus. To sum up, there are two reports of huge meteor showers for 530 and 531 and sandwiched between them was a 'dragon' that was visible for 30 days as reported both in the poem and Chinese observations.[24]

The Effect on Arthur's Army

The Eta Aquariids meteoroids pass through the Earth's atmosphere at a massive speed, 66 km per second, or 237,600 km per hour and hence burn up before they can hit the ground and be classed as meteorites. NASA estimates that Halley sheds material from around its nucleus that is between 1 and 3 metres thick for each perihelion visit. For the specific year 1910, Hughes (1987) estimates that Halley lost about 1.4 metres from around its nucleus.[25]

John Lewis (1996) points out that normally all the meteors from a cometary shower burn up, but speculates as to whether a meteorite-sized chunk of cometary material might survive its fall to Earth. He notes that along with the vast quantities of meteoric dust, there are occasional larger fragments. He also notes that some comets have split up and that this splitting has not occurred where one would most expect it, near perihelion when the comet is subjected to the strong tidal forces from the Sun's gravity and its strong surface heating. Lewis states that the core of comet Halley has now been found to be of low density, 'a vast network of cracks and voids'. Given such fragility, could a sizeable chunk have split off from Halley's nucleus? The poem suggests that some material may have survived the high-speed entry burnup and hit the ground, which is surprisingly called 'churned up' in the poem (Haycock, 2007).[26]

> 119 Broom in the van of the battalion
> 120 was wounded in the churned-up ground.

Furthermore, if Abbott et al. (2014b) are right about the dust in the atmosphere coming from a comet, it could suggest material exploding in the air, similar to the Tunguska disaster in 1908 which flattened the forest trees in Siberia. This dust may have caused the bristlecone pine frost rings in 532, noted in Salzer and Hughes (2007), as there is no volcanic sulphate signal at this time. If the 'blood up to our thighs' line reflects severe injuries or death, this also suggests that some rocky material was getting through. Even if this material were small, it was travelling at 66 km per second, which would do enormous damage. In the battle of the tree tops the bard is praising the trees for fighting off the dragon whose assault seems to have been coming from the sky. It suggests that he observed material raining down that was hitting the tops of the trees and causing great damage.[27]

Prophesying to Arthur

The bard states that when this disaster occurred they were in the fort of Nefenhyr (line 41) which was in the territory of the Novantae tribe. Haycock (2007) endorses the argument of John Lloyd-Jones (1950-2) that Nefenhyr is derived from a form of *Novantorix* and argues that 'kaer Nefenhyr' probably means the fort of the king of the Novantae. So Arthur's men were somewhere in Galloway, from the Rhinns in the west to an unknown eastern point, perhaps bordered by the River Nith. As noted in Chapter 3, this was where Gwalchmai (Sir Gawain), said to be the son of Arthur's sister, was a king. If this disaster is correctly related to the meteoric outburst of AD 531 then it gives a lower-bound estimate for Arthur's departure to Annwfyn – he must have sailed after this date.[28]

Arthur's reaction to the disaster was typical of kings of that era. The *Historia Brittonum* relates that the fifth-century king, Vortigern, was advised by *magi* (sorcerers). The Irish work *Connlae's Adventure* relates how the king is advised by his druid, Corann. Confronted with the dragon's appearance and the related catastrophe, Arthur would have consulted his advisers on its meaning and what it heralded for the future. The poem actually states this near the end in lines 238-9:

> 238   Druids, wise men
> 239   prophesy to Arthur!

This prophesying to Arthur is immediately followed in lines 240-45 by a repeat of the three greatest cataclysms in the history of the world, so that there is little doubt that the advice from the druids and wise men is being linked to the Galloway disaster.

However, this catastrophe and Arthur's death in Annwfyn had occurred decades before the time of composing the poem. The bard, now an old man, is more optimistic in the current situation, being comforted by Virgil's prophecy of a Golden Age to come. Thus he states in the last four lines.[29]

> 246   Like a magnificent jewel in a gold ornament
> 247   thus am I resplendent,
> 248   and I am exhilarated
> 249   by the prophecy of Virgil.

7
DISASTROUS VOYAGE TO AMERICA

The Welsh material in *Spoils of Annwfyn* and *Battle of the Trees* is the bedrock for the hypotheses on Arthur's voyage. However there are later European legends showing that beliefs in Arthur's explorations in the Atlantic were widespread. Without these poems, the European material would probably be discarded as legends having no historical basis. These European accounts are briefly discussed and arguments are given that they were not derived from the works of Geoffrey of Monmouth but preceded him.

LEGENDARY VOYAGES OF ARTHUR

These legends were assembled by John Dee, from Mortlake in west London, a polymath who advised Queen Elizabeth on many matters as mentioned in Chapter 1. In 1569 his friend Gerard Mercator, based in Duisburg, completed his radical wall map to assist navigation, where the world was shown on a flat surface. Mercator added a circular inset of lands around the North Pole with the astonishing text that King Arthur had settled his people in these northerly regions.[1]

Dee sought information about this text and in 1577 Mercator sent him a long letter based on the account of Jacob Cnoyen of Holland, who had explored Asia, Africa and the North. Cnoyen wrote in Old Dutch but Mercator was more comfortable in Latin, so the letter was a mixture of both. In his manuscript *Of Famous and Rich Discoveries* (Cotton MS Vitellius C. VII, British Library) Dee included a transcript of the letter but the manuscript was damaged by fire in 1731, resulting in some missing lines. Mercator's letter was published in 1956 by Eva Taylor with an English translation. It outlines two voyages of Arthur into the northwest Atlantic to an unknown country called Grocland. From these and other legends, Dee presented a case to Elizabeth I in 1578 that Arthur had sailed to America around AD 530.[2]

Jacob Cnoyen's Account
Cnoyen's account is muddled and has several sources whose extent is not clearly defined but the key source for Arthur's voyages is the

Gestae Arthuri (Deeds of Arthur). No copies of this text now survive, but comments made by Mercator and Dee suggest that Mercator was familiar with it and that Dee had at least heard of it. It mentions the 'Little People' in the north whom the Norse called *skraelings*. In a later part it states that Arthur had conquered the Northern Islands but that 4,000 of his people had entered the 'indrawing seas' and had never returned, their fate being unclear. Further on, the *Gestae* gives a brief outline of Arthur's first voyage via Iceland. This is reproduced below (from Taylor, 1956).[3]

> That great army of Arthur's had lain all the winter [of 530 AD] in the northern islands of Scotland. And on May 3 a part of it crossed over into Iceland. Then four ships of the aforesaid land had come out of the North. And warned Arthur of the indrawing seas. So that Arthur did not proceed further, but peopled all the islands between Scotland and Iceland, and also peopled Grocland. [So it seems the Indrawing Sea only begins beyond Grocland] ...
>
> When those four ships returned, there were sailors who asserted that they knew where the *Magnetini* were.

In this quote, the 530 date is inserted over a blank space in the Old Dutch text and appears to be Dee's estimate. The comment in square brackets on the Indrawing Sea is a surmise of Mercator. The indrawing seas appear in Mercator's circular inset, where they lead to the north pole. These were wildly fanciful speculations but in reality there are regions of powerful indrawing currents. James Enterline (2002) states that the Hudson Strait 'has persistent indrawing tidal flows of five to seven knots', especially along the north side. Taylor also quotes Martin Frobisher's lieutenant, George Best, who when in the Davis Strait said 'This place seemeth to have a marvellous great Indrafte'.[4]

The *Magnetini* term refers to the fallacious belief that in certain regions there were magnetic rocks under the water that could attract and wreck ships containing iron. These stories appeared in Ptolemy's *Geographia*, circa AD 150, and in the *Commonitorium Palladii* by Bishop Palladius in the early 400s. Later, the rocks were replaced by magnetic mountains. Dee was familiar with these tales and in giving a shortened version of Mercator's Letter he adds the further detail that

142

8 ships had foundered because of their iron nails and hence in his second voyage, Arthur fitted out 12 ships containing no iron (British Library Additional Manuscript 59681; MacMillan, 2004). It is likely that the added details were Dee's inferences and were not in the letter of Mercator as the Cotton manuscript appears to show only one line missing from fire damage at the top of folio 267 verso which seems too small a space to contain this extra information.[5]

Both features, the indrawing currents and the areas of magnetic disturbance, actually occur in the Hudson Strait and thus reflect real knowledge. In the National Geospatial-Intelligence Agency's *Sailing Directions* (2011) book, three areas of magnetic disturbance in the Hudson Strait are listed – to the north of Akpatok Island, to the north of Charles Island and to the east of Coats Island. These two features do not appear in the Norse sagas, suggesting that the *Gestae Arthuri* was not derived from those accounts.[6]

The *Gestae* then outlines the second voyage of Arthur, and gives surprising detail. As the first line is missing due to fire damage, the beginning in square brackets is a reconstruction by Taylor.[7]

> [Arthur afterwards put on board a fleet of 12 ships about] 1800 men and about 400 women. They sailed northwards on May 3 (sic) in the year following that in which the former ships had departed. And of these 12 ships, five were driven on the rocks in the storm, but the rest of them made their way between the high rocks on June 18, which was 44 days after they had set out.

Taylor gives the departure date as May 3 which is an error. The Cotton handwritten script shows a '5' instead of '3' and there is one other '5' and two other examples of '3' later on the same page to validate this conclusion. So 'May 3' in the quote above should be read as 'May 5'. This also agrees with the 44 days duration. Had Arthur left on May 3, the duration would have been 46 days.

Dating the Gestae Arthuri

The *Gestae* is linked to the second story in the Mabinogi, *Branwen daughter of Llŷr*, where the central character is Branwen's brother, Brân. In Chapter 3, the many specific correlations between Arthur and Brân were given. In *Branwen*, the Irish were attempting to stop Brân's progress and hence destroyed a bridge over the River Shannon. The Irish defenders make the following remark (Ford, 1977).[8]

> There are magnetic stones at the bottom of the river, so that neither ships nor vessels can cross it.

The underwater magnetic stones are the same as the *magnetini* in the *Gestae Arthuri*. *Branwen's* author took details from poetry and legend on Arthur and set them into a similar story about Brân, including the magnetic rocks. As the only known source linking the magnetic rocks to Arthur is the *Gestae Arthuri*, it probably implies that the author of *Branwen* knew this source, or a derivative of it.

It is very unlikely that the borrowing went the other way – that the European author of the *Gestae Arthuri* found a story in Middle Welsh, not about Arthur, with magnetic rocks in an Irish river, and decided to make them a feature of Arthur's voyages into the Arctic. It is also improbable that such a European author would have known Middle Welsh. *Branwen* was probably written around 1120, certainly before Geoffrey's pseudo-history (Breeze, 2018), which suggests the earlier *Gestae* was written in the 1000s, or perhaps even earlier.[9]

The Twelve Hostages from Norway
A further link to Arthur in the north occurs in *Culhwch and Olwen*, where Arthur's gatekeeper, Glewlwyd, notes the adventures they had shared and refers to a battle in Llychlyn where the Britons took twelve hostages. Llychlyn is Norway, but it could also be a more general reference to Scandinavia. *Culhwch and Olwen* has an even earlier date perhaps to around AD 1090-1100, its language being more archaic than that of the four main Mabinogi tales.[10]

Scottish Burial Mounds in Sweden
Swedish legends indicate British raids around Arthur's time. At Greby in western Sweden are 200 burial mounds. An interpretive sign dated 2006, and associated with the Bohuslän Museum, refers to legends of Scottish raiders who came to plunder Bohuslän but were killed and buried in the mounds. The text is headed 'Scottish raiders defeated'. The interpretive sign states that the mounds date to AD 200-600, which encompasses Arthur's time.

Credibility of the Gestae Voyages

These accounts are primitive, incomplete and certainly not a polished product. Although Grocland is not explained, James Enterline (2002) argues that the old Dutch *groc*, the Flemish *krakke*, and the Modern Dutch *krok* mean 'wild pasture'. Dee thought it was Greenland, but changed his mind, in line with Mercator and Ortelius, who viewed it as an island west of Greenland. A possible 'pasture land' site would be Newfoundland. The second voyage ends with the ships sailing through a passage bordered by high cliffs which reads like a factual description. It is odd that the author makes no attempt to glorify Arthur.[11]

The departure dates of 3 and 5 May and the duration of 44 days are plausible. The voyage was slow by 16th century standards but Arthur's ships were more primitive and he did not sail at a nearly constant latitude as Jacques Cartier did, but went north via Iceland. Crossing to Iceland and awaiting a report from ships scouting north is a realistic strategy. However the 2200 crew over 12 ships averages 183 per ship which is suspect unless the ships were larger than expected and very crowded, or the 12 is just a number arbitrarily assigned to the tale. Any crowding could be in line with 'three fullnesses of Prydwen' mentioned in *Spoils of Annwfyn*, as discussed below.

It seems that Arthur had prior advice on the new land as his 'great army' had wintered in the Scottish isles, ready to go. The 400 women implies he intended to start a settlement. In contrast, before Eirik the Red settled in Greenland he explored it for three years in a single boat before returning to Iceland to get his fleet. Unfortunately, the author and his sources are unknown and there can be no corroboration of any details. *Spoils of Annwfyn* shows that Arthur did sail to America but whether the *Gestae* details are true or an imaginative reconstruction is unknown. The *Gestae* doesn't stand alone. There is further material on Arthur's voyages into the northern regions, as follows.

Scandinavian Lands under British Control

A list of Scandinavian lands controlled by Arthur appears in several sources. The earliest one was thought by Liebermann (1894; 1903) to be the *Leges Anglorum Londoniis Collectae*, a collection of laws of England and miscellanea related to London. He dates it to about 1210. Lyn Muir (1968) gives the Latin passage on Arthur's northern lands and Elizabeth Leedham-Green translates it in Ken MacMillan (2004).

This translation is partly reproduced below, but with the Scandinavian lands listed as a column in their Latin names for greater clarity, and with the more modern names taken from Muir (1968).[12]

Arthur, who was anciently the most famous King of the Britons, ... vigorously subjugated the whole of Scantia ...

Norweya	(Norway)
Islandiam	(Iceland)
Grenelandiam	(Greenland)
Suetheidam	(Sweden)
Hiberniam	(Ireland)
Gutlandiam	(Gotland)
Daciam	(Denmark)
Semelandiam	(Semland)
Wynelandiam	(Vinland)
Curlandiam	(Churland, Kurland)
Roe	(Rugen, Riga, Ruhne)
Fenielandiam	(Finland)
Wirlandiam	(Virland)
Estlandiam	(Aestland)
Cherrelam	(Karelien, Corelia)
Lappam	(Lapland)

and all the other lands and islands of the eastern ocean ... and many other islands beyond Scantia ...

... Arthur was a very good Christian, and he saw to it that they were baptised and that one God was worshipped throughout all Norway, and a single faith in Christ adopted and held inviolable forever. And at that time all the Norwegian chieftains took wives from the noble families of Britain, and hence the Norwegians say that they are of the race and blood of this realm. For in those times King Arthur made petition to the Lord Pope and to the Roman curia, that Norway be confirmed in perpetuity to the British crown in augmentation of this kingdom: and the said Arthur called it the vault of Britain. For this reason indeed the Norwegians say that they have a right to live with us in this kingdom, and they say that they are a part of the body of this realm ...

Ultimately they are united with us by the sacraments of faith and by their later taking wives of our race, and by ties of affinity and marriage. So at length King Edward, our last king (who was a great peacemaker) came to an agreement, and granted them concessions through the common council of the whole realm, such that in future they should be able, and have the right, to live alongside us, and remain in the kingdom as our sworn brothers.

146

This astonishing text presents a political argument for the right of the Norse to live in Britain and uses Arthur's authority to underpin it. His renown is emphasized and a blatantly fictitious history is constructed to show that the Norse are 'brothers' to the Britons. After conquering the lands, Arthur made them all Christians. Then he allowed them to take wives from the British nobility so they became the same 'race and blood' as the Britons. Further, Arthur then petitioned the Pope and the Roman curia to make Norway an augmentation of Britain, so that the Norse were in effect British, a nonsense fabrication.

Finally Edward the Confessor, who was their last king, granted them concessions through 'the common council of the whole realm' so that they had the right to live in, and remain in Britain as sworn brothers to the British. Clearly at this date, the Norse were desperate to remain in Britain and live peacefully there.

Dating the Scandinavian lands account

As Edward was their 'last king', this plea was written in the reign of William the Conqueror (1066-1087) at a time when the Norse were helping the English to resist the Norman occupation. Peter Rex (2004) notes that during this period the English 'were in constant negotiation with the Danes' who were assisting them. William's brutal 'harrowing of the north' in 1069-70, which laid the land waste, would have created fear and insecurity in the Norse living in Britain. The probable date of writing this text would have been after the harrowing, from about 1070 onwards, bounded by William's death in 1087.[13]

The political argument relies on Arthur's fame and his conquering these northern lands. The list of lands under his control is crucial to the political text and must have existed about 1070 or just after, before becoming part of the *Leges* which Liebermann dated to around 1210. Arthur's exploits in the north must have been widely known before 1070 for the political argument to have any credibility.

A lower bound for the dating could exist if Muir is correct in translating Wynelandiam as Vinland. This is not implausible but far from certain. If Vinland is correct, then the northern lands author may have taken it from Adam of Bremen's *History of the Archbishops of Hamburg-Bremen*, published about 1075 (Tschan, 1959). This lists nine of the lands, but omits Denmark, Gotland, Finland, Virland, Roe, Cherrelam and Lapland. The northern lands list is much wider than

Adam's as the author tried to maximize the number of lands under Arthur. Keneva Kunz and Gísli Sígurðsson (2008) state that Adam had obtained his knowledge of Vinland in 1068-9 from the Danish king so the northern lands author, if he did intend Vinland, could have derived it from knowledge at the court.[14]

The 1070-75 dating might shock many scholars who assume that Arthur's overseas exploits must derive from Geoffrey's pseudo-history of 1138, or were inspired by it. It seems that much of our picture of Arthur that many attribute to Geoffrey was already in existence and Geoffrey just extended it and elaborated it. The Scandinavian lands author did not borrow from Geoffrey's list of six lands. Given his desire to include as many lands as possible, he would have certainly used all six if he wrote after Geoffrey, but he omits Geoffrey's Orkney, implying that he wrote before Geoffrey. The borrowing was the other way round, with Geoffrey borrowing five of the first seven items, then adding his own contribution, Orkney, and finally padding out his account with his usual fictional details.[15]

The pre-existing list of Scandinavian lands can also account for Geoffrey's puzzling and unexplained claim that Britain had conquered 30 kingdoms (Thorpe, 1966). He probably used the northern lands list as the basis for the 30 kingdoms by including all the extra unnamed islands to get his figure up to 30.[16]

Dating the accounts of Arthur's northern ventures
A summary of dating estimates for the accounts of Arthur's northern activities is shown below.

Arthur in the North	Dating	Reference Point
Voyages in *Gestae*	Before 1120	Before *Branwen*
12 hostages from Norway	Before 1090	Before *Culhwch*
Northern lands	c. 1070-75	In reign of William I

Clearly, the list of Scandinavian lands should not be taken seriously as lands that Arthur conquered, as it has been designed or boosted to support a political argument to aid the Norse in Britain under William the Conqueror. However its existence implies that there must have been previous legends that Arthur had explored the north, as without these, the political argument would have had no credibility.

148

SPOILS OF ANNWFYN

Higham (2018) states that this poem is in Old Welsh but it is actually in Middle Welsh with some archaic remnants identified by John Koch, as noted in Chapter 1. It is the only poem to give an extended coverage of the voyage. Like other Welsh poems it is not a narrative but a series of incidents which are often not in chronological order. These may have been interesting or important to the bard.[17]

Some of the lines may have changed positions in a monorhyming stanza during the period of oral retellings. For example, it is possible that lines 5-6 were originally in the position of lines 3-4 which would have given a much smoother introduction to Gweir. An attempt is made to reconstruct the voyage in chronological order, from both the incidents in this poem and from *Battle of the Trees* to make the broad sequence of events clearer.[18]

Spoils of Annwfyn and *Battle of the Trees* are the only two works to depict the voyage as a horrific disaster. The mention of *Kaer Sidi* in the Book of Taliesin poem *I Petition God* occupies only seven lines and portrays Annwfyn as a paradise, agreeing with early Irish Otherworld tales. The *Spoils of Annwfyn* poem in the unemended Middle Welsh with an English translation is given below. This original Welsh is given so that scholars can check line by line to confirm that the translation is consistent with the Welsh. The changes made by Haycock (2007) in lines 2, 6, 11, 12, 21, 23 and 26 are accepted here but not her emending Cwy to Dwy. Modern punctuation is used for greater clarity. In the Peniarth 2 manuscript, the only punctuation elements available are the full stop and capitalization, the latter only being used for starting a new stanza, not for proper nouns.[19]

The first verse announces the great king, Arthur, who by making this overseas voyage has enlarged his dominion across the world's shores, but is then dominated by Gweir, who has been captured. This shows the importance of Gweir to the bard, by his placing him in the first stanza rather than in the chronological sequence. Despite Gweir's importance, there is no information at all about who he was and why he is singled out, given that very few of the party survived. It seems that the bard's audience already knew who Gweir was and that any introduction was unnecessary.[20]

149

STANZA 1

1 **Golychaf wledic, pendeuic, gwlat ri,**
I praise the sovereign, prince, king of the land,

2 **py ledas y pennaeth dros traeth mundi.**
who has enlarged his dominion across the world's shores.

3 **Bu kyweir karchar Gweir yg kaer sidi**
The prison of Gweir was prepared in the mound fortress

4 **trwy ebostol Pwyll a Phryderi.**
according to the account of Pwyll and Pryderi.

5 **Neb kyn noc ef nyt aeth idi,**
Nobody before him went into it,

6 **yr gadwyn trom las – kywirwas ae ketwi.**
into the heavy blue chain – it restrained a loyal youth.

7 **A rac preideu Annwfyn tost yt geni.**
And for the sake of the spoils of Annwfyn bitterly he sang.

8 **Ac yt Urawt parahawt yn bardwedi.**
And till Judgement (Day) our bardic prayer shall endure.

9 **Tri lloneit Prytwen, yd aetham ni idi.**
Three fullnesses of Prydwen, we went into it.

10 **Nam seith, ny dyrreith o gaer sidi.**
Except seven, none returned from the mound fortress.

STANZA 2

11 **Neut wyf glot geinmyn, cerd ochlywir**
I am honoured with praise, song was heard

12 **yg kaer pedryuan – pedyr ychwelyt.**
in the four-peaked camp – turning (to face) the four.

13 **Yg kynneir, or peir pan leferit.**
My poetry, from the cauldron it was spoken.

14 **O anadyl naw morwyn gochyneuit.**
By the breath of nine maidens it was kindled.

15 **Neu peir pen Annwfyn: pwy y vynut?**
The cauldron of Annwfyn's chieftain: what is its form?

16 **Gwrym am y oror a mererit.**
Dark around its rim and pearls.

17 **Ny beirw bwyt llwfyr: ny ry tyghit.**
It does not boil the food of a coward: it was not so destined.

18 **Cledyf lluch Lleawc idaw ry dyrchit,**
The flashing sword of Lleawc was thrust into it,

19 **ac yn llaw Leminawc yd edewit.**
and in the hand of Lleminawc it was left.

20 **A rac drws porth Vffern llugyrn lloscit.**
And before the door of the gate of Hell lamps burned.

21 **A phan aetham ni gan Arthur, trafferth lechrit.**
And when we went with Arthur, a renowned tribulation.

22 **Namyn seith, ny dyrreith o gaer vedwit.**
Except seven, none returned from the camp of the mead-feast.

150

STANZA 3

23   **Neut wyf glot geinmyn, kerd glywanawr**
I am honoured with praise, songs are heard

24   **yg kaer pedryfan, ynys pybyrdor.**
in the four-peaked camp, land of the strong door.

25   **Echwyd a muchyd kymyscetor.**
Flowing water and jet are mingled.

26   **Gwin gloyw eu gwirawt rac eu gorgord.**
Bright wine their liquor before their retinue.

27   **Tri lloneit Prytwen yd aetham ni ar vor.**
Three fullnesses of Prydwen we went on the sea.

28   **Namyn seith, ny dyrreith o gaer rigor.**
Except seven, none returned from the freezing-cold camp.

STANZA 4

29   **Ny obrynafi lawyr, llen llywyadur.**
I set no value on little men, (merely) concerned with scripture.

30   **Tra chaer wydyr ny welsynt wrhyt Arthur.**
Beyond the glass fortress they did not see Arthur's valour.

31   **Tri vgeint canhwr a seui ar y mur:**
Three-score hundred men were standing on the wall:

32   **oed anhawd ymadrawd ae gwylyadur.**
it was difficult to speak with their watchman.

33   **Tri lloneit Prytwen yd aeth gan Arthur.**
Three fullnesses of Prydwen went with Arthur.

34   **Namyn seith, ny dyrreith o gaer golud.**
Except seven, none returned from the camp of obstruction.

STANZA 5

35   **Ny obrynaf y lawyr, llaes eu kylchwy.**
I set no value on little men, loose their shield straps.

36   **Ny wdant wy py dyd peridyd pwy,**
They do not know who was created on which day,

37   **py awr y meindyd y ganet Cwy,**
what hour of the slender day the Cwy were born,

38   **pwy gwnaeth ar nyt aeth doleu Defwy.**
who made them who did not go to the Devwy meadows.

39   **Ny wdant wy yr ych brych, bras y penrwy,**
They do not know the brindled ox, thick his head ring,

40   **seith vgein kygwng yn y aerwy.**
seven-score joints in his collar.

41   **A phan aetham ni gan Arthur – auyrdwl gofwy.**
And when we went with Arthur – disastrous visit.

42   **Namyn seith, ny dyrreith o gaer vandwy.**
Except seven, none returned from the camp of God's Peak.

STANZA 6

43   **Ny obrynafy lawyr, llaes eu gohen.**
        I set no value on little men, weak their resolve.

44   **Ny wdant py dyd peridyd pen,**
        They do not know which day the chief was created,

45   **py awr y meindyd y ganet perchen,**
        what hour of the slender day the owner was born,

46   **py vil a gatwant, aryant y pen.**
        what animal they keep, with its silvery head.

47   **Pan aetham ni gan Arthur – afyrdwl gynhen.**
        When we went with Arthur – woeful conflict.

48   **Namyn seith, ny dyrreith o gaer ochren.**
        Except seven, none returned from the enclosed camp.

STANZA 7

49   **Myneich dychnut, val cunin cor,**
        Monks draw together, like a pack of dogs,

50   **o gyfranc udyd ae gwidanhor.**
        from a clash with lords who know.

51   **Ae vn hynt gwynt? Ae vn dwfyr mor?**
        Is the wind of one path? Is the sea of one water?

52   **Ae vn vfel tan twrwf diachor?**
        Is the fire, an invincible tumult, of one spark?

STANZA 8

53   **Myneych dychnut, val bleidawr,**
        Monks draw into a pack, like wolves,

54   **o gyfranc udyd ae gwidyanhawr.**
        from a clash with lords who know.

55   **Ny wdant pan yscar deweint a gwawr;**
        [The monks] don't know when darkness and dawn divide;

56   **neu wynt, pwy hynt, pwy y rynnawd;**
        nor wind, what path it follows, what its rushing is;

57   **py va diua, py tir a plawd.**
        what place it destroys, what land it strikes.

58   **Bet sant yn diuant – a bet a llawr.**
        The grave of the saint is lost/annihilated – both grave and champion.

59   **Golychaf y wledic, pendefic mawr,**
        I praise the sovereign, great prince,

60   **na bwyf trist: Crist am gwadawl.**
        that I not be grieving: Christ provides for me.

THE SAILING ROUTE

A Long Voyage on the Ocean

Geoffrey of Monmouth knew of two versions of Arthur's death, one at Camlan and another at a mysterious overseas location. He named this place Avalon, from *afal* (apple) according to Bromwich (2006). This linked it to legends of a distant western paradise that was abundant with fruit. In his *Life of Merlin* Geoffrey described it as the 'island of apples' and the 'Fortunate Isle'. In the first century, Plutarch had mentioned the far west 'abode of the blessed' in the Life of Sertorius, from his *Parallel Lives*, while the Irish tales *Connlae's Adventure* and *Voyage of Bran* had referred to a magic apple and apple tree branch, respectively, in their Otherworld paradises.[21]

Geoffrey preserved both versions of Arthur's death by making him only wounded at Camlan and then carried from the battlefield to his ship which sailed to Avalon. He portrayed the voyage as a long and difficult one by linking it to Brendan's voyage to a distant land in the west. Brendan had been told about the land by Barinthus, who had previously made the voyage, so Geoffrey made Barinthus the expert navigator of Arthur's ship. Several scholars have linked Brendan's voyage to America (Ashe, 1962; Chapman, 1973; Severin, 1978).

The *Spoils of Annwfyn* also makes clear it was a long journey on the ocean. It was also a voyage to an unexplored place. The following lines show these two features:

1   I praise the ruler, prince, king of the land
2   who has enlarged his dominion across the world's shores.

5   Nobody before him went into it.

27   Three fullnesses of Prydwen, we went on the sea.

33   Three fullnesses of Prydwen, we went with Arthur.

In lines 1-2, the ruler, prince and king is Arthur, who by making this long journey over the shores of the world, has enlarged his dominion. This surely rules out rowing a boat through the Glastonbury marshes to reach Avalon. It also rules out merely sailing from the mainland of

Wales to Bardsey Island off the Llŷn peninsula. Line 5, stating that nobody before Arthur went into it, also rules out Glastonbury and Bardsey Island. Prydwen is Arthur's ship as can be seen from its multiple mentions in *Culhwch and Olwen*. The meaning of 'three fullnesses' is unclear, but there are only two realistic options. One is where the capacity of Prydwen is being used as a measure. If all the ships were of the same capacity, then three ships went. This is a rather obscure way of saying this, but it is a poem and it could be for poetic effect. A second option is that the fullnesses refer only to the ship Prydwen and means that it was packed to three times its usual crew size. This would leave open the number and size of any other vessels in the expedition.[22]

Stepping Stones to Iceland

It was earlier shown that Arthur was strongly connected to the north Wales coast, at Dinarth and Chester and hence the most likely point of departure was from the mouth of the Dee at Chester. In line 38 of *Spoils of Annwfyn* the bard mentions the Devwy meadows, saying that the Annwfyn people do not visit there. This suggests that the Britons may have departed from the mouth of the Dee. It is assumed that Arthur followed a northern route, passing the Isle of Man and sailing through the Minch Channel. There may have been a stop at the safe port of Stornoway. From there, they would have sailed to the Faroes, and from there to Iceland.

Iceland

Barry Cunliffe (2001) makes a strong case for identifying Iceland with Thule, the furthest northern land in the writings of the Greeks and Romans. It seems that the Britons knew about it at a very early date. In 320 BC, Pytheas of Massilia (modern Marseille) made his way to Britain and was guided or taken to Thule by the Britons.[23]

Iceland also had visitors who lost four Roman coins (*antoniniani*), minted in the period AD 270-305, a mere 35 years. Three were found separately in the east, at or near Bragdavellir, and one in the south, inland at Hvítárholt. To lose coins at such relatively distant locations in Iceland suggests that those who lost them stayed on the island for a non-trivial duration. It is not unlikely that the Britons lost them as they knew of Iceland and used Roman coins.[24]

There appears to have been an early Christian presence on Iceland as shown by the carving of Christian crosses into rock. Two simple crosses were found in a cave on the mainland of southern Iceland. If found in Britain, these would usually be dated to the 500s or 600s. In addition, two *expanded terminal crosses* were found there, crosses where the end points expanded outwards in triangular-shaped tips. These crosses are linked to the St Columba (AD 521-597) monastery in Iona and would date to the 600s or 700s. In addition, three other expanded terminal crosses were found in the Westman Islands off the south coast. These were cut into the sheltered alcoves of an exposed cliff (Ahronson, 2000; 2003). A reasonable hypothesis is that monks from Dalriada or Ireland were searching for solitary places to worship God and had expanded their search to Iceland.[25]

Further evidence of early British knowledge of Iceland comes from Bede, in his *Thirty Questions on the Book of Kings* where he states that many knew that it was light on midsummer nights on Thule as visitors from there 'abundantly attest'. This is dated to about AD 715 (Meyvaert, 1999). Dicuil, an Irish scholar writing about 825, states that about 30 years ago clerics who lived on Thule told him about the brightness at night, such that they could pick lice off their shirts. This shows they were living there about 795 and probably earlier.[26]

Arthur's northern route

It is unlikely that Arthur would have launched a costly and dangerous voyage into the unknown unless he had received prior information. Perhaps a ship exploring Iceland had been blown west to a hitherto unknown land and this story had reached Arthur. He may have sent scouts to verify this report. As Iceland was almost certainly known to the scouts, they probably took the northern route. Four clues in *Spoils of Annwfyn* suggest that Arthur also took the northern route: (1) the crew saw a large iceberg on the way; (2) they stayed at a freezing-cold camp; (3) they entered the new land via a 'strong door' and (4) they stayed at a camp with four significant peaks.

The Iceberg

Line 30 below implies that the crew saw a 'glass fortress'. Beyond this iceberg sighting (later on the mainland) Arthur's valour in battle was shown, but the monks were ignorant of it.

30   Beyond the glass fortress they [the monks] did not see Arthur's
        valour.

The portrayal of an iceberg as a 'glass' or 'crystal' object in the sea
also occurs in the *Historia Brittonum* and *Navigatio* of St Brendan.
In the *Historia*, Chapter 13, the sailors see a 'glass tower in the middle
of the sea', a clear indication that it was an iceberg. In the *Navigatio*
(Chapter 23) Brendan's crew glimpse a 'crystal pillar' in the sea and
sail up to it, and around it, to try to estimate its size.[27]

   The word 'fortress' implies that the iceberg was large and worthy
of note. This sighting possibly occurred in the iceberg zone off the
Grand Banks of Newfoundland, where the region between 43–48°N
is called 'iceberg alley'. Although this is a likely location, others are
possible. Icebergs travel down Greenland's east coast and currents
then pull them north up the west coast. They are joined by glaciers
breaking off in western Greenland. In a huge loop they then come
down the east coasts of Baffin Island, Labrador and Newfoundland.
South of iceberg alley they diminish by splitting and melting, but
some large icebergs get through, as in the Titanic disaster. So there is
a wide region for an iceberg sighting including Baffin Bay, the Davis
Strait, the Labrador Sea, and the Grand Banks. All of these imply a
northern route, probably via Iceland.[28]

The freezing-cold camp
In lines 26-28, the bard mentions a stop at a freezing-cold camp, an
interpretation suggested by both Patrick Sims-Williams (1982) and
John Koch, in Koch and Carey (2003).[29]

26   Bright wine their liquor before their retinue.
27   Three fullnesses of Prydwen we went on the sea.
28   Except seven, none returned from the freezing-cold camp.

This viewpoint is also supported by the surprising line 26, which
refers to wine being served to Arthur's retinue. The Welsh word for
'bright' in describing the wine is *gloyw*. The Germanic equivalent,
glüh (glow) appears in *glühwein*, a wine that is served heated, which
would have been a very appropriate drink at the freezing-cold camp.
Why did the bard include such a mundane event in what was an epic

voyage? The answer is that the camp was real, not fictional, and the bard was simply recalling his experiences there. This small sign of authenticity suggests that the poem is describing a real voyage.

The 'Strong Door'

In lines 23-24, the bard is being praised for his poetry at the 'four-peaked' camp:

23   I am honoured with praise, songs are heard
24   in the four-peaked camp, land of the strong door.

In line 24, *ynys* is best translated as 'land', as 'isle' would have been used for any unknown land reached by sea and the Britons would have had little concept of its extent. This line links the four-peaked camp with the 'strong door', a metaphor for the entry point into Annwfyn. The 'strong' implies that gaining access to the new land via this door was difficult. It is argued here that this entry point was the St Lawrence river which flows into the Gulf of St Lawrence.

The northern route implied earlier makes it likely that the ships entered the Gulf, either by the Strait of Belle Isle, or the Cabot Strait. It is assumed that after an extensive period of exploring the Gulf they found the St Lawrence River, which would have provided several benefits. It would take the sailors well into the interior of the land, while keeping them safe from an ambush. It would also allow the transport of heavy supplies and allow the ships to easily retrace their route. It is possible that the freezing cold camp was at one of the stops along the St Lawrence.

The 'strong' epithet probably refers to the powerful downstream currents that would make upstream sailing difficult. In 1534 Jacques Cartier entered the Gulf via the Strait of Belle Isle and thoroughly explored it. He ran out of time to enter the St Lawrence river as winter was approaching but had explored north of Anticosti island and in his 1535 return began his journey up the river. Samuel Morison (1971) details the hard struggles of Cartier against the strong currents and dangerous obstacles, waiting for the flood tide and favourable winds in order to make progress. Arthur's crew would have experienced similar difficulties in making their way up the river, prompting the bard to call it the 'strong door'.[30]

The Four-peaked Camp

The four-peaked camp appears with the 'strong door' (the river) in line 24 and Montreal, further upriver is an excellent fit. It has four similar huge hills – Royal, St-Bruno, St-Hilaire and Rougemont, the remains of intrusive igneous rock that had resisted weathering over the millennia (Feininger and Goodacre, 1995). Mont Royal is about a mile west of the river and is the obvious place to climb to see the surrounds as Jacques Cartier did in 1535. From its summit, Cartier saw the Lachine rapids which dismayed him. These were a barrier to large ships progressing further south.[31]

From the top of Royal, the other three peaks stand out. They are part of a chain called the Monteregian Hills. There are other members further out, but the closest of these, Mont Yamaska, is hidden from view behind Mont Rougemont when viewed from Mont Royal. The land there is flat and without today's modern buildings these four peaks would have dominated the area. The 'four-peaked camp' would be a natural name to apply to the site.

Summary of hypothesized Route

Arthur probably sailed from the port at Caer Legion in north Wales and past the western islands of Scotland to the Faroes, and then on to Iceland. The currents west of Iceland would pull southwest, and then pull north up the west coast of Greenland. There were many opportunities to see icebergs which are shown below as triangles.

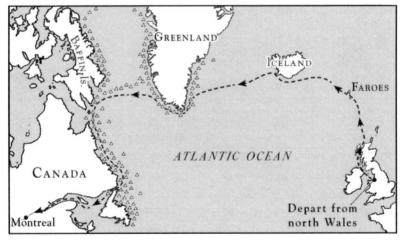

Figure 7.1. The Route: adapted from a map by Sarah Dunning Park.

EXPLORING THE INTERIOR

When the Britons were at the four-peaked camp, spirits were high and the bard was being praised for his poetry:

11   I am honoured with praise, song was heard

12   in the four-peaked camp – turning to face the four.

Like Jacques Cartier, the Britons probably climbed Mont Royal to see the way ahead and the bard appears to have done this. While making his way up the steep slope to Royal's summit it seems that the bard at some point turned 180° and was impressed with the view of the other three peaks, St-Bruno, St-Hilaire and Rougemont across the St Lawrence river. He appears to be describing this in line 12.[32]

The next part of the route is not clear. It is likely that they followed the St Lawrence, perhaps in smaller rowing boats, and carrying these when the river conditions were too difficult. They would have come to the Great Lakes and may have spent some time exploring them. There is some evidence that they may have explored Lake Michigan and then passed through Illinois, as will be discussed later.

The Hopewell

At some stage the Britons saw the extraordinary earthworks built by the Hopewell Native Americans. They had a rich culture that displayed great artistic and geometric skill. Their complex earthworks had walls built in geometrical shapes, including the circle, square, rectangle, octagon, rhombus and ellipse. They were inventive in the way these shapes were connected. A few examples follow: a circle and rectangle that overlapped to form a chord, a circle whose circumference was just touched by the vertex of a square, and a square touching a circle in a tangent. They also built parallel walls to connect the shapes.

William Romain (1991) argues that these mound builders had a practical astronomical knowledge, a method of counting, accurate ways of measuring angles and distance and a basic measurement unit which was about 32 cm. They appear to have built a road with parallel earthen walls from Newark, Ohio all the way to Chillicothe, called the Great Hopewell Road, which has been studied by Lepper (1995) and Schwarz (2016). They also seem to have built mounds in the shape of a comet at the Milford, Ohio site (Tankersley et al., 2022). Valuable images of these mound structures were preserved by Squier and Davis (1848). Fortunately, their structure is now studied by less intrusive methods including Lidar imagery (Burks and Cook, 2011).[33]

Inside these earthwork walls were the burial mounds, some with a dazzling array of treasures placed with the dead, including masses of freshwater pearls, sheets of mica, bear's teeth with inset pearls, shell necklaces, copper breastplates and earspools, smoking pipes carved in the shapes of various creatures, and ornaments of copper and silver. We don't know what they called themselves. Their current name came from earthworks in Ross County, Ohio, called the Hopewell Mounds by Warren Moorehead, as the landowner was Mordecai Hopewell. Moorehead had excavated it in 1891-2. The stunning artifacts found there were thought to be representative of artifacts in other sites and thus the Hopewell name was applied more generally.[34]

Late Woodland Cultures

Arthur possibly sailed to Annwfyn around 535-6 after the Hopewell period had ended. Mound building had then ceased and society was beginning to evolve into the Late Woodland cultures. The gathering of exotic items had ended and there was a shift towards larger villages which were dispersed over a wider area rather than the former pattern of along the major rivers. The bow and arrow was probably beginning to supplement the dart and atlatl which made hunting more efficient and conflict was increasing between groups.[35]

The Buffalo

From Montreal, their route south is unknown but the Great Lakes would have been an attractive place to explore. At some stage they saw the buffalo and must have marvelled at this animal. Lines 39-40 refer to an unusual 'ox' which the bard used to taunt the monks who he was sure had never seen it, as they were ignorant of Annwfyn.

39   They [the monks] do not know the brindled ox, thick his head ring,
40   seven-score joints in his collar.

Here Arthur's bard is speaking poetically with his expressions 'thick his head ring' and 'seven-score joints in his collar'. These aren't actual constraints on the animal but his poetic way of saying that it had a huge head and a massive neck. The brindled part would have referred to the yellow-ochre 'cape' on its shoulders and back (see Reynolds, Gates and Glaholt, 2003). This animal is the American *Bison bison*, more commonly known as the plains buffalo. The Britons had not seen an 'ox' like this before as it was unlike anything in Britain. In early medieval Britain the ox was a common sight as a working animal so it is very unlikely that the bard would have placed a fictional ox in the poem to expose the monks' ignorance. Its inclusion in the poem meant that it became valuable and was seen as knowledge to be preserved. It later became part of the *Welsh Triads* in Triad 45 but by that time no one knew what it was.[36]

Buffalo along the Illinois river, circa AD 500

The distribution of the buffalo across America has varied greatly over the years. By the 1600s they were widely dispersed, including the Ohio region that had the most complex Hopewell earthworks. In 1779-80, Ohio missionary David Zeisberger noted buffalo sightings there:

> ... these animals appeared in great numbers along the Muskingum [river] ... Along the banks of the Scioto and further south, both Indians and whites say that they may be seen in herds numbering hundreds.

Their eastern border was the Allegheny Mountains that run southwest from Pennsylvania through West Virginia, but one cannot assume that this range held in Arthur's time. Plausible arguments have been given that the Hopewell moundbuilders were unfamiliar with the buffalo, especially in Ohio, as it did not appear in their animal effigy pipes and its bones were absent from their mounds and villages. It was thought that in the 500s, the buffalo remained west of the Mississippi.[37]

However, although the Ohio Hopewell never saw the buffalo, the Havana Hopewell in Illinois did. Bruce McMillan (2006) has shown that buffalo had crossed the Mississippi and were present along the Illinois river in the Middle Woodland period. This was probably where Arthur's men saw the buffalo. It suggests that they had explored Lake Michigan and perhaps the other lakes. A buffalo sighting there is also in line with the finding of a worn British Minim coin in Champaign, Illinois in 1885 that had been buried under 4 feet of undisturbed clay. The coin dates approximately to the time of Arthur. Its dating and the details of the find are discussed in Chapter 15.[38]

North American River Otter

Stanza 6 begins similarly to Stanza 5, with the bard continuing to ridicule the monks' ignorance of things and events in Annwfyn. In line 45 the monks do not know what hour the 'owner' was born (*perchen* in Welsh). What does the bard intend by 'owner'? This is clarified in the next line when it is revealed that the people there had tamed an animal with a silvery head – in that sense they owned it.

45   what hour of the slender day the owner was born,

46   what animal they keep, with its silvery head.

47   When we went with Arthur – woeful conflict.

This animal is almost certainly the North American river otter (*Lontra canadensis*), which was plentiful in the rivers of the Hopewell. They made remarkable life-like carvings of the otter in their animal effigy pipes. Photographs of these superb pipes from the Tremper Mound are shown in Lepper (2005), one of which is an otter with a fish in its mouth. Three other otter pipes were also found in the Tremper Mound in southern Ohio, near the Scioto river. Another otter pipe was found at Mound City, a few miles north of Chillicothe, where it is on display in the Visitor Center.[39]

A further otter pipe originally from Mound City is on display in the British Museum in London. This one has slight damage which suggests that the otter originally had a fish in its mouth. Squier and Davis (1848) give drawings of two more Hopewell otter pipes, one badly damaged, but the fish in the mouth can be clearly seen. Of the eight pipes, five show a fish in the mouth.[40]

It is well known that the intelligent otter can be tamed by humans. Eugene Gudger (1927) has surveyed the cultures across the world that have trained the otter to fish. He notes that such otter training in China goes back to a remote past, probably before AD 600. From its mention in this stanza it appears that the Native Americans had tamed the otter to help them catch fish, as the Chinese did.[41]

The North American river otter's muzzle and throat are silvery in appearance, especially if the fur is wet. It also likes to carry its head above water when swimming so that the ears, eyes and nostrils are exposed (Larivière and Walton, 1998). The bard's focus on the otter's head suggests that he was watching it swimming.

Figure 7.2. The 'Brindled Ox'. (Photo: Jack Dykinga).

Figure 7.3. Hopewell carving of river otter with fish.
(Photo: courtesy of Ohio Historical Society).

A Pot decorated with Pearls

In Stanza 2 the bard refers to his poetry as being so inspired that it was produced as though by magic from a cauldron. This imagery then leads him to think of another cauldron, the cauldron of the chief of Annwfyn, which had a dark rim and was decorated with pearls.

15   The cauldron of Annwfyn's Chieftain: what is its form?

16   Dark around its rim and pearls.

17   It does not boil the food of a coward: it was not so destined.

18   The flashing sword of Lleawc was thrust into it,

19   and in the hand of Lleminawc it was left.

The pearl decoration suggests the Britons were in the Ohio Hopewell central region. They would have been freshwater pearls used by the Hopewell and their successors. Olaf Prufer (1964) remarks that 'they were literally heaped into some of the mounds'. The Hopewell site, west of Chillicothe, yielded around 100,000 pearls and the Turner site in Hamilton County yielded around 48,000 pearls. Brad Lepper (2005) notes that about 18,000 freshwater pearls were found at the Seip-Pricer mound, 17 miles west of Chillicothe. The cauldron would have been a ceremonial pot, typical of the fine pottery of the Hopewell, with the pearls giving a beautiful contrast with the dark rim on the outside of the pot. The Hopewell liked using pearls as highlights. They drilled small holes into bears' teeth and glued pearls into the holes for decoration. They also drilled holes into their animal effigy pipes and glued pearls into the holes to represent the eyes.[42]

This stanza implies conflict. The Britons had seized a prized pot and one of Arthur's men, Lleawc, had thrust his sword into it. The pot was then given to Lleminawc to protect. However, there is another possible translation, as rather than a person's name, *lleawc* could be the adjective 'death-dealing', qualifying the sword. So line 18 could be 'The flashing death-dealing sword was thrust into it'. It is difficult to determine which of the two meanings was intended.[43]

Earthen Mounds

The complex Hopewell mounds were most densely concentrated along the rivers of southern Ohio (e.g. Grooms, 1995). They were reached well into the journey, but they appear in the very first stanza as they are linked to a youth named Gweir. He had been captured by the Annwfyn people and the bard was deeply concerned for his safety. Most of this stanza is about Gweir, which shows what the bard thought was important in the poem. A sequenced account was not important, but Gweir was, and his plight dominates the first stanza.[44]

1	I praise the sovereign, prince, king of the land,
2	who has enlarged his dominion across the world's shores.
3	The prison of Gweir was prepared in the mound fortress
4	according to the account of Pwyll and Pryderi.
5	Nobody before him went into it,
6	into the heavy blue chain – it restrained a loyal youth.
7	And for the sake of the spoils of Annwfyn bitterly he sang
8	And till Judgement Day our bardic prayer shall endure.
9	Three fullnesses of Prydwen, we went into it.
10	Except seven, none returned from the mound fortress.

When the bard composed this poem he had returned to Britain, being part of a remnant that had escaped from Annwfyn. Lines 5-6, stating that 'Nobody before him went into it, into the heavy blue chain', refer to Arthur. He led the expedition across the ocean into the unexplored land. The 'heavy blue chain' that they went into is the vast expanse of ocean as can be seen from line 9, where in Arthur's ship, Prydwen, they 'went into it'. Gweir, a loyal youth, remained behind in Annwfyn, effectively imprisoned by this 'heavy blue chain' as a rescue attempt was virtually impossible.

The camp here is the 'mound fortress' (*kaer sidi*). While *kaer* is the Welsh word for fort or camp, *sidi* is a borrowing from Old Irish *síde*, the genitive singular or plural, or nominative plural, of *síd*. It means an 'abode of the gods', later 'fairies', thus a 'fairy-mound' as stated by Sims-Williams (1982). Jackson (1959b) and Bollard (1984) translate it 'faery city' and 'fairy fortress'. Haycock (1983-4; 2007) leaves it as *Caer Siddi* while Koch and Carey (2003) relate it to 'pagan burial mound'. Higley (1996) translates it 'Mound Fortress' and thinks that it would have made a good title for the poem.[45]

In line 4, Gweir's capture was reported by Pwyll and Pryderi, who are father and son in the Mabinogi story, *Pwyll Prince of Dyfed*. The bard probably never saw where Gweir was held captive but imagines him singing bitterly in his prison. As Gweir is portrayed as singing, it is possible that he was a potential bard known to Arthur's bard. He vows to pray for Gweir until Judgement Day which seems an excessive emotional response if Gweir was only a fictional character.

The prominence given to Gweir also implies he was real. In a fiction it would be implausible to have him monopolize an entire verse but not say who he was, but nothing is said of his importance. It implies that at the time the poem was composed he was well known to the bard's associates and the audience listening to the poem.

Thirdly, if it were a fiction with few survivors, why focus on Gweir, just one of many fictional men who died? The bard's grief is a natural reaction to losing a friend and suggests that Gweir was real.

Use of the Old Irish word, *síde*

The borrowing of an esoteric Old Irish word in a poem in Middle Welsh raises the issue of why it was included. Some leading scholars believe that *Spoils of Annwfyn* was composed late, say AD 1000-1200. If this were the case then a Welsh bard was composing a fictional poem in Middle Welsh about Arthur interacting with fairies in a mythical Otherworld. Why would he need an Old Irish word at all, one that was centuries old? The answer is that he wouldn't need it – there were Middle Welsh words to perfectly describe the fairies' surrounds. The second issue is how likely is it that he knew any Old Irish words from the period AD 500-900 that fitted his purpose? It would be very unlikely. Even if the bard did somehow know the Old Irish *síde*, its use would have been generally unintelligible to his audience.

The position argued in this book is that the voyage was real and took place around the mid 530s and perhaps the bard composed the poem not too far from AD 540. Why would Arthur's bard use an Old Irish word? In Annwfyn he saw the impressive Hopewell mounds that were still used by the current inhabitants. He had never met a people like this before in his homeland, north Wales. The latter had once been dominated by the Irish before they were conquered by Einion Yrth, but an Irish influence remained. Lloyd (1911) points out that the Irish language was still used there in the sixth century. To the bard, Old Irish was a contemporary language spoken by people he knew and he may have heard stories of Irish fairies living in great fairy mounds and thought that *síde* best described what he saw in Annwfyn.[46]

Figure 7.4. Entrance to Mound City enclosure, three miles north of Chillicothe, showing the enclosure wall and burial mounds within. (Photo: R. MacCann).

Meeting the Annwfyn People

There is an interesting *Spoils of Annwfyn* reference to the Britons meeting a group of Native Americans as shown below:

30   Beyond the glass fortress they did not see Arthur's valour.

31   Three-score hundred men were standing on the wall.

32   It was difficult to speak to their watchman.

This vivid scene would suit a meeting with the Native Americans. The wall on which they were standing would have been an earthen wall that enclosed their mounds and the precious items buried with their ancestors. They were making sure that these graves and the venerated items were protected. The 6,000 figure is not a literal one. The bard is using a particular number to convey an impressively large number. Similarly the mournful refrain that only seven people returned from the camps just means a small number. This imagery conveys a element of intimidation – a large number of warriors on the wall above the Britons, glaring down at them. The walls surrounding the mounds were then much higher than the walls remaining today.

A longstanding academic view is that the Britons were interacting with fairies, and that the mounds in this fictional Otherworld were fairy mounds, as suggested by the work cited earlier of Sims-Williams, Jackson and Bollard. This view would give the amusing scene of a great number of fairies massing on the wall to intimidate the Britons. As fairies are hardly known for their physical strength, it presents a comical picture.

Line 32 shows that the Britons could not understand the language of the Annwfyn people, an outcome to be expected when peoples from different continents meet for the first time. In contrast, the fairies in the Otherworld stories readily converse with humans. For example in *Connlae's Adventure*, when the fairy woman tells Connlae that she lives in a great fairy mound and wants him to leave his kingdom to live with her, she is easily understood by all the court.[47]

The Bard's pondering their Origin

In the lines below, after first ridiculing the monks for their cowardice, the bard speculates on the origin of the Annwfyn people, about whom the monks were utterly ignorant.

168

35   I set no value on little men, loose their shield straps.
36   They [the monks] do not know who was created on which day,
37   what hour of the slender day the Cwy were born,
38   who made them who did not go to the Devwy meadows.

The Christian bard thought that the Britons were created by God on the Sixth Day of Creation. In line 36 he ponders whether the Annwfyn people, being so different to the Britons, were also created on this day. Even if they were created on the Sixth Day, in line 37 he wonders whether they were created at a different hour. In line 38, he considers the possibility that God didn't create them and wonders who did create them if it wasn't God. The Britons called them *Cwy*, rhyming with 'we', from the rhyme scheme of the stanza. The monks were ignorant of this people, and these issues, as they knew nothing of Annwfyn as the bard makes clear in stanzas 4 to 6. This musing about origins also occurs in *Battle of the Trees*, which he composed as an old man.

The bard's philosophical reflection on the origin of the Cwy is at odds with the poem being a work of fiction. If the Cwy were fictional products of the bard's own imagination, then it would be unrealistic for him to be speculating in the poem about the non-existent origin of his own fictional creations. The fact that the bard spends three lines on this topic strongly implies that they were real people.

Line 38 states that the Cwy do not visit the Devwy meadows in Britain. This suggests that they were a real people who were subject to practical constraints such as a lack of knowledge, time, resources or motivation which could prevent them from visiting a distant place.

The alternative 'fairies' theory is also implausible here as fairies seem to have no limitations on where they can visit. In the stories of their meetings with humans they can appear and disappear at will and can visit any location.

CONFLICT IN SPOILS OF ANNWFYN

It appears that the Britons' relationship with the Native Americans deteriorated after they moved into a former Hopewell region. At the four-peaked camp the Britons' spirits were high, with the singing and praising of the bard. However in the Hopewell region they had seized a ceremonial cauldron decorated with pearls and Gweir had been abducted. A number of lines that mention Arthur suggest that fighting developed and the voyage became a Hell; e.g. 'And when we went with Arthur, a renowned tribulation'; 'Beyond the glass fortress they did not see Arthur's valour'; 'And when we went with Arthur – disastrous visit' and 'When we went with Arthur – woeful conflict'.

The pearl-decorated cauldron that the Britons had seized 'does not boil the food of a coward' which is a poetic way of saying that the owners of the cauldron were not cowards. The bard viewed the Cwy as people like himself with human limitations who bravely faced danger and their willingness to fight courageously against the Britons gave rise to the bard's comment. Like the 'brindled ox' discussed earlier, the cauldron in *Spoils of Annwfyn* also became famous. It appears in *Culhwch and Olwen* in a scene where Llenlleawg, the second half of whose name means 'death-dealing', grabs Arthur's sword and kills the Irish giant Diwrnach and all his men. Then Arthur took the cauldron, full of Irish treasure, to his ship. This scene has clearly been adapted from lines 15-19 in *Spoils of Annwfyn*. Diwrnach's cauldron was later given exalted status in *The Thirteen Treasures of the Island of Britain* but its original meaning had been lost. There it is interpreted literally as an instrument for detecting cowardice. There are two meanings of 'it does not boil the food of a coward' as shown below.[48]

1. It does not boil the food of a coward (*because they are not cowards*).
2. It does not boil the food of a coward (*if they are cowards*).

The first one is the intent of the bard, a poetic way of saying that their opponents were brave men. The second way interprets the line in a literalistic way. Bromwich (2006) reproduces the seventh treasure of the thirteen treasures as follows.[49]

> The Cauldron of Dyrnwch the Giant: if meat for a coward were put in it to boil, it would never boil; but if meat for a brave man were put in it, it would boil quickly.

CONFLICT IN BATTLE OF THE TREES

In *Battle of the Trees* there is a short section on the Annwfyn disaster that confirms the interpretation of bitter conflict given above. This poem gives a fascinating insight into the mind of one who had retained many beliefs of the druids. The bard is now an old man and complains that no one visits him anymore except one friend, Goronwy. It was probably composed about 20-30 years after *Spoils of Annwfyn*. The Annwfyn section begins with the enemy gathering ready for battle by means of the streams, which would exactly fit the Native Americans but would hardly fit the fairy interpretation.

189 In the streams of Annwfyn
190 they come to gather for battle.
191 Four-score hundred
192 I pierced because of their battle lust.
193 They are not older, nor younger
194 than me in their passions (for battle).
195 Everyone born there had the passion of a hundred men
196 and (the passion of) nine hundred did I have.

The bard describes the heated fighting. He pierced four-score hundred men with sword or spear, despite the enemy's aggression, this number being a typical bardic boast. Then he reflects on their passion for battle in an interesting way, relating it to age. He thought of the young braves as having more passion than the older warriors, who had probably experienced wounds and were less inclined to be reckless. By saying that they were 'not older, nor younger than me' in their passion he suggests that they were people like himself, not fictional opponents who were far superior or invincible. He then describes the intensity of the fighting, saying that everyone born there had 'the passion of a hundred', another reference to their courage. Compare this with the *Spoils of Annwfyn* line above that their cauldron 'did not boil the food of a coward'. He then indulges in bardic boasting by saying that he had the passion of nine hundred.

SUMMARY

It is argued that viewing the *Spoils of Annwfyn* journey as a historical visit is the most credible and only viable interpretation. Scholars can see for themselves whether the translations aptly convey the meanings of the Welsh lines and the extent to which the whole gives a coherent account. Those familiar with other translations of the poem will see that these largely do not make sense but as the usual mindset is that the poem is expressing mythology, this incoherence is ignored.

The main points implied from the poems are summarized below:

1. The voyage was a long one 'across the shores of the world', which excludes a voyage to Ireland, or parts of Wales, or rowing a boat through the Glastonbury marshes.

2. The land they went to was unknown to the Britons ('nobody before him went into it').

3. They sailed past a large iceberg the bard calls a 'glass fortress'. This early metaphor prompted later authors to give similar names to icebergs – the 'glass tower in the middle of the sea' (*Historia Brittonum*) and 'crystal pillar' in the sea (*Navigatio* of St Brendan).

4. Somewhere in the northern regions they endured a very cold camp where they drank 'bright (*gloyw*) wine', probably the equivalent of *glühwein* where the wine is served heated.

5. The bard called the entrance to the new country the 'strong door', the St Lawrence river, where to explore the interior of the land they had to sail upstream against strong downstream currents.

6. They stopped at a camp with four peaks, which fits Montreal on the St Lawrence, the peaks being Royal, St Bruno, St Hilaire and Rougemont. There, they were in good spirits. They appear to have continued south and may have explored the Great Lakes.

7. The bard was certain the monks did not know the 'ox' with a huge head and neck, as it was located only in Annwfyn. This 'brindled ox' was the buffalo where the yellow-ochre cape on the shoulders and back contrasted with the other pelage. They probably saw it along the Illinois river after perhaps exploring Lake Michigan.

8. He also saw an animal with a 'silvery head' that was tamed by the people in Annwfyn: the North American river otter. The Hopewell had made life-like carvings of it for their animal effigy pipes.

9. The Britons eventually came to a region of impressive earthworks. The Hopewell had built such mounds, enclosed by earthen walls in geometrical shapes. They were most concentrated along the rivers of southern Ohio suggesting that the Britons had gone south into a region that had been the centre of the Ohio Hopewell culture.

10. The bard speculates on their origin. He believed the Britons were created by God on the Sixth Day and wonders whether the Annwfyn people were created on this day, or another day. Or if it were the Sixth Day, perhaps they were created at a different hour. He then ponders on whether it was God who created them. The bard would not be speculating like this if they were his own fictions. Although they were quite unlike the Britons, they were real people.

11. The Britons captured a ceremonial pot with a dark rim decorated with contrasting pearls. The Ohio Hopewell used freshwater pearls as highlights in their creations and huge amounts of pearls were heaped into their burial mounds. The bard states that the pot 'did not boil the food of a coward'.

12. The Britons met the inhabitants who were standing above them on a wall, probably one enclosing their mounds, to ensure that their precious items and burials were not desecrated. The two peoples with different languages could not communicate. In this stanza the bard says that the monks 'did not see the valour of Arthur'.

13. Conflict began and a youth called Gweir, perhaps a fledgling bard, was captured and held prisoner in the 'mound fortress.' He was left behind in Annwfyn and Arthur's bard vowed to pray for him until Judgement Day.

14. The fighting escalated and the inhabitants gathered together for battle by means of the streams and rivers, implying that the Britons faced a larger, formidable force. The bard remarks on their passion for battle and boasts about his own valour but describes it as a 'woeful conflict'. The expedition became a disaster for the Britons with only a few able to return to Britain.

Arthur's Death

In the next chapter, the three Welsh poems and other material will be analyzed to isolate the references to Arthur's death and build up a complete picture of how he was probably killed. It is argued that the Camlan reference in the *Welsh Annals* was referring to a river in America where he died in a conflict at a 'crooked riverbank'.

8
THE KILLING OF ARTHUR

THE MYSTERY OF ARTHUR'S GRAVE

The Black Book of Carmarthen contains 73 stanzas known as *Stanzas of the Graves*. While the Black Book manuscript is thirteenth century, the stanzas show signs of corruptions and confusions suggesting a long period of oral and written transmission. Thomas Jones (1967), a meticulous scholar, dates them to the 800s or 900s, but some may be earlier, providing information on sixth-century figures. For example, the wife of Maglocunus is given as Sanant, the woman whom Gildas says colluded with him in the killing of his first wife and nephew, but Gildas doesn't give her name. The stanzas record the traditional burial places of early prominent Britons.

Arthur appears in Stanza 44 but he is unique in that his grave site is unknown, as shown in Jones' translation below.[1]

> There is a grave for March, a grave for Gwythur,
> a grave for Gwgawn red-sword;
> The world's wonder, a grave for Arthur.

The unusual Welsh word that Jones translates as 'wonder' is *anoeth* whose exact meaning is not known but it does occur in *Culhwch and Olwen* where its use suggests 'a thing almost impossible to obtain'. Jones' 'wonder' is a suitable shorthand for a mystery that is almost impossible to resolve.

By the time this stanza was composed knowledge of Arthur's death in Annwfyn was lost. No one then knew what the mysterious Annwfyn was and thoughts on Arthur's grave were naturally confined to Britain. Yet a belief in Arthur dying in a distant overseas land appears to have survived in some form, as noted in the Gerald of Wales reference to legends known to the public concerning the end of Arthur's life in a distant unknown place. In his *Life of Merlin* Geoffrey of Monmouth reconciled these legends with Arthur's death at Camlan, supposedly in Britain, using a clumsy hybrid. It did not occur to him that Camlan may not have been in Britain.

ARTHUR'S DEATH IN SPOILS OF ANNWFYN

Arthur's death is mentioned in all three of the poems at the heart of this book, *Spoils of Annwfyn*, *Chair of the Sovereign* (twice) and *Battle of the Trees*. The earliest mention of his death appears in *Spoils of Annwfyn* which describes incidents in Annwfyn and then later in Britain after the bard had returned around 540. Throughout this poem the bard skilfully builds up an atmosphere of dread by the mournful refrain in the first six stanzas, 'Except seven, none returned from ...' where various camps in Annwfyn are named, and by the following expressions of foreboding and despondency:

17	It does not boil the food of a coward: it was not so destined.
20	And before the door of the gate of Hell lamps burned.
21	And when we went with Arthur, a renowned tribulation.
30	Beyond the glass fortress they did not see Arthur's valour.
41	And when we went with Arthur – disastrous visit.
47	When we went with Arthur – woeful conflict.

In Stanzas 7 and 8 the bard's account slowly builds to a climax where the audience senses that something crucial will happen. One begins to wonder whether Arthur himself survives.

Stanza 7

49	Monks draw together, like a pack of dogs,
50	from a clash with lords who know.
51	Is the wind of one path? Is the sea of one water?
52	Is the fire, an invincible tumult, of one spark?

Stanza 8

53	Monks draw into a pack, like wolves,
54	from a clash with lords who know.
55	They [the monks] don't know when darkness and dawn divide;
56	nor wind, what path it follows, what its rushing is;
57	what place it destroys, what land it strikes.
58	The grave of the saint is lost/annihilated – both grave and champion.
59	I praise the sovereign, great prince,
60	that I not be grieving: Christ provides for me.

In Stanza 7, the scene shifts back to Britain where the few survivors of Annwfyn have returned. The bard describes the monks as drawing together like a pack of fearful dogs. They are clashing with the lords who know something important, which the monks don't know. The bard's audience listens in anticipation but are not told the secret. Instead, the bard starts his philosophical riddles about the wind, the sea and fire that have nothing to do with Annwfyn. He is delaying the climax and extending the dramatic tension.

In Stanza 8, the bard starts again, with a slight variation. Now the monks are packing together like wolves, again from a clash with lords who know. Surely the bard will now reveal the secret, but again the audience is held in suspense. The bard continues to spin philosophical riddles, first about when the darkness actually becomes dawn, and then about the mysteries of the wind.

Finally the climax comes in line 58 where he reveals the secret: that the grave of the saint is lost or annihilated, both grave and champion. The audience doesn't need to be told who this is. They know. He is the 'sovereign, great prince' in the next line. The bard's exact meaning is not clear. The key Welsh word is *diuant* which means 'total loss', 'annihilation', or 'dissolution'. Perhaps he meant that as the grave's location was in Annwfyn it was now inaccessible or perhaps it was lost in their desperation to escape. In either case the body would appear to have been left in Annwfyn and not taken back to Britain, as implied by the mystery of its location in *Stanzas of the Graves*.

In line 58 the bard refers to Arthur as a saint, a devout Christian, which agrees with the early church usage for this term – for example, Romans 1:7; 1 Corinthians 1:2; 2 Corinthians 1:2. This usage is also consistent with the way Gildas applies the term in the *De Excidio*. In chapters 28.1, 32.2, 35.4, 65.2 and 66.4 of this work Gildas uses 'saint' simply to refer to devout Christians, not necessarily martyrs. The bard refers to Arthur's reverence of scripture in praising him in line 8 of *Chair of the Sovereign*.

Later works such as the *Historia Brittonum* and *Welsh Annals* also portray Arthur as a Christian. The bard's purpose in composing *Spoils of Annwfyn* was to praise Arthur, to help ameliorate his own grief, as he states in the last two lines. He too was a Christian and he turns to Christ for comfort.

ARTHUR'S DEATH IN CHAIR OF SOVEREIGN

The bard composed this poem when back in Britain after his grief had
subsided a little. After this eulogy to Arthur he mentions a ceremony
where Arthur was blessed and presumably a prayer was said for his
soul. These lines are important as the bard lists Arthur's deeds.

1 **Areith awdyl eglur**
The proclaiming of a clear poem

2 **awen tra messur**
of inspiration beyond measure

3 **am gwr – deu, awdur**
about a man – brave, authoritative

4 **o echen Aladur**
from the family of Aladur/Mars

5 **ae ffonsa ae ffur**
with his staff and his wise nature

6 **ae Reom rechtur**
and his governing of Rheon

7 **ae ri rwyfyadur**
and his royal sovereignty

8 **ae rif yscrythur**
and his honouring of scripture

9 **ae goch gochlessur**
and his bloody defence

10 **ae ergyr dros uur**
and his attack across the wall

11 **ae kadeir gymessur**
and his commensurate chair

12 **ymplith goscord nur.**
amongst the lordly retinue.

13 **Neus duc o Gawrnur**
He took away from Cawrnur

14 **meirch gwelw gostrodur.**
pale horses under saddle.

15 **Teyrnon henur,**
The venerable sovereign,

16 **heilyn, pascadur.**
the provider, feeder.

17 **Treded dofyn doethur**
The third profound (song) of the wise man

178

18 **y vendigaw Arthur.**
(was) to bless Arthur.

19 **Arthur vendigan**
Arthur was blessed

20 **ar gerd gyfaenat:**
in a harmonious song:

21 **arwyneb yg kat**
a defence in battle

22 **ar naw bystylat.**
trampling (his enemies) nine at once.

The bard lauds Arthur – he is brave, authoritative and wise. In line 4 he is likened to Aladur, an obscure Celtic god who is the equivalent of Mars, the Roman god of war. This equating comes from the discovery of a silver gilt plaque in Barkway, Hertfordshire which shows an image of Mars wearing a helmet and holding a spear and shield. The two names, *Marti* and *Alatori* appear as part of a text beneath the figure implying that they are different names for the same god. This is reinforced by the two names *Mar(ti)* and *Ala(tori)* also appearing on the South Shields Roman altar. The Romans made it easier for the Britons to retain their gods by twinning each with a similar Roman god. Apart from the *Chair of the Sovereign*, 'Aladur' doesn't appear anywhere in other Welsh texts: it is absent from *Culhwch and Olwen* which records ancient material on Arthur. If not for the fortuitous discoveries of the plaque and altar, Aladur would be a mystery. This suggests that the poem was composed at an early date, one not too far from the Roman period, when the bard's audience could make sense of the name. The name survives in the wood *Coedladur* (now called Coed-Ladyr in the Ordnance Survey map), about 2 miles south of Cai's fort in Llanuwchllyn and also in the stream, *Nant Ladur*, about 6 miles west of Ruthin, where Arthur beheaded Huail.[2]

In line 5, the word *ffonsa* is here translated as 'staff', which is an option noted by Marged Haycock (2007). This translation is tentative but the idea that Arthur carried a staff does appear in artwork in the Cloisters, Metropolitan Museum of Art, New York where Arthur is holding a rough wooden staff in a medieval tapestry, c. 1400. Line 6 refers to his governing of Rheon, as discussed in Chapter 3. In lines 8-10 Arthur honours scripture but also provides protection through bloody battles. In line 11, his commensurate chair (throne) is noted, a sign that he was seen as a king. In lines 15-16, he is called the venerable soverereign (Welsh: *Teÿrnon*), and the provider and feeder. Then in lines 17-20, his soul is blessed in a song by a wise man. Finally the bard recalls Arthur's valour in defending his people and trampling his enemies nine at once, a sacred number (3 x 3).[3]

Stewards to mind the country

After the eulogy, the bard asks a question which implies that it was anticipated that Arthur would be away from Britain for some time as stewards were appointed to mind the country in his absence.

> 23   **Pwy y tri chynweissat**
> Who were the three stewards
>
> 24   **a werchetwis gwlat?**
> that minded the country?

So before he left for Annwfyn Arthur was aware of the long duration of the journey and that it was a dangerous one. In contrast, Brân's journey was only to Ireland, a trivial distance. The appointment of stewards to mind the country in his case is absurd as he could return to Britain in a few days. This clearly shows that the appointment of stewards in *Branwen* was copied from *Chair of the Sovereign*. Brâns' epithet, 'the blessed' was also copied from Arthur's blessing that is given in lines 17-20 above.[4]

Teÿrnon and Brân

In line 15 Arthur is called Teÿrnon. The copying of Arthurian features into *Branwen*, the second Mabinogi story, also occurs in the first story *Pwyll, Prince of Dyfed*. There, a king called Teÿrnon commands the respect and friendship of Pwyll and Pryderi, who first appear in *Spoils of Annwfyn* as Arthur's men.

Further, the story relates that Pwyll had been one of Teÿrnon's men in the past, so that Teÿrnon well knew his appearance, enabling him to recognize Pryderi as Pwyll's son (Ford, 1977). At the end of this story, Pwyll swears to uphold Teÿrnon and his realm and says that it would be even more fitting for Pryderi to do the same. This suggests that the Teÿrnon in the Mabinogi is depicting Arthur, even though he is not being called Arthur.[5]

The Mabinogi tales were written perhaps c. 1120 but may contain old traditions. Both Teÿrnon and Brân are presented very positively with Teÿrnon being described as 'the best man in the world' while Brân is wise and his acts are mighty. In *Pa Gur*, Arthur's men were also called 'the best men in the world'. The Mabinogi tales were written about 500 years after the three Arthurian poems and borrowed from them. Later in this chapter, inferences are drawn from Arthur's connection to Brân on how Arthur probably died.[6]

Distress at the death of Arthur

In lines 59-67 Arthur's death is mentioned again. The bard begins a new section about the sovereign's throne where the Welsh word, *Teÿrnon*, is again used for sovereign.

59   **Kadeir Teyrnon,**
      The Chair of the Sovereign,

60   **keluyd rwy katwo.**
      he is a skilful one who keeps it.

61   **Keissitor ygno,**
      A renowned fighter will be sought,

62   **keissitor kedic,**
      an aggressive one will be sought,

63   **ketwyr colledic.**
      as our warriors are bereft.

64   **Tebygafi dull dic**
      I am (also) distressed

65   **o diua pendeuic**
      from the annihilation of the prince

66   **o dull diuynnic**
      of the fiery nature

67   **o Leon luryc.**
      with the lorica of Lleon.

This king is Arthur and the theme of this section is that he is now dead, his 'chair' is vacant and the bard asks who could possibly replace him, speculating that a renowned or aggressive fighter would be sought. In line 60, the bard states how difficult it is for a king to retain the throne in that barbarous era, an observation made by Gildas who noted the rapid turnover of kings where one king would be replaced by another even more brutal.[7]

The bard then notes the effect of Arthur's death on his warriors – they were utterly bereft and the bard himself was similarly distressed. Again Arthur's death is described as an annihilation using the same Welsh word *diua* as used in *Spoils of Annwfyn*. Arthur is described as having a fiery nature and wearing the lorica (battle vest) of Lleon, (from 'Legion') meaning Chester itself or the territory associated with it in northeast Wales. The bard's grieving here is similar to that in the last few lines of *Spoils of Annwfyn*.

HUMAN HEADS AS TROPHIES

Beheadings in Europe and Britain

Among ancient peoples, both in Europe and America, the taking of human heads and other body parts as battle trophies was widespread. The beheading of warriors and the mutilation or desecration of the head was a way of intimidating the enemy. It also led to attempts to protect the head of a dying king through his own men beheading him and carrying the head away to safeguard it. The following examples span nearly a millennium.

Livy in his *Founding of the City* describes a slaughter in 295 BC in which a Roman legion was attacked by the Senonian Gauls. After beheading the slain Romans, they hung the heads around their horses' chests and also fixed them on the points of their spears, while they chanted their war songs.[8]

In his *Histories*, Polybius records an attack from 218 BC, in which a Celtic group within the Roman army decided to defect to Hannibal. During the night they ambushed the Romans quartered near them, cut off their heads and brought the heads to Hannibal. He addressed them encouragingly, promising them rewards, and sent them to their cities to declare to their compatriots what they had done and to urge them to make an alliance with him.[9]

Livy also tells of the Boii of northern Italy who in 216 BC massacred the Romans by sawing through trees so that they were barely stable and then pushing them onto the Romans as they passed through the forest. The consul elect, Lucius Postumius, was beheaded and his head was taken to their sacred temple where they cleaned out the skull and covered the scalp with beaten gold. It was used as a drinking cup for the priest and temple ministers and for libations to the gods.[10]

Strabo in his *Geography* describes the behaviour of some Gallic warriors, taken from the work of Poseidonius.[11]

> I mean the fact that when they depart from the battle they hang the heads of their enemies from the necks of their horses, and, when they have brought them home, nail the spectacle to the entrances of their homes ... The heads of enemies of high repute, however, they used to embalm in cedar-oil and exhibit to strangers, and they would not deign to give them back even for a ransom of an equal weight of gold.

Paul the Deacon, in his *History of the Langobards*, describes how the Langobards (or Lombards), under king Alboin, defeated the Gepids in a great slaughter in AD 567. The Gepids were an east Germanic tribe. Their king, Cunimund, was killed and Alboin cut off his head and carried it away to make a drinking goblet out of the skull. Ironically he later married Cunimund's daughter, Rosamund.[12]

As discussed earlier, in Britain in 633 the Saxon king, Edwin, was killed at the battle of Hatfield Chase by Cadwallon and Penda. The Saxons apparently beheaded Edwin to protect the head and it was taken to St Peter's Church, York (Williams, 1980). However his body was buried beside the altar in the Whitby monastery, according to the Whitby *Life of Gregory* (McClure and Collins, 2008).[13]

In about 642 Penda defeated the Saxon king, Oswald (who was Edwin's nephew), at the battle of Maes Cogwy. Penda had the head, arms and hands of Oswald cut off and hung up on stakes. A year later, Oswald's successor, Oswiu, arrived at the site with his army and took them down. He buried the head in the church at Lindisfarne and the hands and arms at Bamburgh, according to Bede.[14]

A poem *On Urien and the Gogledd* describes the beheading of a dead or dying king and carrying away the head to protect it (Ford, 1999). The head is that of Urien Rheged and the person carrying it is Llywarch Hen who was first cousin to Urien in the Welsh genealogies. However Llywarch did not compose the poem, which was probably the work of a Llywarch 'persona' in the 800s. The poet vividly conveys the scene of the carrying away of the head:[15]

> The head I carry at my side, the head of Urien generous in governance of men; and on his blessed breast a villainous crow.

Native American Beheadings
Like the peoples of Europe, the Native Americans took human body parts as trophies from ancient times. Excavations in the Ohio river valley in southern Indiana show cases where beheading and cutting off the forearms have taken place, according to Christopher Schmidt and Rachel Sharkey (2012). These examples come from the Middle Archaic and Late Archaic periods.

In the Hopewell period, two interesting cases of beheadings are shown from their superb carvings. One is the Wray figurine, which was found in 1881 in Newark, Ohio by workers digging the foundations for a building. It was beneath the largest of the Hopewell burial mounds at the Newark Earthworks, in Licking County, and was carved from a solid piece of rock. It shows a shaman dressed in a bearskin, with the bear's head attached. In his lap, he holds a decapitated human head. Both the shaman and the disembodied head wear Hopewell-style ear spools and the decapitated head's hair falls down between the legs of the shaman. Jaimin Weets et al. (2005) comment as follows.[16]

> ... the Wray figurine from the Newark site ... shows a man in bear costume (or wrapped by a bear spirit) with an apparently severed head on his lap and arms placed in a ritual posture.

The second case was excavated from the Seip earthworks, a few miles southwest of Chillicothe. It was a Hopewell smoking pipe, made of dark brown soapstone, and depicts a dog gnawing at a decapitated head, a gruesome scene. The carving is realistic, suggesting that the carver actually watched the dog gnaw at the head that was tossed to him. The head is upside down and the dog is gnawing at the fleshy part of the neck rather than the bone of the skull. Chad Thomas et al. (2005) describe the pipe as follows.[17]

> ... a dog eating a decapitated human head held between his front paws.

The Beheading of Brân
Another case of a dying king who was beheaded by his men appears in *Branwen Daughter of Llŷr*. During Brân's disastrous battle in Ireland he was wounded in the heel by a poisoned spear. Knowing he was dying, he ordered his men to cut off his head, take it to London

and bury it. In the correlations between Brân and Arthur, a beheading for Arthur has not been given. However the ending to Arthur's life in *Battle of the Trees* strongly implies it.

ARTHUR'S DEATH IN BATTLE OF THE TREES

This poem contains 16 lines about Annwfyn that gives the most detail about Arthur's death. It implies that he was badly wounded and in a concealed place when his bard conducted a mercy killing.

189   **Yn Annwfyn llifereint**
In the streams of Annwfyn

190   **wrth urwydrin dybydant.**
they come to gather for battle.

191   **Petwar vgeint cant**
Four-score hundred

192   **a gweint yr eu whant.**
I pierced because of their battle lust.

193   **Nyt ynt hyn, nyt ynt ieu**
They are not older, nor younger

194   **no mi yn eu bareu.**
than me in their passions (for battle).

195   **Aryal canhwr ageni pawb**
Everyone born (there) had the passion of a hundred men

196   **a naw cant oed genhyf inheu.**
and (the passion of) nine hundred did I have.

197   **Yg cledyf brith gwaet**
My bloodspotted sword

198   **bri am darwed,**
brings me honour,

199   **o douyd o golo lle yd oed:**
from the lord from a concealed place where he was:

200   **o dof yt las baed.**
by a meek one was the warrior killed.

201   **Ef gwrith, ef datwrith,**
He (God) made, He remade,

202   **ef gwrith ieithoed.**
He made peoples (again).

203   **Llachar y enw, llawffer:**
Shining his name, strong of hand:

204   **Lluch llywei nifer.**
Brilliantly he governed the host.

Arthur's Beheading

The bard states that his bloodspotted sword brings him an honour which was conferred by the lord in the concealed place, where he was apparently dying of his wounds and too weak to continue fighting. The lord is Arthur, as no other king is associated with Annwfyn. The key line is 200, 'by a meek one was the warrior killed', and there is little ambiguity about this line. It suggests that the warrior king, Arthur, (here called the 'boar') was killed in a merciful way by a close friend and that the honour that Arthur asked of the bard was to kill him, behead him and protect the head. This is the most probable meaning of the bard's 'bloodspotted sword' bringing him honour.[18]

The bard was a devout Christian as can be seen from numerous Christian lines across the three Welsh poems, but he was far from orthodox, retaining many ancient beliefs such as the immortality and transmigration of the soul. In Lines 201-2, he notes that God is in control, making and remaking both individuals and civilisations. He is reflecting on this to soften the tragedy of Arthur's death. Finally he returns to Arthur: 'Shining his name, strong of hand, brilliantly he governed the host', a moving and fitting epitaph.

Arthur's Wounds

There is a further inference that could be true if the author of *Branwen* had access to traditional knowledge of the sort that appears in *Stanzas of the Graves* and *Culhwch and Olwen*. In *Branwen*, the war between the Britons and Irish begins as follows.[19]

> Bendigeidfran grasped her in one hand, his shield in the other; at that, everyone leapt up, and the greatest uproar ever seen by the company of a single house took place, everyone seizing his weapons. Then said Morddwyd Tyllion, 'Warriors of Gwern, beware Morddwyd Tyllion.' As each gathered up his arms, Bendigeidfran held Branwen between his shield and his shoulder.

Here Bendigeidfran (Brân) appears in the first and third sentences, but *Morddwyd Tyllion* appears in the second, his only mention in the entire story. This awkward insertion without any introduction implies that *Morddwyd Tyllion* was important knowledge to the Welsh to be worked into the story in this way. Who was he? John Koch (2006) states that it refers to Brân and describes it as 'an obscure traditional utterance' which means 'pierced thighs'. Although elsewhere in the story Brân was said to be wounded in the heel, this unusual traditional utterance is more significant.[20]

As the author of Branwen was taking things from Arthur's life and putting them into Brân's story, could he have known an ancient saying that associated *morddwyd tyllion* ('pierced thighs') with Arthur and therefore made Brân suffer the same fate? If Arthur was dying from wounds in his thighs, it is easy to understand why. The femoral artery, a large artery, runs down the thigh with the vein behind it. If ruptured, a person could soon bleed to death. He may have been struck by arrows from the Native Americans, but if hit by a spear thrown from an atlatl, great damage could result. The atlatl was a spear thrower that combined with the throwing arm to act as a lever, thus producing a much more powerful throw. Photos of the Native American atlatl in use are given in Lepper (2005). The Hopewell used the atlatl before Arthur's time and their successors may have continued using it after the bow and arrow began to be used. Such a death could be the origin of the expression *morddwyd tyllion*.[21]

Recurring Motifs

In c. 1180, Chrétien de Troyes wrote a poem about the adventures of a knight, *Perceval*, who stayed one night in the castle of the maimed Fisher King. This king had been wounded so badly in battle, by a spear through his thighs, that he could not walk. While in the hall Perceval saw a strange procession, where a servant entered holding a white spear with blood dripping from the iron point. Then followed two servants with candelabra and a girl holding a golden dish (a *graal*) studded with jewels of every kind. The graal glowed with such light that the candles seemed dim. This is the first mention of the dish that was later interpreted as the Holy Grail. In about 1200, Robert de Boron wrote *Joseph d'Arimathie* and reinterpreted the Grail as the cup shared at Christ's Last Supper. In the public mind this view has now supplanted the earlier one of the grail being a dish.[22]

A related account appears in the Welsh prose tale, *Peredur*, written probably in the 1200s. This time, the king is described as lamed and two youths enter carrying a large spear, with streams of blood flowing from the point. Then followed two maidens carrying a large dish on which was a man's severed head, in a profusion of his blood, this replacing the candelabra and graal. It appears that the author of the Welsh version wanted to add the crucial information about the decapitated head that was lacking in the French version. In both stories, the hero is warned not to ask the meaning of wondrous events and so he remains mute, although he is curious to know the meaning. Later in both stories the hero is severely rebuked for failing to ask the meaning of what he had seen – if he had, the King would have been completely restored to health and his lands would have flourished. The three main motifs appearing in these works are features of the death of Arthur and Brân, as inferred here:[23]

(a) a spear dripping blood,
(b) a king pierced by a spear through the thighs, and
(c) a severed head.

CAMLAN

Although the details of Arthur's death cannot be proven, an intriguing picture emerges of how he might have died. The first aspect to consider is the location. Camlan means 'crooked riverbank' (from *Camboglanna*) or 'crooked enclosure' (from *Cambolanda*) according to Bromwich (2006). The 'enclosure' part could have the meaning of village or settlement or the specific meaning of church. The crooked enclosure meaning seems unlikely as the site of a battle in Britain or sixth-century America. However, the 'riverbank' meaning is highly probable for a battle site. In the *Historia Brittonum* battle list, seven of the twelve battles were fought beside a river. An army fighting with the river at its back would have protection from an attack from the rear. On the other hand, a stronger army could hem in its opponents against the river where it would be more difficult to flee.[24]

Spoils of Annwfyn states that Arthur and most of his men were killed in Annwfyn which has many of the features of early America. Given this situation it is likely that Arthur's last battle was not a conventional engagement of two armies massing at a location where both would be aware of the other's presence. A surprise attack by the Native Americans would be more likely, probably while the Britons were camped by a river. The epithet 'crooked' would refer to a point where the river sharply changed direction. As the Britons seemed to be in the Ohio Hopewell region where the large mound structures were complex, then somewhere on rivers like the Scioto or the Ohio would be possibilities. To attempt to pin down a more precise location would only be speculation.

The Native Americans used both the bow and arrow and the atlatl so it is not unreasonable to believe that Arthur died from such wounds. The story of Brân being pierced in the thighs could be yet another example of the many correspondences between him and Arthur. The *Battle of the Trees* states that the lord was in a concealed place when he bestowed an honour on the bard. This honour involved the bard's blood-spotted sword. The natural interpretation of this incident is that it was the dying Arthur's request to behead him and protect the head, another parallel with Brân.

ARTHUR SHOT BY ARROWS

The argument advanced in this section is not essential to the above case but it could be an example that others knew how Arthur was killed. On an interior wall of St Andrew's Church, Stoke Dry, a painting shows a king who is tied to a tree with densely concentrated arrows embedded in his body. There are two archers who are shooting at him who look very much like Native Americans. However the conventional explanation for paintings like this is that the king is St Edmund who was killed by the Danes when they overran East Anglia. Edmund is mentioned in the *Anglo-Saxon Chronicle* for AD 869 where it says that Edmund had fought against the Danes but they were victorious and slew him. Asser's *Life of King Alfred* of 893 seems to imply that Edmund had died in battle.

The most detail on Edmund comes from Abbo of Fleury who wrote his *Life of St Edmund* at Ramsey Abbey in 985, about 116 years after Edmund's death. In this account Edmund was captured, beaten, tied to a tree and shot so many times with arrows that they were like the bristles of a hedgehog. Edmund was then beheaded and the Danes threw his head into a bramble bush. God then sent a wolf to watch over the head to protect it. When his men later searched for it, the head called out 'Here, here, here', allowing the searchers to find it and to see the wolf guarding it.[25]

The Morgan Library Paintings

A number of paintings of St Edmund's death have been made. The earliest extant work was done by an unknown artist working in Bury St Edmunds in the 1130s. It is held in the Morgan Library and Museum in New York (Morgan Library Manuscript M.736). It shows a series of scenes reflecting the Abbo narrative: Edmund being beaten; being tied to a tree and shot with arrows; being decapitated; his head being placed in the brambles, and the finding of his head with the wolf. In the scene where he is being shot, Edmund isn't wearing a crown and is wearing a shorter tunic over a long tunic of a different colour, with hose underneath. Six Danes are shooting him from the left and are dressed in tunics and tight hose around the legs (Figure 8.1).

The St Andrew's Mural

The next extant work is the wall painting in St Andrew's Church. It was painted between 1280 and 1284, according to Clive Rouse, who was familiar with other work of the artist. Like most such paintings on church walls, they had been limewashed over centuries ago. In 1896, restoration work in the church revealed fragments of them and in 1973 they were painstakingly uncovered by Ann Ballantyne of the Victoria and Albert Museum. This mural differs from the 1130s painting as St Christopher is watching the killing, as shown by the Christ child on his right shoulder, and the fish around his feet (Figure 8.2).[26]

St Christopher present at the killing

The St Christopher image is not a separate mural. It is by the same artist, done at the same time, and is placed as close to the king's killing as it is possible to be without obscuring the nearest archer. The Christ child's head is above this archer and the right foot of St Christopher is vertically underneath the left foot of the archer.

Had the artist wanted to present St Christopher as an unrelated mural he could have shifted him to the right, where there is room, and faced him away from the killing. What is the artist's intent by inserting the saint? As he is the patron saint of travellers and mariners, the artist seems to be implying that the king being killed had travelled a long way from home, which is also signified by his vivid depiction of the Native Americans. St Edmund, of course, was killed where he lived, in East Anglia.

Differences between the two paintings

This mural greatly differs from the Morgan Library painting of the killing. In the latter, Edmund is not wearing his crown and is looking up at an angelic hand which is reassuring him. In the later mural, the kingship is being emphasized, rather than saintliness, as shown by the unnaturally large crown on the king's head. The victim is foremost a king, who by the presence of Christopher and the foreign attire of the archers, is shown being killed in a foreign land.

This artist has also made the clothes on the king differ as much as possible from the Edmund in the Morgan Library painting. The king is naked above the waist with his ribs and navel being shown. He is also barefooted whereas Edmund was wearing shoes. Instead of the tight-fitting hose worn by Edmund, the king is wearing what seems to be striped, loose-fitting trousers that stop about halfway down the calf, similar to sailors' pants.

The mural was painted about 210 years before Columbus reached America. The conjecture here is that the artist knew the legends about Arthur dying in a distant land overseas and that he had some idea of the Native Americans' appearance, as discussed below. He probably knew the story of Edmund's death, shot so many times that the arrows looked like hedgehog bristles and he may have seen earlier paintings of this. He has replaced Edmund by Arthur and has left indicators in the mural as to the king's identity. A further sign indicating Arthur is the stylized tree with three branches almost symmetrically distributed about the vertical axis of his body. This effect is achieved by making Arthur face the viewer while the 1130s painting has Edmund side-on with many intertwined branches from the tree. The number 3 and its multiples appear many times in the Arthurian poems, and occur later as the three crowns insignia on his armour.

Gwynedd tradition: Arthur dying under a shower of arrows

The conventional imagery of Arthur fighting his last battle at Camlan is of him wielding a large sword in the thick of the battle. However, Rachel Bromwich (2006) reports a folk tradition in Gwynedd (north Wales), which is Arthur's home territory. Arthur and his men were pursuing an unidentified enemy and Arthur fell dead under a shower of arrows. It is set in Snowdonia and the legend says Arthur was buried under a cairn known as Carnedd Arthur.[27]

The Gwynedd setting is not correct as Arthur's grave is unknown, from *Stanzas of the Graves*, but the tradition of Arthur dying under a shower of arrows or spears could be correct.

Knowledge of the Native Americans

If the artist replaced Edmund with Arthur, how did he gain an idea of the appearance of the Native Americans? These details probably came from the Norse voyages to eastern America. Currently, the only certain Norse settlement is at L'Anse aux Meadows in Newfoundland which was investigated by the Ingstads in the 1960s. A recent study using Bayesian modelling by Ledger et al. (2019) could suggest that sporadic visits continued for a century. Interval estimates for the start and end points of the occupation were AD 910-1030 and AD 1030-1145.[28]

Cnut reigning in Britain

While the Norse were at L'Anse aux Meadows the Danish king, Cnut, (formerly called Canute) invaded England and took the throne in 1016. He reigned until 1035 and ruled over England, Denmark, Norway and southern Sweden. England had a significant Danish population, especially in the north, who aided the English in their resistance to William I. By the end of William's reign (AD 1087) they had been well integrated into the population. This would have made it much easier for news of Norse discoveries to reach England.[29]

Norse exploration in America

It is not known how far south or west the Norse explored in America. Birgitta Wallace (2008; 2009) argues that the pleasant region of Hóp in Eirik the Red's saga could have been in eastern New Brunswick, probably around the Miramichi Bay or Chaleur Bay areas. It is possible that the Norse explored even further inland.[30]

The impressive feathered bonnet on the left Indian looks like a war bonnet worn by the Plains Indians which could suggest exploration, without settlement, much further than expected. The mural of the Native Americans is quite convincing for both the headdresses and the breechcloth of the archer on the right. It is important to note that the breechcloth is warm-weather clothing, not at all appropriate for the Danes. The clothing of the other archer looks to be guesswork, so the painter was probably working from second-hand descriptions.

The massive interest in Arthur

When the artist did the mural there was a huge interest in Arthur. The pseudo-history of Geoffrey of Monmouth about 140 years earlier had fanned the flames. Subsequently, Wace had written *Roman de Brut*, Chrétien de Troyes had written *Lancelot, Perceval,* and *Erec and Enide* and introduced the *graal* while Robert de Boron had written *Joseph d'Arimathie* and *Merlin* and reinterpreted the grail as the cup used at the Last Supper.

Around the time that the mural was painted the English king, Edward I, had commanded that a model of Arthur's Round Table be made and this fictional table is now in the Great Hall of Winchester Castle. It seems that an anonymous artist working in the middle of England had known, in very broad terms, how Arthur had died and had created a memorial to him on a church wall.

Figure 8.1. Morgan Library painting of St Edmund shot
by Danes. He is not wearing a crown and is looking at a
heavenly hand giving him comfort and reassurance.
(Wikimedia Commons).

Figure 8.2. The Stoke Dry mural of Arthur being killed. St Christopher carrying the Christ child is looking on. (Photo: R. MacCann).

9
DECLINE IN ARTHUR'S KINGDOM

CLIMATE DOWNTURN

Around the time that Arthur set sail for Annwfyn, a series of calamities struck his kingdom which, combined with the mysterious nature of his disappearance, eventually led to a view that he was ill-fated. Earlier in c. 531 his army had witnessed such an extreme meteor shower that his bard thought it was a forerunner to Judgement Day. It caused Arthur to ask his wise men to prophesy what it meant for the future.

About five years later a further series of calamities occurred that affected the world's climate for over a decade. It began in AD 536 when both the sun and the moon were mysteriously dimmed for about 18 months, arousing fear and wonder. In Chapter 2 it was argued that Gildas probably witnessed this, and that he was writing in February 537. From that time, the world's climate entered a cooling period from 536 to about 550, causing widespread misery. The 536 dimming was recorded by eyewitnesses as shown below.

Procopius

Procopius was the legal advisor of Belisarius, the military commander of Justinian, and was either in Italy or north Africa when he witnessed the solar anomaly.[1]

> And it came about during this year that a most dread portent took place. For the sun gave forth its light without brightness, like the moon, during this whole year, and it seemed exceedingly like the sun in eclipse, for the beams it shed were not clear nor such as it is accustomed to shed. And from the time when this thing happened men were free neither from war nor pestilence nor any other thing leading to death. And it was the time when Justinian was in the tenth year of his reign. [AD 536-537]

John of Ephesus

John was a sixth-century ecclesiastical historian who was probably in Constantinople when he observed the sun's dimming. His writing on this event is reproduced in the chronicle of Michael the Syrian:[2]

In the year 848 [AD 536/37] there was a sign in the sun the like of which had never been seen and reported before in the world...So it is said that the sun became dark and its darkness lasted for one and a half years, that is, eighteen months. Each day it shone for about four hours, and still this light was only a feeble shadow. Everyone declared that the sun would never recover its original light. The fruits did not ripen and the wine tasted like sour grapes.

The Syriac Chronicle, based on Zachariah of Mitylene

The chronicle of Zachariah is lost but another writer, probably a monk in the sixth century, made a truncated version of it which covers the solar event. This version also notes that the ocean was whipped up.[3]

And he [Pope Agapetus] came with them to Constantinople in the month of March in the year fourteen [536]...And the whole city was disturbed at the arrival of Agapetus and the earth with all that is upon it quaked; and the sun began to be darkened by day and the moon by night, while the ocean was tumultuous with spray (?), from the 24th March in this year till the 24th June in the following year fifteen [537].

Cassiodorus

Cassiodorus was the astute Praetorian Prefect of Italy. In a letter to his deputy, Ambrosius, he notes the strange heavenly events that were affecting the seasons and alarming the people (Barnish, 1992).[4]

How strange it is...to see the principal star (the sun) and not its usual brightness; to gaze on the moon, glory of the night, at its full, but shorn of its natural splendour? All of us are still observing, as it were, a blue-coloured sun; we marvel at bodies that cast no mid-day shadow, and at that strength of intensest heat reaching extreme and dull tepidity. And this has not happened in the momentary loss of an eclipse, but has assuredly been going on equally through almost the whole year... So, we have had a winter without storms, spring without mildness, summer without heat. Whence can we now hope for mild weather, when the months that once ripened the crops have been deadly sick under the northern blasts. For what will give fertility, if the soil does not grow warm in summer? What will open the bud, if the parent tree does not absorb the rain? Out of all the elements, we find these two opposed to us: perpetual frost and unnatural drought...

For this vast inane, which is spread between earth and heaven as the most tenuous element, allows us to see clearly as long as it is pure and splashed with the sun's light. But, if it is condensed by some sort of mixture, then, as with a kind of tautened skin, it permits neither the natural colours nor the heat of the heavenly bodies to penetrate.

Cassiodorus makes a valuable remark that the previous year's harvest was a 'fortunate abundance' and instructs Ambrosius to store crops from the past to overcome the future shortage. To summarize the above accounts, in 536 both the sun and moon were dimmed, lasting for about 15 to 18 months. This cooled the climate and the crops were affected by cold northerly winds, frost and lack of rain. Something in the atmosphere (like a tautened skin) partially blocked both heat and light and gave the sun a bluish tinge.

Cassiodorus' account suggests that he was writing in autumn 536, probably in September or October, as he had noted these effects for the past winter, spring and summer, but not autumn. As it had been happening for nearly a year, it implies that some atmospheric calamity occurred in late 535 or early 536, after the plentiful 535 harvest. There is indeed solid scientific evidence for such a disaster which will be discussed below.

TREE RING AND ICE CORE DATING

Michael Baillie is an expert in the dating of historical events through tree ring dating or dendrochronology (Baillie, 1989; 1994; 1999, 2007, 2008, 2015). Climate disasters can be identified through the annual tree rings being very narrow, or virtually non existent, indicating that the trees showed little or no growth compared to that under a normal climate. Another indicator is frost damage in the tree rings.

Baillie identified the 536 disaster and a slight recovery in 538-9 followed by a severe downturn in 540. The trees suffered badly, with severely restricted ring growth and the effect occurred worldwide: in Irish oak, Finland pine, European oak, USA foxtail and bristlecone, and Argentinian fitzroya. Tree ring dating is valuable because it does not have large standard errors of measurement. The downturn in 540 lasted for at least 10 years but its effect probably differed across the world with some climates suffering more than others.[5]

A second dating system comes from the extraction of ice cores from the Arctic and Antarctic. The cores from Greenland include the American GISP2 and the European Dye3, GRIP and NGRIP. For each core, the ice can be separated into sections representing the yearly deposits. The year by year material found in the ice provides valuable data on climate fluctuations.

The cause of the downturn had been attributed to debris from a comet or asteroid, or from one or more volcanoes. The latter source would give a sulphate anion signal that should show up in the ice cores. Until 2008, no such signal could be found in the critical periods identified by Baillie. Therefore Baillie (1999; 2007) thought that the cause was a comet or comet fragment hitting the earth. Rigby et al. (2004) argued that an airburst high in the atmosphere from a comet fragment could have distributed dust around the globe and calculated the radius that was required to cause the downturn.[6]

In 2008, an important paper by Larsen et al. found strong sulphate signals that were dated to AD 529 ± 2 and 533-534 ± 2. The AD 529 signal did not correspond to any disaster in Baillie's tree rings but it was thought that the 533-534 signal could correspond to the 536 disaster, although it was not a perfect fit. However the mystery was why the tree rings didn't indicate any downturn in 529. The 529 eruption deposited more sulphate in each of the Dye3, GRIP and NGRIP ice cores than did the 533-534 eruption (Table 3, Larsen et al., 2008). There seemed to be a problem with the ice core dating.[7]

BAILLIE'S SOLUTION

Then came a breakthrough paper by Baillie (2008) which suggested that the European ice core chronology was problematic for the sixth century dating and for other dating in the first millennium AD. He was familiar with the work of LaMarche and Hirschboeck (1984) which associated frost rings in American bristlecone pines with explosive volcanic eruptions. He then obtained a list of frost ring damage for bristlecone pines in the sixth century from Salzer and Hughes (2007) and noticed four key dates: 522, 536, 541 and 574. In the European ice cores, volcanic sulphate signals appeared at 515, 529, 533.5 and 567.5. Baillie noticed an approximate 7 year difference between these two sets of figures and hence argued that by adding 7 to the ice core dates, the two dating scales could be reconciled. In my view, he is correct in arguing for this adjustment in the ice core dates. This meant that the huge volcanic eruption initially dated to 529 actually occurred in 536 and the supposed 533-534 eruption actually occurred in 540-541.[8]

Baillie later revisited the issue in Baillie and McAneney (2015) and concluded:[9]

> In this paper we have documented the need for re-dating most of the ice core chronologies for the period before AD 700, and in all probability up to AD 933 ± 1.

Sigl et al. (2015) have broadened the analysis of atmospheric aerosol loading using multi-parameter measurements and agree with Baillie's resolution of the ice core dating problem.

CAUSES OF THE DOWNTURN

As the volcanic sulphate signals now corresponded to downturns experienced by the trees, Baillie abandoned the comet hypothesis and supported volcanoes as the causes.

The 536 Catastrophe

The 536 catastrophe must have come from the northern hemisphere as no volcanic sulphate had drifted far enough south to appear in the Antarctic ice cores. Furthermore, the sulphate deposition in the north of Greenland NGRIP was not much smaller than its deposition in the further south DYE3, a difference in latitude of almost 10 degrees. This also implies a northern volcano. Sigl et al. (2015) think that several north American volcanoes may have erupted at the same time:[10]

> ...individual shards had geochemical compositions that share affinities with volcanic systems in the Aleutian arc (Alaska), Northern Cordilleran volcanic province (British Columbia), and the Mono-Inyo Craters area (California) – indicating at least three synchronous eruptive events, all situated in western North America between 38° N and 58° N.

Loveluck et al. (2018) remark that a volcano in Iceland could have contributed to the catastrophe based on volcanic signals in the Colle Gnifetti ice core on Monte Rosa in the Swiss Alps. As one result of their study, they found volcanic particles from Iceland in the Colle Gnifetti ice core to be chemically similar to those from the NEEM-2011-S1 Greenland ice core, thought to be associated with the 536 eruption (Sigl et al., 2015). It suggests that an Icelandic volcano could be a cause but more research is needed to clarify the relative contributions of the American volcanoes and the Iceland volcano to the catastrophe. These volcanoes were the cause of the mysterious 'cloud' that dimmed the sun and the moon as earlier noted by the ancient writers. Sigl et al. (2015) estimate that from AD 536, European summer temperatures dropped 1.6 to 2.5°C relative to the previous 30 year average.[11]

The 540-541 Eruption

The second eruption in 540-541 happened not far from the Equator as the sulphate appeared in both the Greenland ice cores (Dye3, GRIP and NGRIP) and in the Antarctic ice core DML (Dronning Maud land). In the latter, the dating precision is much lower, giving an estimate of 542 ± 17, which is very close to the 540-541 eruption of the redated Greenland chronology.[12]

Further, in Greenland ice core GISP2 Abbott et al. (2014b) found some tropical marine microfossils that had been blasted into the stratosphere and drifted all the way to Greenland. They also found extremely high levels of calcium in the ice, thought to be a proxy for calcium carbonate dust. Calcium carbonate is the main constituent of seashells. They think that a huge underwater explosion occurred in the tropics or subtropics, probably in water of depth less than 100 metres. Although they date this to 535-536, it is possible that the ice core dating has not been properly recalibrated to conform with Michael Baillie's new chronology and that this event near the Equator refers to the 540-541 eruption.[13]

Some have thought that the Ilopango volcano in El Salvador could have contributed to the climate downturn. Early radiocarbon dates gave AD 260 ± 114 for the eruption but Dull et al. (2001) revised this dating and using the full two standard errors obtained a date range of 408 to 536, which just bracketed the key 536 date. In Dull et al. (2010) they argued for Ilopango causing the 536 event. In a later paper, Dull et al. (2019), they argued that it caused the 540 event. However the most recent study on Ilopango by Smith et al. (2020) dates it to AD 431 ± 2 by identifying the ash layer in a well-dated ice core. Glass shards from the eruption were identified in the TUNU2013 ice core from Greenland. It therefore seems that the 540 volcano has not yet been identified.[14]

This huge eruption gave a global aerosol loading in the atmosphere that was about 10% higher than the massive Tambora eruption in 1815, according to Sigl et al. (2015). They estimate that the summer temperatures dropped again by 1.4 to 2.7°C in AD 541 and that cold temperatures lasted until about AD 550.[15]

The Justinian Plague

After the 540 eruption the Justinian Plague struck. Procopius reports that in 541 it was in Pelusium in Egypt. From there it moved towards Alexandria and the rest of Egypt and also towards Palestine. By the spring of 542 it was in Constantinople. It was a bubonic plague caused by the Yersinia pestis bacterium transmitted by fleas on clothes and bedding and was carried on rats. Recent papers on the plague have disagreed. Mordechai et al. (2019) argue from coin usage, issuing of laws, papyri contents and land use that the plague should be regarded as an 'inconsequential pandemic' but Sarris (2022) argues that their work is flawed in several crucial aspects. He also notes from the Keller et al. (2019) paper that the plague reached Britain around 544 at Edix Hill in Cambridgeshire and that this particular plague strain actually emerged earlier than the strains on the continent.[16]

FLOODING IN CHAIR OF THE SOVEREIGN

Arthur's north Wales domain suffered unusual weather conditions according to *Chair of the Sovereign*. After his death the poem gives two references to extensive flooding, the first in lines 43-4 below.

43   **Pwy enw y teir kaer**
       What are the names of the three forts

44   **rwg lliant a llaer**
       (now) between the sea flooding and low tide?

These two lines suggest that the references to sea flooding and wild weather are not just poetic expressions to convey misery at the death of Arthur. The bard is asking his audience to name the three specific forts now at the mercy of the sea.

It also describes wild weather with violent winds and storms, as follows in lines 53-8.

53 **Tohit gwanec tra gro**
   The wave surges across the sea strand,

54 **tir dylan dirbo**
   sure to become the realm of the sea.

55 **nac eillt nac ado**
   Neither the slopes nor sheltered places,

56 **na bryn na thyno**
   nor hill nor hollow,

57 **na rynnawd godo**
   nor protection from the storm (can be had)

58 **rac gwynt pan sorbo**
   before the angry wind.

Flooding across the Irish Sea

This north Wales flooding was paralleled across the Irish Sea in the north of Ireland. Baillie (1999) refers to an unfinished dugout canoe from Lough Neagh, the largest lake in the British Isles. The oak tree from which the canoe was made was felled in the range AD 506 to 542, from tree ring dating, the range allowing for missing sapwood. Three other oak trees that had been growing near Lough Neagh were dated. Two of the oaks didn't just have reduced tree rings, but actually died in estimates encompassing AD 540. The third had just survived but had a sharp reduction in growth at exactly 540. Baillie speculates that the death of the oaks, the minimum growth of the third oak, and the abandonment of the canoe are consistent with a notable rise in the huge lake's water level around AD 540.[17]

Dating Chair of the Sovereign

The Irish flooding is consistent with an estimated dating for *Chair of the Sovereign*. Although the latter is difficult to date, an estimate can be made as follows. The first assumption is that the 537 date for Gildas' writing is accurate. It may be exactly correct if Woods (2010) is right but is probably close to this even if his conclusion is wrong. Gildas implies that the five kings are controlling the Pharaoh's army which could indicate that Arthur was not in Britain. It suggests that Arthur left for Annwfyn not too long before, possibly 535-536, so that Gildas still thought of him as the overking who may yet return.

What is a reasonable estimate of the duration of the voyage before the survivors returned? Given the time required for exploring the Gulf of St Lawrence, the Great Lakes and further south, it perhaps falls in the 3 to 5 years range. This speculation gives a date of return from about AD 538 to 541.

Spoils of Annwfyn gives an account of the voyage itself and the immediate aftermath where the lords are clashing with the monks as a result of the diatribe of Gildas. It appears that this was the first of the poems. *Chair of the Sovereign* is a tribute to Arthur, describing a eulogy where his soul was blessed. It later refers to the devastation of his men and speculates on who will replace him. It also comments on the flooding, violent storms and wild winds. This could suggest that *Chair of the Sovereign* was composed about 540-541 which is around the time that the Irish flooding occurred.

A further consequence of this reasoning is that Arthur's death date in the *Welsh Annals*, 537/539 may be close to the truth. Arthur had left for Annwfyn not too long before Gildas wrote, perhaps around 535, and died there after a few years of exploring which took him to a region with extensive earthworks. The bard and the remaining crew returned around 540. How his *Annals* death date was obtained is not known but it fits well with other events as understood here.

THE YELLOW PESTILENCE

Although the Justinian Plague did reach Britain as noted earlier, there is no mention of it reaching Wales. However the Welsh lands did suffer from a disease known as the Yellow Pestilence (*fâd felen*). It appears in the *Liber Landavensis* (Book of Llandaff), compiled about 1030. The pestilence appears in the section on the *Life of St Teilo* as shown in the translation of William Rees (1840).[18]

> St. Teilo received the pastoral care of the Church of Llandaff ... in which however he could not long remain, on account of the pestilence which nearly destroyed the whole nation. It was called the Yellow Pestilence, because it occasioned all persons who were seized by it, to be yellow and without blood, and it appeared to men as a column of a watery cloud, having one end trailing along the ground, and the other above, proceeding in the air, and passing through the whole country like a shower going through the bottom of vallies ...

Teilo fled to Brittany and lived with Samson at Dôl until the pestilence was over. A similar account of the pestilence is given in the *Life of St Oudoceus*. The appearance of pestilence as a watery cloud also occurs in Adamnán's *Life of Columba* where St Columba sees a rainy cloud rising from the sea on a clear day and states that the cloud will pour down pestilential rain over Ireland, causing festering ulcers that will kill men and cattle. This prophecy was probably of the bubonic plague, not the Yellow Pestilence, but shares the same belief that disease can arise and spread from a watery cloud. In Ireland, the yellow pestilence was called the *buidhe chonaill* and *crón chonaill*, where *buidhe* means 'yellow' and *crón* is 'saffron coloured'. In Latin it was *flava ictericia*, 'yellow jaundice', from John Colgan in his *Acta Sanctorum*.[19]

William MacArthur (1944; 1949; 1950) argues that the disease was a severe form of relapsing fever which is carried from the sick to the healthy by lice. It propagates strongly in 'conditions of destitution, squalor, cold and overcrowding, which favour the breeding and spread of these insects, and epidemics are outstandingly associated with famine' (MacArthur, 1944). This was likely fostered by the 14-15 years of cold from the climate disaster. In the Irish Annals the dates for the disease are 548 (Four Masters), 549 (Cotton MS Titus A XXV), 550 (Clonmacnoise) and 551 (both Chronicon Scotorum and Inisfallen). The Annals of Ulster date a 'great mortality' at 549 but do not name a disease. But they mention the *crón chonaill* and *buidhe chonaill* for 556, using the same term 'great mortality'. MacArthur (1949) believes that the modifying sentence mentioning the *buidhe chonaill* became detached from the 549 date and was wrongly tacked onto the 556 entry dealing with Pope Pelagius I.[20]

The *Welsh Annals* record the death of Maglocunus in 547-49 using the term 'great mortality'. This dating is consistent with the Irish dates when the Yellow Pestilence was raging. The *Liber Landavensis* also states that the Yellow Pestilence was the cause of Maglocunus' death and that St Teilo had to leave Britain to escape it. I see no reason to doubt this tradition.[21]

> For it seized Maelgwn [that is, Maglocunus] King of North Wales, and destroyed his country; and so greatly did the aforesaid destruction rage throughout that nation, that it caused the country to he nearly deserted.

THE DESERTED LAND IN MABINOGI

The theme of the country being desolate appears in the third story in the Mabinogi. Brân's head has now been buried and Pwyll has died. His widow, Rhiannon, is now with son Pryderi and his wife Cigfa, and also Manawydan, who survived Brân's battle in Ireland. The land then became deserted from a magical enchantment. A mysterious mist descended and after it lifted the country was empty. The only people left were Pryderi, Cigfa, Rhiannon and Manawydan (Ford, 1977).[22]

> Each of them wandered through the land and the realm to see what they could of either houses or habitations, but they could see nothing of any kind except wild animals.

This gives yet another parallel between Arthur and Brân: after their deaths the land became partially deserted. Teilo's flight to Brittany in the *Liber Landavensis* is consistent with the migration to Brittany that Procopius related, c. 551. Thompson (1980) convincingly argues that the *Brittia* in Procopius was Britain and *Britannia* was Brittany. This migration had been ascribed to population pressures in Britain (with little evidence) but in Teilo's case he and perhaps many others were fleeing from the Yellow Pestilence.[23]

INVASION OF THE FOREIGN PEOPLE

In addition to flooding and wild weather, *Chair of the Sovereign* gives two instances of conflict. The first in lines 68-73 cannot be given a clear translation, so it will not be considered further. However the second conflict can be clearly translated as shown below.

74 **Jeithoed edein:**
The foreign peoples:

75 **aches ffyscyolin**
a swift flood

76 **mordwyeit merin**
of sea voyagers

77 **o plant Saraphin,**
from the stock of Saraphin,

78 **dogyn dwfyn diwerin.**
the evil ones of the deep.

79 **Dillygem Elphin.**
Let us free Elphin.

Here the part of Britain known to the bard is being threatened by a 'flood' of sea voyagers from the stock of Saraphin. The latter term is discussed by Marged Haycock (2007) who concludes that it meant 'Saracen' (not the heavenly 'Seraphim'). The term was used well before Islam became established. In the first three centuries AD it referred to an Arab tribe in the Sinai Peninsula and in the centuries after that (including the sixth century) it was used by Christians to cover all Arab tribes in general. Haycock notes that 'the deep' in line 78 probably refers to the depths of Hell. At face value, the astonishing conclusion of these six lines appears to be that Saracens, presumably fleeing from conflict, had sailed to Britain and were holding Elphin prisoner.[24]

The Tale of Taliesin

This conclusion differs from the usual contention that the *Chair of the Sovereign* is a late work and is referring to the spendthrift Elphin in the *Tale of Taliesin*. This amusing tale has Elphin the son of Gwyddno find a coracle that is trapped in his father's fish weir. Inside he finds the baby Taliesin who had been floating in the sea for many years. Elphin and his wife raise Taliesin, who is a promising bard. Later at Maelgwn's court, Elphin's foolish boasts cause the king to imprison him. This leads to a number of cartoonish incidents where Taliesin always gets the better of the king.[25]

For example, in a grand event when Maelgwn's bards are about to proclaim his glory, Taliesin is sitting quietly in a corner of the hall. As the bards pass by he vibrates his lips with a finger to make a *blerum blerum* sound. The bards curtsy before Maelgwn but instead of eloquent praise all they can sing is *blerum blerum,* which angers the king. When Taliesin is identified as the cause, he explains to the king he is there to free Elphin by singing his poetry (unlike the poetry of the historical Taliesin). His poetry amazes the king and also generates a powerful wind so that the king thought that his castle would fall down upon them. After these marvels, Elphin is released.[26]

It is obvious that this tale containing cartoonish incidents bears no relationship to history. It is highly doubtful that the real Taliesin had anything to do with Maelgwn's court, being a northern bard who sang chiefly to Urien and his son, Owain. My view is that the Elphin in this story and two other mentions of Elphin in the Book of Taliesin poems *Song of the Greater World* and *I Petition God* are elaborations from line 79 above in the *Chair of the Sovereign*. The latter poem was highly esteemed as a farewell to Arthur and the poets were trying to add some entertaining substance to this enigmatic line. Although the earliest manuscript of *Tale of Taliesin* is about the mid-16th century the story is much older than that, but not nearly as old as the 6th-century *Chair of the Sovereign*.

Other mentions of Elphin

Another mention of Elphin in the Book of Taliesin *Song of the Mead* is different, as it entreats God (rather than Maelgwn) to release Elphin and presents Elphin as a lord who provided Taliesin with wine, ale and mead as well as powerful horses. The poem ends with the mysterious line 'O Elphin rider, may you possess the North'. A different Elphin is presented in stanza A37 of *Y Gododdin* where he is the epitome of might in battle (Koch, 1997). This Elphin was a sixth-century warrior but it is unknown whether he had any connection with the Elphin of *Chair of the Sovereign*.[27]

Saracens in Britain in other texts

Chair of the Sovereign is the first text to state that a fleet of Saracens sailed to Britain. The poem was important to the Britons and it seems to have influenced later works. The later *Leges Anglorum* has a part where Arthur decrees the *folkmoot* which meets each year to create a common loyalty to king and country to help the king defend the land against foreigners and enemies. It ends with 'By the authority of this law the said Arthur expelled Saracens and enemies from the kingdom'. (Liebermann, 1903-16; Hieatt, 1992). Arthur, of course, did no such thing. In *Chair of the Sovereign* the influx of Saracens occurs after Arthur's death. However many details of the poem were probably not well understood so that the Saracens reference at the end may have been interpreted as just another enemy that Arthur fought.[28]

Geoffrey of Monmouth's *HRB* has a surprising section where both Ireland and then Britain were invaded by a huge fleet of African ships under their leader, Gormund, which devastated the countries (Thorpe, 1966). Geoffrey elaborates with his typically imaginative detail of the African army comprising 160,000 men. However unlike the *Leges Anglorum* author, Geoffrey was aware that this invasion came after Arthur's death and so placed it in the later sixth century. Geoffrey's source is not known. If his source was *Chair of the Sovereign* then he interpreted this poem correctly in placing the Saracen invasions after Arthur's time.[29]

The Moors in Tumult

At around the time *Chair of the Sovereign* was composed there was tumult in northern Africa involving the confederation of native tribes called the *Mauri*. They were noted by Strabo early in the first century who recorded their tribal name, *Mauri*, and the Greek form of the name, *Maurusii* (Jones, 1949). They will be called here by the familiar English name, the Moors. The poet Calpurnius Siculus, composing around the time of Nero, mentioned them raiding southern Spain near the river now known as the Quadalquivir (Duff and Duff, 1934) having crossed over by ship from north Africa.[30]

In 534 the Vandals who had controlled north Africa for nearly 100 years were defeated by Belisarius, the general of Justinian, but one conflict was immediately replaced with another. When Belisarius was replaced by Solomon as commander of the Byzantine army, the Moors began an uprising. They were resilient fighters who had harassed the Vandals and had taken a large amount of former Roman territory off them, all the land west of Caesarea Mauretania, modern Cherchell in Algeria (Bury, 1958; A. H. Jones, 1964).[31]

In 534 the Moors captured the Byzacena fortress (modern Tunisia) and killed commanders Aigen and Rufinus. In 535 Solomon attacked and defeated the Moors at Mammes and returned to Carthage, but the tenacious Moors, boosted by reinforcements, retook Byzacena. Again Solomon met them in battle, dividing his forces so that the Moors faced attacks from behind. The Moors were heavily defeated and the survivors fled south to join the army of Iaudas who was based at Mount Aurasium (Martindale, 1992; Bury, 1958).[32]

Solomon was a very capable battle leader and administrator who tried to subdue the Moors but before he could attack Mount Aurasium his plans were interrupted by a rebellion of his army in 536. He had to return to Constantinople and was replaced by Germanus who resolved the mutiny. In 539 Solomon returned and began a massive building program to fortify all regions under Byzantine control. The formerly open cities were now walled off, the manor houses were fortified and military fortresses were built to reinforce the borders.[33]

In 540 he led his army towards Aurasium but was attacked by the Moors who surprised his advance army. However the Moors had to flee when his main army came to the rescue. Solomon's army met the Moors in the foothills of Aurasium and again defeated them decisively. The surviving Moors fled west to Mauretania or south of Aurasium. Their leader Iaudas remained in a fort called Zerboule. Solomon laid siege to it but found its men had abandoned it, fleeing at night, so he plundered it and took possession. Soon after in 540 he attacked the key fortress of Toumar where his army won an overwhelming victory. Then came another victory where he captured the tower at the 'Rock of Geminianus' where Iaudas had sent his wives and his treasure. The latter helped Solomon to fund his fortifications which included new fortresses in Aurasium (Martindale, 1992; Bury, 1958).[34]

It now looked like the power of the Moors was completely broken. This seems the most likely period when a people whom the bard called Saracens could have fled to Britain. It is possible that the Moors who managed to flee west into Mauretania thought that they would be eventually hunted down by the likes of Solomon and his Byzantine successors and decided to leave. The western Moors along the coast were presumably skilled in sailing and had been raiding Iberia in ships in the first century. If these are the Saracens in Britain mentioned by the bard at the end of his poem, then their likely arrival in Britain would have been around 540-541, given their devastating defeat at Toumar in 540. As noted earlier this was about the time that *Chair of the Sovereign* was composed.

ARTHUR REGARDED AS ILL-FATED

As seen from the events in this chapter, Arthur's kingdom went into a severe decline after his army had been decimated in Annwfyn. At that time in Britain there was a superstitious belief that attributed the prosperity of a country to the personal success and health of its king. The *History of Cambria* (Lhoyd and Powel, 1584) notes that after the death of Owain Gwynedd in 1170, the eldest son, Iorwerth *Drwyndwn*, was not considered fit to govern because of a blemish on his face. The epithet is a compound of *drwyn* (nose) and *twn* (broken). The son looks to have had a broken nose that disfigured it. Van Hamel (1934) mistranslates *Drwyndwn* as 'flatnose'. If a king was perfect in health

211

and character then it was thought that his land would flourish. In both *Perceval* and its Welsh relation, *Peredur,* the Fisher King was severely lame and his country in decline. In both tales if the hero had asked the meaning of what he had seen, the king's health would have been restored and his land would have prospered.[35]

In Arthur's case, his huge reputation as a warrior and battle leader had established him as an exemplar for other warriors as shown by the *Y Gododdin* reference. However, his death overseas was mystifying. Only a few survivors knew what had happened in Annwfyn and when they died off speculation may have arisen that could no longer be corrected. The north Wales people must have wondered how the near invincible Arthur could have been killed and his army destroyed. His long voyage over the ocean to an unknown country and subsequent disappearance were probably superstitiously linked to the tribulations of his country that followed – the cloud that mysteriously blocked the sun and moon, the long-lasting unnatural cold in spring and summer, the flooding and violent weather, the Yellow Pestilence, and the strange 'flood' of Saracens in Britain.

The Superstition against Arthur's Name

Some scholars have put forward the idea that Arthur's name attracted a superstition against its use, a viewpoint that is supported here. Peter Bartrum (1965) correctly notes that the naming of sons 'Arthur' became extremely rare among Welshmen in Wales and could find no occurrences of the name up to the end of the 16th century. Henry VII did name his eldest son Arthur but his son's early death at age 15 probably reinforced the superstition. This fact was discussed by Padel (1994) who argues that Arthur was mythical, considering him to be a figure of folklore who became 'historicized'. Padel thought that the awe associated with Arthur's name stopped fathers from using it for their sons.[36]

Green (2007) presents a similar view to Padel but goes further in thinking that Arthur was really a Celtic god who was eventually thought to be historical. However, no trace of a god with a name like Arthur has been found. Green links the superstition to the belief that Arthur had visited the Celtic Otherworld, an event shown here to be a historical journey. There is no early evidence for the mythological views, as discussed earlier in Chapter 3.[37]

An intriguing exception to the naming superstition is the pedigree of Vortipor, the 'bad son of a good king' who was castigated by Gildas. His great grandson was named after Arthur. However this pedigree is duplicated in an Irish pedigree which implies that members of this family group regarded themselves as Irish. The other three namings of sons after Arthur all appear in Irish areas in western Scotland. It is probable that the geographical separation of Dalriada from north Wales meant that the superstition did not take hold in these distant areas and that they were remembering the fearsome deeds of Arthur in Scotland. The descendants of Vortipor in Ireland were also probably remembering Arthur's earlier glory.[38]

The author of the first two Mabinogi tales used the names Brân and Teÿrnon to refer to two Arthur-like figures which could reflect this superstition, knowing that Arthur had been referred to as Teÿrnon in *Chair of the Sovereign*. But if the author were not deterred by this superstition, it could be just a playful insertion of Arthurian features into the stories to create interest. However the superstition was real. Arthur's enigmatic demise in Annwyn and the series of misfortunes that beset his country afterwards led to the view that he was ill-fated which allowed the superstition against his name to develop.

10
MADOC

THE WELSH EVIDENCE FOR MADOC

This book has argued that Arthur sailed to America around AD 535 and was killed there around 537. It invites the question as to whether any other explorers had reached America before Columbus. John Dee in his 1578 case to Queen Elizabeth based his arguments not only on Arthur's voyage but on the voyages of other British explorers such as John and Sebastian Cabot, the northern voyages of Stephen Borough, Brendan the Navigator, a Friar of Oxford, and Maelgwyn Gwynedd. First on Dee's list were the voyages of Madoc, claimed to be a son of Owain Gwynedd who died in 1170. The Madoc claims were a contested issue for 400 years and the view of scholars is that there is not enough evidence to substantiate the claims that he went to America or that he even existed. However, having met many adamant Madoc supporters myself, I've sometimes wondered whether the scholars have set the bar too high in evaluating the claims and what evidence really does exist for his supposed journeys. This will be explored in this chapter with emphasis on the crucial early material.[1]

The Eisteddfod Essay of Thomas Stephens, 1858

At the 1858 Eisteddford in Llangollen, a competition was held for the best essay on the 'discovery of America in the twelfth century by Prince Madoc ab Owain Gwynedd'. Six essays were entered, five of which took the affirmative view, and one by Stephens which took the unexpected view that Madoc did not discover America. The Eisteddfod Committee decided that Stephen's essay, being not on the *discovery* but on the *non-discovery* of America by Madoc, was not on the given subject and therefore must be excluded from the competition.

The essays had been judged in advance by three judges who resented this decision and one resigned. Another wrote that Stephen's essay was far superior to the others who had failed to establish their points, but this letter was suppressed. The third judge was not called on to read his decision. When the Eisteddfod Committee announced that no award would be given, there was uproar. Stephens stepped onto the platform to speak, against the Committee's wishes. To drown out his voice one member asked the band to start playing but many of the audience wanted to hear his viewpoint. He was allowed to speak following audience support. To mollify him, an Eisteddfod secretary pledged to have the decision reconsidered and thus Stephens agreed to withdraw his protest.

The furore continued in newspapers, with other developments, but no award was ever made. Stephens intended to publish his essay but died in 1875, 18 years before his essay was finally published in 1893. Gwyn Williams (1979) calls Stephens 'one of the sharpest intelligences Wales has ever produced'. Given that his essay was written before Iolo Morganwg's forgeries were exposed, it was his great achievement to largely distinguish the wheat from the chaff and all scholars to follow are in debt to him.[2]

Welsh Evidence around 1170

Clearly the most valuable evidence for the Madoc claims comes from writers who were contemporaries of Owain Gwynedd and met him and his sons. Three main classes of evidence may be distinguished:

(1) poems by north Wales bards who knew Owain and his sons.
(2) the *Brut y Tywysogion* history covering north Wales c. 1170.
(3) an observer who spoke to sons and grandsons of Owain.

It is important to note that Madoc was not an uncommon name so that it needs to determined whether any Madoc under consideration was in fact a son of Owain Gwynedd.

CONTEMPORARY POEMS

Elegy for the Warband of Owain Gwynedd

One early poem that does connect a Madoc to Owain Gwynedd is titled *Marwnat Teulu Ywein Gwynet*. In English this would read 'Elegy for the Warband of Owain Gwynedd'. Here *teulu* would normally be 'warband' but probably also included Owain's retinue. The content of the poem which stresses the fighting ability of Madoc would favour the warband interpretation. The poem is by Cynddelw whose floruit spanned the late 1100s to well into the first half of the 1200s. The relevant Welsh verse is given below.[3]

> *Eny llas madawc mur dygyuorth uar*
> *Meu auar car kynnorth*
> *Oet anwas cas cad ehorth*
> *Oet anwar par yn y porth.*

> Since Madoc, the bulwark of wrathful fury, was slain,
> I mourn a helping friend.
> The violent one was savage in the taxing battle.
> He was a ferocious spear in the gate.

This is the only contemporary poem that connects a Madoc to Owain Gwynedd. At a stretch it might be argued that if Madoc was in the warband then he could have been Owain's son but there is no evidence for this. If he were Owain's son, one would expect the bard to link his valour to that of his famous father, as is usually done. The 'ferocious spear in the gate' seems to be portraying him attacking the entrance to a fort. He had now been slain. There is no mention of him being a sailor and as he died in Wales he could not have discovered America. It will later be shown how the Welsh words in this poem have been badly distorted by associates of Iolo Morganwg, supporters of Madoc, to portray Madoc as a sailor.

Ode to the Hot Iron

Another poem by a poet who was Owain's contemporary also mentions a Madoc – *Awdyl yr Haearn Twymyn* (Ode to the Hot Iron). The bard is Llywarch, Prydydd y Moch (i.e. Poet of the Pigs) who composed around the time of Cynddelw but was perhaps twenty or thirty years younger. It appears that Llywarch was being accused of murdering a Madoc and was dreading being exposed to the ordeal of the hot iron. The belief was that an innocent man would be unharmed due to God's miraculous intervention. The relevant lines follow.[4]

Da haearn diheura pan llas
Lleith madawc nad om llaw y cauas
Noe ae ceif cain ae glas
Rann o nef ae naw ternas.

Good iron exonerate me that when the assassin slew Madoc,
he received not (the blow) from my hand.
And that he who slew the brilliant one
shall have no share of heaven and its nine kingdoms.

Here there is no implication that Madoc was a sailor or Owain's son.
As he was slain in Wales he could not have discovered America.

Praise of Llywelyn ab Iowerth ab Owain Gwynedd

Llywarch also composed this poem to Llywelyn, king of Gwynedd, who
was a grandson (*wyr*) of both Owain and a Madoc as shown below.[5]

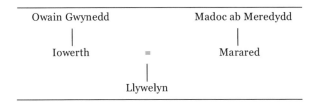

Llyw gwynet ae met hyd y mawddwy
Llaw orthrech wrth rwyfan mordwy
Lloegyr wrthryn tra llynn llwmynnwy
Wyr madawc ermidet uwyuwy
Wyr ywein uirein y auarwy.

The ruler of Gwynedd possesses it (land) to Mawddwy;
the conquering hand, dominion across the sea.
Opposer of Lloegr beyond Loch Lomond,
grandson of Madoc, greater and greater honour;
grandson of Owain, sadness for the splendid one.

This Madoc was not Owain Gwynedd's son, but the son of Meredydd
of Powys. His daughter, Marared (or Marged, i.e. Margaret) married
Iowerth (Edward) and the union produced Llywelyn.[6]

Poem to David ab Owain Gwynedd

The bard Gwalchmai was also a contemporary of Owain Gwynedd and composed poems to Owain and two of his sons, David and Rodri. In the poem to David, with the relevant lines given below, Gwalchmai laments the death of recent lords of high renown, including Owain himself, one of these lords being a Madoc.[7]

> *Owain angerdawl anaw anfeidrawl,*
> *aer wrawl wrhydri.*
> *Cadwallawn cyn ei golli,*
> *nid oed a lludw y llawdai fi.*
> *Cadwaladr cerdgar cerdau cyfarwar*
> *cyfarfu a'm perchi.*
> *Madawg madioed godoli;*
> *mwy gwnaeth uy mod no'm codi.*
> *Un mab Maredud a thri meib grufud*
> *biau bud beird weini.*

Owain the powerful, immensely wealthy,
hero of the vigorous battle.
Cadwallon, before he was lost,
it was not with ashes that he favoured me.
Cadwalader, loving poetry, pleasant song,
honoured me.
Madog kindly gave me gifts;
he did more to please than to offend me.
The one son of Meredydd and the three sons of Gruffudd
had the right to benefit from the bards' service.

Three of the lords being praised by Gwalchmai are Owain Gwynedd and his two brothers, Cadwallon and Cadwalader. All three were sons of Gruffudd (Griffith). The fourth lord was Madoc, son of Meredydd of Powys, identified in the previous poem as the grandfather of Llywelyn. All four lords were contemporaries. The last line, translated literally, may seem understated to us but what Gwalchmai meant was that these lords fully earned their high praise from the bards.

SUMMARY: THE MADOCS IN THE FOUR POEMS

These four poems should give the best evidence for Madoc as the bards personally knew Owain Gwynedd and his sons who would have been Madoc's brothers, had he existed. In the first poem, the Madoc was a warrior in Owain's warband and had been killed in Wales. However, he is not named as a son of Owain Gwynedd which is significant. Had be been such a son, Cynddelw would surely have sung that Madoc derived his valour in battle from his illustrious father, a standard form of praise used by the bards who esteemed a royal ancestry.

The second Madoc seems to be a different one, not slain in battle, but killed by an individual and Llywarch is being accused of this crime. Neither Madoc is called a son of Owain, nor are they said to be sailors, and as they died in Wales they cannot have gone to America.

The third Madoc was the son of Meredydd of Powys, not Owain Gwynedd. He was a grandfather of Prince Llywelyn, the ruler of north Wales, to whom Llywarch addresses the poem. This Madoc's daughter, Marared, married Owain's son, Iowerth, their son being Llywelyn.

The Madoc in the fourth poem is the same as the Madoc in the third poem. He is explicitly named in the poem as the son of Meredydd of Powys and is praised by Gwalchmai as one of a cluster of great lords. Therefore, three distinct Madocs appear in the contemporary poems but none are the son of Owain Gwynedd and no other contemporary poems mention a Madoc son of Owain Gwynedd.

The fact that each Madoc is not Owain's son, is not associated with the sea and is not credited with discovering a new land overseas is surprising given the claims that have been made. This is particularly damning given that the bards well knew and closely interacted with Owain Gwynedd, his sons and grandsons.

If such a Madoc, son of Owain, really did exist he must have been insignificant, achieving nothing of note. Had he discovered a new land overseas and came back to Wales to tell people all about it and actively sought others to join him, it is inconceivable that it would not have been known and praised in poetry by the bards who were closely associated with Owain's sons. The same argument also applies to Riryd, another supposed son who was said to have gone to America. He is completely invisible to the contemporary bards.

THE BRUT Y TYWYSOGION

The monks recorded key events against the years they occurred. They began with the death of Cadwaladr Fendigaid in 682. This material was probably set down in the Strata Florida abbey as annals, but later became more detailed. Other abbeys also contributed. These annals later formed the basis for a Latin document known as the *Cronica Principium Wallie*, the elegant work of a Welsh man. This is now lost but luckily a Welsh translation had been made of it called the *Brut y Tywysogion* (Chronicle of the Princes) which covered events from 682 to the death of Llywelyn ap Gruffudd in 1282. Various Welsh copies were made, giving a number of manuscripts. The *Brut* mainly focused on the kingdoms of Gwynedd, Powys and Deheubarth. As Gwynedd was the home territory of Owain Gwynedd, who ruled it for over 30 years, this gives the best possible historical source for studying events involving the brothers and sons of Owain.[8]

The *Brut* today has two main manuscripts, one in the *Peniarth 20* MS held in the National Library of Wales and one in the *Red Book of Hergest*, held in the Bodleian Library, Oxford. A third version known as *Brenhinoedd y Saeson* (Kings of the English) adds similar Welsh material to an English source. In 1858 Stephens thought that the *Black Book of Basingwerk* was largely identical with the *Brut y Tywysogion*. As mentioned in the *Brut*, Owain Gwynedd founded Basingwerk.[9]

Unfortunately for the Madoc claims, there is no trace of a Madoc son of Owain, nor a Riryd son of Owain in the two main manuscripts of the *Brut*. Nor do these figures appear in the *Brenhinoedd y Saeson* nor the *Black Book of Basingwerk*. Nor in any of these texts is there any mention of a Madoc or Riryd as seafarers, nor any mention of a land discovered overseas.

GERALD OF WALES – JOURNEY THROUGH WALES

Gerald was an eyewitness who travelled through Wales in 1188 with Baldwin, the Archbishop of Canterbury, who preached the Crusade at places on the way. When in the north Wales region, Gerald was able to meet with Owain's sons and grandsons. He was born in Manorbier Castle in Pembroke, southwest Wales, his father being a Norman noble, William de Barri. His mother Angharad was the daughter of

Gerald de Windsor and the beautiful Welsh princess, Nesta, who was the daughter of Rhys ap Tewdr, the last independent prince of south Wales. Although his mother was half English, Gerald identified as a Welshman. He was passionate about Wales and was an intelligent, acute observer whose account vividly captures events. His journey, called *Itinerarium Cambriae*, was published in 1191 and his later Description of Wales (*Descriptio Cambriae*) appeared in 1194.

The Situation in North Wales in 1188

In 1188 Gwynedd was ruled by David (Dafydd) and Roderic (Rhodri), sons of Owain Gwynedd. Owain had first married Gwladus who bore him Iowerth the heir. He later married his first cousin, Christina, who bore him David and Roderic. The Church had judged this marriage to his cousin to be illegitimate but when Owain refused to put her aside, the then Archbishop of Canterbury, Thomas Becket, excommunicated him. Owain also had other legitimate sons and illegitimate sons who would be legitimate under Welsh law if he acknowledged them, one of whom was Hywel, a brave soldier and talented poet.[10]

Iowerth would have been the heir but had a blemish on his nose which could expose him to ridicule. When Owain died, Hywel was a strong contender, despite the fact that his mother Pyfog was an Irish woman. Chaos resulted after Owain's death. David and Roderic forced Hywel to flee to Ireland and when he returned, he was killed in battle in Anglesey. David and Roderic then fought each other for control of north Wales. In 1188 Roderic controlled lands west of the River Conwy and David controlled the east of the Conwy.[11]

Meeting Owain's grandsons, Gruffydd and Meredydd

On the west coast, Gerald's party crossed the Dyfi into Merioneth, 'the land of the sons of Cynan'. Cynan was one of Owain's many sons. They were greeted humbly and devoutly by Cynan's son, Gruffydd. The next day they met his brother, Meredydd, who was attended by his people. Six years later these two would combine with Llywelyn ap Iowerth to defeat David and take control of north Wales. Gerald saw a recently erected stone castle called *Deudraeth* held by these grandsons who were in bitter competition with Owain's sons for land.

Meeting Owain's son, Roderic and his sons

Later they crossed the Menai Strait onto Anglesey where Roderic, the younger brother of David, came 'in a devout manner' to meet them. He was accompanied by nearly all the inhabitants of Anglesey and many others from adjacent territories. In a place near the shore the surrounding rocks formed a huge natural theatre where the large crowd gathered to hear Baldwin preach. Many chosen youths from the family of Roderic were sitting together on a large rock and Baldwin directed his plea to them to 'take the cross', to enter a Christian life and join the Crusade. To his disappointment, none accepted. Gerald, a committed Christian, had a low opinion of them.[12]

Gerald then discusses Roderic himself. He states that only a short time before, Roderic had incestuously married the daughter of Rhys, a wife closely related to him by blood. He had made this marriage to get Prince Rhys' support to help defend himself against the sons of his brothers who had been disinherited by him. For this incestuous union he was admonished by Baldwin, but he paid no attention to the Archbishop. The alliance with Prince Rhys was to no avail and Gerald notes that, not long after, the sons of Roderic's brothers combined to dispossess him of all his lands.[13]

Disgust at Owain's sons and praise for Llywelyn

On the mainland, they were shown the tombs of Owain Gwynedd and his brother, Cadwaladr in Bangor cathedral. These were in a double vault before the high altar. As Owain had been excommunicated by Thomas Becket, Archbishop Baldwin objected to Owain being buried in the cathedral and told the bishop, Guy Ruffus, to remove the body outside when he had a suitable time to do so. It is said that the bishop later made an underground passage from the vault through the south wall of the church to secretly move the body into the churchyard.[14]

Gerald indicates that he knew the details of Owain's death and the vile actions and plotting of his sons in grasping for the throne.[15]

> I shall pass over in silence what was done by the sons of Owain in our days, after his death, or while he was dying, who from the wicked desire of reigning, totally disregarded the ties of fraternity ...

In contrast, Gerald praises Llywelyn, the son of Iowerth, whom he regarded as the true heir. He notes that 'in our days' Llywelyn, from a young age, had began to harass his uncles, David and Roderic, although lacking in lands and funds. He was supported by his cousins Gruffydd ap Cynan and Maredydd ap Cynan, as noted earlier, and in 1194 the three combined to defeat David at a battle at the mouth of the river Conwy. In 1195 Roderic died and Gruffydd and Maredydd ruled north Wales to the west of the Conwy while Llywelyn ruled east of the Conwy. By 1200 Llywelyn ruled all of north Wales. As both David and Roderic were the product of an incestuous marriage, the pious Gerald thought their demise was the work of God.[16]

Meeting Owain's son, David
After crossing the Conwy, Gerald's group arrived at the noble castle at Rhuddlan on the river Clwyd. They had been invited by David himself, to whom the earlier poem by Gwalchmai was addressed. They stayed the night, Gerald remarking that they were 'handsomely entertained that night'. Having met with important grandsons of Owain, and the two sons of Owain who ruled north Wales, the next morning they moved east to stay the night at Basingwerk, founded by Owain.[17]

Opportunities to hear of Madoc
As can be seen from the above, Gerald was intimately acquainted with the history of Owain, his sons, and grandsons and was well placed to hear tales of Madoc's voyages, had he existed. Gerald sought amusing items for his account and notes several ridiculous 'marvels' similar to those in the *Mirabilia* of the *Historia Brittonum*. Rather than writing a dry account he was often like a modern journalist seeking items that capture interest (W. Llewelyn Williams, 1908). The Madoc tale would have been perfect for him to relate, being an unusual important event but apparently no such gossip was related to him.[18]

Further, the overnight stay at Basingwerk was another opportunity to hear stories of Madoc. The monks were recorders of events and these became part of the *Black Book of Basingwerk* which is closely related to the *Brut y Tywysogion* the major history covering Owain's period. However, the monks were apparently unaware of Madoc.

Gerald's comment on Shipping in Descriptio Cambriae

In his *Description of Wales*, Gerald remarks on how the Welsh lived at the time of Owain Gwynedd and his sons.[19]

> Almost all the people live upon the produce of their herds, with oats, milk, cheese, and butter; eating flesh in larger proportions than bread. They pay no attention to commerce, *shipping*, or manufactures ...

Gerald's contemporary comment that the Welsh pay no attention to shipping is of great interest. The small coracle was used on the lakes and rivers of Wales and larger boats were employed for the short journeys between Wales and Ireland. However his comment implies that ships suitable for ocean travel were practically non existent in Wales at that time.

Contrast this point with the late fabrication that Madoc was the commander of Owain's fleet and used this fleet to speedily depart for America, sail back to Wales, and then depart for America again. For example, Bowen (1876) writes of the battle of *Tal y Moelfre* where he puts Madoc in a glorious commander role.[20]

> From all the concurrent evidences which can be gleaned, it appears that Madoc was the commander of his father's fleet, which at that time was so considerable as successfully to oppose that of England at the mouth of the Menai in the year 1142.

Bowen can then explain why a 'son' so insignificant that there is no evidence that he existed was able to sail to America without needing the money, expertise and time to build the ships.[21]

> Being commander-in-chief of the fleet, he was able to take a speedy departure.

These statements are nonsense. Gerald knew the history of Owain and his sons in north Wales. He wrote an account of the battle, two of the leaders of the invasion being his uncles, as he points out. The battle of *Tal y Moelfre* was not fought on the water between two fleets. It was fought on land. The fleet of King Henry II sailed to Anglesey and then anchored off the northeast coast with intent to invade the island.

There was no Welsh fleet. There were only the people living on Anglesey to defend it. Owain Gwynedd and his soldiers were nowhere near the battle on Anglesey. They were based at Basingwerk in order to defend north Wales against an invasion of Henry II who had moved his army into Chester. While Henry advanced up the coastal Roman road towards Owain's camp, his fleet sailed from Chester to Anglesey where his soldiers went ashore and began ransacking the churches. The *Red Book of Hergest Brut* refers to them pillaging the churches of Mary and Peter and many other churches. The account of Gerald of Wales includes the church of St Tyfrydog. The King's soldiers led by Henry, the son of King Henry I, were over confident and didn't expect such resistance from the islanders. The well-connected Gerald vividly describes the disaster for Henry II (Thorpe, 1978).[22]

> Two great noblemen were sent to the island by the king. They were my own uncles: Henry, son of King Henry I and uncle of King Henry II, the child of Nest ... and Robert FitzStephan, Henry's brother ... Henry behaved far too rashly and, with no support from his troops, fell in the first line of battle, pierced by a number of spears, to the great grief of his soldiers. Robert was badly wounded and escaped with great difficulty to his ships, abandoning all hope of defence.

Apart from the glaring error that there was a strong Welsh fleet, when there was no fleet at all, Bowen made other errors. The battle's date was 1157, not 1142. It did not take place at the mouth of the Menai but on land, a considerable distance away. There is today a Moelfre on the coast of Anglesey, north of Red Wharf Bay, which is not far from two of the churches pillaged. About 4 miles west (as the crow flies) is the church of St Tyfrydog while about 4 miles south is the church of St Peter (at Llanbedrgoch).

Bowen's statement is typical of fabrications which use non-specific terms such as 'all the concurrent evidences' or 'an ancient chronicle' or cites authors whose work, when inspected, contains not an iota of the evidence claimed for it. This is not to infer that Bowen was one of these fabricators. He was one of the many misled by deceptions and accretions well before his time. The statements he uses appear to be the inventions of John Williams (1792) as will be discussed later.

THE CRONICA WALLIAE OF HUMPHREY LLWYD

The next evidence to be analyzed are the Tudor claims deriving from the *Cronica Walliae* of Humphrey Llwyd. But first it should be noted that there are Welsh bards from the 1400s whose poetry is often cited as evidence for Madoc. However the manuscripts we have of their work are post-Columbian which means that what they wrote could have been altered, and probably was. A key example involves a poem by Maredudd ap Rhys which influenced the Tudors, including John Dee. This poem will be analyzed at length later in this chapter.

Llwyd's 1559 Manuscript

Llwyd finished writing his chronicle in 1559. When he wrote, the main source for the history of Wales at the time of Owain Gwynedd was the *Brut y Tywysogion* of which there were numerous manuscripts noted by David Powel. Llwyd would not give his main source, merely calling it 'my Welshe author' and other similar terms, but heavily relied on the manuscripts of the *Brut y Tywysogion*. He also used material from Matthew Paris, the *Chronica Majora* and the *Historia Anglorum*, and the chronicle of the Angevin kings of England by Nicholas Trivet. His chronicle, in English, was unpublished in 1559 but was circulated among his friends and was eagerly read and discussed.[23]

Llwyd died in 1568 but his work was 'improved' by Powel and was published in Lhoyd and Powel (1584) where Powel wrote 'Llwyd' as 'Lhoyd'. The work was 'corrected, augmented, and continued out of records and best approved authors'. In a preface Powel notes how the chronicle originated from the work of Caradoc of Llancarvan and the monks from Conwy and Strata Florida added later events. Llwyd then produced a version from the various manuscripts and translated it into English. A modern edition of Llwyd's *Cronica* appeared in 2002 and 2016, edited by Ieuan Williams, assisted by J. Beverley Smith.

In 1559 there was great Madoc fervour amongst the Welsh. Powel presents his joint work with Llwyd as an authoritative history and this history has a section on Madoc sailing to America. What Powel doesn't say is that this section is missing from all manuscripts of the *Brut y Tywysogion*, on which Llwyd relied, from the works of Paris and Trivet, and from all other chronicles.

The Implausibility of Llwyd's section on Madoc

Llwyd wrote his manuscript nearly 400 years after Madoc's supposed journey. Given this, how could he possibly have had real knowledge of the fabled Madoc who didn't appear in any of the histories? There is evidence from Llwyd himself (see below) that his Madoc section was an insertion into his *Cronica*, not originally part of his history.

His Madoc section starts soon after the death of Owain Gwynedd. Instead of finishing with the *Brut*'s scene of Owain undergoing church rituals before his death, the *Cronica* gives a list of the many children Owain left behind. This allows him to insert the *unsourced claims* that Madoc and Riryd were two of Owain's many sons and that Riryd was the Lord of Clochran in Ireland. This Riryd and his Irish title appear in no earlier historical source. As Madoc and Riryd were said to be sons by 'diverse' women, Llwyd is implying that they were illegitimate sons of Owain. Llwyd's account is also given in Lhoyd and Powel (1584) where it says that Madoc sought a land where he could live in peace away from his brothers' wars.

If there really was a Madoc who sought land to live in peace then the obvious option would be to purchase a piece of land elsewhere, say in the Lake District, or in Devon or Cornwall. There are many beautiful and idyllic spots. It would be a tiny fraction of the cost of constructing a fleet of ships and easy to travel to on horseback. Or he could have sailed in a smaller boat to Brittany and settled there, as Britons had done for centuries. The idea of him sailing into unknown western seas for 6 weeks or more (depending on where he went) is ludicrous, as is the notion that an illegitimate son among many offspring would have access to funds to finance the journey. If such money existed, it would have been squandered by the costly wars.

'But to my hystorie'

After finishing the Madoc section, in a new paragraph Llwyd states 'But to my hystorie' and he returns to the type of events in the *Brut y Tywysogion*. This astonishing remark implies that he did not regard the preceding Madoc section as part of his history. This makes sense as his basic sources, manuscripts of the *Brut y Tywysogion*, had no section on Madoc.[24]

Llwyd's Madoc section can be derived from logic

Llwyd remarks that there were many fables about Madoc at the time.[25]

> Of this Madockes passage and returne therbe many fables fayned
> as the common people do use in distance of place and leingth of
> tyme rather to augment rather than dyminish, but sure it is, that
> there he was.

Llwyd was an honest scholar who had become convinced that Madoc
had reached America. Given the many stories circulating about Madoc
some must have convinced him, an issue which will be discussed in a
later section. If he had no information at all on the details of Madoc's
discovery, then he could easily deduce that two voyages were needed
to cement the British claim. The first voyage is needed to discover the
land. However Madoc then had to come back and claim credit for the
discovery so that it would be known in Wales at that time. This would
allow later generations to know he had preceded Columbus. But as his
whole purpose in sailing was to live peacefully on the overseas land,
this required him to go back to do this by a second voyage. Llwyd's
bare-bones account says little more than this.

It is obvious from details in his account that Llwyd was writing it
well after the Spanish discoveries. He was not quoting or paraphrasing
from an authentic ancient document that had somehow eluded all the
other historians. He calls America *Nova Hispania*, the Spanish name.
Possibly a significant factor in creating Llwyd's belief in Madoc was
the Spanish account of the large cross built by the natives on the island
of Cozumel just east of the Yucatan peninsula. To the Spanish and
Llwyd this suggested a Christian influence before the Spanish arrived,
making a Madoc visit much more plausible. When Llwyd refers to this
discovery he mentions Francis Lopez whose account of the cross was
first published in 1553 in Medina. Thomas Stephens (1893) notes that
it was republished in 1554 in Antwerp and that Llwyd was in close
contact with scholars there and therefore found out about it in 1554 at
the earliest. Far from Llwyd accessing ancient information on Madoc
it can be seen that he used Spanish information from 1554 to augment
his two voyages devoid of detail but necessary to argue the claim of
Madoc's primacy.[26]

Other features of Llwyd's Madoc section

Llwyd had Madoc 'leaving Ireland north' which may imply a northern route but a Gwynedd departure would be more likely if he existed. It could mean that Madoc left from Gwynedd, sailed past Ireland and went north. Or it could mean that he was based in Ireland and left from there. The early Atlantic explorers acting for Britain, John and Sebastian Cabot, and Stephen Borough had departed for the north. It is possible that Llwyd also believed that Madoc did so.

However David Powel thought that Madoc had landed in Mexico and that he wouldn't have sailed north from Ireland. In reproducing Llwyd's account in Lhoyd and Powel (1584), Powel 'rewrote Llwyd's original phrase' to insert the words 'so far' (Gwyn Williams, 1979). This made it read 'leaving Ireland [so far] north' which would seem to indicate that Madoc left Ireland for the south. This indirect phrasing is odd and leaves some doubt as to whether Powel's emendment is what Llwyd meant. It shows that Powel was capable of adjusting the data to give greater agreement to his vision of Madoc's journey.[27]

Llwyd also made some inferences. One was that because the Welsh were not many, they were eventually absorbed into the population, living just like the inhabitants and using the natives' language. This is probably what would have happened had a small colony survived in America. But this wouldn't do for the later accounts. It was crucial to the Madoc boosters that the Welsh language existed in America and survived to create the Welsh speaking Indians.[28]

LATER TUDOR ACCOUNTS BASED ON LLWYD

John Dee's account of Madoc

Dee was a brilliant scholar who actively sought out old manuscripts. Where these differed on a point, he studied them diligently to try to establish why the differences occurred (Russell, 2018). He was not a fabricator or a forger. However being honest himself, he was naïve in some instances. For example, he believed Geoffrey of Monmouth's history to be largely a true account of early Britain. He was also unwise in leaving Britain for Prague to investigate the occult, which left his superb library at Mortlake to be ransacked. To him, it was difficult to conceive that people would want to destroy valuable knowledge.[29]

Dee followed Llwyd's manuscript on Madoc, but added the date, circa 1170, a reasonable addition, from his knowledge of the historical situation. His account is given in MacMillan (2004).[30]

> Circa Anno 1170. The Lord Madoc sonne to Owen Gwynedd prince of North Wales, leaving his brothers in contention and warrs for their inheritance, sought by sea (westerlie from Irland) for some forein and apt region to plant hym selfe in with soverainty. Which region when he had found, he retorned to Wales againe & furnished hym selfe with shipps, victuales, armour, men and women sufficient for the colony, which spedely he leed into the province then named *Iaquaza* (but of late Florida) ...

In the 1550s Florida was used as a general name for the Spanish lands north of the Gulf, far more extensive than the current state of Florida. Llwyd had also used Florida in addition to *Nova Hispania*. *Jaquaza* was apparently the native name for Florida before the Spanish arrived and appeared on early maps. Dee's account is pretty much the same as Llwyd's original, with Madoc heading west from Ireland.[31]

Madoc in Mexico

In 1583 Dee set off for Prague, ending his involvement with Madoc. The Tudor accounts then took a strange turn. In 1583 George Peckham wrote *True Reporte* which argued for the British planting of colonies in America. Bizarrely, he identified the colonists of Madoc with the ancestors of Moctezuma (Montezuma) who did give a speech to Cortés which, vaguely expressed, could imply that the Spaniards had a right to sit on the throne that Montezuma had been minding for them. His speech in the *Florentine Codex* contains the following lines.[32]

> I have been worried for a long time, looking toward the unknown from which you have come, the mysterious place. For our rulers departed, saying that you would come to your city and sit upon your throne. And now it has been fulfilled, you have returned.

Peckham gave a different version of the speech in which Montezuma stated that his ancestors were not naturally of Mexico but came from a far country and who would eventually return and govern.[33]

> ... we are not naturallie of this Countrie, not yet our Kingdome is durable, because our Forefathers came from a farre countrie, and their King and Captaine who brought them hither, returned againe to his natural countrie, saying, that he would send such as should rule and governe us ...

Peckham was arguing that Montezuma and his people were descended from the Welsh, giving the British a prior claim to the Spanish. This argument was repeated by David Powel in Lhoyd and Powel (1584). A second novelty from Peckham and Powel was the claim that certain Welsh words existed in the new country, as argued by David Ingram. In the centuries following, this gave rise to the search for the elusive Welsh Indians, some of whom spoke perfect Welsh, according to some accounts. It is not known whether Peckham and Powel thought that Montezuma and his Aztec people also spoke Welsh.

Powel adds detail, stating that Madoc sailed with 'ten sailes' on the second voyage as 'I find noted by Gutyn Owen'. This is the first of a number of new claims, all unsubstantiated and some being obvious inventions. Gutyn Owen was a bard involved in the copying of Welsh language texts. He lived into the late 1400s but it isn't known whether he wrote before or after Columbus. However this is irrelevant as there is nothing in his works about Madoc or his 10 ships. Stephens didn't dismiss the option that the 10 ships had once existed in Owen's works as he was deceived by a forged triad from the Third Series, before Iolo Morganwg's forgeries were exposed (E. D. Jones, 1965).[34]

> Madoc son of Owain Gwynedd, who went to sea with three hundred men in ten ships, and it is not known to what place they went.

Iolo's intent was to 'confirm' Powel's 10 ships. He also invents the 300 men. The 'not known' land was intended to create the belief that the triad was pre-Columbus, but he forged it about 300 years later.

Later accretions to the story
To simplify matters the table below gives some of the many accretions to the Madoc story. Later writers felt unconstrained by considerations of truth but were simply intent on consolidating the story.

Accretions to the Madoc story

Account	Depart	Visit	Date	No. ships	No. crew	Welsh words
Llwyd	Ireland?	America:	-	-	-	No
1559		non specific	-	-	-	
Other: Large cross on Cozumel island						
Dee	Ireland?	America:	1170	-	-	No
1578		non specific	-	-	-	
Other: Dee infers the 1170 date from Owain's death						
Peckham	Coast of	Mexico	1170	-	-	Yes
1583	England		-	-	-	
Other: gives Montezuma's speech						
Lhoyd/Powel	South from	Mexico	1170	-	-	Yes
1584	Ireland		-	10	-	
Other: refers to Montezuma's speech						
Raleigh	-	All parts of	1164	-	-	No
1595		America	1170	-	-	
Other: No evidence for 1164 date; refers to Montezuma's speech						
Howell	Milford	West Indies	1062	-	-	Yes
1630	Haven		-	-	-	
Other: Madoc's tombstone in West Indies; 1062 is before Norman conquest						
Herbert	-	Land in Gulf	1170	-	120	Yes
1634, 1638		of Mexico	-	10	-	
Other: gives Montezuma's speech; Edwall and Eneon went						
Williams	-	Nth America	1170	-	-	Yes
1792		and Mexico	-	-	-	
Other: refers to Montezuma's speech; Welsh Indians; commander of fleet; Riryd went						
Morgan	-	Mexico	1160	8	-	No
1857			1164	18	3000	
Other: Took throne of Mexico; commander of fleet						

As can be seen, from Peckham onwards, the stories changed radically from the simple accounts of Llwyd and Dee. In 1595 Walter Raleigh wrote to Queen Elizabeth from the island of Trinidad. His letter takes the political stance that Madoc had made notable discoveries over all parts of the American continent. He invents an earlier date of 1164 for the first voyage making Madoc sail 6 years before Owain died, thus ignoring the very reason that others used to motivate his sailing, to escape from his brothers' fighting.[35]

James Howell takes a different approach. In a letter to Earl Rivers dated 9 August 1630 he makes the astonishing claim that Madoc's tombstone is in the West Indies, inscribed with his epitaph. This is nonsense and probably reflects one of the partisan tales circulating about Madoc. Howell had little knowledge of Owain Gwynedd and dates Madoc's journey to 1062, about 40 years before Owain was born. He also thought that Madoc's brother, David, was the Prince of south Wales (rather than north Wales) and hence makes Madoc depart from Milford Haven in southwest Wales.[36]

In a later letter to Howel Gwyn he gives the epitaph in Welsh and English, probably taken from Herbert (1638). The four lines are a corrupted version of lines from Maredudd ap Rhys which were well known to the Tudor scholars. The terrible English translation, which rhymes in English, bears little resemblance to the Welsh meaning. This verse is discussed in a later section.[37]

> Madoc ap Owen was I call'd,
> Strong, tall and comely, not inthrall'd
> With home-bred pleasure, but for Fame
> Thro' Land and Sea I sought the same.

Thomas Herbert in his *Travels* (1634, 1638) uses Powel's 10 ships and invents the figure that Madoc left 120 men there to mind the colony. He then describes the second voyage. He states that (1) they managed to find their way back to the colony; (2) that many of the Britons were dead; (3) that they had been killed by the natives or died from the different climate; (4) that with the aid of his brothers Edwall and Eneon, Madoc improved the colony beyond their initial intentions; and (5) that they lived there contentedly and died there. As no one from the colony returned to Wales to relate this detail it is evident that Sir Thomas created this information from his imagination.[38]

John Williams in his *Farther Observations* (1792) shows how the Madoc stories were developing. The Welsh Indians were now of vital importance and he relates the stories of witnesses who met them and conversed with them in Welsh. In some accounts the Welsh Indians produced Welsh Bibles or books that they had kept from long ago but could no longer read. He includes Montezuma's speech and the claim that his ancestors were Welsh. So the Madoc colonists had spread widely, including Mexico and much of northern America. Williams was also a blatant fabricator. He created the fiction that Madoc was commander of Owain's fleet, one so powerful that it defeated the fleet of Henry II. He used this fiction to explain how Madoc was able to bypass the building of ships and speedily depart for America.[39]

Williams takes Riryd from Lhoyd and Powel (1584) and fabricates yet another scenario (citing Brechfa) that Riryd went with Madoc on a second voyage.[40]

> It is said by Ieuan Brechfa, a Bard who flourished about the Year 1480, that Rhiryd, an illegitimate Son of Owen Gwynedd, who, Dr Powel says was Lord of Clochran in Ireland, accompained Madog across the Atlantic (Morwerydd) to some Lands they had found there, and there dwelt. There can be no doubt, therefore, but that some Irish went with Madog to America.

Neither Riryd nor Madoc have been found in the writings of Ieuan Brechfa, despite the extensive searches by Welsh scholars, including those of Thomas Stephens in 1858.

Richard Morgan (1857) in his *British Kymry* repeats the delusion that Madoc was commander of his father's fleet. He also invents dates for the voyages (1160 and 1164), number of ships (8 and 18) and a crew number for the second voyage (3000), unconcerned by figures from earlier accounts. He also states that Madoc took the throne of Mexico but doesn't mention the Welsh Indians.[41]

It's incredible that the bards who knew Owain and his sons, Gerald who knew their history and talked to the sons and grandsons, and the monks nearby who recorded notable events, knew nothing of a Madoc ap Owain Gwynedd. The great Welsh historian, John Lloyd, does not include Madoc as a son in Owain's family tree. If Madoc did exist he was utterly insignificant. Yet from nothing, from just an eagerness to believe, a myth kept growing as shown in the table. Gwyn Williams (1979) rightly remarks of the myth:[42]

> At the heart of the Madoc myth, at its very origins, there is therefore a certain contradiction, an initial blankness.

The Irish Forebears of Owain Gwynedd

Owain's grandfather, Cynan, married Ragnaillt, the Irish daughter of Olaf, who was the son of Sitriuc Silkenbeard (Charles-Edwards, 2013 and Jones, 1910). Cynan was the son of Iago, the north Wales Prince, but when his father was deposed and killed by Gruffydd ap Llywelyn he had to flee to Ireland. He made two attempts to claim the north Wales throne but each time was forced to return to Ireland, as told in Llwyd's *Cronica*. Olaf was apparently a Viking. Cynan's son Gruffydd, born in Ireland, (not the above Gruffydd ap Llywelyn) did reclaim north Wales and was the father of Owain Gwynedd. If Madoc were a son of Owain Gwynedd then he had distant Viking relations.[43]

A second possible Irish connection is that Humphrey Llwyd names Riryd as a son of Owain and states that he was Lord of Clochran in Ireland but there is no previous Irish material that says this. Meredith Hanmer in his *Chronicle of Ireland* gets his information from Lhoyd and Powel which gives no source. Hanmer assumes that Riryd came into this Irish title by marrying a royal Irish woman.[44]

These Irish relations have been used to support the arguments for Madoc's journeys to America as the Vikings were able sailors. Llwyd's account could be interpreted as Madoc leaving from Ireland or could be interpreted as just passing the north of Ireland, either north or south. However if Madoc and Riryd did live in Ireland then they were already safe and distant from the fighting of Owain's sons. The very reason for them sailing west to escape the fighting is negated. They could live in peace in Ireland away from the north Wales strife.

Another argument is that Madoc, with Viking relations, may have gained knowledge of the Norse *Vinland* (de Costa, 1891) but there is no evidence for this and it is never raised in the Tudor accounts as motivating the sailing. The Viking connection leads nowhere. It relies on the assumption that Madoc was Owain Gwynedd's son. Yet in the crucial early sources there is no evidence that such a Madoc existed. Thus the Irish connections do not apply and cannot be used unless it is first established that Madoc was Owain's son. The Viking link is again raised in a 1966 book *Madoc and the Discovery of America* by Richard Deacon which seems to present new material. Unfortunately these have now been shown as misleading fabrications.[45]

THE POEM OF MAREDUDD AP RHYS

As there was nothing on a Madoc ap Owain Gwynedd in early poetry, his advocates relied heavily on four lines in a poem by Maredudd ap Rhys (c. 1480). Both Thomas Stephens and Gwyn Williams thought that these lines showed evidence of a Madoc tradition as a sailor. After finding nothing in the early bards, Stephens examined a six line section on Madoc which he obtained from the *Iolo Manuscripts*. The first four lines are based on a translation by Paul Russell (2018) and lines 5-6 by Stephens (1893).

> 1 Madoc the bold, of ample appearance,
> 2 proper whelp of Owain Gwynedd.
> 3 He did not desire land, my soul was he,
> 4 nor great possessions, but only the seas.
> 5 I am a Madoc to my age and to his passion
> 6 for the seas have I been accustomed.

Stephens commented that 'Here we evidently have a Madoc tradition; and it will be well to bear it in mind'.[46]

Similarly, Gwyn Williams after finding nothing on Madoc in the early material says 'We are left with one poet, Maredudd ap Rhys'. He notes Stephens' belief in a tradition and then speculates on Flemish material, in particular, a work called *Madoc* that was composed by the Willem who wrote *Reynard the Fox*. This work on Madoc is lost but Williams was deceived by Deacon (1966), a modern-day Iolo, who fabricated a story that a copy of a French manuscript of the work had been found in Poitiers in the 1600s and that a local scholar had judged it to belong to the 1300s or even earlier. The source for these details was an Edouard Duvivier but searches have found no trace of Duvivier or the manuscript. More will be said on Deacon later.[47]

Further, Williams was deceived by Iolo Morganwg himself. In the late 1700s Iolo had interpolated the two extra lines (5-6 above) into the poem to bolster the material on Madoc. They do not appear in the manuscript used by Enid Roberts (2003) who presents the entire poem in Welsh. Williams did not realize that they had been forged by Morganwg and actually quotes line 5 as the evidence that suggests the existence of a Madoc tradition. Lines 5-6 should be ignored.[48]

The four Madoc lines are a 1500s interpolation

It is depressing to observe the deceptions about Madoc. Unfortunately to add to these it will now be argued that lines 1-4, on which so many arguments for Madoc's historical existence rely, are a post-Columbian interpolation into the poem, inserted some time in the early 1500s. The poem is the second one of two related poems. In the first poem, Maredudd is begging his patron Ifan (Evan) for the gift of a fishing net. In the second poem, Maredudd is thanking Ifan for his generous gift of the net. From the mundane activity of the poet using his net to fish along riverbanks or beaches, an incongruous comparison is made between the poet and the deeds of Madoc exploring the seas.

Excluding the Morganwg forged lines, the poem comprises 54 lines but to present the argument it is sufficient to give only a few lines preceding the Madoc lines (the latter in italics) and the following lines to the poem's end. To give clarity, the Welsh lines must be given so that scholars can check the translation. The Welsh is that given in Enid Roberts (2003) in which some of the lines differ slightly from those in the *Iolo Manuscripts*.[49]

> Helied Ifan, hael dyfiad
> Ar ei dir teg wir dre tad.
> Mewn awr dda minnau ar ddŵr,
> O fodd hael, a fydd heliwr.
>
> *Madog wych, mwyedig wedd,*
> *Iawn genau Owain Gwynedd,*
> *Ni fynnai dir, f'enaid oedd,*
> *Na da mawr ond y moroedd.*
>
> Minnau rhodiaf hyd yr afon
> Ar hyd eu gro a rhwyd gron.
> Gwell bod yn wraig pysgodwr
> Na'r rhai nid elai i'r dŵr.
> Pedr, mawr ei hap ydoedd,
> Pysgodwr, oreugwr oedd.
> I'r un helwriaeth yr af,
> Mwy no Phedr mi ni pheidaf.

An approximate English translation is given below.

Let Ifan, increasingly generous, hunt
upon his fair land, his true patrimony.
In a suitable hour I also on water,
with the goodwill of the generous one, will be a hunter.

Madoc the bold, of ample appearance,
proper whelp of Owain Gwynedd.
He did not desire land, my soul was he,
nor great possessions but only the seas.

I will walk by sea and river
along the strand with my circled net.
It is better to be the wife of a fisherman
than of one who wouldn't go to the water.
Peter, great was his fortune,
was a fisherman, the best of men.
To the same pursuit will I go,
more than Peter I will not cease.

Maredudd begins by referring to his patron, Ifan, the generous one, hunting on the lands that he had inherited from his father. Thanks to the gift of the fishing net, the poet will also be a hunter, but on water as a fisherman. Here the flow of the text is abruptly interrupted by the Madoc lines which look like an interpolation. If they were removed, then 'will be a hunter' would naturally be followed by 'I will walk by sea and river...'. The latter completes the meaning of 'be a hunter' showing that he will hunt for fish with his new net along the beaches and riverbanks. In the unlikely case that the Madoc lines were in the original poem, it would show unintentional poetic *bathos*, where the poet praises the famous Madoc of great ancestry, sailing the seas, and implies that he is like him – by the triviality of walking along a beach or river to fish.

A second concern is the use of the 'proper' whelp of Owain. If it were well known, when Maredudd wrote, that Madoc was Owain's son, one would expect him to just say 'Madoc ap Owain Gwynedd' similar to his earlier reference to his patron as 'Ifan ap Tudor'. He does not refer to Ifan as the 'proper' or 'true' whelp of Tudor in praising him. The use of 'proper' with Madoc suggests it wasn't written by Maredudd but that the author of the lines was an advocate. He was presenting a view he wanted to reinforce, that Madoc was Owain's son. Contrast this overkill with the understated comparison to St Peter in the last four lines, a much better example as he actually was a fisherman.

A third concern is the reference to Madoc's appearance. Under the assumption he existed, it would have been 300 years before the time of Maredudd and he would have had no idea what Madoc looked like. It again looks like the line was inserted by a Madoc booster. Maredudd didn't give the appearance of his patron, Ifan. The inane reference to Madoc's appearance has no relevance to his alleged sailing. It's just part of a forger's effort to create a historical reality for him.

A fourth concern is the association between the disparate concepts of '*sailing to explore*' to '*fishing on land*'. The bard says nothing about sailing on the ocean to fish or explore. He fishes from a riverbank or beach. Maredudd couldn't afford a net, having to beg for one, so he certainly couldn't afford a boat. It's also hard to believe that Maredudd wrote '*my soul was he*' after saying Madoc '*did not desire land*'. This implication that the poet did not desire land is absurd as he happily lived and fished on land. The Madoc lines are an incongruous fit for Maredudd's situation. It implies that he did not write them.

Llwyd in his 1559 *Cronica Walliae* notes the many fables on Madoc that were in existence at that time. It seems that a Madoc advocate interpolated four extra lines in an attempt to provide a pre-Columbian authority to the body of fables that were circulating.[50]

Further developments regarding the Madoc lines

The first Madoc line begins 'Madoc wych...' where a suitable meaning of *wych* is 'bold'. But the Madoc fervour caused the repeated copying of the four lines, resulting in a scribal error where *wych* became *wyf*, which completely alters the meaning. 'Madoc the bold' then became 'I am Madoc', where Madoc is speaking in the first person. Thus lines 1-2 are now in the first person but lines 3-4 are in the third person, an unrealistic change. This will be called the corrupted version.

Paul Russell (2018) notes that Dee knew this corrupted version and wrote it at the end of a manuscript on the Latin life of Gruffudd ap Cynan, who would have been Madoc's grandfather if Madoc was a son of Owain. That Dee had presumably read Gruffudd's life shows he was trying to research Madoc's history. Russell states that these four lines existed independently of the poem, appearing in this form in at least six manuscripts dating to the 1600s. John Dee presented *Of Famous and Rich Discoveries* to Elizabeth I in August 1578 (MacMillan, 2004) and it seems likely that he knew the verse before this date. In 1583 he was off to Prague and not concerned with Madoc. As Dee knew about the corrupted verse before 1578 then the uncorrupted verse in the full poem must have existed before this, probably in the first half of the 1500s after Columbus' voyages were well known. The corrupted verse was known to Tudor scholars and it was these Welsh lines that James Howell states were on Madoc's tombstone in the West Indies.[51]

Deio ap Ieuan Du: Lament for Jenkin ap Maredudd

Another poem used to claim that Madoc was a sailor before Columbus was composed by Deio ap Ieuan Du, a Cardiganshire poet in the late 1400s. Jenkin was the son of Maredudd of Tywyn. The poem relates that Jenkin was taken prisoner at sea by French pirates and the 'poet' idiotically boasts that, had he been a sailor, he would have put to sea, *like Madoc*, presumably to try to rescue Jenkin.

> fal Madog, marchog y medd,
> baun gwyn, fab Owain Gwynedd.
> Y gŵr siwrneio a gai,
> ar foroedd yr arferai.

> like Madoc, knight of the mead,
> fair peacock, son of Owain Gwynedd.
> The man who journeyed,
> his haunts were the seas.

In a lament for a dead son, the insensitive boast does not belong. It is doubtful the grieving relatives and friends, some of whom may have been sailors, would have taken kindly to the fatuous boast had it been part of the eulogy. It is an inept interpolation to portray Madoc as a sailor. The 'knight of the mead' tells us nothing, put in so that *medd* rhymes with Gwynedd and the 'fair peacock' is yet another pointless reference to Madoc's appearance. The manuscript (NLW MS 6511B) is dated to 1560–1699, allowing a forger to insert a section in the early 1500s. Eleri Davies (1992) gives the poem in Welsh.[52]

RICHARD DEACON'S BOOK

In 1966 Richard Deacon wrote a book on Madoc which was outwardly impressive as it seemed to comprehensively cover the usual material and even introduce new material. It was also well written in contrast to the mind-numbing prose of some historical works. The author was a journalist named Donald McCormick, Richard Deacon being his pseudonym. It wasn't fully known at the time but Deacon displayed a creativity in fabricating new material that rivalled Iolo Morganwg. This new material was often startling, which if true, would greatly bolster the case for Madoc's discovery of America. Over the years there were critics who had suspicions about Deacon but these did not fully surface until a book edited by Leeson (2014) exposed his limitations not only in the Madoc book but in his other works. My view is that nothing he says in presenting new material can be trusted.[53]

His book was reviewed in 1968 by the acute scholar E. D. Jones of the National Library of Wales. Jones was an expert in the early Welsh contemporary material and made the following comment.[54]

> After reading the seventeen chapters, one cannot fail to marvel at the amount of blatant deception, wishful thinking, and human gullibility which went to the making of this legend over the course of four centuries.

When Jones made this comment he thought that Deacon was honestly sifting the evidence for Madoc. He merely thought that Deacon was incompetent in Welsh, incompetent in Latin and too trusting in some cases in accepting certain evidence. Having an expert knowledge of the early Welsh evidence, or the lack of it, Jones was not impressed by Deacon's arguments but was intrigued by new evidence that Deacon had presented. In his summing up Jones states:[55]

> Of all this material, the only manuscript I would like to see published in full is the French precis of 'Madoc', by Willem the Minstrel. This is an important piece of evidence for the early existence of the legend and calls for a close study.

This manuscript did not exist. It was Deacon's invention.

For laypeople unfamiliar with the Welsh material and seeking a reliable guide to the evidence for the Madoc claims, Deacon's book is a dangerous trap. He wrote in a confident style to give the positive case for Madoc using a mass of unreliable data, difficult to check due to his very poor referencing. His misinformation is cleverly presented and expressed so confidently that it looks convincing. In addition to his journalism he wrote around 50 books (see Spence, 2014) giving the impression that he was not too concerned with checking his content with original source material. Robert Leeson (2014) gives some views of eminent scholars on one of his books *The British Connection*.[56]

A. J. P. Taylor, eminent historian
'*No more preposterous book has ever been written*'.

P. Noel-Baker, Professor of International Relations, London University
'*grotesque and ridiculous*'.

E. P. Thompson, eminent historian
'*warmed-up fourth-hand crap*'.

Thompson's words are apt for Deacon's book on Madoc. The sections below show his poor Welsh, his ignorance of key texts, his resorting to imaginary 'authorities' to present false details, his heavy use of fake material, his use of imaginary 'experts' to justify his fake dates, his use of forgers and partisans rather than scholars and his elaborate hoaxes. Despite his poor Welsh he denigrates the work of Thomas Stephens, a noted scholar. *Elegy for the Warband of Owain Gwynedd*, discussed earlier, uses the word *mur*. It means 'wall' or 'bulwark' and the latter is given by Stephens, but Deacon prefers the work of a forger.

A major issue for Madoc advocates is that the verse does not refer to the sea. In 1803 one of Morganwg's cronies, William Owen Pughe, had fudged the line by replacing *mur* by *myr* (seas) in the stanza in his Welsh dictionary, to portray Madoc as a sailor. Deacon presents this blatant falsehood as a 'rival translation' and the disagreement as an 'academic argument'. Jones agrees with Stephens and says that the alteration is 'entirely unwarranted'. Deacon actually knows this from his familiarity with Jones (1965) but it does not fit his intended conclusion that Madoc discovered America, so he ignores it.[57]

Deacon then foolishly tries to discredit Stephens as follows:[58]

> Stephens not only accepted this most unimpressive translation but quite unnecessarily wrote into it after the words 'swelling rage', the verb 'was slain'.

But all Deacon has done is to show his ignorance. The verb 'was slain' (*llas*) is in the Welsh line but not where he expects it as the word order in Welsh is different to English. This Madoc was slain in Wales and therefore could not have discovered America.

A few pages later Deacon blunders twice. In the fake lines that were interpolated into Maredudd, he gives both the Welsh and English of Stephens but includes two extra lines in the English.[59]

> Madoc am I, who throughout my life will seek,
> Upon the water, that which I have been used to.

These lines are not in the Welsh. He then attempts to clinch his earlier 'academic argument' that the *mur* should be *myr* but blunders again when using a fake line interpolated into Maredudd.

> *na da mawr ond y moroedd.*
> nor great possessions but only the seas.

In this line, Welsh *mawr* is the adjective 'great' and *moroedd* means 'seas'. However Deacon is not familiar with the common Welsh word *mawr* and makes his horrible blunder.[60]

> In previous odes one has noted the argument about *mur* and *myr* – bulwark or seas: here there can be no room for doubt, as the translation of *mawr* is clearly 'seas'. If one accepts this indisputable translation in the ode of Maredudd, it is then probable that Cynddelw referred to seas and not a wall or bulwark.

His poor knowledge of Welsh contrasts with his certainty: 'there can be no room for doubt' and 'this indisputable translation'. It puts many of his conclusions in doubt, on top of his Morganwg-type fabrications. His use of *mawr* to decide between *mur* and *myr* is laughable, and like a dreadful movie that is so bad it can be watched as a comedy, this example sticks in the mind as a warning.

Reliance on modern 'inventive' sources

Deacon's book is full of details that are not in scholarly works. A naïve reaction is to be impressed by these details but the reason scholars do not mention them is that they are the deceptive inventions of Madoc advocates. For example, he claims that 'some authorities' list Brenda as a wife or concubine of Owain Gwynedd but that it could be 'bardic hearsay'. He then states positively that Arthur Rhys names Brenda as Madoc's mother but doesn't say who Rhys is, giving the impression he was one of these 'authorities' and an early bard. But his endnote shows that his source is worthless, a modern partisan pamphlet: *Did Prince Madoc Discover America?* by A. Rhys, Chicago, 1938.[61]

He then says a genealogy *'quoting contemporary sources'* such as the Conwy Abbey annals gives Madoc's wife as Annesta and daughter as Gwenllian. But his endnote has nothing on 'contemporary sources'. His 'ibid.' directs us to the previous rubbish – 'pamphlet by A. Rhys, Chicago, 1938'. This fake genealogy is yet another worthless invention. Thompson's earlier colourful assessment is spot on.[62]

Remarks on the validity of texts he has never read

Deacon says that both the *Brut y Tywysogion* and *Annales Cambriae* provide details on Owain Gwynedd's wives and mistresses, but in his view these details in the Brut are *'apt to be faulty'* whereas those in the Annales are *'more accurate'*. He didn't know that Owain's wives and mistresses are not mentioned at all in either the Brut or Annales. His inane remarks are made without knowledge of either text which casts grave doubts about all other statements he makes.[63]

Creating an extra son for Owain Gwynedd

Deacon gives another fake genealogy that includes Madoc as Owain's son, based on 'many authorities'. Owain's first son was Iowerth whose blemished nose prevented him from ruling. The Welsh for the blemish is *drwyndwn* where *drwyn* is 'nose' and *dwn* (→ *twn*) means 'broken'. Iowerth is often called Iowerth Drwyndwn, but Deacon's sloppy work leads to a remarkable discovery – a hitherto unknown son of Owain Gwynedd. In his genealogy he lists Iowerth as the first son, Drwyndwn as the second son, Howel as the third son and so on, thus creating an additional son for Owain called 'broken nose'.[64]

DEACON'S FABRICATIONS ABOUT LUNDY ISLAND

Deacon made much use of a modern bard using the name 'Meiron' who wrote c. 1800 in the midst of Madoc fervour as a Madoc partisan. In his review of Deacon's book, E. D. Jones summed up Meiron.[65]

> If 'Meiron' was responsible for all the additions to Ieuan Brechfa quoted in this book, through J. Morgan Lewis, he cannot have been the least among the forgers and purveyors of forgeries who thrived on Madoc.

It was Meiron who introduced the idea that Madoc sailed from Lundy Island in the Bristol Channel, in the *Monthly Magazine* of December 1796. He states that Madoc and Riryd, in a second journey, left from Lundy Island in 7 ships. To create supporting material for Meiron's claim, Deacon invents 'evidence' for Lundy in a series of fabrications. He begins with a Joan Dane who wrote a novel on Madoc in 1909. He claims she had 'heard mention' of Madoc having an island retreat off the coast of Wales from where he planned his expedition to America. Deacon presents this farcical 'heard mention' as a 'vital clue'.[66]

Fabrication of archive manuscripts on Lundy
He then proceeds through a series of invented evidence which has been exposed by Howard Kimberley (2014). Deacon claims that (1) the archives on Lundy recorded that 'an emissarie of the Prince of Gwynet landed at Lund[y] to seek aide against Henrie of Englande' and that (2) this evidence was supported by the existence of Welsh manuscripts in the archives of Lundy. These documents never existed.[67]

Fabrication that Geraint sailed from Lundy
To boost Lundy's importance, he uses Triad 14 on Three Seafarers of Britain, one being Geraint son of Erbin (Bromwich, 2006). However Morganwg had forged an extra line in the Triad in which each sailor had 120 ships with 120 men on each ship. This became Triad 68 in his notorious Third Series. Unaware of this forgery, Deacon adds his own fabrication. He refers to Geraint as Geraint of Devonshire who was one of the three seamen with six score ships and six score men in each. His fabrication is that Geraint sailed from Lundy.[68]

Fabrications about a Lundy manuscript mentioning Madoc

Deacon claims that a 'faded manuscript' found on Lundy in the 1800s has a poem in which baby Madoc was cast adrift in a coracle and that he later became skilful at sailing it. Deacon says it dates to the 1400s or earlier but doesn't name the 'expert' who dated it. He falsely claims that the poem is cited in the Gwydir papers. The Lundy MS is unknown to scholars and there is no doubt that it never existed.[69]

Fabrication of Lundy Stone mentioning Madoc

After fabricating Lundy archives about a non-existent 'emissarie of the Prince of Gwynet' he declares that this could be Madoc. He then begins a hoax worthy of Morganwg. He says that a Lundy load of granite, sent to Barnstaple in 1865, included a worn tablet in old-style Welsh that translates as: 'It is an established fact, known far and wide, that Madoc ventured far out on the Western Ocean, never to return.' He says that 'experts' dated it to the 1300s but as one of the 'old-style' Welsh words was 'invented' in the 1800s by forger W. Owen Pughe, it is clear that these unnamed 'experts' and the tablet didn't exist.[70]

He claimed his source was: 'letter to the author by Mr D. G. Evans, Bristol, July 4, 1963'. Great efforts were made to find the stone and Mr D. G. Evans but they were never found. When asked for the letter by sceptical archaeologist, Keith Gardner, Deacon could not produce it. The Devon records and Barnstaple Museum knew nothing of such a stone. On 24 July 1967 the *Bristol Evening Post* told the story and asked for details on the identity of D. G. Evans or the inscribed stone. No response was forthcoming. Deacon had made it all up.[71]

DEACON'S FABRICATIONS REGARDING REV. SYNNOTT

To support Meiron's claim that Madoc and Riryd had made a second trip to America, Deacon created a fabrication using a real person, the Rev. E. F. Synnott. He was born in 1870 in Ireland and was learned, obtaining the Master of Arts and Bachelor of Divinity degrees. In 1914 he came to Rusper in West Sussex with his wife to become the vicar. He was a strong personality and was Low Church but after a good start, he alienated the conservative villagers. Rumours and slander were rife about his doings and complaints were made to the Bishop, leading to his trial on a charge of serious misconduct. He was found not guilty. As a result, he wrote *Five Years in Hell in a Country Parish* (1920). Deacon begins his hoax by saying that Synnott bought some charred, mould-infected manuscripts in the village of Rye. He was vague about the date, saying it was 'several years ago'. As his book came out in 1966, one would expect the purchase to have been about 1960, but Synnott had died aged 76 on 16 March 1946. Had the sale really occurred it would have been well before his death, when he was active. The timing doesn't work. It's another of Deacon's hoaxes where he is the only one to know of faded manuscripts, ancient archives, mould-infected manuscripts, a worn tablet etc., all giving new data, which scholars can never find. His selection of Synnott meant his story could not be contradicted as Synnott had died 20 years earlier.[72]

Fabrication of Inventory of Missing Ships

Deacon claims that one of Synnott's manuscripts was an inventory of missing ships from 1166-1183, with Madoc's ship listed as the Guignon Gorn (Gwennan Gorn) and Riryd's ship as Pedr Sant (St Peter), for the date 1171. He says that next to 'Pedr Sant' there was the sign of the cross and an indecipherable word which led him to believe that Riryd's ship had sunk and that the cross had been placed there by the compiler of the inventory to indicate that it was lost at sea.[73]

However Deacon didn't think it through with his fabrication. From Meiron, he had argued that Madoc and Riryd had sailed from Lundy on the *second voyage*. If so, then the ships departed, were never seen again, and it was assumed they reached America. How then did the compiler of the inventory of missing ships know that Riryd's ship had sunk? No one returned from America to tell him.

Had a bona fide inventory really existed, the learned Synnott would have sent it to experts to analyze its writing surface and ink. It would have been a huge newspaper scoop for Deacon, attracting worldwide scrutiny – tangible proof of Madoc. He would have written stories on it, with photos of it, and his role in interpreting it. He would surely have put its photo in his book. It would have been far more important than the 22 illustrations he did include. As none of this occurred, it is clear that the manuscript never existed.

DEACON'S FABRICATIONS ON WILLEM THE MINSTREL

Like Iolo Morganwg, Deacon excelled in taking paltry material used to argue for Madoc and blending it with other fabricated material to give apparent depth to the evidence. In the case of Willem the Minstrel, his fabrications completely deceived the knowledgeable Gwyn Williams into thinking there was an early Madoc tradition in spite of the fact that Williams could find no contemporary evidence at all that a Madoc son of Owain Gwynedd ever existed.

Willem was a Flemish author who wrote *Reynard the Fox*. In it he says he also wrote a book on Madoc: 'Willem die Madocke makede' (Willem the author of Madoc). Unfortunately, his Madoc work is lost. Another Flemish author, Jacob van Maerlant, wrote his *Rijmbijbel* in 1271, a huge serious work on secular and biblical history in verse. He was thoroughly familiar with the Arthurian romances and had written works on Merlin and the Holy Grail. However in his large serious work *Rijmbijbel* he is apparently referring to Willem's book on Madoc when he made the comment (here given in English translation) that in his own book:[74]

> ... there would be no Madoc's dream, neither Reynard's nor Arthur's pranks.

It seems to indicate that Willem's *Madoc* was a light-hearted work, possibly containing satirical elements. This all that is known about Willem's *Madoc*. There is a fundamental assumption that this Madoc was the same as the Madoc son of Owain Gwynedd who circa 1170 was thought to have discovered America. However this identification is not raised in early material. It was not raised by Peckham, Powel, Howell, Herbert, or John Williams who would have seized upon it had it been an early identification. In 1837 this late claim was made by Delepierre according to Gwyn Williams (1979). However there is a more likely candidate for the identity of Willem's Madoc as Arthur himself had a brother called Madoc and this was probably known to the Flemings who had been settled in southwest Wales. When the burgeoning tales about Arthur travelled back to Flanders, the knowledge of his brother may have travelled with them.[75]

There is a six line poem in the Book of Taliesin on Arthur's brother whose wording has affinities to the comment of Jacob van Maerlant. It is called *Madawc Drut* (Madoc the Brave). Marged Haycock (2007) gives the translation below.[76]

1 **Madawc, mur menwyt.**
   Madog, protector of happiness.
2 **Madawc, kyn bu bed,**
   Madog, before he was in the grave,
3 **bu dinas edryssed**
   was a citadel of prowess
4 **o gamp a chymwed.**
   through feat and jest.
5 **Mab Vthyr cyn lleas,**
   Before the son of Uthr was slain,
6 **o'e law dywystlas.**
   he pledged himself by his hand.

Arthur's brother Madoc was known for his feats and jesting (line 4) which were a characteristic of Willem's works which involved 'pranks' from Reynard and Arthur. As the Flemings were a major source of transmission of Arthurian material it is not unlikely that his brother was introduced to add variety to the tales.

A massive problem with Willem's Madoc being Owain Gwynedd's son is that contemporary north Wales witnesses who met the men who would have been his brothers, had he existed, say nothing about him. It is remarkable that such a Madoc is never mentioned and thus it is inconceivable that distant southwest Wales, c. 1200, had any tales at all of a Madoc ap Owain Gwynedd to transmit to the continent.

Fabrication of Willem's Madoc manuscript
In this outrageous fabrication Deacon claims that Willem's long-lost work on Madoc had been found in the 1600s, in a French manuscript. The crucial details of who found the manuscript and who held it for 400 years are ignored and there were no academic accounts of this find which suggests a hoax. His fake source was Edouard Duvivier of Poitiers who 'wrote' to him in December 1965 and who dated the manuscript to the 1300s or earlier, suspiciously in line with Deacon's Madoc claims. It seems that Duvivier was the only one who knew

about it but there is no explanation of how he knew of it when scholars didn't, or why he would even write to Deacon, a non scholar whose book had not yet been published. To complete his hoax, Deacon thanks Duvivier in his Acknowledgements 'for his fascinating contribution on Willem the Minstrel'. Deacon says it was a précis of *Madoc* in medieval French. The 'contents' of course agree with his Lundy claims and say that Madoc's grandfather was 'half a Viking' and refer to a 'garden' in the sea (Sargasso Sea). These 'contents' won't be discussed here as the manuscript didn't exist. Gwyn Williams (1979) was badly deceived by Deacon and called it the 'most riveting evidence'. But the experts at Poitiers University knew nothing of such a manuscript. Kimberley (2104) sums up the results of their enquiries.[77]

> Poitiers University have been unable to trace any record of the above manuscripts or, indeed, the existence of a M. Edouard Duvivier.

E. D. Jones had called for the manuscript to be published. Deacon had ample opportunity in the next 30 years to provide a witnessed photo or photocopy of it. Like all his sources for his new claims, it was never made available to scholars. In the 57 years from when his book was first published to the present day not one of his new sources has been found. Duvivier and the manuscript had never existed.[78]

WHAT CAUSED LLWYD TO BELIEVE IN MADOC?

Humphrey Llwyd was the first to write a simple account of Madoc's two voyages to America and give the fables that were circulating some authority. Dee simply followed him and added the circa 1170 date from his knowledge of Owain Gwynedd. From then on, strongly partisan accounts with unsourced accretions took over. It is interesting to speculate on what caused Llwyd to believe in Madoc although the true answer will probably never be known.

Relating Madoc to Owain Gwynedd

The fables had Madoc as Owain's son and this may have derived from *Elegy for the Warband of Owain Gwynedd*. The meaning of *teulu* has broadened from 'warband' to 'family' and at some stage the belief that *teulu* meant 'family' may have caused some to regard Madoc as one of

Owain's sons. When this belief became common is unknown. If this belief later became detached from the poem then the poem's telling of Madoc's death in Wales may have been forgotten. We are dealing here with what people may have thought rather than the reality.

Madoc as a Sailor

So far there is no link of this courageous warband warrior to the sea. However Madoc was not an uncommon name and there may have been other Madocs who were known as skilled at sailing off the coast of Wales. One of these Madocs was remembered in a local tradition to explain a feature of the waters near Bardsey Island.

This tradition was recorded in 1582. It involved the name *Ffrydiau Caswennan* (currents of Gwennan's Bane), rough waters in Bardsey Sound, east of Bardsey Island. *Caswennan* is a compound from *cas* and *gwennan* where *cas* means 'hated' and *gwennan* refers to the white spume of the waters. *Ffrydiau* means swift current. It is possible that a real sailor named Madoc had damaged his boat in these wild waters and this was locally remembered.

The 1582 tale was created to explain the name of the rough waters. It uses the belief that boats would sink if they contained iron nails that were attracted to magnetic rocks under the water, which would create a vortex. Stag horns were used instead of nails in boat construction. In this tale Madoc built his boat like this and called it *Gorn Gwennan* (white horn) which becomes *Gwennan Gorn* with the adjective placed first. The tale says that this is the reason the sea is called *Ffrydiau Caswennan*, a false explanation. Edward ap John Wynn who told the story to the scribe believed the tradition was quite old. This tale in its original form could have been pre-Columbian.[79]

Equating the two Madocs

So far we have a belief that a warrior Madoc was the son of Owain Gwynedd from one source and that a Madoc was a skilful sailor around Bardsey from another source, possibly from different time periods. As Bardsey was in Gwynedd it would not be hard for a later antiquary to equate the two Madocs, creating a Madoc ap Owain Gwynedd who was a skilled sailor. It's possible that this was done before Columbus.

After Columbus made his Voyages

The Welsh Tudors came to power in 1485 when Henry VII defeated Richard III at the Battle of Bosworth Field. After America was known the British initially made voyages to the north, John Cabot being the first in 1497. Welsh patriotism and a desperation to claim a stake in America led to elaborations in the Madoc fables. By 1582 this Madoc was called Madoc ab Owain Gwynedd and he now was said to have sailed to foreign lands, these two features being part of the tale told by Edward ap John Wynn. While this is speculation, such a process could have created a Madoc who was the seed from which the fables grew.

What may have persuaded Llwyd?

Williams (1979) was interested in this question and states that Llwyd was one of the early scholars who had initiated the scientific study of placenames and would have had no truck with the 'linguistic fantasies' of David Ingram who claimed that Welsh words could be detected in the natives' languages. These claims were used by Peckham, Powel, Howell, Herbert and Williams as shown in the earlier table.[80]

However both Llwyd and the Spanish were impressed by the large cross on Cozumel Island and reports of Christian-like ceremonies, but he cross is not unique to Christianity. Williams notes that for some Indians the cross represents the Four Houses of the Sky. Near Tarlton, Ohio the Native Americans, probably Hopewell, built a large earthen mound in the shape of a cross (Squier and Davis, 1848).[81]

Another element that may have helped persuade him was the four line 'verse' of Maredudd ap Rhys which John Dee had in the corrupted form. Llwyd probably was aware of this, as was Herbert and Howell. This is the verse which in its uncorrupted form I have argued was an interpolation into Maredudd's poem in the early 1500s.

The many fables on Madoc probably had the common element that he was the son of Owain Gwynedd and was a famous sailor. Llwyd probably thought it safe to accept these but his language is sometimes uncertain in making further statements. Williams (1979) wrote:[82]

> It is that 'must needs be' which is central to Llwyd, as is the existence of an *unspecific* popular tradition susceptible to fantasy.

CONCLUDING COMMENTS

The intent of this chapter was to examine the early evidence for Madoc and to keep the chapter within reasonable bounds the later material about the 'Welsh Indians' will not be discussed. The best coverage of this material is the thorough analysis by Stephens (1893). Two major expeditions which should have found them, one by John Evans, and the other by Lewis and Clarke, found no trace of them. There was also Major Long's expedition in 1819-20 from Pittsburgh to the Rocky Mountains which could not find them.[83]

An important point is that the Welsh language of the hypothetical Madoc would have been Middle Welsh but the Welsh of the American settlers was Late Modern Welsh. Further, the two languages would have evolved differently, being exposed to radically different linguistic contexts. If the Welsh Indians did exist, they would have had difficulty communicating with modern Welsh speakers although they may have recognized common words. Any account of fluent conversation with modern speakers would be bogus. So the Rev. Morgan Jones' account of conversing with the Welsh Indians many times and preaching to them three times a week in the British tongue suggests that his story is yet another fabrication.[84]

The low quality 'evidence' created by the Madoc advocates is hardly credible. One example is a letter published in *American Pioneer* from Thomas Hinde to J. S. Williams. Hinde states he had a vast amount of historical notes from persons who knew the facts. One of these 'facts' was that the Welsh, under Owen ap Zuinch (surprisingly not Madoc) had reached America. His proof is the find in his quote below.[85]

In 1799, six soldiers' skeletons were dug up near Jeffersonville; each skeleton had a breast-plate of brass, cast, with the Welsh *coat of arms*, the MERMAID and HARP, with a Latin inscription, *in substance* 'virtuous deeds meet their just reward'. One of these plates was left by captain Jonathon Taylor, with the late Mr. Hubbard Taylor, of Clarke county, Kentucky, and when called for by me, in 1814, for the late doctor John P. Campbell, of Chillicothe, Ohio ... by a letter from Hubbard Taylor, Jr (a relation of mine) now living, I was informed that the breast-plate had been taken to Virginia, by a gentlemen of that state, I supposed as a matter of curiosity.

The italics and capitals in the quote are Hinde's. If the details of the find were true, they would have been of great importance. The cast breastplates could have been studied by experts who would have tried to find similar plates in the historical record. The priority would be to keep them safe for future study but in a short time they had entirely 'vanished'. It is clear that they never existed. Hinde states that one of the six plates was held by Hubbard Taylor and, after he died, by his son Hubbard Taylor Jr. They were relatives of his but he shows little interest in the plate. His quote has detail but only in the parts that are useless for locating the plate. He only knows that a man of Virginia had taken it, no name, no county, no official position, no reason. The details of the plates are obviously fake. Wales wasn't a unified country but various kingdoms often at war with each other: there was no Welsh coat of arms. The claim that a mermaid was part of it is ludicrous. This is similar to the fabrications of Deacon.

It is apparent that the 'Welsh Indian' tales are fabrications. If they did exist, they would not have referred to themselves as 'Welsh'. About 24 years after Owain Gwynedd's death, Gerald wrote that 'Welsh' was a barbarous term applied to them by the Saxons, meaning 'foreigners'. If they really existed, they would have been the *Cymry* and 600 years later, if they had been able to keep their identity, they still would have called themselves this when conversing with settlers.[86]

It is sometimes implied that Roman coins along the eastern rivers were lost from Madoc's men, but the Welsh c. 1170 didn't use Roman coins. Wales was mostly a 'cattle' economy with limited coins. For AD 1040 William of Malmesbury mentions shillings and pence and Gerald of Wales mentions the half-penny, penny and three-pence. Some coins of Henry I, Henry II and Stephen were available. When Llywelyn came to power he began issuing his own coins. The old Roman coins in America are not evidence for Madoc.[87]

In a time when details on Owain and his sons were abundant, there is no evidence that Madoc even existed. This surprises me as I had a small degree of optimism before researching this. I am staggered by the huge number of forgeries, fabrications and creative interpolations by people from the 1500s onwards, all designed to keep the myth alive. These have cruelly deceived the Madoc believers.

11
INSCRIPTIONS ON STONE

IRISH IN AMERICA?

Voyages of Brendan

Some believe that Irish monks reached America in antiquity and that this is reflected in Irish writing (Ogam) on the face of rock formations. This claim seems more reasonable than many other such claims which are obvious fakes. The *Navigatio* of St Brendan relates his voyages into the Atlantic Ocean and contains incidents which appear to show knowledge of Iceland and sailing conditions in the Atlantic. Brendan was a real person, appearing in the *Life of St Columba* by Adomnán. He was a contemporary of fellow monks Cormac and Báetán who also sought places of retreat in the Atlantic. Báetán sailed for 'many miles' over the seas but was unable to find such a suitable place. Cormac also unsuccessfully sought such a place in three voyages into the Atlantic. In one voyage he reached Orkney and in the last may have sailed as far as the Arctic Circle according to Simon Young (2009).[1]

In the *Navigatio* it was Barrind who first discovered the 'Promised Land of the Saints'. It is described as a huge, significant landmass rich in resources, not a small island like those on which the monks usually lived. He sailed *west* from Delightful Island, which was near Slieve League, Donegal. No details are given on the journey itself but towards its end they spend an hour in thick fog just before the Promised Land (O'Meara, 2002). It was too big to fully explore it and on reaching a great river they are turned back by an angel of God.[2]

Barrind tells Brendan about it and he decides to go there. He leaves from the isle of the steward (the Faroes, from its sheep and birds) and sails to island after island in a tedious fanciful account. After seven years of visiting islands he returns to the Faroes. Finally he sets out for the Promised Land of the Saints. The text says they sailed *east* for 40 days and then spend an hour in thick fog, as in Barrind's visit. If the isle of the steward is in the Faroes, sailing east for 40 days can't be correct as a boat sailing east from the Faroes would meet the coast of Norway in several days. As Barrind went west, Ashe (1962) and others argue that 'east' is an error for 'west' in Brendan's visit. This could then explain the fog, as 40 days sailing west may have taken them near to Newfoundland, noted for its thick fogs. It's also in line with knowledge of westward sailing such as the Faroes (Sheep/Birds), Iceland (Isle of Smiths) and an iceberg sighting (crystal pillar in the sea).[3]

The evidence for reaching America is slight but the tale has been given some credence. Morison (1971) thinks that Brendan's historical voyages in the Atlantic were later enhanced by Celtic imagination. He states: 'We are not straining the evidence to conclude that Brendan sailed for several trips, if not for seven years, on the circuit Hebrides-Shetlands-Faroes-Iceland, possibly as far as the Azores'. Gwyn Jones (1986) also thought that Brendan could have reached Iceland and may have witnessed an eruption of a volcano there, possibly Hekla or Katla, or another crater in Öraefi. Given that he sailed in a curragh, it is difficult to believe that Brendan made it all the way there and back, despite Tim Severin's intrepid voyage from Ireland to Newfoundland in a leather curragh with two masts. Severin, however, had the great advantages of safety equipment, crucial communication devices and valuable geographical knowledge.[4]

David Dumville (1988b) dates the *Navigatio* to about 750-775, but cannot rule out the possibility that it was earlier, perhaps as early as the 600s. Brendan's death date is AD 575 in the *Annals of Tigernach* and *Chronicum Scotorum*. Brendan met Columba on the isle of Hinba after AD 563, the year Columba left Ireland (Burgess, 2002).[5]

Great Ireland or White Man's Land

The Norse sagas also suggest an early Irish presence in America. *Eirik the Red's Saga* relates that Thorfinn Karlsefni captured two skraeling boys in Markland who learnt his language while he raised them. They described their own land and another land not far away (Kunz and Sígurðsson, 2008).[6]

> They spoke of another land, across from their own. There people dressed in white clothing, shouted loudly and bore poles and waved banners.

This land was thought to be the land of the white men.

The notion of White Man's Land (*Hvítramannaland*) also appears in *Landnámabók* (Book of Settlements). It concerns an Ari Marsson who drifted in his boat to White Man's Land which some also call Greater Ireland (Pálsson and Edwards, 2007).[7]

> It lies in the ocean to westward, near Vineland the Good, said to be a six-day sail west from Ireland. Ari couldn't get away, and was baptized there. This story was first told by Hrafn Limerick-Farer who spent a long time at Limerick in Ireland. Thorkel Gellisson quoted some Icelanders who had heard Earl Thorfinn of Orkney say that Ari had been recognized in White Man's Land, and couldn't get away from there, but was thought very highly of.

The *Eyrbyggja Saga* gives an account concerning what seems to be White Man's Land although not explicitly stated. It involves Gudleif, a trader intending to sail to Iceland, but west of Ireland he ran into easterly gales and the ship was driven out to sea. Finally land was seen but they had no idea what country it was. The inhabitants seemed to be speaking Irish and were aggressive. They marched them inland and held them prisoner. A group of horsemen arrived and the leader, an old man, spoke to them in Icelandic. Gudlief told him he was from Borgarfjord in Iceland and the leader asked detailed questions about the leading people in Borgarfjord and Breidafjord, and about Snorri, his sister Thurid and young Kjartan. After consulting with advisers the leader decided to release them. He wouldn't say who he was but asked Gudlief to give gifts on his behalf (Pálsson and Edwards, 1989).[8]

> Before he and Gudleif parted, he took a gold ring from his finger and gave it to Gudleif along with a fine sword. Then he said, 'If you're lucky enough to get back to your homeland, give this sword to Kjartan the farmer at Frodriver, and the ring to his mother Thurid.'

Gudleif and his men set out for Ireland and spent the winter in Dublin. The following summer they set sail for Iceland where he found Thurid and Kjartan and handed over the gifts. From this, people now believe the leader, the old man, must have been Bjorn, the lover of Thurid and the father of Kjartan.

Seaver (1996) calls Great Ireland a 'fabled' land and Nansen (1911) also dismisses it. Even if these tales were based on an early Irish colony, its location and settlement date are unknown. It is unlikely to be related to Brendan as the events in these tales are centuries later.[9]

OGAM WRITING IN WEST VIRGINIA?

Ogam is Irish writing, dating from about the 300s, which uses straight lines for the letters. In Britain and Ireland it is carved on stone, usually up a vertical edge which acts as the stem line. Here the stem is shown horizontally. In Table 11.1, 'h' is a single line above the stem while 'b' is a single line below. For a vertical stem, lines on the *left* are *above* the stem and lines on the *right* are *below*. The vowels shown in the first line of 11.1 are small notches that cross the stem.

In English, the shapes comprising each letter are joined, except the dots on i and j. In Ogam, a single letter can comprise several lines that aren't joined to each other. There must be a method of separating to show when it finishes and when the next letter starts. For example, if 'o' and 'u' are adjacent letters then there are 5 identical lines. There must be a separator (an obvious space) after the first 2 lines, otherwise the 'o' and 'u' would be interpreted as an 'i'.

Table 11.1 The Basic Ogam Letters

This is a crucial issue in the interpretation of the 'Ogam' writing in the West Virginia rock formations.

The Luther Elkins site, Wyoming County WV

The issue of possible Ogam in America came to prominence with the March 1983 issue of *Wonderful West Virginia*, published by the West Virginia Department of Natural Resources. The cover showed a photo of rock carvings at the Luther Elkins site in Wyoming County that were chalked to make them clearer. They were claimed to be Irish Ogam and a translation by Barry Fell was shown below the photo. Fell had written *America BC* and *Saga America* where he had argued for early pre-Columbian visitors to America. His translation was a Christmas message and implied that Irish monks had travelled to West Virginia and inscribed it in Ogam. It said:[10]

> At the time of sunrise a ray grazes the notch on the left side on Christmas Day. A Feast-day of the Church, the first season of the (Christian) year. The season of the Blessed Advent of the Savior, Lord Christ (Salvatoris Domini Christi). Behold, he is born of Mary, a woman.

Figure 11.1: Luther Elkins site carvings (Credit: Robert L. Pyle)

How the discovery was made and publicized

The site was formally recorded in 1965 but was known to local people before that. Robert Pyle learnt of the petroglyph from local resident Tony Shields and in 1982 Pyle and Shields were able to find it. Pyle examined the carvings with a magnifying glass and chalked those he thought authentic and made a latex copy of it, helped by Shields.

Pyle later discussed it with the editor of a Morgantown newspaper whose editorial and photo greatly impressed a Morgantown reader. He then clipped it and sent it to Arnout Hyde Jr. the editor of *Wonderful West Virginia*. Hyde then sent the clipping to Ida Jane Gallagher, a former West Virginian living in Connecticut who wanted to see it. On a 1982 November day, Pyle, Shields, Hyde, Gallagher and three others gathered at the site. Gallagher wondered whether the winter solstice sunrise on 21-22 December might be connected to the 'Sun' carving on the left of the rock carvings. She states that from the 4th to the 16th centuries the winter solstice and Christmas Day both fell on the 25 December in the Julian calendar used in Europe.[11]

As soon as possible, Gallagher contacted Barry Fell. What she said to him is not recorded but it appears she discussed her winter solstice idea. From photos of the carvings that he received, Fell produced the above 'Christmas' translation which 'confirmed' Gallagher's sunrise theory. Fell was also given photos of carvings from the Horse Creek site in Boone County which he translated. He wrote up his findings in Fell (1983) which was published in *Wonderful West Virginia*.[12]

Before sunrise on the 22 December 1982 a second group visited the site: Tony Shields, Brad Toler, Ida Gallagher and her father, H. P. Meadows. They report that the Sun's rays hit the 'Sun' symbol on the left and then the entire panel of carvings. This news was given to Hyde, resulting in the *Wonderful West Virginia* papers: a note by Hyde and papers by Fell (1983), Pyle (1983) and Gallagher (1983) giving the details of the discovery and implications.[13]

Are the carvings really Ogam?

While I would be personally delighted if the carvings were Ogam, even a cursory look suggests they are not. There are horizontal cracks in the rock face but no stem lines. There is a profusion of vertical strokes that are densely located but no way of separating one 'letter' from another, or one 'word' from another, if these could ever be defined. There are arrowhead type figures which have no resemblance to Ogam letters. The Ogam characters are clearly defined in Table 11.1 but there are characters carved in this rock face more complex than Ogam.

It looks like Native American rock art which may be portraying a message about the Sun. They conveyed their observations of the sky in various ways, one by building earthen mounds to portray a comet airburst at Milford (Tankersley et al., 2022). The strokes do appear to be meaningful, not random, but their meaning is unknown.[14]

FELL'S TRANSLATION

Ogam Consaine

To create a 'translation' out of rock art lines, Fell claims that the Ogam is one without vowels, just consonants, which he calls Ogam Consaine. It is doubtful that Ogam ever had this form, but if it did, it would be very old and well before the time of Brendan. Languages that have vowels do not later drop them, so that only consonants remain, as it becomes harder to read. There is an example of Ogam with vowels in Silchester, late 300s/early 400s which is not difficult to translate (Fulford et al., 2000). It has two stem lines and clear symbols so that a layperson can verify the translation from Table 11.1. This example is about 150 years before Brendan who, if he ever did get to America to write Ogam, would have used vowels. Fell's claim of Ogam Consaine and other fudging tricks, give him great freedom to manipulate his translation to whatever he wants. He can select any single vowel to suit his purpose, or not insert them, or insert multiple vowels.[15]

Other fudging techniques

Fell uses an array of fudging techniques that will be illustrated by an example below. These include:

- His drawings often differ significantly from photos of the carvings.

- His reading path is idiosyncratic and arbitrary.

- He ignores problems of letter shape, slope and position.

- He invents multiple arbitrary stem lines, often at weird angles.

- His starting point to begin reading the 'writing' is arbitrary.

- His direction of reading the 'writing' is arbitrary.

- He accepts rock art shapes with little resemblance to Ogam letters.

- He invents his own rules, but uses them inconsistently.

Below are the symbols Fell (1983) translated to obtain 'At the time of sunrise a ray grazes the notch on the left side on Christmas Day'. My table of consonants is given underneath as a reference.

He needs consonants **S F G D M R G G R N C B G L T D N T L** to convert to Old Irish to get the above sentence.[16]

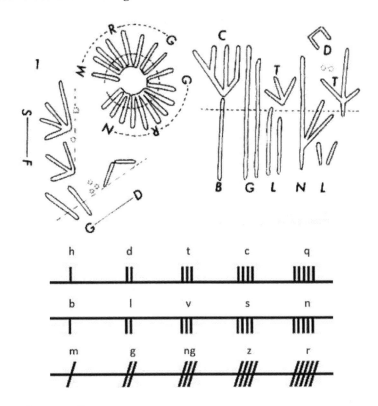

h	d	t	c	q

b	l	v	s	n

m	g	ng	z	r

S and F, G and D

Fell draws a faint vertical stem with two arrowhead shapes on its left, with 4 and 3 lines respectively. In both shapes the lines *aren't parallel* but touch the stem at varying angles. He intends these to be S and F, but letters on the left are *above the stem*, so the 4-line one is C and the 3-line one is T. Fell reads them as *below the stem*, an obvious error, and gets S and F (also his F should be V).

A vertical stem reads from *bottom to top*, as in the Silchester Ogam, but Fell reads from *top to bottom*, an elementary error for starting an Ogam message, because he wants to connect with G and D.

For G and D his stem is arbitrary, through G's midpoint. His G lines have a *negative* slope to the stem but it should be *positive*. Letter D is two parallel lines. In his D, the wide-angled lines meet at a point. Also its point does not face the stem, in contrast to his S, F, C and T!

The 'Sun' Symbol

After an arbitrary route to D, he goes to the 'Sun'. The nearest point is R (see Figure 11.1 photo) but he goes to M. He draws the 'Sun' to create a gap between M and N, but this has no meaning as the 'arrowhead' for S partly fills the gap in the photo. Yet his drawing gives the illusion that M is the best starting point because of the gap. His choice of the stem through the middle of the 'rays' is also arbitrary.

The Sun symbol artist undoubtedly intended that it be symmetrical with no differentiation between the length of the 'rays' and the angles between them. Thus any point on the Sun to continue his 'translation' is utterly arbitrary. So is his division of the 'rays' into 1 line (M), 5 lines (R), 2 lines (G), 2 lines (G), 5 lines (R) and 3 lines (N). This partition of the 'rays' has no more validity than any other random partition.

He ignores other problems. Most Ogam letters are at 90 degrees to the stem and here would be at 90 degrees to the tangent and point to the circle's centre. But his M, R and G belong to the group that meets the stem tangent *at an angle*. They should not point to the circle's centre. Letter N is in the former group and should point to the centre but there are no apparent differences. Further, his N uses 3 lines, but needs 5, which requires 20 'rays'. Alas, there are only 18. A third point is that his N 'rays' should be about half the length of the others and not appear above the stem. He seems oblivious to all this.

The 'Garden Rake' and other nonsense

Having gone left to arrive at N, Fell abruptly moves the opposite way to leap over to C which sits on top of a figure resembling a garden rake. He breaks the rake into two, with the prongs being a grotesque letter C and the handle being B, reaching new heights of absurdity. He is inventing a new Ogam rule where one letter can sit on top of a second one with the top letter read first, here CB. Let's use his new rule on the next letter. His G could be H on top of B, repeated twice to get HB, HB. However being flexible, he reverts to the standard rules to get G, but his parallel lines must meet the stem at an angle. He ignores the fact that they don't. Ever flexible, he again uses his new rule on the next letters, allowing T to sit above L, but this time reads the bottom letter L first to get LT, thus breaking part of his own rule.

New heights of absurdity follow. The next four shapes are so irregular that it is impossible to force them into writing, but he does his best. The next shape doesn't resemble an Ogam letter but he decides it is N. But he doesn't use it next – he wants a D. He finds it in a small upside down 'U' shape, hovering above the others as though it doesn't belong. He creates a stem for one letter! He makes the stem run along the base of the U. A slight clockwise rotation would give the letter L but he doesn't want this and so arbitrarily decides that the sides of the U are above the stem line to get D, even though they are below it. Instead of using the order of the symbols in moving to the right along the stem which would give ND, he reverses the order to get DN.

Moving to the right along the stem the next shape is two small lines way under the stem. If one assumes that they are intended to go to the stem, an absurdity, they could represent the letter B repeated, BB. Fell does use this absurd assumption but arbitrarily chooses L, a needed letter, but he doesn't need it yet, so he temporarily ignores it. He first needs a T and gets it from the 'cactus' figure on the right which differs from his other T as its long central spine goes beyond the two 'arms' in both directions. Instead of LT he arbitrarily uses TL. It can be seen that his translation is contrived to get the result that he wants.

The Second Major Problem – Fell's use of Irish

Fell's arbitrary derivation of the chain of consonants for Luther Elkins is only half the problem. The second half is converting these to Irish. John Carey and Proiseas Ni Chathain, Irish language experts, state that primitive Irish differed from the late medieval and modern Gaelic that Fell used. He used Irish sentence structures and spelling that only developed many centuries later than the 500s-700s.[17]

Horse Creek Carvings

Fell (1983) also relates the Horse Creek carvings to Christmas:[18]

A happy season is Christmas, a time of joy and goodwill to all people. A virgin was with child; God ordained her to conceive and be fruitful. Ah, Behold a miracle! She gave birth to a son in a cave. The name of the cave was the Cave of Bethlehem. His foster-father gave him the name Jesus, the Christ, Alpha and Omega, Festive season of prayer.

In contrast, Edo Nyland (1996) gives a vastly different translation of the Horse Creek carvings. He thought it was Basque, using Ogam letters, and about a buffalo hunt where they are being driven off a cliff. His translation is very long but Ogam is intended for short messages, being laborious to carve into rock. A small part of the translation is given below. His rendering is totally different to Fell's, illustrating the problem of forcing translations onto symbols that are not writing.[19]

To bring about a disturbance we advanced rattling branches and shouting ... we fell back in fear (to avoid) the bad-tempered stampede of the frightened herd of bison (moving into) the entrance of the narrow wooden-fenced passage and into the abyss in flight ... Club blows in abundant measure (were needed) because many which had fallen into the ravine resisted with obviously broken legs.

Professor Meyer and Oin Dia (One God)

Robert Meyer, Professor of Celtic at Catholic University, also thought the symbols were Ogam. He was an scholar of early Christian writings, translating *Life of St. Anthony* by St Athanasius and *Lausiac History* and *Life of St. John Chrysostom* by Bishop Palladius. On 8 April 1983 he visited the Luther Elkins site with Robert Pyle and Ida Gallagher and appears in a photo in Pyle's *All that Remains* (1998) book. He was interviewed at the site by Mike Morachi for the West Virginia Public Television where he stated:[20]

Nobody could have faked this thing unless they had a very deep knowledge of Celtic philology, for this is very archaic, and it will be from the VI or VII centuries. This for Celtic scholars is probably at least as important as the Dead Sea scrolls, I think. Because it shows that Irish monks, I suppose, came here – I would say, about 1500 years ago. For this is very archaic Old Irish.

This is a very strong statement. Morachi asked if he was certain and Meyer said 'yes'. He then said that it has really archaic forms such as as *Oin Dia* (One God). However this phrase has nothing to do with the Luther Elkins carvings. It is in Fell (1983) as a separate part of the Horse Creek, Boone County carvings. Meyer must have read it in Fell's paper but confused it with the Luther Elkins site.[21]

A 'Procrustean Bed' translation for 'One God'

Fell (1983) derives *Oin Dia* in Figure K but only derives *Oin* (one) from the single letter 'N', inferring the *oi*. The stem for his 'N' is in the *middle* of 3 lines and is 45 degrees to the stem for 'God', which is absurd given their proximity. However an N consists of 5 lines *under* the stem, so he does not have an N, but instead an NG. His 'God' derives from a D and an X, a Forfeda letter (later Ogam letters). The stem should go through X's centre but X sits on top of it. It didn't even initially resemble an X! Comparing the Figure J photo and Figure G.3 shows he has added a 'leg' to the X on the left. Comparing Figures G.3 and K shows he has lopped off part of the other leg under the stem and a line projecting from this leg. He also removes a line crossing the stem, on the right, absent in Figure K. Finally the X is a *vowel* sound, EA, which contradicts his claim that it is Ogam Consaine writing.[22]

I think that Meyer trusted Fell and had not studied the carvings in detail when interviewed. It is significant that he did not publish any academic papers on them given his initial strong views. Fell was a fine scholar of marine biology but his translations here are appalling.

The Luther Elkins carvings at Sunrise

The reader might object that Gallagher (1983) states that the Sun first hit the Sun design and then soon bathed the entire panel in sunlight, thus confirming the translation. She also excitedly states: 'A shadow cast by the left wall of the shelter fell to the left of the Sun symbol ... As the group watched the shadow inched from left to right. Before their eyes, light dawned on West Virginia history'.[23]

But this was not replicated. In 2002, on the winter solstice, Roger Wise took photos there. At sunrise the Sun design was not lit up first, the whole panel lit up simultaneously and the creeping shadow failed. After an hour the shadow's point had still not touched the Sun symbol and was not going to, being above it, as shown by his photos.[24]

On 3 March 1983 a letter in the *Charlestown Gazette* stated that originally there was a rock overhang which had prevented light from illuminating the Sun symbol, negating Gallagher's theory. It had now broken off. The author was experienced archaeologist, Sigfus Olafson, author of several publications on West Virginian petroglyphs.[25]

IOLO'S FAKE LANGUAGE – COELBREN

Fell began a trend where amateurs tried similar translations. A second language popular in America is Coelbren, a fake language created by Iolo Morganwg who claims it had existed in antiquity and was used by the bards through the centuries. No linguistic expert believes his claim. If it were true there would be such manuscripts in the National Library of Wales or the British Library but there are none. Further, the letters he created are obvious variations of Roman letters (Stephens in Löffler, 2007). In 1837, the Rev. John Jones thought that Iolo had invented it himself and stated that W. Owen Pughe (Iolo's crony, who had fudged *mur* into *myr*) had admitted inventing five letters to add to the language. So much for it being an ancient language.[26]

In America, some claim that the writing on the Bat Creek stone is Coelbren which is translated as: 'The Ruler Madoc he is distinctly' (Michael, 2004). The Madoc believers in America are split into two groups, one believing in an 1170 Madoc. The second group thinks that Arthur's brother, Madoc, sailed to America in the 500s and that he is referred to on the stone. This section will analyze in detail how the 'The Ruler Madoc' translation was obtained and show the nonsensical inventions that are needed to get the desired result.[27]

Coelbren letters from Iolo's Barddas

Iolo's claims on Coelbren are in his *Barddas*, translated by Williams ab Ithel (1862). Iolo invents a history for Coelbren and claims 'In the time of king Arthur there were introduced twenty primary letters, as at present, by the counsel of Taliesin, the chief of Bards'. As these are Iolo's own letters this is the authoritative source for their exact shape. They are reproduced in Table 11.2 from Williams ab Ithel (1862).[28]

Table 11.2 English and Coelbren

MADOC'S NAME ON THE BAT CREEK STONE?

In 1889 John Emmert found the Bat Creek stone in a Hopewell mound in Loudon County, Tennessee. The writing was originally thought to be Cherokee, but Cyrus Gordon argued that it was being read upside down and that it was ancient Hebrew. The stone is mentioned in Barry Fell's *Saga America* (1980) where Fell claims that it is first century Hebrew. It is thought to be a fake of the 1800s although McCulloch (1988; 1993) thinks the issue is not fully resolved. Mainfort and Kwas (1993; 2004) argue that most of the Hebrew letters were copied by Emmert from a Masonic book by Robert Macoy (1868) which is the obvious and most convincing explanation.[29]

Mangling Hebrew letters to get Coelbren equivalents

The letters are Hebrew and Michael knew this from Cyrus Gordon but despite this, he states that Coelbren was used by the Ten Lost Tribes of Israel as they migrated through the Mediterranean. Table 11.3 gives the Hebrew letters alleged to give Madoc's name in R1. The Coelbren 'equivalents' from Michael (2004) are in R2. Each step is then closely examined to see how Madoc's name was obtained.[30]

Table 11.3 Hebrew/Coelbren letters alleged to give Madoc's name

Step		C1	C2	C3	C4	C5
R1	Hebrew on Bat Creek stone					
R2	Hebrew letters as 'Coelbren'					
R3	Coelbren to English	-	a	-	-	w	c

The most preposterous step of all is the fact that one has to convert the Hebrew letters into the 'equivalent' Coelbren letters, as given in Michael (2004). If the writing on the stone is in Coelbren this should not be necessary. As one can see, the Coelbren letters are very different to the Hebrew with the exception of C3, but this mirror image of 'E' is not even a Coelbren letter. It would be sufficient to stop here to refute the claim, but the analysis is continued to see the reasoning.[31]

In C1, the Coelbren letter has a 'loop' at the bottom but the Hebrew looks nothing like it. The Hebrew letter has no loop, just a vertical line crossed by a sloping line with a hook on the end.

In C2, the curved Hebrew has no resemblance at all to the pointed Coelbren. These are so different that it seems the translator's motive in choosing this Coelbren shape as the second letter is to make the 'a' in Madoc appear, as can be seen from Table 11.2.

C5 illustrates a common way of fudging translations of writing on stone – distorting the letters. The Hebrew letter acute angle between the two arms is increased to roughly a right angle in the Coelbren. Secondly, the letter is also rotated clockwise so that one arm intended to be horizonal now has a negative slope. It can then be interpreted as an English 'c' from Table 11.2. Taking such liberties is common.

I have left C4 to last as it is the most bizarre piece of nonsense I have ever seen in a 'translation'. The Hebrew letter is split into two characters to give two Coelbren letters. The left half of the Hebrew is then rotated clockwise so that the 'spine' is vertical to give the mirror image of 'F', a most extraordinary contortion. But this contortion is all in vain. The mirror image of 'F' is not a Coelbren letter as shown from Table 11.2. The right Coelbren figure is obtained by borrowing the left Hebrew 'spine' and the right 'arm' of the Hebrew to obtain a 'v'. From Table 11.2 the Coelbren 'v' gives the English letter 'w'.

All six Coelbren letters in R2 are given without explanation. From Iolo's *Barddas*, shown in Table 11.2, it can be seen that three of the six are not even Coelbren and cannot be translated into English, so they are shown as hyphens in Tables 11.3, 11.4. Thus the incomplete 'name' is 'awc' not 'Madoc' but this is only obtained if the bizarre contortions in C4 and C5 are used and the obvious planting of the symbol in (R2, C2) to get the English 'a' is accepted. If these are rightly rejected, then not a single English letter is obtained.

Gobbledygook to obtain 'Maefuc'

In the above I have taken the Coelbren row *as given* in Michael (2004) and used Iolo's original table to produce 'awc', a simple task. Surely the translator will get the same result. Alas, the translation obtained by further creative means is 'Maefuc'. However Madoc's name never

271

appears in any of the Welsh literature in the ludicrous form 'Maefuc'. It is again a simple task to see what Coelbren letters are required to give 'Maefuc' by taking each letter in this word and looking up the Coelbren equivalent in Table 11.2. This gives the Coelbren letters in R5 in Table 11.4 below.[32]

Table 11.4 Inconsistent Ad Hoc Procedures

Step		C1	C2	C3	C4	C5	C6
R2	Hebrew letters as 'Coelbren'	_(glyph)_	_(glyph)_	_(glyph)_	_(glyph)_	V	_(glyph)_
R3	Coelbren to English	-	a	-	-	w	c
R4	Translation in Michael (2004)	m	a	e	f	u	c
R5	Coelbren needed to give Maefuc	W	_(glyph)_	_(glyph)_	_(glyph)_	_(glyph)_	_(glyph)_

This table gives the incredible conclusion that only 2 of the Coelbren characters in Michael (2004) match with the correct Coelbren to spell 'Maefuc'. The table does give clues as to how the translation was done. (R2, C3) and (R2, C4) are not Coelbren letters so Table 11.2 can't be used to give the English letters. Undeterred, the translator notes that their mirror images are like the English 'E' and 'F' and so uses these letters as the translation, a preposterous ad hoc invention.

For (R2, C5) the translator should have used Table 11.2 but didn't. He apparently thought the Coelbren 'v' shape resembled an English 'u' and used this English letter, another ad hoc decision. Had he used the conversion table for 'v' he would have obtained 'Maefwc'.

As for the 'M' for Madoc, the Coelbren letter in (R2, C1) is wrong – the correct letter is in (R5, C1), like the English 'W'. To sum up, from Table 11.3 the only 'Coelbren letter' that resembles the Hebrew is C3 but this is not even a Coelbren letter. In this translation it is converted to English with mirror-image fudging. No legitimate form of 'Madoc' can be obtained by claiming the Hebrew is Coelbren. This shambolic approach may be described as 'making it up as you go'.

THE BAT CREEK STONE

So far it has been shown that the name 'Madoc' doesn't appear on the stone in any of its forms. The second claim is that the 'Coelbren' says that Madoc is 'the Ruler' but he isn't a king in the Welsh material. It is shown below that 'the Ruler' translation in Michael (2004) is based on a misconception and farcical inventions. Below, the Bat Creek stone is shown twice. In the careful drawing in Picture (1) the top left corner is blank. In Picture (2) two parallel vertical lines have been added in that corner. The third row shows the Hebrew letters in Macoy (1868). Some of these have been copied onto the stone.[33]

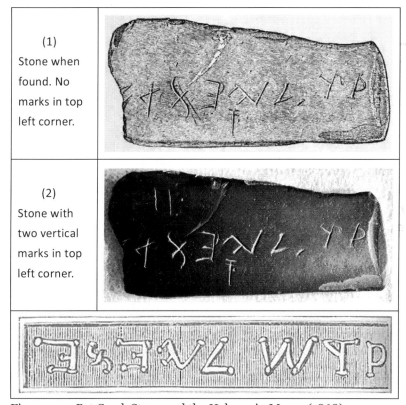

| (1)
Stone when found. No marks in top left corner. | |
| (2)
Stone with two vertical marks in top left corner. | |

Figure 11.2 Bat Creek Stone and the Hebrew in Macoy (1868)

Picture (1) is the original drawing from Thomas (1890), where it was shown upside down in Figure 7. The two lines in the Picture 2 photo were added between 1894 and 1970 by a Smithsonian worker.[34]

'THE RULER' TRANSLATION

Smithsonian marks used in the translation

The two parallel lines weren't there when the stone was dug up but the translator didn't know this and uses them in his translation. In Table 11.2, a vertical line in Coelbren gives the English 'i' so the two lines read 'ii'. This simple use of Iolo's table should have told him something was wrong, but he proceeds with his shambolic inventions.

A Farcical Chain of Associations

The 'ii' for the two lines is useless, so he decides to use their number, 'two', which is *dwy* in Welsh (not Coelbren). He then claims that *dwy* in Welsh also means 'ruler' and so translates: 'the Ruler Madoc'. But the other meaning for *dwy* is 'God' and this could only be translated 'ruler' in a figurative sense (as God rules all). However let's allow this to show the lack of logic. It is obvious that his associations are not transitive like mathematical expressions, as shown below:

$$(\text{'two'} \equiv dwy) \text{ and } (dwy \equiv \text{'ruler'}), \text{ but } (\text{'two'} \not\equiv \text{'ruler'}).$$

That is, if this ludicrous method is applied, the meaning of the two lines is 'two', not 'God' or 'ruler'. There is also no reason for thinking the two lines convey a number rather than a letter as Coelbren has a symbol for 'two'. It is not two parallel lines but is like the letter 'T' with the right horizontal part removed (Williams ab Ithel, 1862). Also note that *nothing in his translation relates to Coelbren* despite the fact that he thinks the two lines are Coelbren. He counts the parallel lines to get 'two' and the rest is just Welsh.[35]

Summary of his translating tricks

In tackling each letter on the stone he invents an imaginative range of fudging tricks. He chooses a Coelbren letter to get the wanted 'a' in 'Madoc' despite the fact that the Coelbren letter bears no resemblance to the Hebrew. He rotates and distorts letters, and even cuts a Hebrew letter into two to create two Coelbren characters, one of which is not even Coelbren. He ignores Iolo Morganwg's table for converting Coelbren to English when it suits, converts non-Coelbren to English by substituting their mirror images as English letters, and directly uses an English letter if similar to the Coelbren shape.

His greatest trick of all is his creation of 'the Ruler' from parallel lines put there by a Smithsonian worker. However as the two lines were not on the stone when dug up they can't be part of any ancient writing. Thus 'the Ruler' vanishes. In summary, the whole translation process can be seen as a farce. Scholars knew this already as they knew that the letters were Hebrew and that Coelbren was invented c. 1791 by prolific forger, Iolo Morganwg. However those who believe that Coelbren was an ancient language should critically study the creative details of the 'making it up as you go' process of a fervent believer.

Discussion

This analysis has taken two translations, one in 'Ogam' and the other in 'Coelbren' and worked through every step, showing what occurred, the rationale, and revealing errors, distortions, inconsistencies and arbitrary decisions. It is the best way to appreciate the farcical nature of the 'translations'. Both are fantasies. To state the obvious, writing is meant to be read, and this requires clear rules. If the writing is in a different alphabet to English then a translation requires that a foreign letter has a unique identification with an English letter or sound that experts can recognize. Each letter should be distinguishable from the next letter. Where letters are worn or damaged, different readings may occur but the logic of the variations should be understood by other experts. Fell's 'translations', however, are not reproducible by other independent translators. For a start, his drawings of the strokes often differ from the photos in ways that aid his translations. The latter are also based on arbitrary choices, absurd letter identifications, ignoring features that do not fit, and comical movements around the symbols. The Coelbren 'translation' to English is even worse.

12
PRE-COLUMBIAN WHITE PEOPLE IN AMERICA

The Rev. John Campbell collected Native American stories about the slaughter of an ancient white people who had once lived in Kentucky. He was known to meticulously check details. For example, when told of six skeletons having breastplates with the 'Welsh coat-of-arms' he asked Thomas Hinde if he could see the plates. Naturally no plates could be found and so Campbell didn't report on them. Further, when told of a witness who had heard an Indian speaking Welsh, Campbell found the man and discovered that he was not a witness (*American Pioneer*, 1842). The five quotes below are from his notes which first appeared in *The Port Folio* (1816). The italics in these are mine.[1]

Thomas Bodley

Thomas Bodley was informed by Indians of different tribes northwest of the Ohio, that they had understood from their old men, and that it had been a tradition among their several nations, that Kentucky had been settled by whites, and that they had been exterminated by war. *They were of opinion that the old fortifications now to be seen in Kentucky and Ohio, were the productions of those white inhabitants.* Wappockanitta, a Shawnee chief near a hundred and twenty years old living on the Auglaze river, confirmed the above tradition.

James Moore

An old Indian, in conversation with Colonel James F. Moore, of Kentucky, informed him that the western country, and particularly Kentucky, had once been inhabited by white people, but that they were exterminated by the Indians. That the last battle was fought at the falls of the Ohio, and that the Indians succeeded in driving the Aborigines into a small island below the rapids, where the whole of them were cut to pieces. He said it was an undoubted fact, handed down by tradition, and that the colonel would have ocular proof of it when the waters of the Ohio became low. This was found to be correct, on examining Sandy Island, when the waters of the river had fallen, as a multitude of human bones were discovered.

George Clark

The Indian chief called Tobacco [a Piankeshaw] told General Clarke, of Louisville, that the battle of Sandy Island decided finally the fall of Kentucky, with its ancient inhabitants. General Clarke says that *Kentucke*, in the language of the Indians, signifies the river of blood.

In addition to the proof of a great battle near the falls of the Ohio, it is said by General Clarke, of Louisville, that there was at Clarkesville a great burying ground, two or three hundred yards in length. This is likewise confirmed by Major John Harrison, who received the tradition from an Indian woman of great age.

Joseph Daviess

Colonel Joseph Daviess when at St Louis in 1800, saw the remains of an ancient tribe of the Sacks [Sac or Sauk] who expressed some astonishment that any person should live in Kentucky. They said the country had been the scene of much blood, and was filled with the manes of its butchered inhabitants. He stated also, that the people who inhabited this country were white, and possessed such arts as were unknown by the Indians.

William McKee

Colonel McKee, who commanded on the Kenhawa when Cornstalk [Shawnee] was inhumanly murdered, had frequent conversation with that chief respecting the people who had constructed the ancient forts. He stated that it was a current and assured tradition, that Ohio and Kentucky had been once settled by white people, who were possessed of arts which the Indians did not know. That after many sanguinary contests they were exterminated ... Col. M. asked him if he could tell who made those old forts, which displayed so much skill in fortifying. He answered that he did not know, *but that a story had been handed down from a very long ago people, that there had been a nation of white people inhabiting the country who made the graves and forts.* He also said, that some Indians, who had travelled very far west or northwest, had found a nation of people, who lived as Indians generally do, although of a different complexion.

The White Moundbuilders

In the 1800s it was wrongly believed that the forts and earthworks had been built by an ancient white people. The early settlers' amazement at their complexity and the fact that the Indians at that time weren't building them led to this myth. These works were so old that who built them was forgotten. Over time, contacts between settlers and Indians allowed the belief in the white moundbuilders to be absorbed into a common Indian tradition, as in the Bodley and McKee quotes above. To explain how the white moundbuilders disappeared, this tradition may have been elaborated to have the whites being massacred.[2]

The Welsh Indians

A second influence on these stories came from the mythical Madoc, a later claim of a white people building forts across America. The 'Welsh Indians' developed as an extension of claims that there were several Welsh words in Native American languages. This has been decisively rejected by linguists. While there are superficial similarities in some cases these are also true of other languages. For example, James Adair (1775) lived among the Indians for forty years and argued that the Indian languages were related to Hebrew.[3]

In the story that was the seed for the Welsh Indians, Morgan Jones said he was saved from being put to death by Indians when one brave thought that Jones' Welsh was his own native language. Jones claims that this occurred in 1660 but didn't tell his story until 1686. It was finally published in 1740 by Theophilus Evans in *Drych y Prif Oesoedd* (Mirror of the Early Ages) and it impressed the Welsh. Gwyn Williams states that 'It was this book, more than any other, which made Madoc into a rooted popular "tradition" among them'.[4]

The sheer improbability of Jones' account was exposed by Thomas Stephens. Gwyn Williams agrees with Stephens and calls Jones' tale a 'complete farrago'. Nevertheless, from then on stories on the Morgan Jones model began to appear, first in a trickle, and later in a flood. By 1753 there were so many such stories that Governor Dinwiddie of Virginia asked for a report on them. This resulted in a claim of the finding of a 'Welsh tribe' and that this was said to be proven by the Welsh Bibles that the searchers brought back from the tribe.[5]

This started a trend. Benjamin Sutton said he had met a tribe west of the Mississippi who were whiter than other Indians and who spoke Welsh. They had a 'Welch Bible' wrapped carefully in skins. Another claim concerns Isaac Stewart who travelled with a Welsh man to a small river called the Post. They came across an Indian nation who were remarkably white and whose hair was of a reddish colour. The Welsh man wanted to stay with them as he understood their language, it being similar to Welsh. As proof they were Welsh they showed rolls of parchment with large characters written in blue ink. These were tied up in otters' skins, a variation of the Welsh Bibles model.[6]

It did not occur to the inventors of such stories that in the 1170s (Madoc's supposed time) there were no Welsh Bibles. They didn't exist then and so could not have been brought to America to be eventually shown to Welsh visitors in the 1700s. This fact destroys the credibility of such stories, which are blatant fabrications.

The Welsh Indians myth was early embedded in the slaughter of the whites at the Falls of the Ohio, as shown from a circa 1783 meeting of Kentucky citizens with historian, John Filson. In Reuben Durrett's *Traditions of the Earliest Visits of Foreigners to North America* under 'The Madoc Tradition in Kentucky' he writes:[7]

> This tradition was especially popular in Kentucky, where the Welsh Indians were believed to have dwelt in early times and where they were finally exterminated at the Falls of the Ohio by the Red Indians. The Kentucky pioneers were full believers in this tradition, and in the family circle, by the warmth and light of the huge log fires of the cabins, the story of Prince Madoc was told on long winter nights to eager listeners who never wearied of it.

Three of the people quoted by Campbell above are linked to the Madoc myth – General Clark, Major Harrison and Colonel Moore. Filson was seeking information on the Madoc colony to put in his history of Kentucky. Durrett describes the purpose of the meeting:[8]

> When the members of the club and their guests had assembled ... it was resolved that each person present ... should have the opportunity to state what he knew about the Madoc tradition.

The statements of Clark, Harrison and Moore were similar to those in Campbell's notes. While it seems likely that there was a battle at the Falls, it appears that beliefs in the white moundbuilders and in Madoc had influenced the viewpoints of both the white settlers and Native Americans that the people exterminated were whites.

Joseph Brant (Thayendanegea)

Brant was a great Mohawk military and political leader who fought on the British side. He initially fought for the British against the French in Canada as part of the Seven Years' War and later fought against the American colonists in the American Revolutionary War. He was a man of strong character and great intelligence whose testimony is valuable as it appears to be independent of the Madoc myth.

His life and the border wars of the American Revolution appear in the two-volume work of William Stone (1865). A friend of Stone, Samuel Woodruff, visited Brant in the summer of 1797 at the Grand River Settlement. He remained with Brant for several days and had frequent and full conversations with him on many subjects. Woodruff asked Brant about the tumuli found near the rivers and lakes from the St Lawrence to the Mississippi and Brant replied that the subject had long been agitated but remained in some obscurity, and then continued as follows.[9]

> A tradition, he said, prevailed among the different nations of Indians ... and had been handed down time immemorial, that in an age long gone by, there came white men from a foreign country, and by consent of the Indians established trading-houses and settlements where these tumuli are found. A friendly intercourse continued for several years; many of the white men brought their wives, and had children born to them; and additions to their numbers were made yearly from their own country. These circumstances at length gave rise to jealousies among the Indians and fears began to be entertained ... that becoming strong, they might one day seize upon the country as their own.

Brant then said that a council of chiefs from the St Lawrence to the Mississippi met to form a coalition for a surprise attack and that this was successful in exterminating the whites. He thought that the whites may have been early French and took the tradition so seriously that he made efforts to find out who they were. While in London he gained letters of introduction to scholars in Paris and on his arrival there they assisted him in researching the matter. All he could find out was that around the year 1520 several ships carrying traders, suitable goods for trading and individuals and families departed for north America. They sailed from L'Orient (now Lorient in Brittany) with the intent to plant a colony. However nothing else is known about them.[10]

A similar story of the fighting is told by another Mohawk, John Norton, of Albany, New York. His account has less detail than Brant's and is tailored to add lustre to the Mohawks. The white inhabitants were at war with the Five Nations, but four nations of the Confederacy were badly repulsed when they attacked without the Mohawks. When the Mohawks joined in, the last fort of the whites was finally taken. Although Brant thought that the whites could have been early French settlers and deserves great credit for actively investigating this, it seems unlikely. To have boatloads going back and forth from Brittany and an annihilation of the settlers in the 1520s would surely have been known to others in France.[11]

Further, Jacques Cartier's voyages in 1534-6 discovered nothing of this story. In 1534 he took two young sons of Chief Donnaconna to France and in 1535 brought them back to Canada. Worse, he then kidnapped Donnaconna and other Indians, ten in total, and took them to France. Donnaconna lived at the court of French king, Francis I, but missed his homeland and after four years he died. Given the close contact of the French and the Canadian Native Americans, the story of an earlier massacre of French settlers would have been known to the French had it really occurred.[12]

Stone, Brant's biographer, thought that the whites were probably from Madoc's party or his American descendants and quotes the Triad that Madoc went to sea in 10 ships with 300 men and discovered land far to the west. Stone didn't know that this fake Triad had been forged by Iolo Morganwg. There is no mention of Madoc ap Owain Gwynedd in the crucial early Welsh material. There is not a shred of evidence that he existed and his popularity is due to a mind-boggling number of fabrications and forgeries in both Wales and America.[13]

Mary Kelly's Story

In 1912 the Washington Post carried a story entitled 'Curse of Yellow Hair'. The reporter isn't given but it was assuredly Herman Rave who had written other stories of events in the Falls of the Ohio area and Rose Island, Charlestown. The story came from Mary Kelly, a Shawnee who was a descendant of Black Hawk Stewart, a warrior who had fought against the white settlers. It was sung to her many times in the Indian tongue by her mother when she was young. She lived on a small farm on the Ohio River, not far upriver from where General Clark's cabin had been located. Rave reported that she had just been robbed and murdered by her grandson who had then killed himself. This ended the Shawnee line that had descended from Black Hawk and much further back to another illustrious ancestor, Hawk Wing.

Her story goes back to Hawk Wing's time, when a powerful white people led by Yellow Hair were living at the Falls and for ages they had fought off the Indians. They were religious and worshipped the Sun. Hawk Wing wanted the Falls area for fishing and hunting and planned a surprise attack to exterminate the white people.[14]

> Just as the sun was breaking ... the canoes of Hawk Wing reached the shores of the island. Yellow Hair and his people were awakening from sleep and were falling on their knees in prayer to their sun god. They were in this position when the yells of my people burst upon them. Many were slain as they knelt, but Yellow Hair was a warrior, and though taken by surprise, he seized his battle-ax and valiantly defended his subjects.

The slaughter of the whites continued until all, including women and children, were dead. The Shawnee then took possession of the houses and lands of the vanquished people.

Yellow Hair had earlier met with Hawk Wing's representatives who had threatened war, and his reply was that if war occurred then a curse would be on any Indian that took part and on their descendants. Mary Kelly believed in this curse as her family had died in violent circumstances and her house had mysteriously burned down. As she sat in the roadway at the front gate, viewing the smoldering ruins, Mary Kelly solemnly said: 'It is the curse of Yellow Hair.'

The Stone-Lined Graves

Rave notes that Kelly's farm was bounded by a bubbling spring on the east side, identifiable as Cane Run. Her eastern neighbour was Edward Commines whose land contained a large graveyard where occasionally a skull or a portion of a skeleton was dug up by the plow. These people were of medium stature and were all buried facing the rising sun.

On the river edge of Kelly's farm were 50 graves of people of large stature whom Kelly called the 'kings'. Their tombs were made of rough hewn stone and the occupants were all men, not one of whom was less than six and one half feet tall. George Green, a former Indiana State Geologist, was allowed to open two of these graves with Rave present on one occasion. The kings were in the sitting posture, with their faces turned toward the rising sun and the left temple of each had been crushed in by some blunt instrument. At the time when Green opened two graves (in the 1890s) more than 40 remained. The high water of the Ohio river had washed away some of them.

Rave notes that similar stone-lined graves had also been found by Charlestown archaeologist W. F. Work, 13 miles away, putting them near Devil's Backbone. These also had the left temple of each man crushed in and the bones were those of men of large stature.

William Borden who worked with the State Geologist E. T. Cox on geological surveys, including Devil's Backbone, had observed the slate-lined burials over 20 years earlier.[15]

> The most extensive field for pre-historic research is at Clarkesville below the Falls where there is an ancient burial ground on the river bank. During high water, large masses of the bank are undermined and topple into the river exposing the skeletons, which lie about two feet below the surface. At this place I have frequently found human bones protruding from the bank. The skeletons are enclosed by pieces of slate placed on edge. They are buried in a sitting posture and are covered with shells, and fragments of pottery.

Kelly places the final slaughter on Corn Island where General Clark had initially settled six families. However, by 1873, this island was 'now almost washed away' (Borden, 1874). Colonel Moore and General

Clark place the final slaughter on Sand Island, further downstream. Although Kelly didn't relate the dead warriors to the Madoc myth, others did. According to Rave, Dr Work believed that Yellow Hair's people were the Mandan Indians who are often associated with the descendants of Madoc. Rave further notes that learned archaeologist, Orlando Hobbs, also held this view.[16]

Devil's Backbone

Devil's Backbone is a huge landform in Clark County, Indiana, next to the Ohio River, fourteen miles upstream from the Falls. From the top it gives superb views along the river. On the river side, the cliff face is nearly vertical. On the western side the cliff face is also steep in most parts making the hill very difficult to access. The top of about seven acres is fairly flat and is pear-shaped, rounded at the southern side and narrowing to barely 20 feet at the 'neck' on the northern side. On the west, Fourteen Mile Creek runs close to the hill and curves around towards the Ohio River on the southern side, emptying into the river. There, between the creek and the landform's base, is a flat area called Rose Island. Like the Falls of the Ohio, Devil's Backbone became strongly associated with the Welsh Indians.[17]

By 1786, stories of the Welsh Indians had become commonplace and 'everyone' knew that they existed. Through the late 1700s and into the 1800s 'a Madoc fever burned through America' (Gwyn Williams, 1979). On Boxing Day 1792 John Evans, a young Welshman, while in Baltimore sent a letter to his brother in Carnarvonshire, Wales saying that he was planning to find his 'brethren', the Welsh Indians.[18]

During the period 1795 to 1797 he went 1800 miles up the Missouri River, mapping it, and found the Mandans whom many thought were descendants of Madoc. He traded with them until his goods ran low and thought highly of them (Witte, 2006). However his conclusion on the Welsh Indians was devastating to the Welsh, especially since Evans was Welsh: he had been unable to meet with any such people as the Welsh Indians and had concluded from his meeting with various tribes that there were no such people in existence. The later Lewis and Clark expedition of 1804-1806, using Evans' map, also came to the same negative conclusion.[19]

Despite this, belief in Madoc and the Welsh Indians persisted. In 1841, George Catlin, well known for his writings about and portraits of Native Americans added to the speculation about Madoc:[20]

> Now I am inclined to believe that the ten ships of Madoc ... entered the Mississippi River at The Balize, and made their way up the Mississippi, or that they landed somewhere on the Florida coast, and that their brave and persisting colonists made their way through the interior, to a position on the Ohio River, where they cultivated their fields, and established ... a flourishing colony; but were at length set upon by the savages ... until it was necessary to erect these fortifications for their defense, into which they were at last driven by a confederacy of tribes ... and they in the end have all perished, except perhaps that portion of them who might have formed alliance by marriage with the Indians.

By placing the colony on the Ohio River he reinforced the belief that the Falls of the Ohio region was where they were slaughtered.

Cox's Reports on Devil's Backbone

Devil's Backbone first came into prominence when it was investigated in 1873 by the Indiana State Geologist, E. T. Cox and William Borden, accompanied by a number of citizens of Charlestown. Cox stated that it 'surpasses any antiquity of the kind which has yet been found in the state.' His investigation was rudimentary as it was just a part of other explorations of unusual earthworks and forts. He provided diagrams of the fort by 'stepping over the ground' and in the circumstances did a reasonable job as a starting point. He saw it as a place of refuge that could resist attack: 'The locality selected for this fort presents many natural advantages for making it impregnable to the opposing forces of pre-historic times' (see Cox, 1874; 1875).[21]

His claim that a two-part limestone wall, in total 75 feet high, was built near the 'neck' has been disputed. The first part of the 'wall' was stone laid against the surface of the sloping ground that rose from the hill's base near the creek, covering 65 feet. This terminated at a flat part on the side of the hill on which a 10 foot stone and rubble vertical wall was built. This is my tentative understanding of what he meant, which is unclear because he gave no diagram of the wall.

In 1902, 29 years later, Gerard Fowke gave a vitriolic critique of Cox's 'wall'. He was probably disgusted at the continuing association of the fort with the mythical Madoc and resorted to ridicule.[22]

> The worst publication of this character which has ever appeared in a scientific disguise is that of a former State Geologist of Indiana, who furnishes a report and figure of a most remarkable "Stone Fort" at the mouth of Fourteen Mile Creek, in Clark County, near Charleston ... Both the plan and description of this so-called fort are entirely imaginary ... The reported "walls" of ten and seventy-five feet in height are only the natural outcrop of the heavy, evenly-bedded lime-stone. It seems incredible that a person connected in any capacity with a geological survey, even as cook or mule-driver, could ever have made such a ridiculous blunder as to suppose them artificial.

Witnesses to the 'wall' were Cox and Borden in 1873 and F. W Putnam in 1874 (taken by Cox) who from their other reports were very able men. Three reports appear in Putnam's name (one in *Nature*) which implies that he endorsed it. Modern archaeological methods should be able to resolve the issue. If Fowke is right the evenly-bedded limestone should still be there in the location joining the 'neck' and a judgement could be made as to whether it could be mistaken for laid stone. If Cox is right then most of the loose stone would have been taken away as it was valuable for construction in the 1800s and early 1900s.[23]

Regardless, back in 1874 Cox's report and the imagery of a 75 foot wall implied a huge fortification effort and that the ancient inhabitants had been defending themselves against frequent attacks. This fitted well with the Madoc narrative of the Welsh Indians and with the slaughter of the whites at the nearby Falls of the Ohio.

Who were the Stone-lined Graves People?

The fact that the people in the stone-lined graves were covered with shells and fragments of pottery (Borden, 1874) implies that they were not white people but Native Americans. Recent research identifies them as Native Americans of the Mississippian culture (Munson and McCullough, 2004). There are Mississippian sites near the Falls and further north, including Prather, Devil's Backbone and Rose Island, the area at its southern base. These are all part of the Mississippian Prather complex, the name derived from the important Prather site which is located within the triangle formed by State Road 62, the Charlestown-Jeffersonville Pike and the Salem-Noble Road. It is the best preserved of such sites. Another site of interest is the Elrod and Newcomb site between Clark's Cabin and Silver Creek. It is probably the large burial ground that General Clark mentioned. Guernsey (1942) identifies it as the site in Borden's quote above, with the buried in a sitting posture, covered with shells and fragments of pottery. Guernsey recognized that this culture was shared with other sites such as Prather, Koons, and Willey indicating that the Mississippian culture was spread over quite a large area.[24]

Radiocarbon date ranges (2 standard errors) are given below for three Falls of the Ohio sites. For the Newcomb site, the range is AD 1180 to 1290. For Shippingport, based on a median of nine measures, the range is AD 1310 to 1400. For Eva Bandman, on the floodplain on the Kentucky side opposite Jeffersonville, the dates ranged between AD 1270 to 1470. In contrast, the northern Prather dates are earlier, from AD 1000 to 1250. These dates are from Arnold and Graham (2011), a summary of dates from earlier research.[25]

The Mississippian culture featured a strong centralized control by a chief or by a small group. This led to increased conflict between tribes and stockades were frequently built for defence. Munson and McCullough (2004) speculate on whether a log palisade was built around the central Prather site. Munson et al. (2006) state that these palisades were typically well planned and stoutly constructed, often with bastions spaced at intervals, as opposed to non-Mississippian palisades which were often constructed of smaller diameter posts, typically without bastions. A battle at the Falls between Mississippian tribes would fit the aggression present at that time.[26]

Native American sites were frequently settled and reused by later cultures and Devil's Backbone appears to have been used by the earlier Middle Woodland culture. On the top of Devil's Backbone three flint quarry pits have been discovered on the Fourteen Mile Creek side, along with a flint chipping station, and it shares several other features with Middle Woodland sites (Sipe, 2004).[27]

Madoc myth absorbed into Cherokee Lore

To summarize, we have seven reports from Native Americans that say there was an ancient white race living in America that was eventually exterminated by their ancestors. Six reports put them in Kentucky, of which three specifically mention the Falls of the Ohio. Joseph Brant doesn't give a specific location. Two are Shawnee and the others are Piankeshaw, Sauk and Mohawk. One is 'different tribes northwest of the Ohio' and another is 'an old Indian', presumably in Kentucky, as he spoke to Colonel Moore of Kentucky.

If the white moundbuilder belief and the Madoc mania in America did not exist before these reports were given, then these reports would have to be taken very seriously. However, these beliefs did exist and the question is how far did it influence these reports. Gwyn Williams (1979) is in no doubt that the statements of white Madoc believers had been accepted by Native Americans, incorporated into the lore of a tribe and attributed to their ancestors. He remarks: [28]

> A beautiful illustration of the way minds were working in the late eighteenth century – and of the power of suggestion which white minds could exercise over red – is provided by the account John Sevier ... gave of his talks with Oconostota, a chief of the Cherokee.

Sevier spoke to Oconostota in 1782 but his story wasn't published until Amos Stoddard's (1812) history. He asked Oconostota who had built the forts in his country. The chief replied that his forefathers said that white people, who had formerly inhabited the country, built them. The Cherokees had lived lower down in the country, now South Carolina, and had fought the white people for many years. Finally a truce was called and the whites agreed to leave, making their way to the Missouri River and 'then up that river to a very great distance' and that they are 'now on some of its branches'. This story of the northwest retreat of the whites can be traced back to Cornstalk in his 1776 talks with McKee but Cornstalk had applied it to the white moundbuilders. [29]

It is obvious that Oconostota's tribe had just absorbed the Madoc tradition at that time. As the 'forts' were built about 1300 years ago, his ancestors would have had no idea who built them, as some other Indian tribes truthfully stated. Second, Oconostota was just repeating the whites' belief that Madoc's descendants had made their way up the Missouri River, a very great distance, and were now on some of its branches. How could the Cherokee possibly know this as they were in North America's southeast in South Carolina while Madoc's supposed descendants were in obscurity in the far northwest?

Sevier asked Oconostota if his ancestors knew the nation to which the white people belonged. He replied that his grandfather and other old people said that they were a people called Welsh and that they had crossed the great water to land near the mouth of the Alabama River, but that the Mexican Indians had driven them north, to the heads of its waters, and even to the Hiwassee River. These Mexican Indians had been driven out of their own country by the Spaniards.

As noted earlier in this book, the term 'Welsh' was a derogatory name given to the Britons by the Saxons and meant 'foreigners'. In the late 1100s, Gerald of Wales said that their own name was the *Cymry* which appears early in poetry c. 632. If the mythical Madoc did exist, they would have been *Cymry* in America. This implies that Oconostota was taking the term 'Welsh' from late current beliefs. Also the notion above that Mexican Indians drove the Welsh north seems to allude to the fiction that the Welsh were in Mexico.[30]

Oconostota also told Sevier that Peg, an old Cherokee woman, was given a book by an Indian *living high up the Missouri River* whom she thought was Welsh. It had been 'consumed by fire' but others claimed to have seen it and claimed it was worn and disfigured. This is hardly a real ancient tradition of Cherokee ancestors.[31]

One may ask how Peg obtained the book. Did the old woman travel for thousands of miles from the southeast to the far northwest to find a Welsh tribe that no one else could locate, to then be allowed to take away one of their most precious items, and then bring it all the way back to Oconostota?

This is just another 'Welsh Bible' fabrication. It is telling that this precious Welsh book was also no longer available. Despite the various tales of Welsh Bibles, books or manuscripts written in ink, not one has ever been made available to a Welsh linguist or placed into a museum. It is similar to the six Welsh brass breastplates which disappeared as soon as John Campbell asked to see them.

White moundbuilders absorbed into Mohawk Lore

The Mohawk accounts in the north seem to have greater credibility as there are apparently no associations with the Madoc myth in their traditions. Joseph Brant was a man of sharp intelligence who believed the Mohawk tradition of the extermination of a white race, which he thought were early French, and went to Paris to find out about them. His theory of visitors from Brittany is insufficient to account for the legend. However the Mohawks were influenced by the white mound builders myth and part of Brant's earlier statement implies that white people had built the tumuli (mounds).

> A tradition ... had been handed down time immemorial, that in an age long gone by, there came white men from a foreign country, and by consent of the Indians established trading-houses and settlements where these tumuli are found.

Joseph Brant says that the tradition had been handed down from time immemorial but the tradition that the moundbuilders were white only probably developed after white settlement. The white moundbuilder myth did influence the Mohawk accounts and this tradition, thought to be ancient, became embedded in Indian lore within 200 years.

Summary

Probably all the Indian stories mentioned earlier were influenced by either the white moundbuilder myth, or the Madoc myth, or by other stories derived from these myths even though the stories were thought to be part of the traditions of their ancestors.

The burials in the stone-lined graves, covered in shells and pottery fragments, imply they were Native Americans, not white outsiders. Modern research has identified them as Native Americans of the Mississippian culture and the radiocarbon dates confirm this. They lived in a time of conflict where they built sturdy wooden palisades around their central areas for protection and there were Mississippian sites around the Falls of the Ohio and further north including Prather and Devil's Backbone. It seems inescapable that the bodies at the Falls were not white visitors as the legends state.

13
IRISHMAN IN WEST VIRGINIA
AD 710

In 2018, while I was in the United States, a friend told me of a 2004 paper in *Ancient American* with the title 'An 8th century Irishman in West Virginia'. The author was Robert Pyle whose role in discovering the rock carvings there was earlier discussed. The magazine's front cover featured a colour photo of an ancient partial skull still having some of its teeth. Its heading was '700 AD European in West Virginia'. As I had not heard of this find before, I sent a letter to Pyle, giving my email, and enquiring about the skull, but did not receive a prompt response. Months later I had returned to Australia and had forgotten about it when I received an email from a friend of Pyle's family who had worked with him for many years. She told me that Robert Pyle had passed away in December 2017 and she was helping his family decide what to do with his effects. She kindly sent me many of his papers on the analyses done on the bones.[1]

The Cook site: where the skeletal remains were found

After the 1983 *Wonderful West Virginia* articles Pyle kept looking for promising sites. One such site was only about 10 miles away from the Luther Elkins site. The land was owned by Lowell and Eve Cook and had similar Indian rock art patterns including a pattern that some thought looked like a boat, which Pyle called a 'Boat Rebus'. Barry Fell didn't translate it and the two 'translations' given in Pyle (1998) are utterly different.[2]

In May 1989 Pyle did a test dig in front of a rock shelter not far from the site and discovered the skeletal remains. They were at a depth of 35 inches and were close to the back wall of the shelter which had a low roof. He recovered parts of long bones in various sizes and about one third of the skull, with some teeth still in place and some displaced near the skull. He also found projectile heads, tools such as scrapers and pottery sherds. In a 2002 paper Pyle gives a plan of the site which has the buried bones 224 ft (74 m) east from the 'Boat Rebus'.[3]

Analysis from Brigham Young University

Pyle kept possession of the bones until the year 2000 when he found a benefactor, Earl Hill, to pay for the analyses. Hill's name and his email address had appeared in Pyle's correspondence and so I was able to obtain further information from him. Four teeth and a long bone had been sent to Scott Woodward, Professor of Microbiology at the Archaeological/Genetic Laboratory, Brigham Young University, Utah whose lab did the DNA work on one of the teeth.[4]

The mitochondrial DNA sequence

In May 2001 a segment of the mitochondrial DNA sequence from the tooth was printed – a long row of 277 base pairs between nucleotide positions 16137 and 16413. The base pairs are shown by the letters A (adenine), T (thymine), C (cytosine) and G (guanine) in which A pairs with T and C pairs with G.

As well as the tooth DNA, another 21 DNA sequences were given for comparison, including British, European and Native American sequences. These pages gave each sequence name on the left followed by a pattern of 277 letters, each from the A, T, C, G set. There were 22 such rows. These were photocopied for Pyle but on one page of the photocopies many of the base pairs were not legible and I could not make much use of it.[5]

Coloured DNA sequences

Fortunately Earl Hill also had various printouts from his work with Pyle which he kindly sent me. It included a coloured set of sequences printed with the four bases (A/T, C/G) in different colours making it easier to distinguish them. This had been printed in June 2001. The coloured set had only two sequence rows, the tooth sequence and the Anderson reference sequence for comparison.[6]

Absolute Difference Matrix

Also enclosed in the various material was an *absolute difference matrix* with 22 rows and 22 columns where all possible combinations are compared. For example (Col. 2, Row 20), would show how many base pair differences occurred between Sequence 2 and Sequence 20.

As Sequence 2 is the tooth, looking down Column 2 allows one to see the rows where the differences are minimal and the most like the tooth. The closest matches were from England, Wales, Sardinia and Finland, each with 3 differences from the 277 nucleotide positions. The Native American sequences for the haplogroups A, C and D had 7 differences from the tooth sequence, while the Native American haplogroup B sequences were closer with 4 differences.

Pyle used this difference matrix to infer that the closest matches were not Native American. In his letter to Pyle dated 24 March 2002, Woodward gave no conclusion on the implications of the tooth DNA, simply describing the various sequences to Pyle and the meaning of the absolute distance matrix.[7]

The Dating of the Bones

The C14 dating was performed by Tom Stafford of Stafford Research Laboratories using a long bone passed on to him by Scott Woodward in December 2000. He used the accelerator mass spectrometry (ams) technique which gave the interesting result that the long bone dated to AD 710 ± 60 at two standard errors. That is, the 95.4% confidence interval was AD 770 - 650.[8]

The Checking Process

Tom Stafford is a rigorous scientist who was aware of the potential political situation brewing and urged great caution and the checking of everything before announcing any results. In his letter to Pyle giving the AD 710 date, he lists activities that should be performed to check the results and mentions Doug Owsley, a physical anthropologist from the Smithsonian, as a person who could help.[9]

Terry Melton's Review

This checking process began when Pyle requested that Terry Melton, President of Mitotyping Technologies, in Pennsylvania, review the mitochondrial DNA analysis report from Scott Woodward. On 27 November 2002 she wrote to Owsley stating that Pyle had asked for the review and that she had seen the 277 base pair sequence. She noted that it was 'not very closely related to any sequences from the many international populations surveyed to date'. She then recommended that a second lab attempt to reproduce and possibly augment the data already collected.[10]

Eventually, Terry Melton's lab was asked to perform this additional analysis task but some time elapsed before this was decided. Others were interested in what was happening and were keen to be kept informed. For example, Catherine Sipe (2004) knew of the Brigham Young DNA results, the AD 710 dating by Stafford and the existence of petroglyphs thought to be Irish Ogam, not far from where the bones were found. In 2003 she had contacted Doug Owsley in a personal communication to get an update:[11]

> However, Doug Owsley, forensic anthropologist of the Smithsonian Institution, fears there may have been contamination in the samples and from his examination, he feels the skull is Native American.

Confusion about the Dating of the Bones

Another source of confusion at this time concerned the date of the skeleton. While Stafford's report is clear and precise, Pyle didn't know how the dating worked. He thought the uncalibrated radiocarbon year (which was 780) was the date to use and somehow got the idea that the AD date was obtained by subtracting the radiocarbon year from the current calendar year. So in a 2002 paper he dated the skull to AD 1222 (i.e. 2002 – 780) but in other papers he dated the skull to AD 1220 (i.e. 2000 – 780).[12]

The latter became part of the Smithsonian official record. In his formal acceptance of the bones, Doug Owsley states 'These remains, radiocarbon dated at 1220 AD, are an important addition to the human skeletal collection for West Virginia.' Similarly, when Terry Melton was asked to review the DNA sequence she uses the 1220 AD dating provided by Pyle. The analyses of the bones found by Pyle were also placed on the Prehistoric Planet website with the 1220 dating. Earl Hill, who helped Pyle extensively, was later able to get this changed to the correct 710 date. Another less serious error is that Pyle used the uncalibrated standard error of ± 40. This should be changed to ± 30 (or ± 60 for two standard errors).[13]

The Second DNA Analysis, Mitotyping Technologies

On 1 August 2003 Terry Melton received a different tooth from Owsley to do the second DNA analysis. On 6 November she sent a report giving her results (labelled Case 2346) to both Pyle and Owsley. She obtained a mitochondrial DNA sequence for the nucleotide positions 15998 to 16374. This DNA segment is not available in the papers I have received but her analysis in the report is sufficient to show how her results differed from the Woodward lab, as shown below.

Table 13.1 Differences in the two DNA analyses

	Nucleotide Position							
	16197	16223	16290	16306	16313	16319	16362	16363
Stand.	C	C	C	C	C	G	T	C
Lab 1	C	C	C	C	C	G	T	C
Lab 2	Y	T	Y	Y	Y	A	C	Y
		*				*	*	

In Table 13.1, Lab 1 is Scott Woodward's and Lab 2 is Terry Melton's. The Standard row is a comparison sequence. A characteristic of the Lab 2 row is the inconclusive base results that Melton denotes by 'Y'. It means that *both* a 'T' and a 'C' were observed. Melton remarks that this may be characteristic of very old DNA, but there are three clear results, shown by my asterisks. These three deviations from the Standard indicate a Native American origin. Melton observes that this profile is most closely related to Native American haplogroup A(1,2). However the Lab 1 results are just identical to the Standard Sequence for these nucleotide positions. Melton also states[14]

'the sequence we have observed in this sample is not similar to a profile obtained from a tooth from the same site analyzed by Dr Scott Woodward at Brigham Young University in 2001'.

A Typo error in Melton's Report

Unfortunately in Melton's report to Owsley a typo was made in one of the important comparisons. In nucleotide position 16362 the typist had reversed the bases for the Standard and the Lab 2 sequences, incorrectly giving 'C' for the Standard and 'T' for Lab 2. This has now been corrected above in Table 13.1 to show 'T' for the Standard and 'C' for Lab 2. As this mistake is part of the Smithsonian official correspondence it should be noted.[15]

Summary of the Current Situation

My view is that the case for an Irishman being in West Virginia in circa AD 710 has now been fatally weakened. The elements that looked so promising to Robert Pyle at one stage have collapsed.

Firstly, the inscriptions on stone believed by many to be Celtic Ogam do not appear to be writing, but Native American rock art. The proponents of the Ogam belief like Barry Fell, Robert Meyer and others have passed away and later more critical scholars have strongly attacked the notion that it is Ogam. This nullifies a major part of the argument that early visitors from the British Isles were implied from the inscriptions.

Secondly, Doug Owsley's worry that the first sample may have become contaminated is probably correct. Its sequence differs greatly from that derived by Melton and frequently agrees with the reference sample. Melton's analysis implies that the man was probably a Native American from haplogroup A(1,2).

A Third DNA Analysis?

DNA labs interested in performing a third analysis should contact the Smithsonian's National Museum of Natural History Anthropology *Collections Advisory Committee* (CAC) to get guidelines on how to present a request. In the last two decades one would expect that such techniques would have been further improved and that such an analysis should give scientific clarity. Perhaps more information on the ancient man can be obtained. In my view it would be appropriate to have a third test and have the results (alongside the initial two results) published in a journal to make it openly available.

The Smithsonian appears to be at stage where it is looking to return material to Native Americans who can successfully claim ownership. While the early 710 date might make it hard to establish ownership, another tooth from the collection could be released for analysis under the condition that, after it was done, the entire collection would be respectfully reburied at the Cook site where it was found. In 2001 Robert Pyle held a reinterment ceremony with the other material he found there that the Smithsonian didn't take. The catalogue number for the remains is Physical Anthropology #2028586.[16]

14
ANCIENT ROMAN COINS IN AMERICA

There have been three waves of belief that a white people had been in America before Columbus. The earliest was the white moundbuilders myth later followed by a Madoc fever in which more and more details accrued to the story which at its heart had no substance at all. As Gwyn Williams states, at one stage 'everyone' knew that the Welsh Indians existed. These stories became absorbed into the beliefs of the Indian tribes and stories were told of the massacre of the whites in Kentucky. But now it seems that the graves thought to be the slain whites were instead Native Americans of the Mississippian culture.

A third wave of interest in pre-Columbian visitors was created by Barry Fell from his books, *America BC* (1976), *Saga America* (1980) and *Bronze Age America* (1982). Fell's thesis included not just white people but multiple samples of different peoples visiting America at various times. His books appear to be packed with evidence but each piece, it seems to me, is superficially treated before moving on to the next and most scholars think his case is far-fetched. However he did attract supporters who were interested in finding further evidence to support his claims. Such evidence includes the finding of ancient coins in inland America which could suggest ancient visitors. In response to these claims Jeremiah Epstein (1980) performed a valuable task in assembling and analysing a list of such coins. His paper also included commentary from those of differing beliefs about the probability of pre-Columbian voyages to America. In this chapter only Roman coins are considered, which dominate his list.

Epstein concludes that the presence of these coins is explained by modern (post-Columbian) coin losses. This was contested by some of the commentators on his paper. While his conclusion seems plausible for most of the coins in his list, are there any such coins which cannot be explained in this way? Epstein's paper does not include a number of batches of Roman coins which he did not know about at the time of writing and other batches were only discovered after he published. These batches will now be considered.[1]

Coins found on Indiana side of Sherman Minton Bridge

In 1963 a construction engineer found a small hoard of coins while excavating the north bank of the Ohio River during construction of the Sherman Minton Bridge. The coins seemed to be grouped as though they were originally in a leather pouch that had disintegrated away. The discoverer kept most of the coins for himself, but gave two of them to another engineer working there. This engineer told his wife of the discovery and kept the two coins at his house. Not long after the find, the discoverer moved south to work on another bridge, taking the bulk of the coins with him. Decades passed and the second engineer died.

In 1997, his widow brought the two coins to Troy McCormick, then the manager of the new Falls of the Ohio Museum, who put them on display in an exhibit. The widow couldn't remember the name of the first engineer who had found the coins so now only the two coins are available. One is a bronze of Claudius II who reigned from AD 268-270. The second is a follis of Maximinus II from AD 310-313. Troy McCormick gave this information to Hu McCulloch who preserved it on his Ohio State University website.[2]

Coins found in Cave in Breathitt County, Kentucky

In a Kentucky cave Michael Griffith found a group of heavily corroded Roman coins. The three best preserved are shown on McCulloch's website. It's hard to make out the images but Norman Totten, a former History Professor and expert in identifying Roman coins, said that two were antoniniani, a bronze coin from AD 238-305. The emperors were wearing the 'solar crown'. One of these appears to have Provident on the reverse, facing left and holding a baton and cornucopia. A Claudius II coin has a solar crown and such a reverse. The third coin is thicker, and the emperor wears a laureate wreath rather than a crown. Totten thought that this coin probably dates to a similar period.[3]

Coins found by Fred Kingman along the Wisconsin River

During the 1970s, Fred Kingman who lived near Wisconsin Rapids, was exploring along the banks of the Wisconsin River with his metal detector. When it gave a strong signal he found a batch of 10 coins that appeared to be Roman. He took no action on the coins until early 1994, when he contacted Fred Rydholm who lived in Marquette, Michigan. Rydholm then rang James Scherz who invited Kingman to give a talk on the coins on 18 May 1994 at the University of Wisconsin-Madison. One is too corroded to be identified. Another shows an 'emperor' with a moustache but hasn't been identified. Scherz (1994) identified four coins and suggested two others, another Claudius II and Tetricus. The latter appears to have Spes on the reverse raising the hem of her robe. Of the ten coins, I tentatively identify six.[4]

Coins found by David Wells near Rose Island

In early 2009, David and Don Wells of Charlestown, Indiana went exploring along the Ohio River. Don was looking for arrowheads but David had brought his metal detector. On the riverbank about 300-350 yards east of Rose Island he got a hit from the detector and found eight weird-looking coins. He didn't know they were Roman coins. At a coffee gathering at McDonalds, David showed the coins to a friend who suggested that David contact Bob Gallman, the president of the Clarks Grant Historical Society. Gallman recognized them as Roman and alerted Lee Pennington. They then met with Wells to photograph and identify the coins. Lee Pennington (2009) gives this account and relates the discovery to the Sherman Minton, Wayne Griffith, and Fred Kingman coins. Of the eight coins, I tentatively identify five.[5]

Second set found by Wells near Bethlehem, Indiana

On 14 June 2009, David Wells found a second batch of Roman coins near Bethlehem. They were about a mile north of Bethlehem and Don went upriver while David went downstream. Before lunch, he found three coins with his metal detector and after lunch went back to the same spot and found eight more. They were about four to six inches deep and spread over about 30 feet along the shore. Lee Pennington also took colour photos of these and discussed them in Pennington (2010). Of the eleven coins, I tentatively identify seven.[6]

In Table 14.1 the various finds are presented together for comparison, with the coins sorted by date from the earliest to the latest. The Roman coins found in Iceland are also included.

Table 14.1 Roman coins by location and date

Iceland	Date (AD)	Wisconsin River in the 1970s	Date (AD)
Aurelian	270–275	Claudius II	268-270
Tacitus	275–276	Claudius II	268-270
Probus	276–282	Tetricus	270-273
Diocletian	284–305	Tetricus	270-273
		Diocletian	284-305
		Constantine II	337-340

Rose Island, IND February 2009		Bethlehem, IND 14 June 2009	
Claudius II	268-270	Claudius II	268-270
Claudius II	268-270	Claudius II	268-270
Aurelian	270-275	Probus	276–282
Constantine I	306-337	Probus	276–282
Constantine II	337-340	Constantine I	306-337
		Constantine I	306-337
		Constans	337-350

Sherman Minton Bridge IND, 1963		Breathitt County, Kentucky	
Claudius II	268-270	Claudius II?	268-270
Maximinus II	310-313	Solar Radiate	Unknown
		Laureate wreath	Unknown

At first glance, the finding of so many batches of Roman coins dating to the third or fourth century seems to suggest one or more ancient expeditions to America by people who used these coins. It could be the Romans themselves, or Britons who had been under Roman rule for nearly four centuries, but the widespread use of such coins makes it difficult to narrow it down to a particular people. A further point of interest is that with the exception of the Kentucky find, the coins were found alongside rivers, the probable way ancient travellers would have explored the interior of America. Three of these batches were found through the use of the metal detector.

However, there are unexpected features in the coin patterns. Dr T. Buttrey, an eminent scholar and President of the Royal Numismatic Society from 1989-94, makes a comment which implies that a typical early hypothetical visitor to America would have been carrying coins limited in minting date and geographical location:[7]

> Although Greek and Roman coins were produced in incredible quantity and variety, at any given moment or place the actual circulation was normally limited to certain denominations, types, and mints and to one specific monetary system.

In a modern example in Western societies, a household on 1 January 2000 would have had the bulk of its coins from the 1990s, less from the 1980s, even less from the 1970s, and perhaps a few from the 1960s or earlier. The dating distribution would be negatively skewed.

Anomalous Patterns in the Coin distributions

In the Wisconsin case a hypothetical visitor to America had a coin of Constantine II, of earliest possible date, 337. Most of his coins should have been around this date and tapering off for earlier dates but this is not the case. He has two of Claudius II which are at least 67 years earlier. The very early coins are occurring at about the same frequency as the latest coins. It is even worse when we include Tetricus, giving four early coins compared to the one late Constantine coin.

The locations of the emperors differ widely. In 306, Constantine I was proclaimed emperor in Britain and by 330 had moved the capital to Constantinople where his son Constantine II ruled. Claudius II was declared emperor near Milan, northern Italy, and is famous for his massive defeat of the Goths at Naissus, in modern Serbia. Tetricus was the last emperor of the Gallic empire in the far west and was defeated by Aurelian at Châlons, in modern France.

Although the samples are small, the pattern of having more than expected early coins also occurs in the Bethlehem and Rose Island samples. This pattern is not typical of coins expected to be held by an ancient visitor but is more like modern coin collections which are expected to vary in date and geography.

Improbabilities

Norman Totten agrees that the Venezuelan hoard of Roman coins in Epstein's paper was likely a collection but argues that art-collecting Romans would also have had coin collections. His implication seems to be that an ancient Roman took his coin collection to Venezuela. The latter seems highly improbable. If America were known circa 350 and the visit was intentional exploration (rather than a ship being blown off course) it would hardly be the place to bring one's coin collection because of the potential dangers and the unknown. A large part of the pleasure obtained from owning such a collection would be to display them for similarly cultured aristocrats to admire. There was a shortage of the latter in ancient America. Similar considerations apply to the batches of Roman coins in Table 14.1.[8]

If an ancient ship was taking a collection to another destination, perhaps to sell, and was blown off course and landed on the east coast of America then it cannot explain the inland batches of coins. The crew would hardly set about exploring the inland rivers. After ensuring that the ship was still seaworthy, and perhaps a brief coastal exploration, they would set sail for their original intended destination.

The Planting of Coins

Epstein's explanation of coin losses by modern collectors seems the most likely for individual coins, but not for the batches in Table 14.1 which are not in his paper. It's hard to imagine a man in Wisconsin taking his coin collection with him for a walk along the Wisconsin River and inexplicably losing it without being aware of the loss. It's also difficult to imagine modern people taking their coin collections to spots alongside the Ohio River in Indiana and losing them.

If one accepts that hypothetical ancient visitors to America would be unlikely to be carrying coins with date patterns like the ones found, and that modern coin collectors would be unlikely to have taken them to riverbanks, then the deliberate planting of coins should be considered. The reasons for the planting of coins and other artifacts may be grouped into two categories. One is unfocused, perhaps to play a joke, or hoping to confuse or mislead future discoverers, or simply for one's private amusement. The coins themselves are not expensive and not very difficult to obtain, as Norman Totten points out. One interesting example of this is given by Buttrey:[9]

> Fraud is possible, as in the case of a Roman coin recently discovered during water-pipe excavations. The homeowner laboriously did his own work, and his neighbour, a professor of classics, made it more interesting by planting an inexpensive Roman coin where it could easily be dug up – as it was.

Madoc and Ancient Roman Coins

The second category for such planting is to convince people of the credibility of a certain belief. This could have motivated a planting of the three coin batches found along the Ohio River at the sites of the Sherman Minton Bridge, Rose Island and Bethlehem. The Sherman Minton site is close to Sand Island a Madoc hotspot near the Falls. Similarly, the Rose Island location is at the foot of Devil's Backbone, another Madoc hotspot. Devil's Backbone is in the middle, about 16 miles downriver from Bethlehem and about 16 miles upriver from the Sherman Minton Bridge. If people believed that Madoc used ancient Roman coins and these were found at exactly the sites linked to Madoc then this would surely convince them that Madoc had actually been there and was the discoverer of America.

The Association of Madoc with Ancient Roman Coins

The belief that Madoc used ancient Roman coins in Wales and brought them to America is absurd. In the supposed time of Madoc, the Welsh had a mainly cattle economy but for coins used halfpennies, pennies and shillings, not Roman coins. The Roman coins in America were over 800 years before Madoc's time. Had he existed, he would have found it hard to find such old Roman coins in Wales.

At some point, the weird linking of Madoc to Roman coins became well established. If this time can be found, it sets a lower limit for the time that Madoc-motivated planting of coins along the Ohio River could have occurred. The early finding of Roman coins in America is discussed in Caleb Atwater (1820) and John Haywood (1823). Atwater was scathing about such finds: 'That some persons have purposely lost coins, medals etc. in caves which they knew were about to be explored;

307

or deposited them in tumuli, which they knew were about to be opened, is a well known fact, which has occurred at several places in this western country'. Haywood, however, speculates that sailors from east Asia brought the coins to America, obtained through Roman trade with China. Neither connected the coins to Madoc. A search of the 1700s, 1800s Madoc material failed to find any sources linking him to Roman coins. Similarly, the early 1900s yield nothing.[10]

Apparently the first association of Madoc with Roman coins occurs in a footnote in *Dawn of Tennessee Valley and Tennessee History* by Samuel Cole Williams (1937). After mentioning Madoc's discovery and settlement in America, he remarks on a Roman coin mentioned by Haywood which had been found about 1818, on the site of Fayetteville, Tennessee on the Elk River. In his footnote he asks:[11]

> Who but Madoc's men or De Soto's men could have brought the coin
> to that place?

He then notes that Haywood's argument had ruled out the coin being lost by De Soto or anyone subsequent to the discovery of Columbus. This left Madoc. This footnote would probably have gone unnoticed had not Zella Armstrong began to write a *History of Hamilton County and Chattanooga Tennessee* and used Samuel Cole Williams' book above for material. In her Appendix she thanks him for the data and writes about 'the discovery in Tennessee of Roman coins which must have been brought there by the Welsh'. This was published in 1940 but was still obscure. However she later referred to the Roman coins in a non scholarly book *Who Discovered America? The Amazing Story of Madoc* (1950) which was widely read. From then on the Roman coins began to be linked to Madoc.[12]

In 1953 the Daughters of the American Revolution (DAR) erected a Prince Madoc plaque at Fort Morgan near Mobile, Alabama. It cites evidence for the Madoc claims and one was the finding of Roman coins in forts in Tennessee. Non scholarly works on Madoc began citing the coins as evidence; e.g. Ellen Pugh (1970), Dana Olson (1987), James Callahan (2000). It is interesting that a current belief not sufficiently credible for use by the Madoc boosters of the 1700s/1800s derives from a footnote by Samuel Cole Williams in 1937.[13]

When were the Ohio River coins planted?

Two reasons suggest that the Roman coins were planted after 1950. The first is that the Roman coins were only connected to Madoc in the public mind after 1950 from Armstrong's book and the DAR plaque at Fort Morgan in 1953 shows that the idea had taken hold. The second is that after World War II the volume of Roman coins in America had massively increased as pointed out by Epstein (1980):[14]

> The striking increase in coin discoveries comes after World War II; ... This coincides with a time when Americans, whether as inductees or as tourists, traveled to Europe in great numbers ... The number of coins purchased by Americans is hard to estimate, but it must be quite large. ... Coin collectors and dealers tell me that the growth of coin collecting in America is essentially a post-World War II phenomenon.

The most plausible explanation for the Sherman Minton, Rose Island and Bethlehem batches is that they had been planted along the 32 mile stretch of the Ohio to include key Madoc sites by a Madoc enthusiast, this occurring around the early 1950s. The Wisconsin coins are distant from the Ohio River coins which suggests they were not planted by the same person, although it's not impossible. It is pointless to speculate on how they got there. The Kentucky cave coins were badly corroded and may have been there for a long time. They could be an example of the coins planted in caves noted by Atwater in 1820. The coin finders were not the planters, merely the discoverers, this being made much easier by the metal detector.

There is no evidence that Madoc ap Owain Gwynedd existed, but if he did, he certainly wouldn't have used Roman coins. Yet these coins occur at two Madoc hotspots on the Ohio and a third place upriver. If ancient visitors, c. 340, lost Roman coins at precisely these Madoc hotspots it would be an amazing coincidence. It strongly implies that they are Madoc plants. The notion that ancient people using Roman coins explored American inland rivers is interesting but the onus is on the advocates to establish this. I have argued that the coin finds currently available are not adequate as evidence for this task.

15
ARTHUR IN AMERICA

The American section of this book has analyzed claims that there were pre-Columbian visitors to America. The Norse are not discussed here as their legends and their settlement in Newfoundfound have been extensively covered by others. The other pre-Columbian claims are mainly non literary. With the exceptions of Brendan and Arthur, there is no early tale that says 'X' sailed to an unknown land that can be identified as America. Brendan's *Navigatio* has many weaknesses. It has marvelous events and is vague on locations and directions. On the key voyage to the 'Promised Land of the Saints' it gives few details, but when all his voyages are considered, it gives enough hints to suggest a knowledge of far voyaging into the Atlantic in the sixth century.

The first Madoc story was finished by Humphrey Llwyd in 1559 but was unpublished. This was 67 years after Columbus and it is almost bereft of details, being an attempt to put the fables into writing. It says that Madoc went, returned and went again, with further details being Llwyd's suppositions or knowledge derived from the Spanish. His story was not published until 1584 by David Powel and by then the unwarranted accretions were beginning to be added.

Fell's cases in his books rely on artifacts – inscriptions, drawings, coins, and so on. He provides masses of data but treats each item only briefly. It is difficult to trust many of his assertions. To satisfy my own curiosity I decided to take just one sentence out of his *Wonderful West Virginia* translations and analyze every step. The result was far worse than I expected which raises doubts about his other conclusions.

In Arthur's case, the evidence that he sailed to America is purely literary, coming mainly from one poem, *Spoils of Annwfyn* and I have argued that it was orally composed very early, c. AD 540. Like early Welsh poems in general, this doesn't give a narrative in chronological order but a series of scenes that describe the journey. From these, features of early America can be recognized. The events in this poem are supported by a section in *Battle of the Trees* which deals with the enemy gathering for battle by the streams, the torrid fighting and the death of Arthur. Are there any indicators, other than literary allusions, that Arthur reached the interior of America? As he sailed nearly 1500 years ago it seems unlikely that any solid evidence could be found. My belief is that the literary allusions are convincing and are sufficient to establish a case that he was killed there. However there is perhaps one indicator, while not strong enough to be classed as evidence, that could provide support for the literary case.

AN ANCIENT BRITISH COIN IN AMERICA

In *Saga America* (1980) Barry Fell relates the story of the finding of an unusual coin in Champaign, Illinois, a British minim. In May 1885 it was found in a lump of clay by an eight-year-old boy, Alexander, during the digging of a trench in the reconstruction of a street. His father then made a notarized statement about the find. Fell remarks that the statement gave the important information that the minim had been 'under 4 feet of undisturbed clay'. The coin and the notarized statement were then passed down to a descendant of the boy, Gordon A. Price of Wiggins, Colorado. Price had made a number of efforts to have it identified but these proved fruitless. He later sent a letter, the coin, and a copy of the notarized statement to Fell.[1]

Fell shared this information with Norman Totten who added the additional information that above the clay layer in which it was found was a thick layer of black soil. This fact is given by Donal Buchanan in Epstein (1980). Unfortunately Fell doesn't reproduce the notarized statement or give exact quotes from it. He also doesn't give a photo of the coin but gives a drawing of it and states that its diameter is 12 mm. It is a minim of poor workmanship. The obverse side has part of a man's face, facing right with what could be a laurel wreath for a crown but this is far from certain. The reverse side has the winged Victory holding up a laurel wreath in her right hand.[2]

British coins in the time of Gildas

In the time of Gildas, a cattle economy and barter were in use although some coins were available. Gildas makes three references to coins. In section 66.3 he berates the current clergy: 'They preach, lip-deep, that the poor should be given alms, but themselves contribute not a groat'.

Gildas calls this coin the 'obol', the name of the smallest silver Greek coin, but according to Philip Hill (1949-51) he wasn't referring literally to the Greek coin but to tiny British copper coins of similar low value, the minimi, a coin here called the British minim. In translating 'obol' as 'groat' Winterbottom (1978) uses the same approach as the groat was a very low-value coin that was common in the Middle Ages.[3]

Gildas also refers to the minim coin in 107.4. He compares Judas' betrayal of Christ with the appalling wickedness of the current clergy: 'He [Judas] thought the price for the saviour of all men was thirty silver pieces; your price is but a single groat'.[4]

Gildas refers to a second coin as the denarius, probably a silver coin (siliqua) reduced in size by clipping around the edges, the clippings being taken for their silver value. Winterbottom translates this higher value coin as a 'penny'. Gildas berates the greed of the clergy: 'If they lose a single penny, they grieve; if they gain one, they cheer up'.[5]

Barbarous imitations

Fell refers to Hill's paper on the minimi and dates the mimim sent by Price to the late 300s, early 400s, before the arrival of the Saxons. He doesn't say how he obtained these early dates and gives the impression the dates came from Hill's paper, but Hill does not imply this. While these small barbarous imitations were produced over a wide date range, the most probable date for this coin was much later, as argued below. After the Romans had left Britain by AD 410 the Britons had to rely mostly on their existing coin supply. By 450 and later, the scarcity of coins and the metal to make them was critical. The Britons had to make their own coins that were far inferior to the ones produced in the Roman mints. Hill gives an example of how barbarous copies were made from existing coins:[6]

> ... the source of supply for their flans was the orichalcum sestertii and dupondii of the Early Empire hammered out, often into the thinness of a wafer, and roughly cut up with a chisel or shears, usually without any regard for neatness of execution. One sestertius would in that way produce metal for quite a substantial number of new coins at a time when metal was at an ever-increasing premium.

The minim was crudely made. The man's face on the obverse is not centred but is on the far left. The back of his head is cut off so that it's uncertain whether he wore a solar radiate or wreath. About 60% of the obverse side is blank. On the reverse, Victory is better positioned but too far to the right with much of the side blank. The Briton who made it had little skill. To the layman, it looks like a crude fake coin.

The likely dating of the minim

Hill examines Dark Age British coins in the following date intervals: I. 410-450; II. 450-550; III. 550-600. In his 'List of Hoards' he gives statistics describing the hoards that were buried in each interval. Although minims appear in each period, the percentage of barbarous coins in each hoard increases sharply in period II. For example, the Somerset hoard of AD 400 yielded 1139 coins of which only 46 were barbarous. Other early large hoards were similar to this. Later hoards around AD 500 and after are shown for comparison.

Burial date	Location	No. coins	No. barbarous
400	Somerset	1139	46
420	Icklingham	1064	46
420-30	Kiddington	1176	26
500	Hayle	Many 1000s	All
500-50	Richborough	1238	All
550	Lydney	1646	All

These figures reflect the extreme coin and metal shortages around 500 and after and suggest that Fell's minim could have been circulating in that period. Fell measured its diameter at 12 mm (0.47 of an inch). In the hoards above, around the AD 500 date, the minim diameters in inches were 0.25 to 0.45 (Hayle) and 0.15 to 0.50 (Richborough). For the later Lydney hoard the diameters were only 0.10 to 0.35. The latter minims (minimissimi) were so tiny they were almost useless as coins. Fell's minim would likely have been made when barbarous coins were common, c. 500, but not when coin diameters had shrunk to absurdly tiny sizes. The coins were used in Gildas' time, circa 537.[7]

Embedded in clay

Donal Buchanan in Epstein (1980) states that 'The coin was in a lump of clay thrown out of a trench being dug by the city'. He adds that 'above the clay layer in which it was found was a thick layer of black soil'. Clay takes a long time to form and if the coin was in a layer of clay, about 4 feet deep, below a thick layer of soil, then it implies that the coin wasn't carelessly lost by an 1885 collector. Fell concluded that the coin was probably lost in America by an ancient Briton.[8]

It is unlikely that anyone in 1885 Champaign had such a coin as it is rarely, if at all, in early collections, unlike Roman coins. However, assuming a man did have the coin, one could say he dropped it in the trench as he passed by. But why would it be in his pocket if he could not buy anything with it? Or perhaps he planted it in the trench, at night, to mislead people that it was lost by pre-Columbian visitors, as others did with Roman coins. But he would only do this if it was seen as a convincing ancient coin. A barbarous coin that looks like a crude fake would hardly succeed in convincing anyone. The irony is that the coin was genuinely old and, if he believed this, he may have kept it. Irrespective of this, it is improbable that he would bother to plant a coin that most people would dismiss as a badly-made fake.

It appears that the boy's father was an educated man. He may have recognized winged Victory on the coin and thought it was connected to Rome. The boy probably saw the coin partly embedded in a clay lump near the trench and retrieved it. His father may then have noted how deep the clay lump had been in the trench. The fact that he made a notarized statement implies that he thought it a genuine find and told his family that it was important, as his descendant, Gordon Price, repeatedly took it to experts, but none could identify it.

Further speculation on Arthur's route

If the coin was dropped in ancient times it's possible that it came from one of Arthur's men as these coins were used in Arthur's floruit. The location of the coin in Illinois is of considerable interest. If they passed through the site where the city of Champaign would later be built it is likely that they also explored Lake Michigan. Given that this lake is well to the west of the St Lawrence river it could suggest that the expedition spent much time exploring the Great Lakes. This surmise is consistent with the bard seeing the plains buffalo there, as Bruce McMillan (2006) refers to archaeological evidence that the buffalo were present along the Illinois river in the Middle Woodland period. He also presents convincing evidence from others that the buffalo at that time had not yet reached Ohio.[9]

FEATURES OF EARLY AMERICA IN THE POETRY

As the argument for Arthur in America primarily rests on the allusions in *Spoils of Annwfyn*, the key points for identifying the journey to Annwfyn as a voyage to America are summarized below.

Land unknown to the Britons

The new land that they reached was unknown to the Britons, as shown by line 8, 'nobody before him went into it'.

Long Voyage across the shores of the world

The voyage was not an easy one to familiar locations, but a long one 'across the world's shores' (line 2). Geoffrey of Monmouth got this right in his *Vita Merlini* when he required an expert navigator to guide Arthur's ship 'to whom the seas and the stars of heaven were well known'. Geoffrey was also correct that Arthur died there but expressed it as a euphemism in which Arthur was being treated for his terrible wounds. From this arose the belief he would later return. Geoffrey also knew the *Navigatio* story that Barinthus had sailed to the far west and discovered the 'Promised Land of the Saints' and told Brendan about it. Geoffrey thus made Barinthus Arthur's expert navigator. These beliefs were present 350 years before America was discovered.

Voyage to the north where Icebergs were seen

The crew saw a large iceberg which the bard poetically called the 'glass fortress' (line 30). In Brendan's voyage, perhaps around 560, the author of the *Navigatio* used the expression 'crystal pillar' in the sea. A later work, 830-31, the *Historia Brittonum*, used the expression 'glass tower in the middle of the sea'. *Spoils of Annwfyn* was a poem which used a metaphor and the later authors of prose works may have been influenced by it in their similar use of 'crystal' or 'glass'.

Very Cold Conditions
At some point in the journey, Arthur's men experienced a freezing cold camp where they drank *gloyw* wine, the equivalent of the Germanic *glühwein*, in which the wine is heated (lines 26-28).

So far these allusions have Arthur going on a long sea voyage to a land unknown to the Britons. That they went north is inferred from the large iceberg and cold conditions. The poem doesn't say they sailed to the north *west*, so to nullify the idea that Arthur reached America a pedant could say that they may have sailed north *east*, going up the coast of Norway, and then sailing along the north coast of Russia, the latter land being presumably unknown to the Britons. But it is a poem which is not concerned with giving navigational details, but important images. The European legends recorded by Jacob Cnoyen had Arthur exploring to the north west, passing Iceland, and finally arriving at Grocland. After studying Cnoyen's work, Dee, Mercator and Ortelius placed Grocland to the west of Greenland on their maps, roughly in the position of Baffin Island. Below are further allusions that clearly identify the new land as part of Canada/North America.

The 'strong door' entry – St Lawrence river
The hint that they entered via Canada is the 'strong door' (line 24), the entry point to the new land. Rivers as entry points were familiar to the Britons and offered many advantages. When Cartier explored Canada he sailed up the St Lawrence, a natural entry point, but it was hard to make progress against strong downstream currents, requiring rowing, waiting for the flood tide and favourable winds. Arthur must have had similar difficulties, prompting his bard to call it the 'strong door'.

The 'strong door' and the 'four-peaked camp' – Montreal
Although 'strong door' is not a specific term and could perhaps refer to other rivers, it is linked to the St Lawrence through the 'four-peaked camp'. Both appear in line 24: 'in the four-peaked camp, land of the strong door'. There are four prominent peaks in Montreal – Royal, St-Bruno, St-Hilaire and Rougemont. Without the modern buildings of today, these peaks would have been the main feature of the site. Montreal is on the St Lawrence river.

The Great Lakes

Following the St Lawrence to the south of Lake Erie was an old traders' route and it's possible that they went this way. However if the British minim was lost by one of them it puts them considerably to the west in Illinois. This suggests that they may have explored Lake Michigan and possibly other members of the Great Lakes.

The Buffalo (Bison bison)

The ox was a common working animal in early Britain, but the Britons in Annwfyn saw an 'ox' they had never seen before, the buffalo. The bard taunts the monks' ignorance in the poem with 'they do not know the brindled ox, thick his head ring, seven-score joints in his collar' (lines 39-40), these constraints being poetic expressions to refer to the huge head and neck. The 'brindled' epithet would refer to the 'yellow-ochre 'cape' on the buffalo's back. From McMillan (2006) it is likely that they saw the buffalo along the Illinois River.

Massive Earthworks and Mounds

It's not known where the Britons saw the Hopewell earthworks but the Scioto river has a dense concentration along its banks and could be a possibility. Earthen walls in various geometrical patterns were built with their burial mounds inside. These walls were much higher than today and fit the scene where the Britons confronted the inhabitants who were standing on a wall, probably to protect their sacred items in the mounds. As the two languages were different, the Britons could not understand them (lines 31-2). A member of the party, Gweir, was also held prisoner in a 'mound fortress' (line 3).

The Extensive use of Pearls

The burial mounds were associated with masses of freshwater pearls that were buried with the dead. Many thousands of pearls were found in sites in Ohio. Pearls were also used in decorations, as the 'eyes' in their animal carvings and glued into holes made in bears' teeth. The poem notes the Britons' capture of a ceremonial pot (cauldron) with a black rim and contrasting pearl decoration. The bard remarks of this cauldron that 'it did not boil the food of a coward', acknowledging the bravery of the Native Americans (lines 15-19).

The North American River otter

To further taunt the monks about their ignorance of Annwfyn the bard observes that the natives kept an animal with a silvery head (line 46). This is a perfect fit for the North American river otter. They were plentiful in the rivers and streams at that time and the Hopewell made very realistic carvings of them. The muzzle and throat were silvery in appearance. They are intelligent and playful and have been tamed by many cultures. The ancient Chinese tamed them to catch fish and the Hopewell carvings often depict them carrying a fish in the mouth. They like to hold their head above water when swimming. As the bard focused on the head, he may have been recalling them swimming.

Spoils of Annwfyn as a historical text

I am convinced that the interpretations above from *Spoils of Annwfyn* give a true picture – that it is highly probable that Arthur explored the inland of America. This extraordinary claim directly opposes modern views that Arthur was a myth who later came to be seen as a historical figure. However these scholars have not engaged deeply with the early Welsh poetry but have focused on Irish legends and the late Latin texts where Arthur had already accrued legendary features. For the above interpretations to be valid, three conditions must be met:

- *Spoils of Annwyn* must be a contemporary poem which is based on an eyewitness account and its surviving form must be close enough to the original to allow valid translations.

- The English translation given here accurately renders the Welsh meaning, as far as possible.

- The allusions in the poem are interpreted correctly as features of ancient America.

The first point is addressed in Chapter 1 and also in MacCann (2016). In essence, the poem has remnants of archaic language, is consistent with Gildas in giving a north Wales location, and its attacks on the monks in the last 5 stanzas (of an 8 stanza poem) are a credible early reply to the slanders of Gildas in his *De Excidio*. In general, the lines make sense and give a coherent picture of the expedition.

For the other points, the modern translations have been studied closely and each line checked with the GPC Welsh dictionary. For opaque lines I've tried to use the context of nearby lines to decide the translation. But in line 25 two options are difficult to separate. One is 'Flowing water and jet are mixed' where 'jet' is a type of lignite, a dark material used in jewelry and is probably a proxy for darkness. The other is 'Midday is confused with jet-blackness' implying that it was dark around midday. I've used the first, visualizing a waterfall flowing down on the black sand of Iceland, or water flowing across the black sand, but with not much confidence.[10]

A book suitable for the general reader, as this is, would normally omit the Welsh, but as it is essential to my case it must be included so that experts can check the translation and the interpretations. In this, it is unlike Fell's books where usually not enough information is given to allow any checking to be made. The general reader can skip over the Welsh while the experts can thoroughly scrutinize it.

THE FANTASY INTERPRETATION

I am the only academic that has argued that *Spoils of Annwfyn* refers to a real journey to a land unknown to the Britons. An alternative view is that it is a late fantasy, related to the Irish Otherworld stories or inspired by them. The early attempts to translate the poem made little sense and appeared at a time where Arthur was thought to be a Celtic god, Solar Hero, or god of sun and storm. John Lloyd, a great scholar who wrote a definitive history of Wales, was unimpressed by these weird theories and maintained that Arthur was historical.

The problem with a fantasy viewpoint is that it is hard to refute and can last for many years as an agreed consensus, even if badly wrong. The usual criteria of coherence, logic, plausibility, etc. for accepting or rejecting are hard to apply, as it is a fantasy. A fortress is usually made of stone but in a fantasy the scholars can interpret the 'glass fortress' in the poem as a fort literally made of glass (e.g. Roger Loomis, 1956) and make no attempt to relate it to similar objects in the *Navigatio* and *Historia Brittonum*. Even items that contradict each other can be explained away as acceptable, the contradiction being asserted as a delight to the Celtic mind.[11]

The 'brindled ox' had a huge head and neck, and a brindled coat. In the absence of further data, one wonders why the monks should be ignorant about this as oxen were commonplace, and if some had brindled coats, what does it matter? However, if additional data shows that the animal was seen in America, it can be identified as the buffalo and the bard's reason for taunting the monks about not knowing this particular 'ox' becomes evident.

Under the fantasy model the animal can just be explained away as a 'magical animal'. But this fantasy explanation does not explain how the bard can triumph over the monks from exposing their ignorance of something that does not exist.

The other animal with a silvery head that was 'kept' also presents problems under the fantasy model. In the absence of further data that shows that this animal was in America, this could be another 'magical animal' with a head that was literally silver, as in some translations. As above, there is hardly any point in exposing the monks' ignorance of an animal that does not exist.

Fantasy Model: the taunts do not belong

A major problem for the fantasy view is the bard's taunting the monks about their ignorance of what happened in Annwyfn. For example, in line 30 the bard says 'Beyond the glass fortress they did not see the valour of Arthur'. There are 8 lines like this in Stanzas 4–6. In addition there are 3 lines that just belittle the monks; e.g. 'loose their shield straps'. If the poem is a fairy-tale fantasy then the taunts are jarringly out of place. They don't belong. The taunts imply that the bard had a strong emotional involvement in what happened and this further suggests that what happened was real.

In the fantasy model, one can visualize a bard, c. AD 1000, reciting his fantasy poem to an eager audience. Afterwards the audience would be puzzled, wondering what grudge the bard had against the monks to merit the relentless taunts. However if the poem was composed shortly after the *De Excidio* (c. 540), the reason for the bard's ridicule is obvious. It was a retaliation for the slanders of Gildas. John Lloyd states that Gildas apparently did not impress his fellow Britons and notes that not a single church in Wales is dedicated to him.[12]

THE CRUCIAL LAST TWO STANZAS

The last two stanzas are different to the rest in that the survivors have returned to Britain and the lords are clashing with the monks – 'from a clash with lords *who know*'. This clash, with the monks withdrawing in fear, appears in the opening lines of both stanzas. In the first they are likened to a pack of dogs; in the second to a pack of wolves. This scene is not adequately explained by the fantasy model although that model is so elastic as to have an 'explanation' for anything. The theme of the monks' ignorance is also in Stanza 8 where it is explicitly stated they don't know the mysteries of darkness and dawn and the workings of the winds. In Stanza 7 their ignorance of the actions of the wind, the sea and fire is implied. These examples appear to be unrelated to what happened in Annwfyn but are used to further denigrate the monks.

Apart from exposing the monks' ignorance, the last two stanzas have historical content. There is strong dissension between the lords and monks and the monks appear to be physically threatened. If *Spoils of Annwfyn* was composed by Arthur's bard, the time of composition would be shortly after Gildas' *De Excidio*. The obvious inference is that the lords were furious about that publication. They may have been pressuring the monks to give up the author.

What do the lords know?

The most intriguing part of these two stanzas is that the lords, who are clashing with the monks, know something significant which the monks don't know. This is clearly important as it is repeated twice. The answer is not revealed immediately as the bard holds the audience in suspense with his riddles that denigrate the monks. In line 58 he finally reveals the secret – that Arthur (the saint) is dead and his grave is lost. The Welsh is: *Bet sant yn diuant, a bet allawr*.

In the first part of this line, all scholars take *sant* as 'saint' and *diuant* as 'lost', or similar. I take *bet* as 'grave' and obtain 'the grave of the saint is lost'. Coe and Young (1995) and Higley (1996) also take *bet* as 'grave' and obtain 'the lost grave of a saint' and 'the grave of the saint is hidden (lost, vanishing)'. But Haycock (2007) takes *bet* as *pet* ('how many') as does Bollard (1984). They obtain 'how many saints are in the void' and 'how many lost saints', a different meaning.

In the second part I take *bet* as 'grave' and *allawr* (*a llawr*) as 'and champion', giving 'both grave and champion'. However I note that the GPC also gives 'ground' for *llawr and* Higley takes this meaning to get 'both grave and ground', which also makes sense. She also notes the 'hero or champion' alternative. The other translations diverge here. Coe and Young and Haycock both take *allawr* as 'altar' and obtain 'and the grave of an altar' and 'and how many altars'. Bollard does not use 'altar' and obtains 'and how many others'. The latter three make little sense as isolated lines. More importantly, they don't relate to the lines around them or to anything in the poem.

My version 'the grave of the saint is lost, both grave and champion' does relate to the poem, revealing what the lords knew. The poem is all about Arthur in Annwfyn, a hero and a Christian king as shown by his 'reverence of scripture' in *Chair of the Sovereign*. The bard refers to Arthur in the next two lines: 'I praise the sovereign, great prince, that I not be grieving; Christ provides for me'. It is doubtful that the bard would be grieving about lost altars.

As the whole poem is about Arthur's voyage to Annwfyn it makes sense that the 'sovereign, great prince' is Arthur (not God) and that the grave lost in Annwfyn is his. As the bard went with Arthur to Annwfyn, he must be Arthur's bard and an eyewitness to the events there. Given the bard's grief, he seeks refuge in Christ. This ending is consistent with the distress in the rest of the poem – it is coherent.

SUMMARY OF ARTHUR

The Welsh texts reveal new details about Arthur. I show that Uthr, Arthur's father, was probably the great Einion Yrth who subdued the Irish that occupied north Wales and was the founder of the Gwynedd dynasty. Einion was based in Rhôs, possibly in the Dinarth hillfort, although that name would not have applied until Arthur took control. Henben, the father of Arthur's mistress, Garwen, lived at nearby Dinorben. Uthr's defence of Henben in *Marwnat Uthr Pendragon* was against the Irish. This data puts Arthur into a historical setting in which he was probably a half uncle of Maglocunus and this allowed him to take control of Dinarth when Maglocunus resigned to become a monk. It also explains how Dinarth received its name.

A speculative picture of Arthur is given below. As a youth Arthur probably aided his father to subdue the Irish in north Wales and began to build his great reputation. Einion died and was succeeded by Owain Danwyn, but circa AD 495, Maglocunus killed him and took the throne of Rhôs. After a short reign he resigned, about 500. As Arthur was the half brother of Owain, and a military hero, he was able to take over the throne. He was probably about 30. His military strength and strong leadership eventually allowed him to gain the loyalty of the five kings, becoming the 'Pharaoh'. He also subdued other Britons like the sons of Caw. If the battles in *Linnuis* are his, then he made some aggressive strikes against the Angles in the east. Later, perhaps responding to a plea for aid, he established an army in Galloway to help restore order against the Irish or Picts. His deeds there impressed the north Britons so much that his fame spread across Scotland and babies began to be named after him. He was in Galloway c. 531 when many of his men were killed in the 'battle of the treetops', a barrage of stones.

The *Historia* lists Badon Hill as Arthur's victory but I show that its underlying battle-list poem was not composed by his bard. This does not disprove that he won Badon, but it devalues the key text used to claim he did. I argue that the Badon siege did not have the importance assigned to it by later historians; e.g. the patriotic view of Morris.

Neither Merlin nor Taliesin was Arthur's bard. There were two 'Merlins' as Gerald of Wales knew 800 years ago. One was a composite of two figures: a non-existent Merlin created to explain the name of Carmarthen and the Ambrosius with legendary details in the *Historia*. Geoffrey of Monmouth merged these two into 'Merlin Ambrosius'. The second was a Scottish man whose name was probably Llallawg. He was born after Arthur died and thus had no contact with him. He went mad after seeing the slaughter in the battle of Arfderydd but the details of his life are legendary. Geoffrey in *Vita Merlini* made a farcical effort to merge this Scottish Merlin with his 'Merlin Ambrosius'.

Taliesin was a bard of the north, distant from Dinarth. His poems are different in style to the Arthurian poems and he was too late to be Arthur's bard. The latter was Talhaearn ('iron brow'), a warrior bard. In the *Historia* he was the leading bard of the sixth century, the 'father of inspiration'. His village, Tre Talhaearn, was close to Dinarth.

324

The early poetry shows that Arthur courageously led an expedition to North America in which he was killed. The voyage occurred around the time when a climate crisis was starting. Earlier, c. 531, many of his men were killed in Galloway, as noted earlier. He consulted his druids to tell him what it meant. Then in 535/536 volcanic eruptions started a severe climate downturn. This was about the time he set out for Annwfyn but it can't be determined if this motivated his exploring into the north Atlantic. Knowledge of Arthur's deeds travelled far. His voyage to Grocland was known in Europe and appears in the *Gestae Arthuri*, mentioned by Jacob Cnoyen. I have shown that this material was independent of Geoffrey of Monmouth.

Today many take it for granted that Arthur was a myth who at some time before the *Historia Brittonum* was written came to be thought of as a historical figure. The field of historical Arthurian studies is now confined to rehashing the inadequacy of late Latin texts that mention him and arguing that *Y Gododdin* can't be shown to be early or that its Arthurian reference could be an interpolation. But it is remarkable that the same degree of rigour is not applied to the 'Arthur is a myth' view. This is based on late texts 600 years after his time and tells us nothing on how he was seen in 537. It extensively uses the *Mirabilia*, attached to the *Historia*, but ignores the fact that this text is 300 years after Arthur's floruit and that other historical people such as Illtud and Meurig also appear in the *Mirabilia*.

It also fails to mention the glaringly obvious case of Ambrosius who developed incredible legendary features. In AD 537 he was seen as a historical warrior but by 830 he was seen as a wizard, born of a virgin mother, who predicted the future, whose magic was superior to that of Vortigern's *magi* and yet whose father was a Roman consul ('worn the purple' in the *De Excidio*). In comparison, by 830, Arthur's accrual of legendary features was rather tame.

There no early evidence for 'Arthur was a myth' and the poetry of his bard shows it to be false. It is a notable example of a False Negative error. Arthur's deeds as a warrior and explorer were remarkable and were the very cause of his widespread fame. He deserves his place as a great hero of the Britons and their descendants, the Cymru.

NOTES

Chapter 1 Arthurian Texts

1. Squire (1905: 273-4) for Arthur and his knights as Celtic gods, and p. 321 for his interpretation of the Otherworld; also see Loomis (1927: 350).
2. Haycock (1983-4: 52-78; 2007: 174-86, 295-9, 435-8); Bollard (1984: 21-3); Koch and Carey (2003: 309-11); Higley (1996: 43-53). Ford (1977: 183-7) for Battle of the Trees. A valuable addition from Haycock is her *Prophecies from the Book of Taliesin* (2013).
3. Thorpe (1966) for Geoffrey's *HRB*; Parry (1925) for *Vita Merlini*.
4. Thorpe (1966: 259-61) for Camblam; Bromwich (2006: 167) for the meanings of the Camlan name.
5. O'Meara (2002: 25-64) for *Navigatio*. For America, see McCarthy (1848), Little (1945), Pohl (1961), Ashe (1962), Chapman (1973) and Severin (1978).
6. Parry (1925: 85).
7. Thorpe (1978): p. 117-8 for Meilyr; p. 281 for Arthur's grave.
8. Taylor (1956: 62; 64).
9. Woolley (2001: 38; 54-5).
10. MacMillan (2004: 7, 46).
11. Charles-Edwards (1991: 29).
12. Jarman (1988: lxiv).
13. Rowland (1990: 180).
14. Line 46 requires that 'Artir' be emended to 'Artur', which was first proposed by Ifor Williams (1932-33: 140). This was supported by Bromwich (1975-6: 177), Gruffydd (1982: 23), Bromwich et al. (1991: 5, 13), Koch and Carey (2003: 379) and Green (2007: 252). The translation is by Koch (2006: 119). See Rowland (1990: 186) for her emending of *artir wras* to *arddyrnfras*.
15. See Bromwich (1975-6: 177) on MS 4973, NLW; Green (2007: 53).
16. See Rowland (1990: 459) for the Welsh and p. 505 for the English translation. See Sims-Williams (1991: 47-8) for his discussion on the original verse which he thinks had Arthur's brave men being slain.
17. Bartrum (2009: 472).
18. Sharpe (1995: 38, 111); Rowland (1990: 388-9); Koch (1994: 1127).
19. Chadwick and Chadwick (1932: 161-2). There is a first century Lucius Artorius Castrus (Malone, 1925). He was from Dalmatia (modern Croatia) and came to Britain as leader (*praefectus*) of the sixth legion, stationed at York. While he was at York, a rebellion broke out in Brittany (Armorica) and he was sent there to fight against the rebels. Malone states that when he was no longer able to fight he was given a lucrative civil service post in North Dalmatia.
20. See Dumville (1986: 5-7) for synchronizing history. See Davies (1982: 205) for her statement that it's not possible to generalize about its value.
21. Chadwick and Chadwick (1932: 155) for the poem origin; Jones (1964: 10). For the battles as a miscellaneous list see Lloyd (1911: 126), Bromwich (1975-6: 170-2). For Field's analysis of the meagre evidence see Field (2008: 8-11).
22. Alcock (1971: 45).
23. Chambers (1927: 1-2).

24. The scuit/scuid issue was raised long ago by Stephens (1849: 17). If it did occur, Dumville (1986: 13) notes the poem must have been in a written form.
25. Alcock (1971: 45).
26. Lloyd (2017: 18-19).
27. Loomis (1956: 141). This Bran (Febal's son) is different to another Bran (the Blessed) who has parallels with Arthur. The *Voyage of Bran* was composed in the 600s or early 700s whereas Bran the Blessed appears in a Mabinogi tale of c. 1120. Both are unhistorical literary figures. *Annwfyn* comprises the prefix *an-* and *dwfyn* where *dwfyn* means 'deep' or 'world'. The prefix can mean 'very', an intensifier or 'un', the opposite. Thus two possible meanings are 'very deep' or 'opposite world'. See Haycock (2007: 440); Koch (2006: 75).
28. Koch (2006: 1653).
29. See Koch (1985-6: 57, 59; 1988: 37; 1996: 264-5; 2006: 1456).
30. Koch and Carey (2003: 291) for the *Historia* iceberg. Jackson (1959b: 17); Sims-Williams (1991: 55-6) and Haycock (2007: 446) compare it to lines 30-2. O'Meara (2002: 53-4) translates the *Navigatio* event. Dumville (1988b: 101-2) dates the *Navigatio* to about 750-775, but cannot rule out an earlier date.
31. Meyer (1895: xvi); Thrall (1917: 450); Breatnach (1977: 101-3); Carney (1976: 174) & (1983: 178); Mac Mathúna (1985: 411); McCone (2000: 29, 45-7).
32. Cross and Slover (1936: 589) for the white bronze pillars; Haycock (2007: 277) line 49 for *banneu* translated as turrets around which the sea swirls.
33. Cross and Slover (1936: 490) for glass ship; Stokes (1888: 489) for glass bridge.
34. Stokes (1889: 81) for the fiery revolving rampart; Cross and Slover (1936: 273) for the *Bricriu's Feast* revolving fort. A simpler explanation is that the bard was turning to face the four large hills at the 'four-peaked camp', the large hills argued in Chapter 7 to be features of Montreal.
35. For dating of *Cú Roí* see Cross and Slover (1936: 328); Sims-Williams (1982: 251). For the iron doors, see Cross and Slover (1936: 352).
36. Cross and Slover (1936: 352) for the pit of Hell from which serpents emerge.
37. Winterbottom (1978: 36) for the Pharaoh over the five kings and pp. 31 for the Bear's Stronghold.
38. Haycock (2007: 437) for Devwy meadows and p. 298 for the lorica of Lleon.
39. See Haycock (2007: 436-8) for the ferocious attack on the monks by the bard.
40. For the old form *gwrith* see Koch (1991: 116).
41. Haycock (2007: 172, 206); Haycock (1990: 307).
42. Most (2018: 69-73); Rouse (1940: 39, 41, 63, 73, 83, 91).
43. For a description of the beast in the poem, see Ford (1977: 184); Coe and Young (1995: 145, 147) and Haycock (2007: 175-6).
44. Cross and Slover (1936: 352).
45. Koch (1988: 27); Koch (1997: 144).
46. Chapter 9 in MacCann (2016: 129-51).

Chapter 2 Gildas

1. Ó Faoláin (2006: 621) for the biform Dumnonia/Damnonia. Winterbottom (1978: 29-30) for Constantine.
2. Winterbottom (1978: 30-1); Jackson (1982: 31); Lloyd (1911: 132).
3. Winterbottom (1978: 31). For the Vortipor stone see Jackson (1982: 32).

4. Winterbottom (1978: 31-2). See Jackson (1982: 32-3) for Gildas' distorting the translation to give 'tawny butcher'. See Jackson (1982: 33-4) and Sims-Williams (1990: 218) for Gildas translating *Dineirth* as *receptaculum ursi*. Jackson also locates *Dineirth* in Rhôs, north Wales.

5. In the *Harleian* genealogies Maglocunus was the son of Cadwallon Lawhir while Cuneglasus was the son of Owain Danwyn. Owain and Cadwallon Lawhir were brothers, the sons of Einion Yrth. For Maglocunus, Winterbottom (1978: 32-6). For *avunculus*: Lloyd (1911: 128); Winterbottom (1978: 33); Morris (1978: 153); Miller (1975-6: 108); Dumville (1984a: 58); Bartrum (2009: 500). For *atavus* as 'ancestor' see Gruffydd (1989-90: 13-14, footnote 65).

6. For the two murders of Maglocunus, see Winterbottom (1978: 34).

7. Winterbottom (1978: 34).

8. Winterbottom (1978: 18).

9. Williams (1899: 45).

10. Winterbottom (1978: 29).

11. Bede's *Ecclesiastical History*, Bk. 3, Ch. 9; McClure and Collins (1994: 124).

12. For the 'rain showers of the hostile' and the protection given to Gildas by his faith, see Winterbottom (1978: 36, 52). The Picts were located in the north of Britain as shown on p. 21. In addition, they were located in the 'far end' of the island as shown on p. 24. This surely eliminates any northern location for Gildas.

13. Koch (2013: 122).

14. McClure and Collins (1994: 71-3); Koch (2013: 108). See Corning (2006) for the differences in religious customs.

15. McClure and Collins (1994: 73-4); Tolley (2016: 83); Koch (2013: 108-9).

16. McClure and Collins (1994: 74); Bromwich (2006: 232-3).

17. Winterbottom (1978: 28).

18. See Morris (1978: 1); Dumville (1984b: 83-4); MacCann (2016: 14-5); Woolf (2018: 95); Stancliffe (2018: 125). See also Stancliffe (1997: 178-80).

19. Woods (2010: 228-9); Winterbottom (1978: 70).

20. Stevens (1941: 362-3).

21. Higham (2018: 156) reproduces his earlier quote from Higham (1994: 137).

22. See Morris (1978: 150-1). He notes that these early dates derive from Section 66 in the *Historia Brittonum* and points out that archaeology does not admit significantly later dates.

23. See Koch and Carey (2003: 405-6) for the Breton legend.

24. Morris (1973: 48, 71, 73-4).

25. Padel (1994: 17); Wood (1999: 34-9). Apart from the other difficulties, the MS is 400 years after the time of writing and is an extremely flimsy prop to support this argument.

26. See Winterbottom (1978: 34).

27. Winterbottom (1978: 32).

28. Dark (2000a: 144).

29. Winterbottom (1978: 31); Anderson (1928: 404-5); Koch (1983: 209).

30. Winterbottom (1978: 36).

31. Winterbottom (1978: 33).

32. MacCann (2016: 287).

33. Jackson (1982: 34); Dark (1994: 126).

34. Higham (2002: 78); Higham (2018: 163-5).
35. Jackson (1982: 33-34); Sims-Williams (1990: 218). Gildas' translation using the genitive singular of 'the Bear' must be given a huge weighting. No amount of desperate theorizing can dismiss 'the Bear'. Are we really to believe that the fort was owned by a *single* animal bear? Are we really to believe that the fort was named after another person with Arth in the name, perhaps like Arthmael, despite zero evidence for this hypothetical person's existence there and despite the many other links to Arthur in this region.
36. Jackson (1953: 5, 691); Sims-Williams (1990: 260).
37. Haycock (2007: 449); Winterbottom (1978: 30, 34).

Chapter 3 Arthur

1. Jackson (1982: 33-4); Longley and Laing (1997: 90). For the first mention of the Camelot name (as *Camaalot*) see Frappier (1959: 176), the name occurring around 600 years after Arthur's time.
2. Kelliwic in Kernyw appears in the very first Welsh Triad (Bromwich, 2006: 1) and five times in *Culhwch ac Olwen*. Kernyw is usually translated as Cornwall but this location is unlikely in some cases. John Koch argues that the Kernyw in the poem on Kynan Garwyn lies in the area centred on Wroxeter, the civitas of the Cornovii tribe (see Koch, 2013: 121-7) and derives Kernyw from Cornovii. Charles-Edwards (2013: 389) argues that the Cornovii annexed Chester no later than the 400s. It is quite possible that the Llangernyw name was derived from this tribe although the village is about 37 miles west of Chester. The tribe's name comes from *corn* (meaning horn) but there are two schools of thought on how this occurred. Watson (1926:16) and Watts (2004: 158) think the name derives from people associated with horns of land (promontories) but Ross (1967: 189) thinks it comes from worshippers of the horned god *Cernunnos*. My proposal that Arthur's Kernyw came from the Great and Little Orme 'horns' belongs to the 'horns of land' school but it could possibly derive from the Wroxeter Cornovii who are known to exist with that name.
3. Longley and Laing (1997: 90); Laing (2006: 34-5), and Simon Denison in *News: British Archaeology*, no 29, November 1997, partly reproduced in *The Heroic Age*, Issue 1, Spring/Summer 1999.
4. For *Gwy* see Geiriadur Prifysgol Cymru (GPC). For *Devwy* see Koch and Carey (2003: 365), line 34.
5. Snyder (1998: 167); Koch (2013: 116).
6. Haycock (2007: 309).
7. For Hennin Old Head see Jones (1967: 113-4). For the *morfa* and mention of Garwen and Sanant see p. 114. Stanzas 70, 71 are on p. 132 (Welsh) and p. 133 (English). See Bromwich (2006: 164) for Triad 57.
8. Bartrum (1966: 85); see also *Culhwch and Olwen*, Ford (1977: 127), for Iaen and his sons being men of Caer Dathl. For the location of Caer Dathl in Arfon see Ford (1977: 91).
9. See Jones (1964: 14) for Branwen as a 'rationalized form of an earlier story' told in *Spoils of Annwfyn*. For the stewards appointed to mind the country in *Branwen* see Ford (1977: 65-6). In *Chair of the Sovereign* the stewards appear in lines 23-4 (Haycock, 2007: 296). For the stewards in Triad 13, see Bromwich

(2006: 25-6). For the magnetic rocks under the river Shannon water see Ford (1977: 67). The *magnetini* appear in Taylor (1956: 58). See Chambers (1927: 228-9) for Arthur's soul residing in the crow.

10. Dark (1994: 133).

11. RCAHMW, Vol. 4 (1914: 117) gives the co-ordinates of the two *Ffynnon Arthur* as 52°57'20"N, 3°7'19"W and 52°57'20"N, 3°7'22"W. They visited the sites in June 1911. In the same RCAHMW volume, *Croes Gwenhwyfar* is on p. 124. For Gogfran's fort see *Tours in Wales*, Pennant (1883: Vol. 1, 300-1), this edited by John Rhŷs. 'Gogfran' is spelt in several ways. Bromwich (2006: 161-2) favours Gogfran or Ogfran. Ford (1977: 126, 131) for Gwenhwyfar as Arthur's wife.

12. Williams (1899: 323-7) for Arecluta, Caunus and Huail in the first *Life*. See Winterbottom (1978: 21; 24) for the Antonine wall and the 'far end'. Bartrum (2009) details these children of Caw separately in alphabetical order. See p. 127 for Caw and Edeirnion.

13. See online https://historicplacenames.rcahmw.gov.uk/placenames/recorded-name/905f9211-48d5-4298-847f-910f607d292d for RCAHMW giving the peak Bron Bannog in Lluyd (1699). See RCAHMW, Vol. 4 (1914: 182) for the Stone of Huail. For Arthur's conflict with Huail in the second *Life* see Williams (1899: 401-5). It says that Gildas was in Ireland when he heard of the killing.

14. Thorpe (1978: 259); Williams (1899: 67).

15. Dark (2000a: 170); Gardner and Savory (1964: 216).

16. See Dark (1994: 134) for the high status forts; for Arthur fighting at Caer Fenlli see Rhian Andrews in Andrews and McKenna (1996: 619).

17. RCAHMW, Vol. 6 (1921: 135-6), Merioneth; Roberts (1941-4: 14).

18. Dumville (1986: 5, 15, 26); Hanning (1966: 120); Higham (2018: 178-215) are sceptical about the *Historia*. For less pessimistic views see Davies (1982: 205); Jackson (1963); Koch (1996); Field (2008).

19. Chadwick and Chadwick (1932: 155); Jones (1964: 10); Jackson (1949: 46); Jackson (1959a: 6).

20. Jackson (1945: 53).

21. Bachrach (1990: 22).

22. Williams (1968: xliv).

23. Jackson (1945). For *Glein* p. 46; for *Bassas* p. 48; for *Guinnion* p. 49-50.

24. Rowland (1995: 18). There seems to be a consensus that stirrups were not used at that time which would make such skills difficult to master. In Welsh tradition Arthur's horse was a mare, Llamrei (Ford, 1977: 152).

25. For *rechtur* see Koch (1988: 27; 1997: 144). For *Rheon* see Watson (1926: 34); Crawford (1935: 285); McCarthy (2004: 125) and Haycock (2007: 300-1). For *Pen Rhionydd* see Bromwich (2006: 4); Haycock (2007: 300).

26. For Novantarum promontory, Ptolemy's *Geographia*, Book 2: 3.1. For *Nefenhyr*: Lloyd-Jones (1950) and Haycock (2007: 170). For Caer Nefenhyr in *Culhwch and Olwen* see Ford (1977: 125).

27. Koch (1997: 23) for B2.39. For Nouant, pp. lxxxii- lxxxiii. Jackson (1945: 48).

28. Chambers (1927: 17).

29. Jones (1967: 119). See Sims-Williams (1991: 50) for *Peryddon* as another name for the River Dee or part of it. An alternative site is the Rhôs in southwest Wales where there is a Walwyn's Castle, but this is not on the 'sea shore'.

30. See Bromwich (2006: 9-10) for the Triad 4 on Gwalchmai.

31. Laing and Longley (2006: 157). For Pictish symbols see Cessford (1994: 86) and Forsyth and Thickpenny (2016: 83-90).
32. See Koch (1997: 8-9; 22-3) for the translations.
33. Koch (1997: xlviii).
34. Dumville (1988a: 2-4). See also Cessford (1997) for an account of the issues.
35. Dark (2000b) speculates that Vortipor's great grandson may have been King Arthur himself but this is far too late.
36. Morris (1973: 114).
37. Winterbottom (1978: 28).
38. In *Battle of the Trees* the bard says that he had sung from when he was small and in the next two lines that he had sung in the battle of the treetops before the lord of Britain (lines 25-7) suggesting that he was fairly young when that event took place. See Haycock (2007: 175). In the last two lines of the poem he says that he is exhilarated by the prophecy of Virgil (Haycock (2007:108).
39. Snyder (2005: 12).
40. Bromwich (1975-6: 181).
41. Bartrum (1966: 9-10, 94) for *Bonedd yr Arwyr*.
42. Chadwick (1953: 165); Bromwich (1975-6: 181). See also Bromwich (2006: 153) for Triad 54 on Aeddan the Treacherous.
43. Winterbottom (1978: 28) for Ambrosius. For the boy wizard in the *Historia* see Koch and Carey (2003: 295-7) and pp. 299-300 for Arthur's battle list.
44. See Winterbottom (1978: 31-2) for Cuneglasus, the son of Owain, and p. 33 for Maglocunus in the 'first years' of his youth killing Owain.
45. Williams (1968: 10) in Poem VIII, line 17 and p. 98 note 17 for *gorlassawc*, 'clad in blue-grey armour'. Haycock (2007: 507-8), note 3.
46. Koch (1997: 74-5).
47. See Rees (1840: 386) for Athrwys becoming king after the Yellow Pestilence which killed Maglocunus c. 547-9. See Davies (1979: 76) for Athrwys' later floruit and her argument that he did not survive Meurig.
48. For the battle of Tintern ford see Rees (1840: 383-4).
49. See Rees (1840: 381-2) for Meurig as the father of Athrwys. Arthur's father was Uthr (Einion Yrth) as discussed in Chapter 4.
50. See Bartrum (1966: 9-10, 94) for Eigyr as Arthur's mother. See Rees (1840: 381-2) for Onbrawst as Athrwys' mother. See Bartrum (2009: 31) for Arthur's brothers. See Rees (1840: 382) for Athrwys' brother Idnerth and p. 391 for the other brother, Frioc.
51. For Arthur's children see Bartrum (2009: 31) and for Athrwys' children see Rees (1840: 399) for Morgan and p. 401 for Ithael. For Gwenhwyfar see Triad 56, Bromwich (2006: 161-2). For Cenedlon see Bartrum (2009: 35). For Arthur's 'son' Amr probably not being historical, see Higham (2002: 89).
52. Turner (1852: 246), Vol. 1.
53. Gwyn Williams (1979: 99-100) writes of Iolo Morganwg: 'He was ultimately to create the gorgeous Glamorgan-that-never-was ... to throw in the teeth of sundry supercilious and superior north Walians and sneering Englishmen, and to charm later generations of addicts'.
54. National Museum of Wales (2010). Retrieved on 27 September 2023 from: https://museum.wales/articles/1139/Our-own-pageantry-and-peacockry-the-Gorsedd-of-the-Bards/

55. Ifor Williams (1944: 60-1) for the quote.
56. Morganwg (1848: 550).
57. Mierow (1915: 118).
58. Thorpe (1974: 132).
59. Ashe (1981: 310-1); Higham (2018: 153).
60. Dalton (1915: 76). Book III, Letter IX. To his friend Riothamus.
61. Ashe (1995: 15); Higham (2018: 153).
62. Ashe (1981: 315-6); Ashe (1995: 14).
63. Rhŷs (1891: 13-4); Squire (1905: 273-4); Loomis (1927: 350); For the Lloyd quotation see Lloyd (1911: 128).
64. Morris (1980: 42); Van Hamel (1934: 220); Padel (1994: 4); Green (2007: 71).
65. Bromwich and Evans ((1992: lxvi). See Jarman (1989-90: 24). Also see Koch (1987: 273).
66. See Miller (1916: 426-37) for the Ovid translation.
67. Green (2007: 122).
68. Jackson (1959a: 2); Padel (1994: 7-8) for Cadog and Carannog.
69. Rowley (2005: 69) for Illtud and Meurig; Higham (2018: 228).
70. Winterbottom (1978: 28); Koch and Carey (2003: 296-7).
71. Jackson (1959b: 15); Koch and Carey (2003: 313), line 64.
72. Padel (1994: 12). Higham (2018: 229) notes that of the 158 Arthur placenames in Lloyd (2017: 159-63) only 27 are evidenced before 1535.

Chapter 4 Arthur's Father

1. Haycock (2007: 503; 507); Koch (2006: 1722).
2. See Thorpe (1966: 203-8) for Uther impersonating Gorlois.
3. Haycock (2007: 512); Ashe (1982: 142-3).
4. Roberts (1991: 78); Sims-Williams (1991: 39).
5. Haycock (2007: 506).
6. Gruffydd (1989-90: 2); Koch and Carey (2003: 301).
7. Chadwick (1958: 34); Dumville (1977: 181-3); Lloyd (1911: 120-1).
8. Gruffydd (1989-90: 3).
9. Bartrum (2009: 262).
10. Gruffydd (1989-90: 11).
11. Koch (2013: 47-52, 95, 98).
12. For *Cunedaf* see Gruffydd (1989-90: 11); Koch (2013: 89).
13. Koch (2006: 519); Koch (2013: 73-4, 77).
14. *Ecclesiastical History* (*EH*) Bk 1, Ch 34. McClure and Collins (1994: 61).
15. Kirby (2000: 71). Triad 26 WR lists Edwin as an oppressor of Anglesey who was 'nurtured therein' (Bromwich, 2006: 52) reflecting a tradition that he grew up there and knew Cadwallon as a youth.
16. Koch and Carey (2003: 301-2); McClure and Collins (1994: 78, 84).
17. Gruffydd (1978: 25-43); Koch (2006: 315); Bromwich (2006: 192-3).
18. Bartrum (2009: 92).
19. For Stanza 5 and the Breiddin Hills see Bromwich (2006: 158). For Triad 55 see Bromwich (2006: 156).
20. Koch (2006: 316). Bromwich (2006: 62-4) for Triad 29 on the faithful warband.
21. Kirby (2000: 71-2); Koch (2013: 171).

22. Breeze (2001: 149-50), Koch and Carey (2003: 374-7), Koch (2013: 188-93) for the translations. Williams (1951: 85-6) for his estimated 632 date.
23. Breeze (2001: 152); Dumville (1988a: 15), note 72.
24. See Koch (2013: 189, 191) for lines 14-15, 34-35 and 43.
25. Breeze (2001: 151); Ekwall (1960: 86).
26. Koch (2013: 189).
27. *EH*: Bk 2, Ch 20, Bk 3, Ch 1. McClure and Collins (1994: 105, 110-1).
28. Stenton (1971: 81). For Penda's victory over Oswald see *EH*: Bk 3, Chs 9 and Ch 12. McClure and Collins (1994: 124, 129).
29. Koch (2013: 192). The 'Enniaun Stone' in Margam has a Christian inscription but it is not certain that it refers to Einion Yrth (RCAHMW, 1976: 48-9).
30. Koch (2006: 1722); Bromwich (2006: 513).
31. Morris (1973: 55, 73-4).
32. Haycock (2007: 505-6).
33. Lloyd (1911: 117).
34. Jones (1967: 132-3) for Stanza 71.
35. Ford (1977: 171); Haycock (2007: 509).
36. Bartrum (2009: 621); Winterbottom (1978: 32-4).
37. Lloyd (1911: 120); Bromwich (2006: 176-8); Gruffydd (1989-90: 9).
38. Willoughby Gardner, who excavated Dinorben in 1912-22 states that Henben's grave may be the cromlech near Dinorben farm, about 600 yards south of Dinorben (Gardner and Savory, 1964: 15), note 20.
39. Haycock (2007: 506); Coe and Young (1995: 151).

Chapter 5 Arthur's Bard

1. Bromwich (2006: 228).
2. Koch and Carey (2003: 295-7) for Sections 39-42 of the *Historia*.
3. See Jarman (1991: 137; 1959: 29) for the 'sea-fort' meaning of the Brittonic *Moridunon* and the Latin forms *Moridunum* and *Maridunum*.
4. For *merda* see Bartrum (2009: 563). For Geoffrey's account of the fatherless boy who became Merlin Emrys see Thorpe (1966: 166-71). For the *Prophecies of Merlin* see pp. 171-85. For Merlin and Stonehenge see pp. 195-8. For Merlin changing Uther's shape into that of Gorlois see pp. 203-8.
5. The English names given by Jarman (1959: 20) for the poems are used here. These four poems and three other poems relating to Merlin are translated by Bollard (1990a) in Section I, Chapter 2 of *The Romance of Merlin*. The seven poems in their Welsh names are: *Yr Afallennau*, *Yr Oianau*, *Ymddiddan a Thaliesin*, *Cyfoesi Myrddin a Gwenddydd*, *Y Bedwenni*, *Gwasgardgerdd Myrddin* and *Peiran Faban*. Some stanzas from these also appear in Bollard (1990b) and Jarman (1959). The *Lailoken and Kentigern* story appears in Clarke (1973: 227-31) in Appendix 1. Three stanzas from Jarman's translation of *Yr Afallennau* are also reproduced in Appendix 2 of Clarke (1973).
6. The Armterid entry comes from *Annales Cambriae*, Manuscript B. The *Bonedd Gwŷr y Gogledd* pedigree stating that Gwrgi and Peredur were sons of Eliffer comes from Peniarth MS 45. For a useful pedigree chart of showing Eliffer's relations see Tim Clarkson (2016: 65). William Skene's identification of *Caer Wenddolau* as Carwinley appears in Skene (1865: 97-8).

7. Breeze (2012: 5-6) for the battle site. For the vision, see Clarke (1973: 227).

8. The notion that Rhydderch fought against Gwenddolau appears in Chalmers (1807: 246-7), Skene (1865: 95); Lloyd (1911: 166-7) and Parry (1955: 27). Miller (1975: 113-5) omits Rhydderch from the battle and thinks that Gwrgi and Perdur were from the south in Yorkshire or Lancashire. Unfortunately there is not enough evidence to say precisely who the combatants were and why the battle was fought.

9. *Lailoken and Kentigern* (Lailoken A) and *Lailoken and Meldrum* (Lailoken B) are in Appendix 1 of Clarke (1973) on pp. 227-31 and pp. 231-4 respectively. The theme of the 'wild man' is ancient; e.g. Enkidu in the legend of Gilgamesh and Nebuchadnezzar in the Bible. There is an Irish counterpart of Lailoken, Suibhne Geilt (Wild Sweeney) in *Buile Shuibhne* (The Frenzy of Suibhne). In this tale he travels to Britain and there meets Alladhán 'a man of the woods' and the two wild men become friends. The Alladhán name was probably based on Lailoken (Carney, 1950: 101). In another Irish story, *Cath Maige Rátha* (Battle of Moira) Suibhne was a prince who survived the battle but like Lailoken was driven mad and fled into the forest to live. The Scottish tale of Lailoken was probably known to the Irish storytellers who then created a similar Irish tale.

10. See Thomas (2000) for how Geoffrey in his *Vita Merlini* modified his Merlin figure to downplay the guilt Lailoken suffered and rendered his Merlin more as a Celtic holy man. See Parry (1925: 31-5) for Geoffrey's account of the battle and Merlin fleeing to the woods.

11. Parry (1925: 47-51).

12. Parry (1925: 75-85).

13. See Parry (1925: 71) for the incident where Merlin explained to Vortigern the meaning of the fighting dragons. For the Gerald of Wales statement that there were two Merlins see Thorpe (1978: 192-3).

14. Huws (2000: 79).

15. Williams (1968) is an English translation by Caerwyn Williams of the Welsh *Canu Taliesin* (1960) by Ifor Williams. The poems have been left in Welsh but the Introduction and Notes are in English. Urien and Gwallawg appear together in Chapter 63 of the *Historia Brittonum* along with Rhydderch and Morgan in their battles against the Angles.

16. Koch (2006: 1653); Lewis (1968: 298). Williams (1968: xii). Koch (2013: 144-5). *EH* in Bk 2, Ch 3 (McClure and Collins, 1994: 74). McCarthy (2002: 373-4) argues for a small western Rheged. Others centre it around Carlisle.

17. Nora Chadwick (1963: 173) states that 'Nothing would be more natural at this period than for Brocfael, who had been king of Powys and the natural defender of the Valley of the Dee, to take part in defence of the kingdom'. However, Lloyd (1911: 180) thinks that the Brocmail at the battle was not the Powys king as the latter's grandson was at the battle and that Brocmail was a common name. If this were the case, it doesn't explain how an ordinary man named Brocmail came to be known by Bede. Brocmail wasn't even at the battle site. He was at a separate location with the praying monks and had a few guards with him as nearly all the soldiers were needed for the battle. Under such a scenario there is no reason for the monks to know the names of their guards as their focus was to pray for the Britons in the battle. The monks would not normally have known the guards as they were separately based at Bangor-on-Dee and the two groups

were together only for this special purpose. They didn't expect to be attacked. However if the Brocmail was the former king the monks would certainly have known his name, from his reputation as a powerful king and his distinctive facial features involving his teeth which gave rise to the epithet 'Brochfael of the tusks' (*Ysgrithrog*) as discussed in Williams (1968: xxxiii).

18. Koch (1997: xiii-xlii); his emendment in Koch (1997: xxviii). Ford (1999: 164); Pennar (1988: 51). *Garanwynyon* is usually *granwynyon*.

19. See Isaac (1998: 62-3) for the existing syllable counts and p. 68 for his dating of the poem based on his prosthetic vowels argument.

20. Koch (2013: 12-3).

21. For Gwallawg and Elfed, Williams (1968: 14), line 21 and Pennar (1988: 118). For Gwallawg at Catraeth see Koch (2013: 190), lines 30-1.

22. See Williams (1968: xlii) for *Erechwydd*; p. xlix for *Idon* (Eden) and p. xliv for *Llwyfenydd* (Lyvennet). For the latter also see Hogg (1946: 210-1). For *Eirch* as the Ark, see Williams (1968: xlv).

23. Pennar (1988: 99-100).

24. Williams (1968: 81); Pennar (1988: 83).

25. Pennar (1988: 69-70).

26. Koch (2013: 148).

27. For example, Koch and Carey (2003: 301).

28. Gruffydd (1989-90: 10).

29. Williams (1980: 44), footnote 8.

30. Gruffydd (1989-90: 10); also Jackson (1963: 29) for the name.

31. Williams (1968: xviii).

32. Williams (1968: lxvii); Koch (1997: 93).

33. See Loomis (1941: 887) for Ifor William's comment. See Koch (1985-6: 59); Koch (1996: 265) for a 700s dating.

34. For Strabo, see Jones (1923: 245). A similar account is also in Diodorus Siculus (Oldfather, 1939: 178-9).

35. See Haycock (2007: 185) for the bard on his horse, Melyngan. See Koch and Carey (2003: 359-60) for Taliesin's worry about Urien.

36. Romer (1998: 115).

37. Parry (1925: 85).

Chapter 6 Catastrophe in Scotland

1. See Haycock (2007: 192) for the 'battle of the treetops' translation, rendering the line as it stands.

2. Coe and Young (1995: 144-7). The bard's indirectness has left scholars puzzled as to the identity of the enemy. Benozzo (2004: 111) assumes that the trees are fighting 'an army of Britons'. Green (2007: 66) considers the enemy to be the monstrous forces of the Lord of the Otherworld opposed by Arthur leading an army of trees animated by magic. Haycock (2007: 169) comments that 'It is disappointing that the enemy here is not identified'. However the dragon beast is described in the poem just prior to the start of the battle in Lines 30-40.

3. Most (2018: 68-73). For Typhoeus ravaging the heavens, Rouse (1940: 15-21), Book 1. He then left the air and flogged the seas (pp. 21-5). After being tricked by Cadmos, the furious Typhoeus then ravaged the earth, Rouse (1940: 47-51),

Book 2. He battles Zeus and is ultimately defeated in pp. 63-93. See also Ogden (2013) for an account of dragons in the Greek and Roman worlds.

4. Revelation, 12: 3-4. Isaac (2002: 84).

5. Rackham (1938: 91), Volume I, Book 2, Chapter 23.

6. See Clube and Napier (1990: 189), Bailey, Clube and Napier (1990: 69) and Napier (2006).

7. Haycock (1990: 325) for the translation. While I assumed in the main text that Arthur's bard had introduced the humorous lines about the small vegetation, the structure of the poem would allow later bards to easily add such lines. If the poem is early then it may not have been in a fixed form for many years as bards retold it to show their own virtuosity by adding entertaining lines.

8. Haycock (2007: 177) for the translation.

9. See Yeomans et al. (1986: 78) for Halley's AD 530 appearance and also Tsu (1934: 195). For Halley's 530 closest distance to the Earth see Yeomans et al. (1986: 73).

10. Hughes (1987: 102).

11. For the description of the Eta Aquariids see Egal et al. (2020: 1). The years of the ancient Eta Aquariids outbursts appear on p. 3.

12. Egal et al. (2020: 3) for the Minimum Orbital Intersection Distance graph in Figure 2 giving the MOID values near the ascending and descending nodes over a 4000 year period.

13. Egal et al. (2020: 3) for the closeness of the comet around AD 500.

14. Abbott et al. (2014a: 415-8).

15. For the Zachariah of Mitylene statement on the dancing stars, Hamilton and Brooks (1899: 231), Book IX, Chapter VII. See also Baillie (1999: 199).

16. See Abbott et al. (2014b: 428) for the Eta Aquariids as the source for the dust particles in the ice.

17. See Abbott et al. (2014b: 427), in Figure 4, for the drop in the volume of the extraterrestrial material over time.

18. Yeomans et al. (1986: 78); Tsu (1934: 195).

19. Yeomans and Kiang (1981: 643).

20. Sekhar and Asher (2014: 53).

21. See Sekhar and Asher (2014: 55) for the 6 or 13 resonant zones and for the comet itself being resonant and also moving through the zones. See p. 54 for the greater chance of ejected meteoroid particles being trapped in resonance if the comet is trapped.

22. Hasegawa (1993: 212), Table 1.

23. Dall'Olmo (1978: 125).

24. Sekhar and Asher (2014: 55) for the 1-2 years for a 2:13 resonant zone.

25. For NASA: https://solarsystem.nasa.gov/asteroids-comets-and-meteors/comets/1p-halley/in-depth/; Hughes (1987: 353).

26. See Lewis (1996: 39-40; 48-9) for high-speed cometary material burning up and not surviving to be meteorites. See p. 44 for the low density of Halley's nucleus and p. 139 for comets splitting up. See Haycock (2007: 180) for the 'churned-up ground' translation.

27. Salzer and Hughes (2007: 62), Table 2.

28. Haycock (2007: 170).

29. Haycock (2007: 186).

Notes

Chapter 7 Disastrous Voyage to America

1. Taylor (1956: 62) presents an image of the circular inset and the accompanying text box. On pp. 64-5 she gives the Latin text and Richard Hakluyt's (1589: 249) translation of the text.
2. Taylor (1956: 56-61). See MacMillan (2004: 7, 46) for Dee presenting his case to Queen Elizabeth I.
3. See Taylor (1956: 58) for Arthur's first voyage of settlement. Not shown in the main text is the statement that there were people there who were 23 feet tall, a height which is both unrealistic in size and absurdly specific for these Arctic inhabitants. This is obviously a corrupted element from another part of the account in which 23 people who were not above 4 feet tall were observed. See Taylor (1956: 59). For the 'little people', Seaver (2008).
4. Enterline (2002: 59); Taylor (1956: 68) for Best's statement.
5. Ptolemy's *Geographia* mentions ten islands off the coast of India, the Maniolae, where the nearby magnetic stones could attract and wreck boats with iron nails (Nobbe, 1966: 170, in Greek; Stevenson, 1932: 157). This theme also appears in the *Commonitorium Palladii* by Bishop Palladius of Helenopolis, written in the early 400s. The relevant text is reproduced in Latin in Kübler (1891: 211). It states that magnetic stones that attract iron are found near Taprobane (Sri Lanka) and that ships which travel in this area are built entirely without iron nails. The 'magnetic mountain' appears in Book of the Marvels of India written by Buzurg ibn Shahrijar in c. 950. The text appears in Lecouteux (1984: 36) and refers to 'montagnes d'aimant' that stopped ships with iron from navigating on the stream, for fear the mountains would attract them. The magnetic mountain is in *The Arabian Nights* (Tuczay, 2005: 273-4) and *The Adventures of Abulfuaris* an early Persian tale (Blamires, 1979: 89-90). See MacMillan (2004: 83-5) for Dee's account that Arthur fitted out 12 ships containing no iron.
6. National Geospatial-Intelligence Agency (2011: 299).
7. Taylor (1956: 58) for Arthur's second voyage.
8. Ford (1977: 67).
9. Breeze (2018: 49, 59-60).
10. Ford (1977: 124-5).
11. Enterline (2002: 65).
12. See Liebermann (1894: 91, 97-8), in German, for dating the *Leges Anglorum Londoniis Collectae* and Liebermann (1903: 659-60), Vol. 1, for the Latin text of the *Leges Edwardi Confessoris* Arthurian section. Lyn Muir (1968: 255-6) also gives this Arthurian material in Latin. Elizabeth Leedham-Green's translation of the *Leges Edwardi* Arthur section is in MacMillan (2004: 57-8). The *Leges* Arthurian material also appears in Latin in the Miscellanea section of William of Worcestre's *Itineraries* of circa 1480. This is in Harvey (1969: 390). It also appeared in William Lambarde's *Archaionomia* in 1568, from where John Dee obtained it. Hakluyt took it from Lambarde and published it in his *Principall Navigations* of 1589. An 1885 version of this work in 16 volumes was edited by Edmund Goldsmid with the Latin and English translation. The *Leges* Arthurian material is in Volume 1, Hakluyt (Goldsmid, Ed.), 1885: 46-9. In 1907 an Everyman's Library set appeared in eight volumes called *Richard Hakluyt: Voyages* providing only the English, with an Introduction by John Masefield, and

was reprinted several times in the 1900s. The *Leges* Arthurian material is in Volume 1, Hakluyt (Masefield, Intro.), 1939: 54-5.

13. Rex (2004: 62). Peter Rex gives the various elements of the Norse involvement in the English resistance. When William defeated Harold at Hastings there was a Danish contingent that supported Harold, according to William of Poitiers (Rex, 2004: 95). The Danes then assisted the English revolt against William in 1069, when Edgar sought help from Sweyn Estrithson of Denmark who sent his large fleet to Northumbria. The rebels with the aid of the Danes then captured York, before William regained control and the Danes departed. The Danes were later involved in the revolt at Ely, joining forces with Hereward in the attack on Peterborough Abbey in 1071. They also supported Ralph, Earl of East Anglia, in the Revolt of the Earls and recaptured York in 1075 after the failure of the revolt. In 1085, the persistent Danes again raided York and managed to capture it (Rex, 2004: 101).

14. Tschan (1959: 219). Kunz and Sígurðsson (2008: xxvii).

15. Geoffrey's account of Arthur conquering the six northern lands is given in Thorpe (1966: 221-3). Although Muir's (1968) paper is a useful account of an important topic, she made several errors. First, she copies the wrong departing date of 3 May from Eva Taylor (1956) for Arthur's second voyage. Second, she attributes the flimsy speculation that Arthur's voyages were fabrications based on Eirik the Red's voyages to Raleigh Skelton whereas it was made by George Painter (see Painter, 1995: 244). Third, she remarks 'Of the seventeen places mentioned [in the lands list] six are included among Arthur's conquests in the *Historia Regum Britanniae* ...' This is incorrect: only five of Geoffrey's lands are in the lands list, which didn't copy from Geoffrey and didn't include the sixth item, Orkney. Had it been written after Geoffrey it would certainly have copied Orkney in order to maximize the list. Fourth, she bases her entire analysis on a fundamentally false assumption as shown by this statement: 'The original idea for this account must obviously spring from Geoffrey of Monmouth's narrative of Arthur's northern wars.' This 'obvious' assumption is false and skews her whole discussion.

16. Thorpe (1966: 248).

17. Higham (2018: 236); Koch (1996: 264-5).

18. A clear separation of Arthur and Gweir would introduce the great king (Arthur) who had increased his dominion across the world through undertaking a long voyage that no Briton had done before. He was the first to penetrate the heavy blue chain (the ocean). Then it would note poetically that the blue chain was restraining a loyal youth, which introduces Gweir, who was being held in the mound fortress. The bard visualizes Gweir singing bitterly in his prison and vows to pray for him until Judgement Day.

> *I praise the sovereign, prince, king of the land,*
> *who has enlarged his dominion across the world's shores.*
> *Nobody before him went into it,*
> *into the heavy blue chain – it restrained a loyal youth.*
> *The prison of Gweir was prepared in the mound fortress*
> *according to the account of Pwyll and Pryderi.*
> *And for the sake of the spoils of Annwfyn bitterly he sang.*

19. See Haycock (2007: 277) for lines 45-51 of *I Petition God* and pp. 435-7 for her emendments to *Spoils of Annwfyn*.
20. By the time *Culhwch and Olwen* was written, knowledge of Gweir was forgotten and four Gweirs were listed as Arthur's uncles (Ford, 1977: 129).
21. Bromwich (2006: 274). For 'the island of apples' see Parry (1925: 85-6). For Plutarch's 'Isles of the Blest' see Perrin (1919: 23).
22. *Traeth* is singular for 'shore' but the bard's intent was 'shores' unless he was thinking of a single landmass for the north. For *Prydwen*, Ford (1977: 149, 152, 154). It means 'white face', probably referring to the sail. Arthur's shield was *Wynebgwrthucher* in tradition (Ford, 1977: 126) but to Geoffrey of Monmouth this was too complex so he used *Pridwen* for the shield (Thorpe, 1966: 217).
23. Cunliffe (2001: 130). For Pytheas and Thule, see Whitaker (1981-2).
24. Eldjárn and Friðriksson (2000) and Magnússon (1973) for the four Roman *antoniniani*. Alonso-Núñez (1986) for how the coins arrived in Iceland.
25. Campbell (1987); Ahronson (2000); Ahronson (2003).
26. Foley and Holder (1999: 129-30) give Bede's statement about the 'people of our own age who have come forth from those parts' [Thule and the north]. For the 715 dating of Bede's work see Meyvaert (1999: 275). For Dicuil's statement see Tierney (1967: 76-7).
27. Haycock (2007: 446) for the 'glass fortress'; Koch and Carey (2003: 291) for the 'glass tower'; O'Meara (2002: 53-4) for the 'crystal pillar'. The type of ship Arthur used is unknown but Caesar saw that the Veneti, close associates of the Britons, had large sturdy ships that impressed him in a naval battle against the Romans. Prior to the battle the Veneti asked for help from the Britons who would have been familiar with their ships (Hammond, 1996: 60-3).
28. Diemand (2001: 1256) and Marko (1996: 553) give the iceberg paths and Marko et al. (1994: 1336) give the westward current branches across the Davis Strait. See Ebbesmeyer, Okubo and Helseth (1980: 976) for the percentage of icebergs that originate from each location.
29. Patrick Sims-Williams (1982: 244) thinks that the key word *(f)rigor* should be connected with the Latin *frigus, frigoris*. John Koch in Koch and Carey (2003: 310) agrees with Sims-Williams, translating it as the 'Frigid Fort'. Haycock (2007: 123) calls it the Petrification fort from *rigor* (rigidity) but does note the possibility of frigor (cold).
30. Morison (1971: 401-5) for the dangers and difficulties that Cartier faced.
31. Feininger and Goodacre (1995: 1351) give details on the Monteregian hills and Morison (1971: 414-5) relates Cartier's climb of Mount Royal and his dismay at seeing the Lachine rapids.
32. Line 12 mentions two 'fours', the first one in 'the four-peaked camp' and the second one in 'turning to face the four'. This is taken to mean that the bard turned to view all four peaks while staying at the four-peaked camp. However it has long been misunderstood in the literature as referring to a 'revolving fort'. Higley (1996: 50) has the first four in the line refer to the number of peaks and the second four refer to the number of times that the mythical fort revolved. Haycock (2007: 435) on the other hand thinks that the first four refers to the four quarters of the fort and the second four refers to the revolving fort turning to face the four directions of the compass.
33. Romain (1991: 2). See Tankersley et al. (2022: Figure 25) and Squier and Davis (1848: facing p. 94) for the comet-shaped earthwork at Milford.

34. The following works are excellent general sources on the Hopewell and the progression to the Late Woodland successors: Pacheco (1996); Romain (2000); Woodward and McDonald (2002); Milner (2004), Lepper (2005), Carr and Case (2005), Case and Carr (2008), Lepper (2011) and Lynott (2015).
35. Arthur's arrival date is speculation based on his being in Galloway in 531 when he endured 'the battle of the treetops'. An end date would be his death c. 537. Lynott (2014: 23) has the Ohio Hopewell ending c. AD 500 and the widespread adoption of the bow and arrow as c. 600. Blitz and Porth (2013) argue that it was available in the Eastern Woodlands as early as 300-400.
36. Moore (1961) for the common working ox. Bromwich (2006: 124) for Triad 45. Reynolds, Gates and Glaholt (2003: 1013) for the 'yellow-ochre' cape.
37. Hulbert and Schwarze (1910: 59) for Zeisberger. Reynolds et al. (2003: 1012) for the eastern boundary. McMillan (2006: 68) for the absence of buffalo in the east c. 500.
38. McMillan (2006: 76-7; 83).
39. Higley (1996: 52) for *perchen* as 'the owner'. Lepper (2005: 126-7).
40. Squier and Davis (1848: 256-7).
41. Gudger (1927: 199).
42. Prufer (1964: 93); Lepper (2005: 143); Squier and Davis (1848: 257) state that pearls were inserted for the eyes in the effigy pipes.
43. Higley (1996: 51) and Haycock (2007: 436) take the first option whereas John Koch in Koch and Carey (2003: 310) takes the second option.
44. See Grooms (2005: 93) for Mill's map showing the very high mound density along the Scioto river.
45. Sims-Williams (1982: 244); Jackson (1959b: 16); Bollard (1994: 20); Haycock (1983-4: 55-6, 59; 2007: 439); Koch and Carey (2003: 418); Higley (1996: 45).
46. Lloyd (1911: 120-1).
47. Cross and Slover (1936: 488-90); McCone (2000: 121-3; 175-93).
48. For Llenlleawg's killing of Diwrnach see Ford (1977:152-3).
49. Bromwich (2006: 259-60) for the Cauldron of Dyrnwch, Treasure Seven.

Chapter 8 The Killing of Arthur

1. Jones (1967: 126-7).
2. Barkway plaque: Collingwood and Wright (1995: 70-1; RIB no. 218). South Shields altar: Collingwood and Wright (1995: 353; RIB no. 1055).
3. Haycock (2007: 300). The tapestry of Arthur with the staff appears in the frontispiece of Loomis (1959).
4. In *Branwen daughter of Llŷr*, the cartoonish Brân is a giant who is so large that he simply wades across the Irish Sea to travel to Ireland. In his case the appointment of stewards to mind the country is unnecessary and is obviously borrowed from *Chair of the Sovereign*.
5. Ford (1977: 54-6).
6. For Teÿrnon Twrf Liant as 'the best man in the world' in *Pwyll, Prince of Dyfed* see (Ford, 1977: 52). For Arthur's men as 'the best men in the world' in *Pa Gûr*, see Sims-Williams (1991: 40). 'Twrf Liant' means the 'noise of the waves' according to John Rhŷs (1891: 283), possibly suggesting that Teÿrnon had won fame as a sailor.

341

Notes

7. In lines 59-67 *kadeir* is translated as 'chair', the long-held interpretation where the 'chair' is the 'throne'. When this is done the 9 lines are coherent and follow logically from each other. Line 59 refers to the throne of *Teÿrnon*, who is Arthur, as the introductory part is about Arthur and a eulogy to him after his death. Arthur is linked to Pwyll and Pryderi in *Spoils of Annwfyn* and *Teÿrnon* is linked to them in *Pwyll Prince of Dyfed*. The eulogy implies that Arthur is dead leading naturally to later lines that his throne is vacant. Line 60 notes that it is difficult for a king to retain the throne in that barbaric age, a point made also by Gildas. Then the bard speculates on who best could take the throne and mentions a renowned fighter, or an aggressive one, who may be able to hold onto it. Line 63 then follows logically – the warriors are bereft as Arthur (*Teÿrnon*) is dead. The bard then expresses his own grief and states the reason for it – that the prince with the fiery nature has been killed. All of these lines cohere and imply that *kadeir* means 'chair' here rather than the alternative 'song'.
8. Foster (1989: 458-9), *Livy, History of Rome*, Book 10, Chapter 26.
9. Paton (2010: 178-9), *Polybius, The Histories*, Book 3, Chapter 67.
10. Yardley (2020: 82-5), *Livy, History of Rome*, Book 23, Chapter 24.
11. Jones (1923: 247), *Geography of Strabo*, Book 4, Chapter 4.
12. Foulke (1907: 49-51), *History of the Langobards by Paul the Deacon,* Book 1, Chapter 27.
13. Williams (1980: 143). Bede's *EH*, Book 2, Chapter 20. McClure and Collins (1994: 105-6; 384).
14. *EH*, Book 3, Chapters 12-13. McClure and Collins (1994: 129-31).
15. Ford (1999: 177, 184-7).
16. Dragoo and Wray (1964: 196); Weets et al. (2005: 552); Lepper (2005: 124).
17. Shetrone and Greenman (1931); Thomas, Carr and Keller (2005: 369).
18. To create extra rhyme Haycock (2007: 231) emends 'brith' to 'brith*wed*' and moves gwaet (blood) to line 198, hence her line 197 translates as 'My stained sword'. As the probable meaning in this section is 'blood-stained sword' this emendation is not supported here. The bard was an old man of very limited mobility (as he relied on people to visit him) and he was relating something important to him before he died. The poem appears to be far from a polished product and the message he was conveying seems to be more important than a strict rhyme. His line 195 ends in 'pawb' which doesn't rhyme with the lines before and after. The Welsh at the beginning of line 199, *o douyd*, could mean a secular 'lord, governor' or 'the Lord, God' according to the GPC dictionary. Patrick Ford's (1977: 186) translation of an earthly 'lord', who bestows an honour on the bard, makes good sense and is used here. This lord was in a concealed place, which is inappropriate for God, but which is consistent with previous lines of a fierce battle with many fighters killed.
19. See Ford (1977: 69) for the Branwen incident that started the war between the Britons and the Irish.
20. Koch (2006: 236) for the obscure traditional utterance, *morddwyd tyllion*.
21. Lepper (2005: 60-1).
22. Raffel (1999: 101-3).
23. Guest (1849). See https://d.lib.rochester.edu/camelot/text/guest-peredur
24. Bromwich (2006: 167); Koch and Carey (2003: 299-300). Dubglas (4 battles), Glein, Bassas and Tribruit were fought near rivers.

25. Winterbottom (1972: 67-87).
26. Rutland Times (newspaper), Friday 22 March 1996, p.12.
27. Bromwich (2006: 97) for *Bwlch y Saethau* (Pass of the Arrows).
28. The Ingstads' discoveries and investigations at L'Anse aux Meadows appear in Ingstad and Ingstad, 1986, *The Norse Discovery of America*. The estimated time of the Norse occupation there appears in Ledger, Girdland-Flinck and Forbes (2019: 13342) where the intervals are based on 2 standard errors, hence the wide error bands.
29. Hugh Thomas (2003: 29) states that: '... Danish identity disappeared so quickly after the conquest because assimilation and acculturation had proceeded sufficiently far that the remaining ethnic boundaries easily dissolved under the shock of the Norman Conquest and the common oppression at the hands of the Normans.'
30. Wallace (2008: 610; 2009: 119).

Chapter 9 Decline in Arthur's Kingdom

1. Dewing (1916: 328-9).
2. Chabot (1901: 220-1). Translations from the French are given in Stothers and Rampino (1983: 6362) and Arjava (2005: 78-9).
3. Hamilton and Brooks (1899: 267).
4. Barnish (1992: 179-81).
5. Baillie (1999: 58, 67-8).
6. Rigby, Symonds and Ward-Thompson (2004: 1.26).
7. Larsen et al. (2008: 3-4).
8. The frost ring damage years are in Salzer and Hughes (2007: 62) in Table 2. Baillie (2008: 2), Table 1, gives the 7 year differences between the volcanic acid signals in the ice cores and the years of frost ring damage.
9. Baillie and McAneney (2015: 112).
10. The quote about at least three synchronous eruptive events occurs in the online version of Sigl et al. (2015) in the supplementary data section. It appears under 'Methods, Cryptotephra analyses of the 536 CE sample from NEEM-2011-S1'. In the printed version, the multiple volcanic eruptions also appear on p. 547 as: *'Geochemistry of tephra filtered from the NEEM-2011-S1 ice core at a depth corresponding to 536 CE indicated multiple North American volcanoes as likely candidates for a combined volcanic signal'*. See also p. 543 for the 7 year offset between the volcanic sulphate signals and the tree-ring growth reduction between AD 1 and AD 1000.
11. See Loveluck et al. (2018: 1575) for the Colle Gnifetti Swiss Alps ice core volcanic signals. For the 1.6° to 2.5° C drop in summer temperature after AD 536 see Sigl et al. (2015: 547).
12. Larsen et al. (2008: 3-4).
13. Abbott et al. (2014b: 430-1).
14. Dull, Southon and Sheets (2001: 39); Dull, Southon, Kutterolf et al. (2010), Figure 6 in poster; Dull, Southon, Kutterolf, Anchukaitis et al. (2019: 4-6). Smith et al. (2020: 5-6).
15. For the additional drop in summer temperature of 1.4° to 2.7° C after AD 541 see Sigl et al. (2015: 548).

16. Dewing (1914: 453-5). Mordechai et al (2019: 25546), 'inconsequential' in title. Keller et al. (2019; 12368-9) for 544 date. Sarris (2022: 318, 321).
17. Baillie (1999: 75).
18. Rees (1840: 343).
19. Sharpe (1995: 156-7), *Adomnán's Life of St Columba*, Book 2, Chapter 4. See Shrewsbury (1949: 22) for John Colgan's (1645) *flava ictericia*.
20. MacArthur (1949: 173).
21. Rees (1840: 343-4).
22. Ford (1977: 77).
23. Thompson (1980: 499-502).
24. Haycock (2007: 310) for Saracen.
25. Ford (1977: 165-9).
26. Ford (1977: 171-4).
27. Haycock (2007: 351-2) for the *Song of the Mead* Elphin and Koch (1997: 93) for the *Y Gododdin* Elphin.
28. Folkmoot is Germanic, not British. Liebermann (1903-16: 655) presents the folkmoot section in Latin. Kent Hieatt (1992: 79-80) gives the Latin and his translation to English from Lambarde.
29. Thorpe (1966: 263-5).
30. Jones (1949: 157); Duff and Duff (1934: 246-7).
31. Bury (1958: 138-9); Jones (1964: 273-4).
32. Martindale (1992: 1170-1); Bury (1958: 142-3).
33. Martindale (1992: 1172-3); Bury (1958: 143-5).
34. Martindale (1992: 1174-5); Bury (1958: 145).
35. Lhoyd and Powel (1584: 166); Van Hamel (1934: 226).
36. Bartrum (1965: 242); Padel (1994: 24).
37. Green (2007: 241).
38. Bromwich (1975-6: 177-9). The Irish pedigree is from *Expulsion of the Déisi*.

Chapter 10 Madoc

1. MacMillan (2004: 46) for Dee's list of explorers acting for Britain.
2. Stephens (1893: v-xv): Preface by Llywarch Reynolds. Williams (1979: 200).
3. Welsh taken from *Myvyrian Archaiology* (Jones et al., 1870: 164).
4. Welsh from Jones et al. (1870: 205).
5. Welsh from Jones et al. (1870: 213).
6. In Stephens (1893: 202) the daughter of Madoc ap Meredith is Marged. John Lloyd (1911: 587, 766) calls her Marared and anglicizes it to Margaret.
7. Welsh from Jones et al. (1870: 146).
8. The earliest copy we have of the *Brut y Tywysogion* (in Peniarth MS 20) dates to circa 1330.
9. An early Red Book version edited by John Williams ab Ithel (1860) is available on the internet. Modern scholarly versions have been translated and edited by Thomas Jones. See Jones (1952) for the Peniarth 20 version and Jones (1955) for the Red Book version.
10. Gerald places Roderic on Anglesey and David in Rhuddlan, east of the Conwy (W. L. Williams, 1908: 118, 128-9). He also mentions Owain's marriages to Gwladus and Christina (Williams, 1908: 126), as does Lloyd (1911: 587).

11. Lloyd (1911: 549-52) for the death of the warrior-poet Hywel in Pentraeth in Anglesey and the struggles of David and Roderic for control of north Wales.
12. W. L. Williams (1908: 118-9). In 1187 Jerusalem was captured by the Saracens and Baldwin was seeking young men from Wales to join the Crusade.
13. Williams (1908: 119).
14. Williams (1908: 125). In his footnote, Richard Colt Hoare takes the story of the underground passage from a Hengwrt MS.
15. Williams (1908: 126) for Gerald's comment on the vile plotting.
16. Williams (1908: 126-7) for the rise of Llywelyn against David.
17. Williams (1908: 128-9) for staying the night at the Rhuddlan castle of David.
18. Williams (1908: xix-xxi). In his Preface, Williams describes Gerald's style as similar to that of a modern newspaper reporter – 'His impressions of the men and events of his time, his fund of anecdotes and bon mots, his references to trivial matters, which more dignified writers would never deign to mention, his sprightly and sometimes malicious gossip, invest his period with a reality which the greatest of fiction writers has failed to rival.'
19. Williams (1908: 166) for Gerald's comment on shipping.
20. Bowen (1876: 28).
21. Bowen (1876: 29).
22. Thorpe (1978: 189-90); Thomas Jones (1955: 135-7).
23. For Llwyd's own references to his source material see Williams and Smith (2016: 16-17). See pp. 33-4 in the Introduction for comments on his sources. His use of Paris and Trivet is discussed in pp. 42-59.
24. The conclusion of the Madoc section and the new paragraph starting 'But to my hystorie' is in Williams and Smith (2016: 168).
25. Williams and Smith (2016: 168) for the comment on the many fables.
26. See Stephens (1893: 181, 184).
27. See Lhoyd and Powel (1584: 166) for the 'so far north'. See Llwyd's original phrasing in Williams and Smith (2016: 167-8) and Gwyn Williams' comment about the alteration in Williams (1979: 64).
28. See Williams and Smith (2016: 168) for Llwyd's surmise that they 'used the language that they founde there'.
29. Dee's thorough engagement with the manuscripts is well illustrated in Russell (2018: 407-8).
30. MacMillan (2004: 46).
31. *Jaquaza* as an earlier name for Florida appears in J. Cowley's 1746 edition of Hübner's *Geographie* on p. 241 and also in a heading (in German) for an antique map of north America by Johann Ulrich Müller of Frankfurt in 1692.
32. Bernardino de Sahagún, *Florentine Codex*, Book 12, Chapter 16. Translation by Nancy Fitch from the Spanish in Francisco del Paso y Troncoso (1905). For another account, see Prescott (1973: 305-6), originally published in Prescott (1843) with later reprints. Unfortunately it is doubtful that we'll ever know the true intent of Montezuma's speech.
33. A third account is given by Peckham (1583: 459-60).
34. *Myvyrian Archaiology* (Jones et al., 1870: 401), Triad 10. E. D. Jones (1965: 124) says that 'Iolo was able to get his Madog safely embedded in the spurious Triad without creating suspicion.'
35. For Raleigh's letter see Kimberley (2014: 211-12).

36. Howell's 9th August 1630 letter to Earl Rivers is in his *Epistolae Ho-Elianae* (Familiar Letters) in Book II, letter LV (Jacobs, 1892: 459-62). The Welsh Indies Epitaph and Madoc's 1062 departure are on p. 461. This letter was reprinted in the *Cambro-Briton* (1822), Vol 3, No 30, 462-5.
37. Howell's later letter to his cousin, Howel Gwyn is in his Familiar Letters in Book IV, letter XXX (Jacobs, 1892: 608-9). It includes the four Welsh lines that were interpolated into Maredudd ap Rhys and the terrible English translation that Howell appears to have taken from Thomas Herbert (1638: 360).
38. Herbert (1634: 221).
39. John Williams (1792: 49) for the fabrication that Madoc was the commander of his father's fleet, victorious over the fleet of Henry II.
40. John Williams (1792: 28) for the fake Ieuan Brechfa statement that Riryd went with Madoc on the second voyage.
41. Morgan (1857: 166).
42. Lloyd (1911: 766); Gwyn Williams (1979: 64).
43. Charles-Edwards (2013: 334) gives a convenient pedigree chart. See Arthur Jones (1910: 39-40) for Gruffydd's Irish ancestors through Ragnaillt.
44. Meredith Hanmer, an Anglican churchman of Welsh descent, wrote a history of Ireland but relies on Lhoyd and Powel (1584) for the Irish relations of Cynan and the claim that Riryd was lord of Clochran. He speculates that Riryd received the latter royal title by 'right of his wife' (Hanmer, p. 221).
45. De Costa (1891: 5) constructs the following imaginary scenario: 'The Welsh, on the contrary, did not exhibit surprise on reaching a land at the west. In fact, everything would seem to indicate that they knew of that land, probably by contact with the Northmen, and that Madoc sailed expecting to reach some part of the region known as Vinland.'
46. Russell (2018: 406-7). The 6 lines are in the Iolo MS, Morganwg (1848: 323-4). Stephens (1893: 19) remarks on the evident tradition.
47. Gwyn Williams (1979: 51-5) for his thoughts on the Willem Madoc material as given by Deacon.
48. Gwyn Williams (1979: 49) for 'A Madoc am I to my age' as evidence.
49. Roberts (2003: 39-40) for the poem, with the Madoc lines on p. 40.
50. Williams and Smith (2016: 168) for the fables.
51. Russell (2018: 406-7).
52. E. D. Jones (1965: 123); Eleri Davies (1992: 13).
53. For example see the chapters in Leeson (2014) by Kimberley, pp. 201-13, and Spence, pp. 236-56.
54. E. D. Jones (1968-9: 185) for the blatant deception, wishful thinking etc.
55. E. D. Jones (1968-9: 187) for his desire to see in full Willem's Madoc precis.
56. Spence (2014: 236) for the 50 books; Leeson (2014: xi-xii) for the comments.
57. For W. Owen Pughe's fudging of *mur* to *myr* see Stephens (1893: 9). E. D. Jones (1965: 122) says that this substitution is 'entirely unwarranted'. For Deacon presenting this blatant falsehood as an 'academic argument' see pp. 16-17.
58. Deacon (1967: 17).
59. Deacon (1967: 26).
60. For his appalling blunder and absolute certainty, see Deacon (1967: 26-7).
61. For the 'some authorities' and Arthur Rhys as the bard see Deacon (1967: 24). For the Rhys endnote pamphlet see p. 246.

62. Deacon (1967: 24-5). For the endnote 'ibid.' see Deacon (1967: 247).
63. Deacon (1967: 24) for his hilarious claim that the *Annales* are more accurate in giving detail on the wives and mistresses (which don't mention them).
64. Deacon (1967: 23); E. D. Jones (1968-9: 187).
65. E. D. Jones (1968-9: 187).
66. Deacon (1967: 247) gives a source for the 'heard mention' clue of Joan Dane as 'Letter from Joan Dane to Mrs Grafton S. Porter, Cincinatti (sic), May 23, 1910', a source both worthless and inaccessible, if it existed.
67. Kimberley (2014: 202-4).
68. Bromwich (2006: 28-9) for Triad 14. See *Myvyrian Archaiology* (Jones et al., 1870: 407) for Triad 68 containing Iolo's forgery. See Deacon (1967: 51) for his fabrication that Geraint sailed from Lundy Island.
69. Deacon (1967: 82-3).
70. Deacon (1967: 86) for the emissary and pp. 86-7 for the tablet. The old-style Welsh he took from a late source. E. D. Jones (1968-9: 185) says that the word 'ffaith' in the Welsh was one of W. Owen Pughe's inventions.
71. Kimberley (2014: 203-4, 209-10) relates the efforts to find the Lundy archives, the stone tablet and D. G. Evans. Keith Gardner tried to get Deacon to show his sources but Deacon was evasive, saying that all his notes were in America, an implausible excuse for a British resident. He never produced the letter from D. G. Evans. If his notes were in America, he had 30 years to retrieve them but never gave them to Gardner. For the *Bristol Evening Post* enquiry, see Bernard Knight (2013), Madoc International Research Association.
72. Sources for Synnott's life include Slyfield (2000), the *Leeds Mercury* (Tuesday 6 January 1920) about the trial and his exoneration, and the *West Sussex County Times* (Friday 18 October 1946) for his death. He was survived by his daughter Miss Harriett J. Fitzgerald Synnott who had lived with him at the Iden Rectory and was granted 'Letters of administration'. Nothing in Slyfield or any of the newspapers says that he possessed old papers mentioning Madoc. Deacon (1967: 98) for the 'several years ago' purchase.
73. Deacon (1967: 99-100).
74. Gwyn Williams (1979: 50-1).
75. Gwyn Williams (1979: 51).
76. Haycock (2007: 461-2).
77. Deacon (1967: 166-73); Gwyn Williams (1979: 51-4); Kimberley (2014: 207).
78. E. D. Jones (1968-9: 187).
79. E. D. Jones (1965: 123-4).
80. Gwyn Williams (1979: 46).
81. Gwyn Williams (1979: 46). Squier and Davis (1848: 99), Plate XXXVI.
82. Gwyn Williams (1979: 46).
83. Stephens (1893: 100-171).
84. For Morgan Jones, see Stephens (1893: 128-33); Gwyn Williams (1979: 75-7).
85. J. S. Williams (1842: 373) for the breastplates in T. S. Hinde's Letter of 30 May 1842 in the *American Pioneer*.
86. W. L. Williams (1908: 164-5).
87. The Daughters of the American Revolution mention Roman coins on the plaque for Madoc (Knight, 2013). Giles, 1847: 289, 511) and W. L. Williams (1908: 16) for the coins. Also see Martin Allen (2017: 80-1).

Chapter 11 Inscriptions on Stone

1. Sharpe (1995: 118, 127, 196-8, 219); Young (2009: 131-9).
2. O'Meara (2002: 26-7) for Barrind's journey.
3. For Brendan's voyage for 40 days, the fog, and reaching the wide land with a great river see O'Meara (2002: 62-3). Ashe (1962: 321-2) argues that east is a mistake for west.
4. Morison (1971: 25); Jones (1986: 33-4); Severin (1978).
5. Dumville (1988b: 101-2); Burgess (2002: 8).
6. Kunz and Sígurðsson (2008: 48).
7. Pálsson and Edwards (2007: 61).
8. Pálsson and Edwards (1989: 162-3).
9. Seaver (1996: 27); Nansen (1911: 47-56).
10. Fell (1983: 17).
11. See Pyle (1983: 5-6) for the chalking of the lines and publicizing the site. See Gallagher (1983: 7-9) for her winter solstice theory.
12. Gallagher (1983: 8) for contacting Fell and his translation.
13. Gallagher (1983: 9) for the group observing the first glimmer of light striking the left side of the petroglyph.
14. Tankersley et al. (2022: 15-16).
15. Fulford et al (2000: 11).
16. See Fell (1983: 17), Part 1, for this section of the inscriptions.
17. See Oppenheimer and Wirtz (1989: 12-15). They also point out Fell's arbitrary decisions, how his sketches can be different to the actual carvings and how a line of consonants can give different translations. They state: 'Gallagher's own account leaves little question but that she reported her fairly extraordinary "hunch" to Fell before he ever saw the pictures of the petroglyph'.
18. Fell (1983: 18) for the Horse Creek Carvings.
19. Nyland's 1996 translation is given in Wise (2003). Nyland used Fell's own derived consonants but a Basque dictionary.
20. Pyle (1998: 70) for Meyer's television interview and p. 69 for a photo of him with Pyle at the Luther Elkins site.
21. Fell (1983: 16) for *Oin Dia – One God*. It's on the same page as the Luther Elkins petroglyphs photo which probably accounts for Meyer's mistake.
22. Fell's layout and explanation is very poor. The strokes from which he derives 'Father, Son and Holy Spirit, *One God*' are first given in a hand-drawn Figure G, as part 3 of three sets of strokes. The title for G is 'Pious symbols used by early Christians', but nothing about Horse Creek. A photo of the chalked carvings next appears in Figure J entitled 'Rebus with Ogam strokes that are incorporated in a hand', again nothing about Horse Creek. For the 'one God' part, by comparing Figures G and J it can be seen that he has added a 'leg' to the 'X' in G. Figure K, to the right of J, shows the final pruned 'X' above the letters IA. The extra leg on the left is there but the leg on the right has been pruned off under the stem and the projection from this leg that is in J has been pruned off. The shift from the photos to Fell's hand-drawn figures is another area ripe for fudging.
23. See Gallagher (1983: 9). She never clarifies where the 'notch' is in the photos, surely a vital part of her argument, and never says what the creeping shadow is supposed to do in terms of her theory.

24. Wise took his photos at the site in 2002 and an unpublished version of his paper was available in 2003, eventually published in Wise (2019). He is critical of Gallagher's lack of clear criteria. He displays 8 photos taken over a one hour period which show that nothing of interest happens to the 'Sun' design.
25. W. H. Lesser (1983) relates Olafson's letter and lists his research papers.
26. Löffler (2007: 188) for Stephens' comments that Coelbren letters are derived from Roman ones. The Rev. John Jones' statements about Morganwg inventing Coelbren and Owen Pughe inventing 5 extra letters are in *Gwaith Lewis Glyn Cothi* (1837: 260). See Jones and Davies (1837, eds.).
27. Michael (2004: 41).
28. Williams ab Ithel (1862: 57, 71).
29. Fell (1980: 168); Mainfort and Kwas (2004: 765).
30. Michael (2004: 40) for the Ten Lost Tribes using Coelbren as their language.
31. Michael (2004: 41) for the Coelbren equivalents of the Hebrew.
32. Michael (2004: 41) for 'Maefuc'.
33. Macoy (1868: 134) for the Hebrew, translated 'Holiness to the Lord'.
34. Thomas (1890: 36) for the drawing of the Bat Creek stone without the parallel lines. It was originally thought to be in Cherokee and was read upside down.
35. Williams ab Ithel (1862: 113).

Chapter 12 Pre-Columbian White People

1. Williams, J. S (1842: 373-4) in *American Pioneer*. Campbell (1816: 460-1) for the five quotes in *The Port Folio*.
2. General Clark was an exception, arguing that the mounds were built by the Indians' ancestors (Thomas and Conner (1967: 208-11).
3. Mooney (1910: 931-2) says '... there is not a provable trace of Welsh, Gaelic or any other European language in any native American language, excepting for a few words of recent introduction ...'. Adair (1775: 37-74), Argument 5.
4. Gwyn Williams (1979: 75-9). The 1660 date probably should be 1669.
5. Stephens (1893: 127-33); Gwyn Williams (1979: 76, 80-1).
6. Gwyn Williams (1979: 82-3).
7. Durrett (1908: 46).
8. Durrett (1908: 49).
9. Stone (1865: 484-5).
10. Stone (1865: 486).
11. The John Norton story appears in a footnote in Stone (1865: 486).
12. Morison (1971: 420, 430).
13. Stone (1865: 487-8) for Stone relating Brant's white people to Madoc.
14. Rave (1912: 3). It is odd that the whites are kneeling in prayer to the sun in the Shawnee song but the origins of this are lost to us.
15. Borden (1874: 185-6).
16. Borden (1874: 148); Rave (1912: 3).
17. Cox (1874: 122-3) gives sketches of Devil's Backbone.
18. For the 'Madoc fever' see Gwyn Williams (1979: 84); Stephens (1893: 105) for the John Evans' letter.
19. Witte (2006: 88, 96). Gwyn Williams (1979: 183).
20. Catlin (1841: 296).

21. See Cox (1874: 125-7); Cox (1875: 25-6).
22. Fowke (1902: 65-6).
23. Putnam (1875a, b and c). In the last two, he goes beyond Cox (1874) re the 75 ft wall. He says the stones were laid overlapping each other, breaking joints, without cement or mortar. It puts him directly at odds with Fowke (1902).
24. An overview of Prather sites is given in Munson and McCullough (2004: 5-12). Guernsey (1942: 62-3).
25. Arnold and Graham (2011: 27).
26. Munson and McCullough (2004: 81-3); Munson et al. (2006: 159-60).
27. Sipe (2004: 94-5).
28. Gwyn Williams (1979: 86).
29. Stoddard (1812: 483-4); Draper (1912: 259) for the white Indians moving to the far west or northwest.
30. Stoddard (1812: 484). For Gerald of Wales, see W. L. Williams (1908: 164-5).
31. Stoddard (1812: 485) for the old Cherokee woman, Peg, and her book.

Chapter 13 Irishman in West Virginia, AD 710

1. Pyle (2004: 2-6), Vol. 9, Issue 56 in *Ancient American*.
2. Pyle (1998: 84-5) for the two 'translations'.
3. The most detailed description of Pyle's excavating the bones is in a document *Petroglyph Research: Cook Petroglyph Site, Wyoming County, West Virginia. DNA/C14 Tested Skeletal Remains, Site 46-WYO-43* an unpublished paper dated December 2002. This is 13 years after the excavation.
4. In a letter to Scott Woodward dated 23 March 2000 Pyle says that he is sending one partial femur and four teeth from the lower mandible of the skull.
5. The comparison sequences included Cromwell (England); Wales; Sardinia1; Sardinia2; Sardinia3; Sardinia4; Bulgaria; Finland98; FinSaami; Finland127; Turk; Chile10; Chile18; Albania and five Native American sequences, 2419A; 2361B; 9219B; 2305C and 9269D.
6. The Anderson reference sequence comes from Anderson, Bankier, Barrell et al. (1981) and is usually called the Cambridge Reference Sequence (CRS). It was revised in 1999 as the revised Cambridge Reference Sequence (rCRS).
7. Woodward made no comment on the significance of the result. He ended his letter to Pyle as follows: 'I have also included a copy of the absolute difference matrix comparing the DNA sequences for absolute differences. It indicates the number of sequence differences found between the various samples'. He didn't say that the man was not Native American.
8. Stafford's report is dated 27 September 2001. He also obtained a C14 dating of a small bone needle as well as the long bone and gained a very early BC date for it. It was found in a different location at the Cook site by Paul Browning in 1997 but apparently has no relation to the skeleton (Pyle, 1998: 82).
9. Stafford outlined six actions he thought necessary to safeguard the tentative findings. One was to compare chemically the sediments from the Cook site where the bones were excavated with sediments from the skeleton to verify that the bones were from the Cook shelter and not another location.
10. Terry Melton may have been recommended to Pyle by Doug Owsley who would have been aware of labs based much closer to the Smithsonian than Utah.

11. Sipe (2004: 97).
12. For example, in his *Affidavit* of 21 March 2002 he dates the bones to AD 1222 (2002 – 780) but usually just takes the AD 2000 date as the reference point, as the analyses began then, to get AD 1220 (2000 – 780).
13. Owsley's quote on the remains dating to AD 1220 appears in his letter to Pyle of 1 December 2003 which was Owsley's formal acceptance of the bones.
14. Melton's 2003 report, Case 2346, page 2.
15. Melton's 2003 report, page 2, Table 1, nucleotide position 16362.
16. In his *Affidavit* of 21 March 2002 Pyle states that in 2001 the remains not taken by the Smithsonian were reinterred at the Cook site shelter in the presence of about 40 witnesses.

Chapter 14 Ancient Roman coins in America

1. Epstein (1980: 11-12).
2. See https://www.asc.ohio-state.edu/mcculloch.2/arch/coins/fallsoh.htm
3. See https://www.asc.ohio-state.edu/mcculloch.2/arch/coins/breathit.htm
4. Scherz (1994: 32-8).
5. Pennington (2009: 46-7).
6. Pennington (2010: 34-5).
7. T. V. Buttrey in Epstein (1980: 12).
8. N. Totten in Epstein (1980: 18).
9. T. V. Buttrey in Epstein (1980: 18).
10. Atwater (1820: 120-1), Haywood (1823: 173-7) and Commentary XLV-XLIX.
11. S. C. Williams (1937: 3), footnote 6.
12. Armstrong (1940: 279) in Appendix; Armstrong (1950: 63).
13. The Madoc plaque blew down in 1979 and was put into storage. In 2008 it was decided to resurrect it and a restored version now sits in the yard of the DAR headquarters in N Joachim St Mobile, Alabama. For the Roman coins, see Pugh (1970: 118); Olson (1987: 48); Callahan (2000: 53).
14. Epstein (1980: 4).

Chapter 15 Arthur in America

1. Fell (1980: 120-1).
2. Epstein (1980: 12); Fell (1980: 153).
3. Winterbottom (1978: 52; 118); Hill (1949-51: 5-6).
4. Winterbottom (1978: 107; 140).
5. Winterbottom (1978: 53; 119).
6. Fell (1980: 120); Hill (1949-51: 8).
7. Hill (1949-51: 21-5).
8. Epstein (1980: 12); Fell (1980: 121).
9. MacMillan (2006: 106).
10. Coe and Young (1995: 137) for midday and jet-blackness.
11. Loomis (1956: 166-7).
12. John Lloyd (1911: 134) footnote 43.

REFERENCES

Abbott, D., Breger, D. et al. (2014a). Calendar-year dating of the Greenland Ice Sheet Project 2 ice core. In G. Keller and A. Kerr (eds.) *Volcanism, Impacts, and Mass Extinctions*. Boulder: Geol. Society of America; 411-20.

Abbott, D., Breger, D.et al. (2014b). What caused terrestrial dust loading and climate downturns between AD 533 and 540? In G. Keller and A. Kerr (see above). Boulder: Geol. Society of America; 421-37.

Adair, J. (1775). *The History of the American Indians*. London: Dilly.

Ahronson, K. (2000). Further Evidence for a Columban Iceland: Preliminary Results of Recent Work. *Norwegian Archaeological Review*, 33, 117-124.

Ahronson, K. (2003). Crosses of Columban Iceland: a survey of preliminary research. In S. Lewis-Simpson (ed.) *Vinland revisited*. Historic Sites; 75-82.

Alcock, L. (1971). *Arthur's Britain: History and Archaeology AD 367-634*. Harmondsworth: Penguin.

Allen, M. (2017). First Sterling area. *Economic History Review*, 70, 1, 79-100.

Alonso-Núñez, J. (1986). A note on Roman coins found in Iceland. *Oxford Journal of Archaeology*, 5, 121-2.

Anderson, A. (1928). Varia. 1. The dating passage in Gildas's *Excidium*. 2. Gildas and Arthur. *Zeitschrift für Celtische Philologie*, 17, 403-406.

Anderson, S., Bankier, A., Barrell, B. et al. (1981). Sequence and organization of the human mitochondrial genome. *Nature*, 290, 457–65.

Andrews, R. and McKenna, C. (1996). Gwaith Bleddyn Fardd. In R. Andrews, N. Costigan et al. (eds.). *Gwaith Bleddyn Fardd a Beirdd Eraill Ail Hanner y Drydedd Ganrif ar Ddeg*. Vol. 7. Cardiff: UOW Press; 519-63.

Arjava, A. (2005). The Mystery Cloud of 536 CE in the Mediterranean Sources. *Dumbarton Oaks Papers*, Vol. 59; 73-94.

Armstrong, Z. (1940). *History of Hamilton County and Chattanooga Tennessee*. Vol II. Johnson City, Tennessee: Overmountain.

Armstrong, Z. (1950). *Who discovered America? The Amazing story of Madoc*. Chattanooga: Lookout.

Arnold, C. and Graham, C. (2011). Archaeological investigations at the Ellingsworth site (12 Cl 127), a Mississippian hamlet of the Falls Mississippian complex of southeastern Indiana. *Indiana Archaeology*, 6, 1; 24-48.

Ashe, G. (1962). *Land to the West*. London: Collins.

Ashe, G. (1981). 'A Certain Very Ancient Book'. *Speculum*, 56, 301-323.

Ashe, G. (1982). *Avalonian Quest*. London: Methuen.

Ashe, G. (1995). Origins of the Arthurian Legend. *Arthuriana*, 5, 1-24.

References

Atwater, C. (1820). *Archaeologia Americana. Transactions of the American Antiquarian Society, 1:* 105-299.

Avilin, T. (2007). East European Meteor Folk-Beliefs. *WGN, journal of the International Meteor Organization,* 35, 5, 113-16.

Bachrach, B. (1990). The Questions of King Arthur's Existence and Romano-British Naval Operations. In *The Haskins Society Journal,* 2, 13-28.

Bailey, M., Clube, V. and Napier, W. (1990). *Origin of Comets.* Pergamon.

Baillie, M. (1989). Do Irish Bog Oaks Date the Shang Dynasty? *Current Archaeology,* 117, 310-313.

Baillie, M. (1994). Dendrochronology raises questions about the nature of the AD 536 dustveil event. *The Holocene,* 4, 212-217.

Baillie, M. (1999). *Exodus to Arthur: Catastrophic Encounters with Comets.* London: Batsford.

Baillie, M. (2007). Tree-Rings indicate global environmental downturns that could have been caused by Comet Debris. In P. Bobrowsky and H. Rickman (eds.) *Comet/Asteroid Impacts and Human Society.* Berlin: Springer.

Baillie, M. (2008). Proposed re-dating of the European ice core chronology by seven years prior to the 7th century AD. *Geophysical Research Letters,* Vol. 35, L15813.

Baillie, M. and McAneney, J. (2015). Tree ring effects and ice core acidities clarify volcanic record of the first millennium. *Climate of the Past,* 11, 105-14.

Barnish, S. (1992). *The Variae of Magnus Aurelius Cassiodorus Senator. Translated Texts for Historians 12.* Liverpool: Liverpool University.

Bartrum, P. (1965). Arthuriana from the genealogical manuscripts. *National Library of Wales Journal,* 14, 242-5.

Bartrum, P. (1966), ed. *Early Welsh Genealogical Tracts.* Cardiff: UOW.

Bartrum, P. (2009). *A Welsh Classical Dictionary: People in History and Legend up to about A.D. 1000.* Aberystwyth: NLW.

Beijing Astronomical Observatory (1988). *General Collection of Ancient Chinese Astronomical Records.* Nanjing: Jiangsu Press.

Benozzo, F. (2004). *Landscape Perception in Early Celtic Literature.* Aberystwyth: Celtic Studies Publications.

Blamires, D. (1979). *Herzog Ernst and the Otherworld Voyage.* Manchester: Manchester University Press.

Blitz, J. and Porth, E. (2013). Social Complexity and the Bow in the Eastern Woodlands. *Evolutionary Anthropology,* 22, 89-95.

Bollard, J. (1994). Arthur in the early Welsh tradition. In J. Wilhelm (ed.) *The Romance of Arthur.* NY: Garland; 11-23. First published 1984 when edited by J. Wilhelm and L. Gross with the same title. NY: Garland; 13-25.

Bollard, J. (1990a). Gwyn eu Byd: Some Comments on the Myrddin Poetry. *Proceedings of the Harvard Celtic Colloquium,* 10, 69–87.

Bollard, J. (1990b). Myrddin in Early Welsh Tradition. In P. Goodrich (ed.) *The Romance of Merlin.* New York: Garland: 13-54.

Borden, W. (1874). In E. Cox, *Fifth Annual Report of the Geological Survey of Indiana in 1873;* 134-89.

Bowen, B. (1876). *America Discovered by the Welsh in 1170 AD.* Philadelphia: Lippincott.

Breatnach, L. (1977). Suffixed Pronouns in Early Irish. *Celtica,* 12, 75-107.

Breeze, A. (2001). Seventh-Century Northumbria and a Poem to Cadwallon, *Northern History,* 38, 1, 145-52.

Breeze, A. (2012). The Name and Battle of Arfderydd, near Carlisle. *Journal of Literary Onomastics.* Vol. 2, Issue 1, 1-9.

Breeze, A. (2015). The Arthurian Battle of Badon and Braydon Forest, Wiltshire. *Journal of Literary Onomastics,* 4, 20-30.

Breeze, A. (2018). The Dates of the Four Branches of the Mabinogi. *Studia Celtica Posnaniensia,* Vol. 3 No. 1, 47-62.

Bromwich, R. (1975-6). Concepts of Arthur. *Studia Celtica,* 10-11, 163-181.

Bromwich, R. (2006), ed. and trans. *Trioedd Ynys Prydein: The Welsh Triads* (3rd edition). Cardiff: University of Wales Press.

Bromwich, R. and Evans, D. (1992), eds. *Culhwch ac Olwen:* Cardiff: UOW.

Bromwich, R., Jarman, A., Roberts, B. and Huws, D. (1991). Introduction. In R. Bromwich et al. (eds.) *The Arthur of the Welsh.* Cardiff: UOW; 1-14.

Burgess, G. (2002). The Life and Legend of Saint Brendan. In W. Barron and G. S. Burgess (eds.) *The Voyage of Saint Brendan.* University of Exeter; 1-12.

Burgess, R. (1990). The Dark Ages return to fifth-century Britain: the 'Restored' Gallic Chronicle exploded. *Britannia,* 21, 185-95.

Burkitt, T. and Burkitt, A. (1990). The Frontier Zone and the Siege of Mount Badon: a Review of the Evidence. *Proceedings of Somerset Archaeological and Natural History Society,* 134, 81-93.

Burks, J. and Cook, R. (2011). Beyond Squier and Davis: rediscovering Ohio's earthworks with geophysical remote sensing. *American Antiquity,* 76, 667-89.

Bury, J. (1958). *History of the Later Roman Empire: from the Death of Theodosius I to the Death of Justinian.* Vol. 2. New York: Dover.

Callahan, J. (2000). *Lest We Forget: the Melungeon Colony of Newman's Ridge.* Johnson City, Tennessee: Overmountain.

Campbell, E. (1987). A cross-marked quern from Dunadd and other evidence for relations between Dunadd and Iona. *Proceedings of the Society of Antiquaries of Scotland,* 117, 105-117.

Campbell, J. (1816). Aborigines of the Western Country. *Port Folio*, 1, 458-63.

Carney, J. (1950). 'Suibne Geilt' and 'The children of Lir'. *Éigse, 6*, 1948/52, (part. 2, 1950), 83–110.

Carney, J. (1976). The Earliest Bran Material. In J. O'Meara and B. Naumann (eds.) *Latin Script and Letters AD 400–900*. Leiden: Brill; 174-93.

Carney, J. (1983). Dating early Irish verse texts, 500-1100. *Éigse, 19*, 177-216.

Carr, C. and Case, D. (2005), eds. *Gathering Hopewell: Society, Ritual, and Ritual Interaction*. New York: Kluwer Academic/Plenum.

Case, D. and Carr, C. (2008), eds. *The Scioto Hopewell and their Neighbors*. NY: Springer.

Catlin, G. (1841). *The North American Indians*. Vol. I. London: Catlin.

Cessford, C. (1994). Pictish Raiders at Trusty's Hill? *Trans. Dumfriesshire and Galloway Natural History and Antiquarian Society, 69*, 81-8.

Cessford, C. (1997). Northern England and the Gododdin poem. *Northern History, 33*, 218-22.

Chabot, J. (1901). *Chronique de Michel le Syrien*, Vol 2. Paris: Ernest Leroux.

Chadwick, N. (1953). The Lost Literature of Celtic Scotland: Caw of Pritdin and Arthur of Britain. *Scottish Gaelic Studies, 7*, 115-83.

Chadwick, N. (1958). Early culture and learning in North Wales. In Chadwick et al. (eds.) *Studies in the early British Church*. Cambridge: CUP; 29-120.

Chadwick, N. (1963). Battle of Chester: a Study of Sources. In Chadwick (ed.) *Celt and Saxon: Studies in Early British Border*. Cambridge: CUP; 167-85.

Chadwick, H. and Chadwick, N. (1932). *The Growth of Literature, 1*. Cambridge: Cambridge University Press.

Chalmers, G. (1887). *Caledonia: a Historical and Topographical account of North Britain*. Vol. 1, Paisley: Gardner. First published in 1807.

Chambers, E. (1927). *Arthur of Britain*. London: Sidgwick and Jackson.

Chapman, P. (1973). *The man who led Columbus to America*. Atlanta: Judson.

Charles-Edwards, T. (1991). The Arthur of History. In R. Bromwich et al. (eds.) *The Arthur of the Welsh*. Cardiff: UOW Press; 15-32.

Charles-Edwards, T. (2013). *Wales and the Britons 350-1064*. Oxford: OUP.

Clarke, B. (1973), ed. and trans. *Life of Merlin (Vita Merlini)*. Cardiff: UOW.

Clarkson, T. (2016). *Scotland's Merlin: a Medieval Legend and its Dark Age Origins*. Edinburgh: John Donald.

Clube, S. V. and Napier, W. (1990). *The Cosmic Winter*. Oxford: Blackwell.

Coe, J. and Young, S. (1995), eds. and trans. *The Celtic Sources for the Arthurian Legend*. Felinfach: Llanerch Publishers.

Collingwood, R. and Wright, R. (1995), eds. *Roman Inscriptions of Britain, I: Inscriptions on Stone. Addenda, Corrigenda*, R.S.O. Tomlin. Stroud: Sutton.

Corning, C. (2006). *The Celtic and Roman Traditions: conflict and consensus in the early medieval church*. NY: Palgrave Macmillan.

Cowley, J. (1746). *An Introduction to the study of Geography by way of Question and Answer*. London: T. Cox.

Cox, E. (1874). *Fifth Annual Report of the Geological Survey of Indiana made during the year 1873*. Indianapolis: Sentinel.

Cox, E. (1875). *Sixth Annual Report of the Geological Survey of Indiana made during the year 1874*. Indianapolis: Sentinel.

Crawford, O. (1935). Arthur and his battles. *Antiquity, IX, 277-279*.

Cross, T. and Slover, C. (1936), eds. *Ancient Irish Tales*. NY: Holt.

Cunliffe, B. (2001). *The Extraordinary Voyage of Pytheas the Greek*. Penguin.

Dall'Olmo, U. (1978). Meteors, meteor showers, meteorites in Middle Ages: European Medieval Sources. *Journal for the History of Astronomy*, 9, 123-34.

Dalton, O. (1915), trans. *The Letters of Sidonius*. Vol. 1. Oxford: Clarendon.

Dark, K. (1994). *Discovery by Design: the identification of secular elite settlements in western Britain A.D. 400-700*. BAR 237. Oxford: Hadrian.

Dark, K. (2000a). *Britain and the End of the Roman Empire*. Brimscombe Port: Tempus.

Dark, K. (2000b). A Famous Arthur in the Sixth Century? Reconsidering the Origins of the Arthurian Legend. *Reading Medieval Studies*, 26: 77-96.

Davies, E. (1992). *Gwaith Deio ab Ieuan Du a Gwilym ab Ieuan Hen*. Caerdydd: Gwasg Prifysgol Cymru.

Davies, W. (1979). *The Llandaff Charters*. Aberystwyth: NLW.

Davies, W. (1982). *Wales in the Early Middle Ages*. Leicester: LUP.

Deacon, R. (1967). *Madoc and the Discovery of America: Some New Light on an Old Controversy*. London: Muller. First published in 1966.

De Costa, B. (1891). *Myvyrian Archaiology: The Pre-Columbian Voyages of the Welsh to America*. Albany: Joe Munsell's Sons.

Dewing, B. (1914). *Procopius: History of the Wars*. Volume 1, Books 1-2. The Persian War. Loeb Classical Library 48. Cambridge, MA: HUP.

Dewing, B. (1916). *Procopius: History of the Wars*. Volume 2, Books 3-4. Loeb Classical Library 81. Cambridge, MA: HUP.

Diemand, D. (2001). Icebergs. In J. Steele, S. Thorpe and K. Turekian (eds.) *Encyclopedia of Ocean Sciences*. London: Academic Press; 1255-1264.

Dragoo, D. and Wray, C. (1964). Hopewell figurine rediscovered. *American Antiquity*, 30, 195-199.

Draper, L. (1912). Sketch of Cornstalk, 1759–1777. *Ohio Archaeological and Historical Quarterly*, 21, Numbers 2 and 3: 245–62.

Duff, J. and Duff, A. (1934), trans. *Minor Latin Poets.* Vol. 1. This includes Calpurnius Siculus: Bucolica. LCL 284. Cambridge, MA: Harvard University Press.

Dull, R. et al. (2001). Volcanism, Ecology and Culture: A Reassessment of the Volcán Ilopango Tbj eruption. *Latin American Antiquity,* 12, 25-44.

Dull, R., Southon, J. et al. (2010). *Did the TBJ Ilopango eruption cause the AD 536 Event?* American Geophysical Union Meeting, 13-17 December.

Dull, R., Southon, J., Kutterolf, S. et al. (2019). Radiocarbon and Geologic evidence reveal Ilopango volcano as source of the colossal 'mystery' eruption of 539/40 CE. *Quaternary Science Reviews*, 222, 1-17.

Dumville, D. (1972-74a). The Corpus Christi 'Nennius'. *Bulletin of the Board of Celtic Studies,* 25, 369-380.

Dumville, D. (1972-74b). Some aspects of the chronology of the Historia Brittonum. *Bulletin of the Board of Celtic Studies* 25, 439-45.

Dumville, D. (1975-6). 'Nennius' and the Historia Brittonum. *Studia Celtica* 10/11, 178-95.

Dumville, D. (1976-7). On the North British section of the Historia Brittonum *The Welsh History Review*, 8, 345-54.

Dumville, D. (1977). Sub-Roman Britain: history and legend. *History,* 62, 173-92.

Dumville, D. (1984a). Gildas and Maelgwn: Problems of Dating. In M. Lapidge and D. Dumville (eds.) *Gildas: New Approaches.* Boydell; 51-9.

Dumville, D. (1984b). The chronology of De Excidio Brittaniae, Book 1. In M. Lapidge and D. Dumville (eds.) *Gildas: New Approaches.* Boydell; 61-84.

Dumville, D. (1985-1988), ed. *The Historia Brittonum.* Vols. 2, 3 and 7. Vol. 2 Chartres Recension; Vol. 3 Vatican Recension; Vol. 7 Sawley and Durham Recensions. Cambridge: Brewer.

Dumville, D. (1986). The historical value of the Historia Brittonum. *Arthurian Literature,* 6, 1-26.

Dumville, D. (1988a). Early Welsh poetry: problems of historicity. In B. Roberts (ed.) *Early Welsh Poetry: Studies in the Book of Aneirin.* NLW; 1-16.

Dumville, D. (1988b). Two approaches to the dating of the 'Nauigatio Sancti Brendani'. *Studi Medievali,* 29, 87-102.

Dumville, D. (1994). Historia Brittonum: an Insular History from the Carolingian age. In A. Scharer and G. Scheibelreiter (eds.) *Historiographie im frühen Mittelalter.* Wien/München: R. Oldenbourg Verlag; 406-434.

Durrett, R. (1908). *Traditions of the Earliest Visits of Foreigners to North America.* Louisville: Filson Club.

Ebbesmeyer, C., Okubo, A. and Helseth, J. (1980). Description of iceberg probability between Baffin Bay and the Grand Banks using a stochastic model. *Deep-Sea Research,* 27A, 975-986.

Egal, A., Brown, P., Rendtel, J.et al. (2020). Activity of the Eta-Aquariid and Orionid meteor showers. *Astronomy and Astrophysics,* 640, A58.

Ekwall, E. (1960). Concise Oxford Dictionary of English Place-Names. Oxford: Oxford University Press.

Eldjárn, K. and Friðriksson, A. (2000). Kuml og haugfé úr heiðnum sið á Íslandi (2nd ed., revised by Friðriksson). Reykjavík: Mál og menning.

Enterline, J. (2002). *Erikson, Eskimos and Columbus.* John Hopkins.

Epstein, J. (1980). Pre-Columbian Old World Coins in America: An Examination of the Evidence. *Current Anthropology,* 21, 1; 1-20.

Fell, B. (1980). *Saga America.* New York: Times Books.

Fell, B. (1983). Christian Messages in Old Irish Script Deciphered from Rock Carvings in W. Va. *Wonderful West Virginia,* March, 47, 1; 12-19.

Feininger, T. and Goodacre, A. (1995). The eight classical Monteregian hills at depth and the mechanism of their intrusion. *Canadian Journal of Earth Sciences,* 32, 1350-64.

Field, P. (2008). Arthur's battles. *Arthuriana,* 18, 3-32.

Foley, W. and Holder, A. (1999), eds. *Bede:a Biblical Miscellany.* Liverpool: Liverpool University Press.

Ford, P. (1977), ed. and trans. *The Mabinogi and other Medieval Welsh Tales.* Los Angeles: University of California.

Ford, P. (1999), trans. *The Celtic Poets.* Belmont, MA: Ford and Bailie.

Forsyth, K. and Thickpenny, C. (2016). The Rock Carvings. In R. Toolis, and C. Bowles (eds.) *The Lost Dark Age Kingdom of Rheged: the Discovery of a Royal Stronghold at Trusty's Hill, Galloway.* Oxford: Oxbow; 83-102.

Foster, B. (1989), trans. *Livy, History of Rome.* Vol. IV, Books 8-10. Loeb Classical Library 191. Cambridge, MA: Harvard University Press.

Foulke W. (1907), trans. *History of the Langobards by Paul the Deacon.* Philadelphia: University of Pennsylvania.

Fowke (1902). *Archaeological History of Ohio: the mound builders and later Indians.* Columbus, Ohio: Heer.

Francisco del Paso y Troncoso (1905) ed. *Bernardino de Sahagún: Historia general de las cosas de Nueva España.* Madrid: Fototipia de Hauser y Menet.

Frappier, J. (1959). Chrétien de Troyes. In R.S. Loomis (ed.) *Arthurian Literature in the Middle Ages.* Oxford: Clarendon; 157-91.

Fulford, M., Handley, M. and Clarke, A. (2000). An Early Date For Ogham: Silchester Ogham Stone Rehabilitated, *Medieval Archaeology,* 44:1, 1-23.

Gallagher, I. (1983). Light Dawns on West Virginia History. *Wonderful West Virginia*, March, 47, 1; 7-11.

Gardner, W. and Savory, H. (1964). *Dinorben: a hill-fort occupied in early Iron Age and Roman times*. Cardiff: National Museum of Wales.

Giles, J. (1847). *William of Malmsbury's Chronicle of the Kings of England*. London: Henry G. Bohn.

Green, T. (2007). *Concepts of Arthur*. Chalford, Stroud: Tempus.

Grooms, T. (2005). Ohio's First True Pottery. In B. Lepper, ed. *Ohio Archaeology*. Wilmington: Orange Frazer; 88-93.

Gruffydd, R. (1978). Canu Cadwallon ap Cadfan. In R. Bromwich and R. Brinley Jones (eds.) *Astudiaethau ar yr Hengerdd*. Cardiff: UOW; 25-43.

Gruffydd, R. (1982). Marwnad Cynddylan. In R. Gruffydd (ed.) *Bardos*. Cardiff: UOW; 10-28.

Gruffydd, R. (1989-90). From Gododdin to Gwynedd: reflections on the story of Cunedda. *Studia Celtica*, XXIV/XXV, 1-14.

Gudger, E. (1927). Fishing with the Otter. *American Naturalist,* 61, 193-225.

Guernsey, E. Y. (1942). The Culture Sequence of the Ohio Falls Sites. *Proceedings of the Indiana Academy of Science*, 51; 60-7.

Guest, C. (1849). Peredur the son of Evrawc. In *The Mabinogion from the Llyfr Coch o Hergest;* 297-383. London: Longman, Brown, Green and Longmans. First published in 1839 in a series as Part 2 of 7 parts.

Hakluyt, R. (1589). *The Principall Navigations, Voiages and Discoveries of the English Nation*. London: Bishop and Newberie.

Hakluyt, R. (E. Goldsmid, ed.,1885). *The Principal Navigations, Voyages, Traffiques and Discoveries of the English Nation*. Edinburgh: Goldsmid.

Hakluyt, R. (J. Masefield, 1939). *Richard Hakluyt: Voyages*. London: Dent.

Hamilton, F. and Brooks, E. (1899), trans. *The Syriac Chronicle, known as that of Zachariah of Mitylene*. London: Methuen.

Hammond, C. (1996), trans. *Caesar: The Gallic War*. Oxford: OUP.

Hanmer, M. and editors (1633). *Chronicle of Ireland: Collected by Meredith Hanmer in the Yeare 1571*. First printed 1633. Reprinted Dublin 1809.

Hanning, R. (1966). *The Vision of History in Early Britain*. New York: Columbia University.

Harvey, J. (1969), ed. *Itineraries: William Worcestre*. Oxford: Clarendon.

Hasegawa, I. (1993). Historical Records of Meteor Showers. In J. Stohl and I.P. Williams (eds.) *Meteoroids and their Parent Bodies*. Bratislava: Astronomical Institute of the Slovak Academy of Sciences; 209-23.

Haycock, M. (1983-4). 'Preiddeu Annwn' and the Figure of Taliesin. *Studia Celtica*, 18-19, 52-78.

Haycock, M. (1990). The Significance of the 'Cad Goddau' Tree-List in the Book of Taliesin. In M. Ball, J. Fife, E. Poppe and J. Rowland (eds.) *Celtic Linguistics: Readings in the Brythonic Languages for T. Arwyn Watkins.* Amsterdam: Benjamins; 297-331.

Haycock, M. (2007), ed. and trans. *Legendary Poems from the Book of Taliesin.* Aberystwyth: CMCS.

Haycock, M. (2013), ed. and trans. *Prophecies from the Book of Taliesin.* Aberystwyth: CMCS.

Haywood, J. (1823). *The Natural and Aboriginal History of Tennessee.* Nashville: Wilson.

Herbert, T. (1634 and 1638). *A Relation of Some Yeares Travaile, Begvnne Anno 1626.* London: Stansbury and Bloome.

Hieatt, A. (1992). King Arthur in William Lambarde's *Archaionomia* (1568). *ANQ: A quarterly journal of short articles, notes and reviews,* 5, 78-82.

Higham, N. (1994). *The English Conquest: Gildas and Britain in the Fifth Century.* Manchester: Manchester University Press.

Higham, N. (2002). *King Arthur: Myth-making and History.* Routledge.

Higham, N. (2018). *King Arthur: Making of the Legend.* New Haven: Yale.

Higley, S. (1996). Spoils of Annwn: Taliesin and Material Poetry. In K. Klar, E. Sweetser and C. Thomas (eds.) *A Celtic Florilegium. Studies in Memory of Brendan O Hehir.* Lawrence: Celtic Studies Publications; 43-53.

Hill, P. V. (1949-51). The coinage of Britain in the Dark Ages. *British Numismatic Journal,* 26, 3, 1-27.

Hogg, A. H. A. (1946). Llwyfenydd. *Antiquity,* 20, 210-11.

Hughes, D. (1987). History of Halley's Comet. *Philosophical Transactions of the Royal Society of London Series A,* 323, 349-367.

Hulbert, A. and Schwarze, W. (1910), eds. *David Zeisberger's History of the northern American Indians.* Columbus, Ohio: Heer.

Huws, D. (2000). *Medieval Welsh Manuscripts.* Cardiff: UOW and NLW.

Imoto S. and Hasegawa I. (1958). Historical records of meteor showers in China, Korea, Japan. *Smithsonian Contributions to Astrophysics 2:* 131-44.

Ingstad, A. and Ingstad, H. (1986). *The Norse Discovery of America.* V.1: *Excavations at L'Anse aux Meadows, Newfoundland 1961-1968.* V.2: *The Historical Background and Evidence of the Norse Settlement Discovered in Newfoundland.* Oslo: Norwegian University Press.

Isaac, G. (1998). Gweith Gwen Ystrat and the northern Heroic Age of the sixth century. *Cambrian Medieval Celtic Studies,* 36, 61-70.

Isaac, G. (2002). Gwarchan Maeldderw: A 'Lost' Medieval Welsh Classic? *Cambrian Medieval Celtic Studies,* 44, 73-96.

Jackson, K. (1945). Once again Arthur's battles. *Modern Philology,* 43, 44-57.

Jackson, K. (1949). Arthur's battle of Breguoin. *Antiquity*, 23, 48-9.

Jackson, K. (1953). *Language and History in Early Britain*. Edinburgh: Edinburgh University.

Jackson, K. (1953-58). The Site of Mount Badon, *Journal of Celtic Studies*, 2, 152-55.

Jackson, K. (1959a). The Arthur of History. In R.S. Loomis (ed.) *Arthurian Literature in the Middle Ages*. Oxford: Clarendon; 1-11.

Jackson, K. (1959b). Arthur in Early Welsh Verse. In R. Loomis (ed.) *Arthurian Literature in the Middle Ages*. Oxford: Clarendon; 12-19.

Jackson, K. (1963). On the northern British section in Nennius. In N. Chadwick (ed.) *Celt and Saxon:* Cambridge University; 20-62.

Jackson, K. (1982). Varia: II. Gildas and the Names of the British Princes. *Cambridge Medieval Celtic Studies,* 3, 30-40.

Jacobs, J. (1892), ed. *Epistolae Ho-Elianae: The Familiar Letters of James Howell*. Books II to IV. London: David Nutt.

Jarman, A.O.H. (1959). The Welsh Merlin Poems. In R.S. Loomis (ed.) *Arthurian Literature in the Middle Ages*. Clarendon: 20-30.

Jarman, A.O.H. (1988), ed. and trans. *Aneirin: Y Gododdin, Britain's Oldest Heroic Poem*. Llandysul: Gomer.

Jarman, A.O.H. (1989-90). The Arthurian allusions in the Book of Aneirin. *Studia Celtica*, 24-25, 15-25.

Jarman, A.O.H. (1991). The Merlin legend and the Welsh tradition of prophecy. In R. Bromwich et al. (eds.) *Arthur of the Welsh*. UOW; 117-45.

Jones, A. (1910). *The History of Gruffydd ap Cynan: Welsh Text with Translation, Introduction and Notes*. Manchester: MUP.

Jones, A. H. M. (1964). *The Later Roman Empire 284-602*. Vol. 1. London: Blackwell. Reprinted 1986, 1992 by John Hopkins Press.

Jones, E. D. (1965). The Reputed Discovery of America by Madoc ap Owain Gwynedd. *National Library of Wales Journal, XIV, News and Notes*; 122-4.

Jones, E. D. (1968-9). Madoc and the discovery of America, some light on an old controversy: Book review. *Welsh History Review,* 4, Nos. 1-4; 185-87.

Jones, G. (1986), ed. and trans. *The Norse Atlantic Saga*. Oxford: OUP.

Jones, H. L. (1923), trans. *Geography of Strabo*. Vol. 2. Books 3-5. LCL 50. London: Heinemann. First published in 1923 and reprinted in 1949.

Jones, H. L. (1949), trans. *Geography of Strabo*. Vol. 8. Book 17. LCL 267. London: Heinemann. Published 1932, revised 1935, 1949; reprinted 1967.

Jones, J. and Davies, W. (1837). eds. *Gwaith Lewis Glyn Cothi*. Oxford: The Cymmrodorion.

Jones, M. and Casey, J. (1988). The Gallic Chronicle restored: chronology for the Anglo-Saxon invasions and end of Roman Britain. *Britannia,* 19, 367-98.

Jones, O. (Myvyr), Williams, E. (Iolo Morganwg) and Owen Pughe, W. (1870). *The Myvyrian Archaiology of Wales.* Denbigh: Thomas Gee.

Jones, T. (1952), ed. and trans. *Brut y Tywysogyon or the Chronicle of the Princes: Peniarth 20 Version.* Cardiff: UOW.

Jones, T. (1955), ed. and trans. *Brut y Tywysogyon or the Chronicle of the Princes: Red Book of Hergest Version.* Cardiff: UOW.

Jones, T. (1964). The early evolution of the legend of Arthur. *Nottingham Medieval Studies,* 8, 3-21.

Jones, T. (1967). The Black Book of Carmarthen 'Stanzas of the Graves'. *Proceedings of the British Academy,* 53, 97-137.

Keller, M., Spyrou, M. et al. (2019). Ancient Yersinia pestis genomes from across Western Europe reveal early diversification during the First Pandemic (541–750). *PNAS,* 116, 25, 12363-12372; DOI: 10.1073/pnas.1820447116

Kimberley, H. (2014). 'Deacon' McCormick and the Madoc Myth. In R. Leeson, ed. *Hayek: A Collaborative Biography. Part III.* Palgrave; 201-13.

Kirby, D. (2000). *The Earliest English Kings.* (Revised edition). London: Routledge. First published in 1991 by Unwin Hyman, London.

Knight, B. (2013). Madoc International Research Association (MIRA). https://web.archive.org/web/20130920083118/http://madocre-search.net/MoreInfo.html

Koch, J. (1983). The Loss of Final Syllables and Loss of Declension in Brittonic. *Bulletin of the Board of Celtic Studies,* 30, 201-33.

Koch, J. (1985-86). When was Welsh Literature first written down? *Studia Celtica,* XX/XXI, 43-6.

Koch, J. (1987). *Llawr en assed* (ca 932) 'the laureate hero in the war-chariot': some recollections of the Iron Age in the Gododdin. *Études Celtiques,* 24, 253-278.

Koch, J. (1988). The Cynfeirdd Poetry and the Language of the Sixth Century. In B.F. Roberts (ed.) *Early Welsh Poetry: Studies in the Book of Aneirin.* Aberystwyth: NLW; 17-41.

Koch, J. (1991). Gleanings from the Gododdin and other Early Welsh texts. Bulletin of the Board of Celtic Studies, 38, 111-18.

Koch, J. (1994). Review of R. Bromwich et al. (eds.) The Arthur of the Welsh. *Speculum,* 69, 1127-29.

Koch, J. (1996). The Celtic Lands. In N. Lacy (ed.) *Medieval Arthurian Literature: a Guide to Recent Research.* New York: Garland; 239-322.

Koch, J. (1997), ed. and trans. *The Gododdin of Aneirin: Text and Context from Dark-Age Northern Britain.* Cardiff: University of Wales.

Koch, J. (2006), ed. *Celtic Culture: A Historical Encyclopedia*. ABC-CLIO.

Koch, J. (2013). *Cunedda, Cynan, Cadwallon, Cynddylan: Four Welsh Poems and Britain 383-655*. Aberystwyth: University of Wales.

Koch, J. and Carey, J. (2003), eds. and trans. *The Celtic Heroic Age,* (4th edition). Aberystwyth: Celtic Studies Publications.

Kübler, B. (1891). Commonitorium Palladii. *Romanische Forschungen*, 6, 203-37.

Kunz, K. and Sígurðsson, G. (2008), ed. and trans. *The Vinland Sagas: The Icelandic Sagas about the First Documented Voyages across the North Atlantic*. London: Penguin.

Laing, L. (2006). *The Archaeology of Celtic Britain and Ireland c. AD 400–1200*. Cambridge: Cambridge University Press.

Laing, L. and Longley, D. (2006). *The Mote of Mark: a Dark Age Hillfort in South-West Scotland*. Oxford: Oxbow.

LaMarche, V. and Hirschboeck, K. (1984). Frost rings in trees as records of major volcanic eruptions. *Nature*, 307, 121–126.

Larivière, S. and Walton, L. (1998). Lontra Canadensis. *Mammalian Species*, No. 587, 1-8.

Larsen, L., Vinther, B. et al. (2008). New ice core evidence for a volcanic cause of the A.D. 536 dust veil. *Geophysical Research Letters,* 35, 1-5.

Lecouteux, C. (1984). Die Sage vom Magnetberg. *Fabula*, 25, 35-65.

Ledger, P., Girdland-Flinck, L. and Forbes, V. (2019). New Horizons at L'Anse Aux Meadows. *PNAS*. Vol. 116, No. 31, 15341-3.

Leeds, E. (1933). The Early Saxon Penetration of the Upper Thames Area. *Antiquaries Journal,* 13, 229-51.

Leeson, R. (2014), ed. *Hayek: A Collaborative Biography. Part III. Fraud, Fascism and Free Market Religion*. London: Palgrave MacMillan.

Lepper, B. (1995). Tracking Ohio's Great Hopewell Road. *Archaeology,* 48, 52-6.

Lepper, B. (2005), ed. *Ohio Archaeology*. Wilmington, Ohio: Orange Frazer.

Lepper, B. (2011). *People of the Mounds: Ohio's Hopewell Culture*. (Ohio Historical Society). Eastern National.

Lesser, W. H. (1983). Cult Archeology Strikes Again: Case for Pre-Columbian Irishmen in the Mountain State? *West Virginia Archeologist*, 35, 2: 48-52.

Lewis, J. (1996). *Rain of Iron and Ice:* New York: Helix Books.

Lewis, S. (1968). The Tradition of Taliesin. *Transactions of the Honourable Society of Cymmrodorion*, 293-98.

Lhoyd, H. and Powel, D. (1584). *The Historie of Cambria*. London.

Liebermann, F. (1894). *Leges Anglorum: Londoniis Collectae.* Niemeyer.

Liebermann, F. (1903). *Gesetze der Angelsachsen*. Halle: Niemeyer.

Little, G. (1945). *Brendan the Navigator: an Interpretation*. Dublin: Gill.

Lloyd, J. E. (1911). *A History of Wales from the Earliest Times to the Edwardian Conquest*. Vol. I, pp. 1-356; Vol. II, pp. 357-771. London: Longmans, Green and Co. Second edition published 1912.

Lloyd, S. (2017). *The Arthurian Place Names of Wales*. Cardiff: University of Wales.

Lloyd-Jones, J. (1950-2). Nefenhyr. *Bulletin of the Board of Celtic Studies*, 14, 35-7.

Löffler, M. (2007). *The Literary and Historical Legacy of Iolo Morganwg, 1826-1926*. Cardiff: UOW.

Longley, D. and Laing, L. (1997). Bryn Euryn Hillfort, Llandrillo-yn-Rhos. *Archaeology in Wales*, 37, 88-91.

Loomis, R. (1927). *Celtic Myth and Arthurian Romance*. New York: Columbia University Press.

Loomis, R. (1941). The Spoils of Annwn. *PMLA*, Vol. LVI, No. 1, 887-936.

Loomis, R. (1956). *Wales and the Arthurian Legend*. Cardiff: University of Wales Press.

Loomis, R. (1959), ed. *Arthurian Literature in the Middle Ages*. Clarendon.

Loveluck, C. et al. (2018). Alpine ice-core evidence for the transformation of the European monetary system, AD 640-670. *Antiquity*, 92, 366, 1571-85.

Lynott, M. (2015). *Hopewell Ceremonial Landscapes of Ohio*. Oxford:Oxbow.

MacArthur, W. (1944). Famine Fevers in England and Ireland. *Journal of the British Archaeological Association*, 9, 1; 66-71. An appendix to 'Epidemics during the Anglo-Saxon Period', by Wilfrid Bonser.

MacArthur, W. (1949). The Identification of Some Pestilences Recorded in the Irish Annals. *Irish Historical Studies*, 6, 23; 169-88.

MacArthur, W. (1950). Comments on Shrewbury's 'The Yellow Plague'. *Journal of the History of Medicine*, 5, 2; 214-15.

MacCann, R. G. (2016). *King Arthur's Voyage to the Otherworld: Was Arthur killed in America?* Sydney: Imperator.

Mac Mathúna, S. (1985). *Immram Brain: Bran's Journey to the Land of the Women*. Tubingen: Max Niemeyer Verlag.

MacMillan, K. (2004), ed. *John Dee: The Limits of the British Empire*. Westport, Connecticut: Praeger.

Macoy, R. (1868). *General History, Cyclopedia and Dictionary of Freemasonry*. 3rd Edition. New York: Masonic Publishing.

Magnússon, Þ. (1973). Sögualdarbyggð í Hvítárholti. Árbók hins Íslenzka Fornleifafélags (1972), 5-80.

Mainfort, R. and Kwas, M. (1993). The Bat Creek Fraud: A Final Statement. *Tennessee Anthropologist*, 18 (2): 87-93.

Mainfort, R. and Kwas, M. (2004). The Bat Creek Stone Revisited: A Fraud Exposed. *American Antiquity*, 69 (4): 761-69.

Malone, K. (1925). Artorius. *Modern Philology*, 22, 4, 367-74.

Marko, J. (1996). Small Icebergs and Iceberg Fragments off Newfoundland: relationships to deterioration mechanisms and regional iceberg population. *Atmosphere-Ocean*, 34, 549-79.

Marko, J., Fissel, D., Wadhams, P., Kelly, P. and Brown, R. (1994). Iceberg Severity off Eastern North America: Its Relationship to Sea Ice Variability and Climate Change. *Journal of Climate*, 7, 1335-51.

Martindale, J. (1992). *The Prosopography of the Later Roman Empire. AD 527-641.* Vol. IIIB. Cambridge: Cambridge University Press.

McBeath, A. (2003). An Introduction to the Meteor-Dragons special. *WGN*, 31, 6, 189-191.

McCarthy, D. (1848). The voyage of St. Brendan. *Dublin University Magazine*, 16, 60-74.

McCarthy, M. (2002). Rheged: an Early Historic Kingdom near the Solway. *Proceedings of the Society of the Antiquaries of Scotland*, 132, 357-81.

McCarthy, M. (2004). Rerigonium: a lost 'city' of the Novantae? *Proceedings of the Society of the Antiquaries of Scotland*, 134, 119-29.

McClure, J. and Collins, R. (1994), trans. and eds. *Bede: The Ecclesiastical History of the English People*. Oxford: Oxford University Press.

McCone, K. (2000), ed. and trans. *Echtrae Chonnlai and the beginnings of vernacular narrative writing in Ireland*. Maynooth: National U. of Ireland.

McCulloch, J. H. (1988). The Bat Creek Inscription: Cherokee or Hebrew? *Tennessee Anthropologist*, 13 (2): 79-123.

McCulloch, J. H. (1993) The Bat Creek Stone: a Reply to Mainfort and Kwas. *Tennessee Anthropologist*, 18 (1): 1-26.

McMillan, R. (2006). Perspectives on the Biogeography and Archaeology of Bison in Illinois. In R. McMillan (ed.) *Records of Early Bison in Illinois*. *Illinois State Museum Scientific Papers*, Vol. 31, Springfield; 67-146.

Meyer, K (1895), trans. *The Voyage of Bran son of Febal*. London: Nutt.

Meyvaert, P. (1999). 'In the Footsteps of the Fathers': The Date of Bede's Thirty Questions on the Book of Kings. In W. Klingshirn and M. Vessey (eds.) *The Limits of Ancient Christianity:* Ann Arbor: Univ. of Michigan; 267-86.

Michael, J. (2004). *Ancient Kentucke Inscriptions. Prince Madoc: Fact or Fiction*. Louisville: Chicago Spectrum Press.

Mierow, C. (1915), trans. *The Gothic History of Jordanes*. Princeton: Princeton University Press.

366

Miller, F. (1916), trans. *Ovid: Metamorphoses*. Vol. 1, Books 1-8. Revised by G. Gould. Loeb Classical Library 42. Cambridge MA: HUP.

Miller, M. (1975). The Commanders at Arthuret. *Trans. of the Cumberland and Westmorland Antiquarian and Archaeological Society*, 75: 96-118.

Miller, M. (1975-6). Date Guessing and Pedigrees. *Studia Celtica* 10-11, 96-109.

Miller, M. (1978). The last British entry in the 'Gallic Chronicles'. *Britannia*, 9, 315-18.

Milner, G. (2004). *The Moundbuilders: Ancient Peoples of Eastern North America*. New York: Thames and Hudson.

Mooney, J. (1910). In F. W. Hodge (ed.) *Handbook of American Indians North of Mexico*. Vol.2. Washington: Smithsonian; 931-32.

Moore, J. (1961). The Ox in the Middle Ages. *Agricultural History*, 35, 90-3.

Mordechai, L., Eisenberg, M., Newfield, T. et al. (2019). The Justinianic Plague: an inconsequential pandemic? *PNAS*, 116, 51, 25546-554.

Morgan, R. (1857). *British Kymry or Britons of Cambria*. Ruthin: Clarke.

Morganwg, I. (1848), *The Iolo Manuscripts*. (ed.) Taliesin Williams. Llandovery: William Rees.

Morison, S. (1971). *The European Discovery of America: The Northern Voyages*. New York: Oxford University Press.

Morris, J. (1973). *The Age of Arthur*. London: Weidenfield and Nicholson.

Morris, J. (1978). Historical Introduction and End Notes. In Winterbottom (trans and ed.). *Gildas: the Ruin of Britain*. London: Phillimore.

Morris, J. (1980), ed. and trans. *Nennius: British History and the Welsh Annals*. London: Phillimore.

Most, G. (2018), ed., trans. *Hesiod. Theogony. Works and Days. Testimonia*. Loeb Classical Library 57. Cambridge, MA: Harvard University Press.

Muhlberger, S. (1983). The Gallic Chronicle of 452 and its authority for British events. *Britannia*, 14, 23-33.

Muir, L. (1968). King Arthur's northern conquests in the Leges Anglorum Londoniis Collectae. *Medium Aevum*, 37, 253-62.

Munson, C. and McCullough, R. (2004). *Archaeological investigations at the Prather site, Clark County Indiana: the 2003 Baseline Study*.

Munson, C., Strezewski, M. and Stafford, R. (2006). *Archaeol. Investigations at the Prather Site, Clark County, Indiana: The 2005 Survey and Excavations*. Indiana University-Purdue University at Fort Wayne.

Nansen, F. (1911). *In Northern Mists:* Vol II. New York: Stokes.

Napier, W. (2006). Evidence for cometary bombardment episodes. *Monthly Notices of the Royal Astronomical Society*, 366, 977-82.

National Geospatial-Intelligence Agency (2011). *Sailing Directions (Enroute) Newfoundland, Labrador, and Hudson Bay* (13th ed.) Bethesda: NGIA.

Nobbe, C. (1966), ed. *Claudii Ptolemaei Geographia.* Vol.2. Hildesheim: George Olms. First published in 1843 by Teubner.

Ó Faoláin, S. (2006). Dumnonia. In J. Koch (ed.) *Celtic Culture: A Historical Encyclopedia.* ABC-CLIO; 619-21.

Ogden, D. (2013). *Drakōn: Dragon Myth and Serpent Cult in the Greek and Roman Worlds.* Oxford: Oxford University Press.

Oldfather, C. (1939), trans. *Diodorus Siculus. Library of History,* Vol. III: Books 4.59-8. Loeb Classical Library 340. Cambridge, MA: Harvard University Press.

Olson, D. (1987). *The Legend of Prince Madoc and the White Indians.* Jeffersonville: Olson.

O'Meara, J. (2002). Latin Version: Translation. In W. Barron and G. Burgess (eds.) *The Voyage of Saint Brendan.* Exeter: University of Exeter; 26-64.

Oppenheimer, M. and Wirtz, W. (1989). A Linguistic Analysis of Some West Virginia Petroglyphs. *West Virginia Archeologist,* 41, 1: 1-16.

Pacheco, P. (1996), ed. *A View from the Core: A Synthesis of Ohio Hopewell Archaeology.* Columbus: Ohio Archaeological Council.

Padel, O. (1994). The nature of Arthur. *Cambrian Medieval Celtic Studies,* 27, 1-31.

Painter, G. (1995). The Tartar relation and Vinland map: an interpretation. In R. Skelton, T. Marston and G. Painter (eds.) *The Vinland Map and the Tartar Relation* (new edition). New Haven: Yale; 241-262. First ed. in 1965.

Pálsson, H. and Edwards, P. (1989), trans. *Eyrbyggja Saga.* Penguin.

Pálsson, H. and Edwards, P. (2007) trans. *The Book of Settlements: Landnamabok.* Winnipeg: University of Manitoba.

Parry, J. (1925). The Vita Merlini: Geoffrey of Monmouth. *University of Illinois Studies in Language and Literature,* 10 (3).

Parry, T. (1955). *A History of Welsh Literature.* Oxford: Clarendon.

Paton, W. (2010), trans. *Polybius, The Histories.* Vol. 2, Books 3-4. Revised by F. Walbank and C. Habicht. LCL 137. Cambridge, MA: Harvard University Press. First pubished in 1922.

Peckham, G. (1583). Sir George Peckham's True Reporte. In D. Quinn (1940), intro. and notes. *The Voyages and Colonising Enterprises of Sir Humphrey Gilbert.* Vol. II, Chapter VI. London: Hakluyt Society; 435-82.

Pennant, T. (1883). (J. Rhys, ed.). Pennant's Tours in Wales, I. Carnarvon: Humphries.

Pennar, M. (1988). (trans.) *Taliesin Poems.* Lampeter: Llanerch Enterprises.

Pennington, L. (2009). New Hoard of Roman Coins found on Ohio River near Louisville, KY. *Ancient American*, 13, 83; 46-7.

Pennington, L. (2010). Second Hoard of Roman Coins found along Ohio River. *Ancient American*, 14, 87; 34-5.

Perrin, B. (1919), trans. *Plutarch's Lives. Sertorius and Eumenes. Phocion and Cato the Younger*. Vol. 8. LCL 100. Cambridge, MA: HUP.

Pohl, F. (1961). *Atlantic Crossings before Columbus*. New York: Norton.

Prescott, W. (1973). *History of the Conquest of Mexico and History of the Conquest of Peru*. New York: The Modern Library. First published 1843.

Prufer, O. (1964). The Hopewell Cult. *Scientific American*, 211, 90-102.

Pugh, E. (1970). *Brave his soul: the story of Prince Madog of Wales and his discovery of America in 1170*. New York: Dodd, Mead.

Putnam, F. (1875a). Archaeological Explorations in Indiana and Kentucky. *American Naturalist*, 9, 7; 410-15.

Putnam, F. (1875b). Archaeological Researches in Kentucky and Indiana, with description of Salt Cave. *Proceedings of the Boston Society of Natural History*, 17; 314-32.

Putnam, F. (1875c). Archæological Researches in Kentucky and Indiana. *Nature*, 13, 319; 109–10.

Pyle, R. (1983). A Message from the Past. *Wonderful West Virginia*, 47, 1; 3-6.

Pyle, R. (1998). *All That Remains:* Morgantown, WV: Archaeol. Archives.

Pyle, R. (2004). An 8th century Irishman in West Virginia. *Ancient American*, 9, 56; 2-6.

Rackham, H. (1938), trans. *Pliny: Natural History*, Vol. 1, Books 1-2. Loeb Classical Library 330. Cambridge, MA: Harvard University Press.

Raffel, B. (1999), trans. *Perceval, the Story of the Grail: Chrétien de Troyes*. London: Yale University Press.

Rave, H. (1912). Curse of Yellow Hair. *Washington Post*, Sunday, 27 Oct. p. 3.

RCAHMW (1914). Royal Commission on Ancient and Historical Monuments in Wales. *Wales and Monmouthshire. Vol IV. County of Denbigh*.

RCAHMW (1921). Royal Commission on Ancient and Historical Monuments in Wales. *Wales and Monmouthshire. Vol VI. County of Merioneth*.

RCAHMW (1976). Royal Commission on Ancient and Historical Monuments in Wales. *Glamorgan. Vol I: Pre-Norman; Part III Early Christian Period*. Cardiff: Her Majesty's Stationers.

Rees, W. (1840), trans. *Liber Landavensis*. Llandovery: Welsh MS Society.

Rex, P. (2004). *The English Resistance: the Underground War against the Normans*. The Mill, Stroud: History Press.

Reynolds, H., Gates, C. and Glaholt, R. (2003). Bison (Bison bison). In G. Feldhamer et al. (eds.) *Wild Mammals of North America*. (2nd ed.). Baltimore: John Hopkins University Press; 1009-60.

Rhŷs, J. (1891). *Studies in the Arthurian Legend*. Oxford: Clarendon.

Rigby, E., Symonds, M. and Ward-Thompson, D. (2004). A comet impact in AD 536? *Astronomy and Geophysics,* 45, 23-6.

Roberts, B. (1991). Culhwch ac Olwen, The Triads, Saints' Lives. In R. Bromwich et al. (eds.) *Arthur of the Welsh*. Cardiff: UOW; 73-95.

Roberts, E. (2003). *Gwaith Maredudd ap Rhys a'i gyfoedion*. Aberystwyth: Canolfan Uwchefrydiau Cymreig a Cheltaidd Prifysgol Cymru.

Roberts, T. (1941-44). Y Traddodiad am y Brenin Arthur yng Nghaergai. *Bulletin of the Board of Celtic Studies,* 11; 12-14.

Romain, W. (1991). Evidence for a basic Hopewell unit of measure. *Ohio Archaeologist,* 41, 4, 28-37.

Romain, W. (2000). *Mysteries of the Hopewell: Astronomers, Geometers, and Magicians of the Eastern Woodlands*. Akron: University of Akron.

Romer, F. (1998), trans. *Pomponius Mela's Description of the World*. Ann Arbor: University of Michigan Press.

Ross, A. (1967). *Pagan Celtic Britain*. London: Routledge.

Rouse, W. (1940), trans. *Nonnos Dionysiaca: Books 1-15*. Loeb Classical Library 344. Cambridge, MA: Harvard University Press.

Rowland, J. (1990), ed. and trans. *Early Welsh Saga Poetry: a Study and Edition of the Englynion*. Cambridge: Cambridge University Press.

Rowland, J. (1995). Warfare and horses in the Gododdin and the problem of Catraeth. *Cambrian Medieval Celtic Studies,* 30, 13-40.

Rowley, R. (2005). *Historia Brittonum: History of the Britons*. Llanerch.

Russell, P. (2018). "Divers evidences antient of some Welsh princes". Dr John Dee and the Welsh context of the reception of Geoffrey of Monmouth in sixteenth-century England and Wales. *L'Historia regum Britannie et les "Bruts" en Europe. Production, circulation et réception (XIIe-XVIe siècle),* Tome II; 395-426.

Salzer, M. and Hughes, M. (2007). Bristlecone pine tree rings and volcanic eruptions over the last 5000 yr. *Quaternary Research,* 67, 57-68.

Sarris, P. (2022). New Approaches to the 'Plague of Justinian'. *Past and Present,* No. 254, ; 315-46.

Scherz, J. (1994). The Kingman Coins. *Ancient American,* 2, 7; 32-8.

Schmidt, C. and Sharkey, R. (2012). Ethical and Political Ramifications of the Reporting/Non-Reporting of Native American Ritualized Violence. In R. Chacon and R. Mendoza (eds.) *Ethics of Anthropology and Amerindian Research*. NY: Springer; 27-36.

Schwarz, K. (2016). The Great Hopewell Road: New data, analysis and future Research Prospects. *Journal of Ohio Archaeology*, Vol. 4, 12-38.

Seaver K. (1996). *The Frozen Echo: Greenland and the Exploration of North America ca. A.D. 1000-1500*. Stanford University Press.

Seaver, K. (2008). "Pygmies" of the far north. *Journal of World History*, 19, 63-87.

Sekhar, A and Asher, D. (2014). Resonant behavior of comet Halley and the Orionid stream. *Meteoritics and Planetary Science*, 49, No. 1, 52–62.

Severin, T. (1978). *The Brendan Voyage*. New York: McGraw-Hill.

Sharpe, R. (1995), trans. *Adomnán of Iona: Life of St. Columba*. Penguin.

Shetrone, H. and Greenman, E. (1931). Explorations of the Seip group of pre-historic earthworks. *Ohio Archaeological and Historical Quarterly*, 40, 343-509.

Sigl, M., Winstrup, M., McConnell, J. et al. (2015). Timing and climate forcing of volcanic eruptions for the past 2,500 years. *Nature*, 523, 543-49.

Sims-Williams, P. (1982). The Evidence for Vernacular Irish Literary Influence on Early Mediaeval Welsh Literature. In D. Whitelock, R. McKitterick, and D. Dumville (eds.) *Ireland in Early Mediaeval Europe: Studies in Memory of Kathleen Hughes*. Cambridge: CUP; 235-57.

Sims-Williams, P. (1990). Dating the transition to Neo-Brittonic: phonology and history, 400-600. In A. Bammesburger and A. Wollman (eds.) *Britain 400-600: Language and History*. Heidelberg: Carl Winter; 217-61.

Sims-Williams, P. (1991). The early Welsh Arthurian poems. In R. Bromwich et al. (eds.) *The Arthur of the Welsh*. Cardiff: UOW; 33-71.

Sipe, C. (2004). Stone Forts: Did Prince Madoc Build Them? *Currents of Change: Journal of Falls of the Ohio Archaeological Society*, 2, 1; 93-8.

Shrewsbury, J. (1949). The Yellow Plague. *Journal of the History of Medicine and Allied Sciences*, 4(1), 5-47.

Skene, W. (1865). Notice of the Site of the Battle of Ardderyd or Arderyth. *Proceedings of the Society of Antiquaries of Scotland*, 6, 91-98.

Skene, W. (1868), ed. and trans. *The Four Ancient Books of Wales*. Edinburgh: Edmonston and Douglas.

Slyfield, B. (2000). Five Years' Hell in a Country Parish. *The Horsham Society Newsletter, November 2000*; 64-5.

Smith, V., Costa, A. et al. (2020). The magnitude and impact of the 431 CE Tierra Blanca Joven eruption of Ilopango, El Salvador. *PNAS*. https://www.pnas.org/doi/10.1073/pnas.2003008117

Snyder, C. (1998). *An Age of Tyrants: Britain and the Britons A.D. 400-600*. Thrupp, Stroud: Sutton.

Snyder, C. (2005). Arthur and Kingship in the Historia Brittonum. In N. Lacy (ed.) *The Fortunes of King Arthur*. Woodbridge: Brewer; 1-12.

Spence, R. (2014). Donald McCormick: 2 + 2 = 5. In R. Leeson, ed. *Hayek: A Collaborative Biography. Part III*. London: Palgrave; 236-56.

Squier, E. and Davis, E. (1848). *Ancient Monuments of the Mississippi Valley*. Washington DC: Smithsonian Institution.

Squire, C. (1905). *Mythology of the British Islands*. London: Blackie.

Stancliffe, C. (1997). The Thirteen Sermons attributed to Columbanus and the question of their Authorship. In M. Lapidge (ed.) *Columbanus: Studies on the Latin Writings*. Woodbridge, Suffolk: Boydell; 93-202.

Stancliffe, C. (2018). Columbanus and Shunning: The Irish peregrinus between Gildas, Gaul and Gregory. In A. O'Hara (ed.) *Columbanus and the Peoples of Post-Roman Europe*. Oxford: OUP; 113-142.

Stenton, F. (1971). *Anglo-Saxon England. The Oxford History of England*. (3rd ed.). Oxford: Clarendon. First published in 1943.

Stephens, T. (1849). *Literature of the Kymry*. Llandovery: William Reese.

Stephens, T. (1893). *Madoc: an Essay on the Discovery of America by Madoc ap Owen Gwynedd in the Twelfth Century*. London: Longmans.

Stevens, C. (1941). Gildas Sapiens. *The English Historical Review*, 56, 353-73.

Stevenson, E. (1932), ed. and trans. *Claudius Ptolemy: The Geography*. New York: New York Public Library. (Reprint, 1991, New York: Dover).

Stoddard, A. (1812). *Sketches, Historical and Descriptive, of Louisiana*. Philadelphia: Carey.

Stokes, W. (1888), ed. Voyage of Mael Duin (Part 1). *Revue Celtique*, Vol. 9, 447-95.

Stokes, W. (1889), ed. Voyage of Mael Duin (Part 2). *Revue Celtique*, Vol. 10, 50-95.

Stone, W. (1865). *The Life of Joseph Brant, Thayendanegea*, II. Albany: J. Munsell.

Stothers, R. and Rampino, M. (1983). Volcanic Eruptions in the Mediterranean before A.D. 630 from Written and Archaeological sources. *Journal of Geophysical Research*, 88, 6357-71.

Tankersley, K., Meyers, S. et al. (2022). The Hopewell Airburst Event, 1699-1567 years ago (252-383 CE). *Nature: Scientific Reports* (2022) 12.1706.

Taylor, E. (1956). A letter dated 1577 from Mercator to John Dee. *Imago Mundi*, 13, 56-68.

Thomas, C. (1890). *The Cherokees in Pre-Columbian Times*. New York: N.D.C. Hodges.

Thomas, C., Carr, C. and Keller, C. (2005). Animal-Totemic clans of Ohio Hopewellian peoples. In C. Carr and D. Case (eds.) *Gathering Hopewell*. NY: Kluwer/Plenum; 339-85.

Thomas, H. (2003). *The English and the Normans: Ethnic Hostility, Assimilation and Identity 1066-c. 1220.* Oxford: Oxford University Press.

Thomas, N. (2000). The Celtic Wild Man Tradition and Geoffrey of Monmouth's "Vita Merlini": Madness or "Contemptus Mundi?" *Arthuriana,* 10(1), 27-42.

Thomas, S. and Conner, E. (1967*)*. George Rogers Clark [1752-1818]: Natural Scientist and Historian. *Filson Club History Quarterly,* 41, 202-26.

Thompson, E. A. (1980). Procopius on Brittia and Britannia. *The Classical Quarterly,* 30, 2; 498–507.

Thorpe, L. (1966), trans. *Geoffrey of Monmouth: The History of the Kings of Britain.* Harmondsworth: Penguin.

Thorpe, L. (1974), trans. *Gregory of Tours: History of the Franks.* Harmondsworth: Penguin.

Thorpe, L. (1978), trans. *Journey through Wales and Description of Wales.* Penguin.

Thrall, W. (1917). Vergil's Aeneid and the Irish Imrama: Zimmer's Theory. *Modern Philology,* Vol. XV, No. 8, 65-90.

Tierney, J. (1967), ed. *Dicuili: Liber de mensura orbis terrae.* Dublin: DIAS.

Tolley, C. (2016). Æthelfrith and the Battle of Chester. *Journal of the Chester Archaeological Society,* (ed. P. Carrington). Vol.86, 51-95.

Tolstoy, N. (1960-62). Nennius, Chapter Fifty-Six. *Bulletin of the Board of Celtic Studies,* 19, 118-62.

Tschan, F. (1959), trans. *History of the Archbishops of Hamburg-Bremen, by Adam of Bremen.* NY: Columbia University Press.

Tsu, W. (1934). The Observations of Halley's Comet in Chinese History. *Popular Astronomy,* Vol. 42, 191-201.

Tuczay, C. (2005). Motifs in the Arabian Nights. *Folklore,* 116, 272-91.

Turner, S. (1852). *History of the Anglo Saxons,* Volume I (7th edition). London: Longman, Brown, Green and Longmans.

Van Hamel, A. (1934). Aspects of Celtic Mythology. *Proceedings of the British Academy,* 20, 207-48.

Wallace, B. (2008). The Discovery of Vinland. Chapter 44. In S. Brink and N. Price (eds.) *The Viking World.* New York: Routledge; 604-12.

Wallace, B. (2009). L'Anse Aux Meadows, Leif Eriksson's Home in Vinland. *Journal of the North Atlantic.* Special Volume 2; 114-25.

Warner, E. (2003). Dragons as Meteors or Comets in Russian Folk Beliefs. *WGN,* 31, 6, 195-98.

Watson, W. (1926). *History of the Celtic Place-Names of Scotland.* Edinburgh: Blackwood and Son. Reprinted in 2004 by Simon Taylor.

Watts, V. (2004), ed. *The Cambridge Dictionary of English Place-Names.* Cambridge: Cambridge University Press.

Weets, J., Carr, C., Penney, D. et al. (2005). Smoking Pipe Compositions and Styles. In C. Carr and D. Case (eds.) *Gathering Hopewell.* NY: Kluwer; 533-52.

Whitaker, I. (1981-82). The Problem of Pytheas' Thule. *The Classical Journal,* 77, 148-64.

Williams, G. (1979). *Madoc: the Making of a Myth.* London: Eyre Methuen.

Williams, H. (1899), ed. and trans. *Gildas: Cymmrodorion Record Series,* No. 3. London: David Nutt.

Williams, I. (1932-3), ed. Marwnad Cynddylan. *Bulletin of the Board of Celtic Studies,* 6, 134-141.

Williams, I. (1944). *Lectures on Early Welsh Poetry:* Dublin: Dublin Institute for Advanced Studies (reprinted 1954).

Williams, I. (1951). Wales and the North. *Transactions of the Cumberland and Westmorland Antiquarian and Archaeological Society,* 51, 73-88.

Williams, I. (1968). *Poems of Taliesin.* Trans. J. E. C. Williams. This is Caerwin Williams' 1968 translation into English of Ifor Williams' 1960 *Canu Taliesin.* The poems are left in Welsh but the commentary and notes are in English. Dublin: DIAS.

Williams, I. (1980). *The Beginnings of Welsh Poetry.* Ed. R. Bromwich, (2nd edition). Cardiff: University of Wales. First edition in 1972.

Williams, I. M. and Smith, J. B. (2016), eds. *Cronica Walliae: Humphrey Llwyd.* Cardiff: UOW. First published in hardback in 2002.

Williams, J. (1792). *Farther Observations on the Discovery of America by Prince Madog ab Owen Gwynedd about the Year 1170.* London: J. Brown.

Williams ab Ithel, J. (1860), ed. *Brut y Tywysogion or the Chronicle of the Princes.* London: Longman, Green, Longman and Roberts.

Williams ab Ithel, J. (1862). *Barddas with Translations and Notes.* Vol. I. Llandovery: D. J. Roderic.

Williams, J. S (1842), ed. T. S. Hinde's Letter (30 May 1842). *The American Pioneer,* Vol. I, No. XI; 373-5.

Williams, S. C. (1937). *Dawn of Tennessee Valley and Tennessee History.* Johnson City, Tennessee: Watauga Press.

Williams, W. L. (1908), ed. *Itinerary through Wales & Description of Wales by Giraldus Cambrensis.* Trans. and notes by R. C. Hoare. London: Dent.

Winterbottom, M. (1972). Life of St. Edmund. In M. Winterbottom, *Three lives of English saints;* 67-87. Toronto: Pontifical Institute of Mediaeval Studies.

Winterbottom, M. (1978), ed. and trans. *Gildas: the Ruin of Britain and other works.* London: Phillimore.

Wise, R. (2003). A Disagreement Translating the Horse Creek Petroglyph. *Council for West Virginia Archaeology* archived paper at: https://cwva.org/pmwiki.php?n=Resources.Ogam

Wise, R. (2019). Solstice Observations at the Luther Elkins Petroglyph (46WM3). *West Virginia Archeologist*, 59, 1: 15-20.

Witte, K. (2006). In the Footsteps of the Third Spanish Expedition: James Mackay and John T. Evans' Impact on the Lewis and Clark Expedition. *Great Plains Quarterly*, 26, 2; 85-97.

Wood, M. (1999). *In Search of England*. London: Viking.

Woodward, S. and McDonald, J. (2002). *Indian Mounds of the Middle Ohio Valley*. Blacksburg, Virginia: McDonald and Woodward.

Woolf, A. (2018). Columbanus's Ulster Education. In A. O'Hara (ed.) *Columbanus and the Peoples of Post-Roman Europe*. Oxford: Oxford University Press; 91-102.

Yardley, J. (2020), ed. and trans. *Livy, History of Rome*. Vol. 6, Books 23-25. Loeb Classical Library 355. Cambridge, MA: Harvard University Press.

Yeomans D. and Kiang T. (1981). The long-term motion of comet Halley. *Monthly Notices of the Royal Astronomical Society*, 197: 633-46.

Yeomans D., Rahe, J. and Freitag, R. (1986). The History of Comet Halley. *Journal of the Royal Astronomical Society of Canada,* 80, 2: 62-86.

Young, S. (2009). *The Celtic Revolution*. London: Gibson Square.

Zhuang Tian-shan (1977). Ancient Chinese records of Meteor Showers. *Chinese Astronomy,* Vol. 1, Issue 2, December 1977, 197-220.

Ziegler, M. (1999). Artúr mac Aedán of Dalriada. *The Heroic Age*, Issue 1.

INDEX

A

Abbott, D. 134, 138
Adair, J. 349
Adomnán, 9, 257
Aethelfrith, 29, 91, 96
Aetius, appeal to, 33, 35
Ahronson, K. 155, 340
Aircol, 24, 100
Aladur/Mars, 14, 178–79
Alcock, L. 70, 327–28
Allen, M. 347
Alonso-Núñez, J. 340
Ambrosius Aurelianus
    historical, 23-24, 33, 35–36, 71
    legendary in Historia, 81
    in Pa Gur, 81
Anderson, A. 329
Andrews, R. 331
Aneirin, 79, 119, 121
Annales Cambriae (Welsh Annals), 10-11
Annwfyn, 149-170
Archfedd, 74
Ardd Nefon, 94
Arfderydd (Arthuret), 107–8, 111
Arfon, 48, 102, 330
Arjava, A. 343
Armstrong, Z. 308
Arnold, C. and Graham, C. 288
Arthur
    bard, Talhaearn, 119-125
    battle list 56–59
    battle vest, 47
    brother, Madoc 74, 249-50
    Christian, 10-11, 21, 177-78, 323
    death, 13, 82, 153, 173, 175–77, 181–82, 185–95
    death date, 205
    father, 97–103
    fortress, 39-41, 45-46
    grave, 175–77
    horsemen, 59
    king, 38-39, 70
    kingdom, 45-56
    men named after him, 9, 66
    mistresses, 47–48, 55, 87
    northern court, 20, 62
    parallels with Brân, 48-50
    Pharaoh, 38–39
    ship, 145, 150–54, 156, 165
    throne, 14, 70
    voyages, 141-46, 150-58
Artuir, 9, 66
Artur, 9, 66, 70–71, 327

Artur emended from Artir, 327
Ashe, G. 76–78, 86, 153, 219, 258
Athrwys ap Meurig, 73–75
Atwater, C. 307, 309
Aurasium, 211
Avalon, 3, 77, 111, 153
Awen, Tad, 120

B

Bachrach, B. 58, 331
Badon Hill, 11–12, 30–31, 34–35, 59, 67–68
Baillie, M. 129, 134, 199–201, 204, 337, 343
Baldwin, Archbishop, 221, 223
Bangor-on-Dee monastery, 17, 28–30, 45, 47
Bannog, 51
Bardsey Island, 252
Barinthus (Barrind), 3, 153, 257–58, 316, 348
Barnish, S. 198-99, 343
Bartrum, P. 8, 26, 48, 50, 74, 92, 100, 102, 212
Basingwerk, 221, 224, 226
Bat Creek Stone, 269–75
Becket, Archbishop of Canterbury, 222–23
Bedd Geraint, 9, 103
Bede, 23, 28–30, 58, 67–68, 90–91, 95–96, 113
Belisarius, General, 197, 210
Belle Isle strait, 157
Bernicia, 65, 89, 91, 96
Black Book of Basingwerk, 221, 224
Blamires, D. 338
Blitz, J. and Porth, E. 341
Bollard, J. 1, 165, 168, 322–23, 327
Borden, W. 284, 287–88, 349
Bowen, B. 225–26, 345
Bran, voyage of (Irish, early), 15–16, 153, 328
Brân the blessed (Welsh) 48–50, 143–44, 180–81, 184–89, 207
    Brân's battle, 49, 184, 207
    Branwen his sister, 48, 143–44, 148, 180, 186
Brant, J. 281–82, 289, 291
Braydon Forest, 59
Breeze, A. 59, 94–95, 144, 334–35
Brendan, 3, 15, 153, 156, 172, 215, 257–58, 263, 311
    Promised Land of Saints, 3, 257
Bricriu's Feast, 328

British minim, 312–15, 318
Brittany, 28, 76, 111, 206, 228, 282
Brittonic, 14, 17–18, 29, 40, 82
Brocmail (Brochfael) 29, 112–14, 119
Bromwich, R. 7, 10, 48–9, 59, 63, 69, 71, 92–3, 97, 102, 105, 191
Brychan Yrth, 99
Burgess, G. 258
Burgess, R. 34
Burkitt, T. and Burkitt, A. 59
Burks, J. and Cook, R. 160
Buttrey, V. 305, 307, 351
Bwrdd Arthur, 51, 54, 83, 93

C
Cadoc, 51
Cadwallon, 9, 26, 28, 90–96, 102, 183, 219
　Marwnad Cadwallon, 91–93
　Moliant Cadwallon, 94–96, 116
Cadwallon Lawhir, 100–102
Caer Dathl, 48, 330
Caer Nefenhyr, 20, 60, 138–9
Cai, 56, 81
　Cai's father, 56
　Cai's fort, 179
Camelot name, 45, 330
Camlan, 3, 11–12, 73, 111, 153, 175, 188, 191
Campbell, J. 254, 277, 280–81, 290
Carey, J. 266
Carney, J. 15, 328, 335
Cartier, J. 145, 157–59, 282, 317
Carwinley, 109, 334
Cassiodorus, 31, 198–99
Cat Coit Celidon, 57, 60
Catlin, G. 286, 349
Catraeth (Catterick) 6, 65, 115–16,
　battle location, 65
　Urien ruler of, 116
Caw (Cawrnur), 50–51, 87
　Caw's children, 50
　Arthur and Cawrnur, 51, 87
　Uthr and Cawrnur, 86
Celtic Otherworld, 14, 42, 212
Cessford, C. 65
Chadwick, H. and N. 9, 56, 66
Chadwick, N. 71, 88, 113
Chambers, E. 49
Chapman, P. 153
Charles-Edwards, C. 6, 236
Chester, 10, 12, 17, 28–30, 47–48, 58, 63, 114, 154, 226
Clark, G. 278, 280–81, 283–85, 288
Clark's Cabin, 283, 288
Clarkson, T. 334
Climate downturn, 197–207

Clube, S. V. and Napier, W. 129
Clwyd, river, 51
Cnoyen, J. 4–5, 141, 317, 325
Cnut, King, 192
Coe, J. and Young, S. 102, 128, 322–23
Coelbren, 75, 269–75
　Iolo's Barddas, 269, 271
　Coelbren letters, 269
Coit Celidon, 58, 60, 68
Columba, St. 9, 109, 206, 258
Commonitorium Palladii, 142, 338
Conwy, river, 47, 102, 222, 224
Cook Petroglyph Site, 350
Cornovii, 45, 330
Cornstalk, 278, 289
Cox, E. 284, 286–87
Crawford, O. 59, 331
Cronica Principium Wallie, 221
Cronica Walliae, 227, 240
Cú Chulainn, 16
Culhwch and Olwen, 60, 79, 81, 144, 170, 175, 179, 186
Cunedda, 26, 69, 87–90, 96
　Foundation legend, 88
　Marwnad Cunedda, 88–90
Cuneglasus, 17, 24, 30, 37–39, 41, 69–70, 72, 85, 97–98, 101–2
Cunliffe, B. 154
Cú Roí, 16, 328
Cydfan, 48, 74
Cymry, 92, 255, 290
Cynddelw, 217, 220, 244
Cynddylan, 7

D
Dafydd ap Gwilym, 99, 117
DAR (Daughters of the American Revolution), 308, 309, 347
Dark, K. 37, 39, 50–51
Davies, E. 241, 346
Davies, W. 10, 73, 327, 331–32
Deacon, R. 236-37, 242–51
Deathsong of Cunedda, 88-90
Deathsong of Cynddylan, 7
De Costa, B. 236, 346
De Excidio, 17, 27–31, 34, 36, 41–43, 78, 80, 82, 106, 321–22
Dee, J. 4–5, 141–2, 144–5, 215, 230–31, 233, 240–41, 251, 253, 317
Dee, river, 17, 20, 28–30, 45–7, 50–51, 63, 82, 88, 154
Deira, 65, 91, 96, 115
Devil's Backbone, 284–88, 291, 307
Devwy meadows, 46–7, 151, 154, 169
　Deva (Chester), 47
Dewing, B. 343–44

Dicuil, 155
Diemand, D. 340
Dinarth (Dineirth) 17, 40–1, 45–8,
51–2, 69, 82, 87, 100, 103, 120
Dinas Brân, Llangollen, 48, 50–51
Dinorben, 47–8, 82, 87, 100, 102,
120
Dragoo, D. and Wray, C. 342
    Wray figurine, 184
Draper, L. 350
Duff, J. and Duff, A. 210, 344
Dumnonia, 23, 86
Dumville, D. 10, 26, 30, 56, 65, 88,
94, 258
Dún Scáith, 13, 16, 18–19
Durrett, R. 280
Duvivier, E. (fake source by
Deacon), 237, 250–51

E
Eanfrith, 96
Edeirnion, 50, 88, 331
Edmund, St. 189–91
Edward ap John Wynn, 252–53
Edwin, 91–93, 95–96, 183
Egal, A. 133, 337
Eidin (Edinburgh) 4, 6–7, 20,
64–66, 83, 89
Einion Yrth, 17, 82, 85, 87–88, 90,
96–98, 100, 103, 323,
    Einion Yrth and Uthr, 103
    Einion Yrth/Uthr hypothesis, 100
Ekwall, E. 95, 334
Eleirch, 48
Eliffer, 108–9, 334
Elmet, 91, 113, 116
Elphin, 121, 208–9, 344
Enterline, J. 142, 145
Epstein, J. 301, 306, 309, 312, 351
Eta Aquariids, 132–37, 337
Evans, T. 8, 279
Evans, J. 254, 285

F
Fell, B. 261, 263, 269–70, 293, 298,
301, 312, 315
    Christmas translation, 263–6
Field, P. 10, 327
Finn (Irish myth), 79, 81
Foley, W. and Holder, A. 340
Ford, P. 1, 48–9, 180, 183
Forsyth, K. and Thickpenny, C. 64
Fort Morgan, 308–9
Foulke, W. 342
Fowke, G. 287
Frappier, J. 330
Fulford, M. 263, 348

G
Gallagher, I. 261–62, 267–8
Gallic Chronicles, 33–35
Galloway, 20, 58–61, 62–64, 67, 83,
103, 127, 139, 341
Garwen, 47–48, 55, 87, 100–101,
103, 323, 330
Garwyn, Kynan, 112–13, 119, 330
Geoffrey of Monmouth, 2–5, 86,
105–7, 110–11, 123, 148, 153, 175,
209, 221, 316, 324–25
    Arthur, 3, 77, 123, 153, 175
    Merlin, 105–7, 110–11, 324
Geraint, son of Erbin, 8–9, 103
Geraint, the seafarer, 246
Gerald of Wales, 4, 51, 111, 175, 221–
26, 235, 255
Gestae Arthuri, 5, 48–9, 142–5, 148
Gildas, 17, 23–43, 45–46, 50–51,
67–72, 80–83, 175, 204–5, 312–13
(Y) Gododdin, 6–7, 9, 12, 64, 73, 80,
82, 86, 115-6, 121
Gorchan Cynfelyn, 79
Gorddur, 6, 64, 66
Gorlois, 86, 334
GPC (Geiriadur Prifysgol Cymru),
97–99, 323, 328, 330
Great Ireland, 258, 260
Great Orme, 45, 51, 54–55
Green, T. 79–81, 212
Gregory of Tours, 37, 76, 80, 183
Grocland, 5, 141–42, 145, 317
Gruffydd, G. 26, 88–9, 91, 94, 102–
3, 120, 222, 224
Gudger, E. 162
Guinnion, 11, 57, 331
Gwalchmai, (Walwen, later Sir
Gawain), 60, 63, 78, 139, 219–20,
224, 331
Gwallawg, 112–13, 116, 335–36
Gweir, 149, 165–66, 169, 173, 318,
Gwenddolau, 109–10, 335
Gwenddydd, 108, 110–11, 334
Gwenhwyfar, 12, 50, 72, 74, 332
    Kroes Gwenhwyvar, 50, 331
Gwrgi, 108–10, 334–35
Gwynedd, 46, 88, 90–91, 93, 110,
191–92, 218, 221–22, 230, 241

H
Hakluyt, R. 338–39
Halley's comet, 130–33, 135–36,
138, 337
    MMR of Halley, 135
    MOID, 133
    intense Eta Aquariids, 137
    meteoroid clumping, 135

Hanmer, M. 236, 346
Hanning, R. 331
Hasegawa, I. 136, 337
Hawk Wing, 283
Haycock, M. 1, 15–16, 18, 43, 47, 59,
85–6, 88, 179, 208, 250, 322–3
Haywood, J. 307–8
Hennin Henben, 47-8, 82, 87, 98,
100-103
Herbert, T. 234, 346
Hesiod, 18–19, 129
Hieatt, K. 209
Higham, N. 34, 39, 41, 50, 76–7, 80,
149, 329–33
Higley, S. 1, 165, 322–3, 327, 340–1
Hill, E. 294, 296
Hill, P. 313
Historia Brittonum, 9, 15, 33–4, 58,
65, 67, 71, 73, 78–9, 109, 112
Historia Regum Britanniae (HRB)
3–5, 86, 106–7, 110–11, 209
Hopewell, 159, 162, 164, 172–73,
187, 253, 319, 341
  earthen mounds, 159–60
  otter pipes, 162–63
  use of pearls, 164
Horse Creek site, 266–67, 348
Howell, J. 233–34, 241, 253, 346
Huail, 50–51, 53, 331
Hulbert, A. 341
Humber, river, 58
Huws, D. 112

I
Iaen, father of Eleirch, 48, 330
Iaudas, 210–11
Ieuan Brechfa, 235, 246
Illtud, 80–81, 333
Ilopango, 202
Ingram, D. 232, 253
Ingstad, H. 192, 343
Iolo Morganwg, 216–7, 232, 237–8,
242–3, 246–7, 249, 282
  Barddas, 269
  fake language, 269–75
  greatest forger of Welsh, 75
  Iolo MS, 75, 237–38
Irish flooding 540 AD, 204–5
Irish language, 88, 166
Irish Otherworld, 149, 320
Isaac, G. 115-16, 129

J
Jackson, K. 39–40, 45, 56, 59–60,
80–81, 165, 168
Jarman, A. 6, 79, 327, 333–34
Jenkin ap Maredudd, 241

Jones, G. 258
Jones, J. 269, 349
Jones, M. 254, 279, 347
Jones, T. 47–8, 55–6, 175, 210, 242–
3, 246, 279
Jordanes, 76–77
Judgement Day, 18, 58, 130–31,
165–6, 197
Justinian Plague, 203, 205

K
Keller, M. 203, 342, 344
Kelly, Mary, 283–85
Kentigern, 108, 110, 334–35
Kernyw, 45, 82, 330
Kiang, T. 135, 337
Kimberley, H. 246, 251, 345–47
Kingman, F. 302–3
Kirby, D. 91, 94
Koch, J. 1, 14, 17–20, 28-9, 47, 59,
64, 89–97, 113, 115, 121, 149, 156
Kübler, B. 338
Kunz, K. 148, 258, 339

L
Laing, L. 45–46, 330, 332
LaMarche, V. 200
Lambarde, W. 338
Larivière, S. 162
Larsen, L. 200, 343
Lecouteux, C. 338
Ledger P. 192, 343
Leedham-Green, E. 145
Leeson, R. 242–43
Leges Anglorum Londoniis
Collectae, 145
Lepper, B. 160, 162, 164, 187
Lewis, J. 138, 254, 285
Lewis, S. 113
Lhoyd H. and Powel D. 211, 227–28,
230, 232-33, 235–36, 249, 253, 311
Lhuyd, E. 50–51
Liber Landavensis, Book of Llandaff,
73-74, 205–7
Liebermann, F. 145, 147, 209
Linnuis (Lindsey) 12, 57–58, 83, 324
Little Orme, 45, 47, 52, 55
Livy, 182, 342
Llamrei (Arthur's mare) 331
Llanborth, 8, 73
Llandrillo-yn-Rhôs, 40, 45
Llanfair Talhaiarn, (previously Tre
Talhaearn), 120
Lleawc, 150, 164
Lleminawc, 150, 164
Lleon, 17, 20, 47, 58, 182
  lorica of, 47, 181, 328

Llongborth, battle, 8
Lloyd, J. 10, 17, 24, 26, 78, 88, 99, 102–3, 166, 235, 320–21
Lloyd, S. 11
Llwyd, H. 227–31, 233, 236, 240, 251, 253
Llychlyn, 5, 144
Llywarch, 183, 217–18, 220
Llywelyn, 218–220, 222–224
Loch Ryan, 20, 59, 62–63, 83
Longley, D. and Laing, L. 64
Loomis, R. 1, 13, 78, 121, 320
Lundy Island, 246–48
Luther Elkins site, 261, 267, 293
Lydus, John, 31
Lynott, M. 341

M
MacArthur, W. 206
MacCann, R. 21, 25, 30, 39, 52–5, 62, 167, 195, 319
MacMillan, K. 5, 143, 145, 231, 241
Macoy, R. 270, 273, 349
Madoc, 74, 215–55, 269, 271–74, 279–82, 286–87, 307–9, 311
Mael Duin, 16
Maglocunus, 17, 24, 26, 30, 33, 36–38, 40–41, 69–70, 72, 100–103
   as Maelgwn, 88, 119, 123, 208–9
Magnetic rocks, 49, 142–4
Mainfort, R. 270, 349
Manawydan, 49, 59, 207
Mandan Indians, 285
Maredudd ap Rhys, 227, 234, 237, 238-40, 244, 253
Marko, J. 340
Martindale, J. 210–11, 344
Marwnad Cadwallon Cadwallon, 92
Marwnad Cunedda, 88, 90
Marwnad Cynddylan, 7, 9
Marwnat Uthr Pendragon, 85–6, 97–8, 102, 323
McCarthy, M. 59
McClure, J. and Collins, R. 183, 329, 333–5, 342
McCone, K. 15, 328, 341
McCulloch, H. 270, 302
McMillan, B. 161, 316, 318
Medrawd (Mordred), 3, 11–12
Meiron, 246–8
Melton, T. 295–98, 350
Mercator, 4–5, 141–3, 145, 317
Meredydd, 218–20, 222
Merlin (Myrddin) 3, 105, 107–8, 110–11, 193, 249, 324
   Merlin Ambrosius, 106-7, 111, 324
   Merlin Emrys – same as above.

Lailoken, Llallawg, 107–10, 324
   Vita Merlini, 110–11, 316
   Myrddin name, 107
   Poems attributed to him, 108, 334
Meurig, father of Athrwys, 70, 73–4, 80–81
Mexico, 230–31, 233, 235, 290
Meyer, R. 267–68, 298
Meyvaert, P. 155, 340
Michael, J. 197, 269–73
Mierow, C. 76, 333
Milford, Ohio, 160, 262
Milford Haven, Wales, 233–4
Miller, F. 79
Miller, M. 26, 34, 335
Milner, G. 341
Mirabilia, 74, 79–81, 224, 325
Mississippian culture, 287–91, 301
Mitochondrial DNA, 294–98
Moel Arthur, 56
Moel Fenlli, 56
Moelfre, 225–26
Moliant Cadwallon, 94, 96, 116
Monteregian Hills, 158, 172, 317
Montezuma, 231–34
   his speech, 233–4, 345
Mooney, J. 349
Moors (Mauri), 210-11
Morddwyd Tyllion (pierced thighs) 186-7, 342
Morgan, son of Athrwys, 74-5
Morgan (Morgen) le Fay, 111, 123
Morgan Library, 190-91, 194
Morgan, R. 233, 235
Morison, S. 157, 258, 340
Morris, J. 26, 30, 67, 70, 97
Morris-Jones, J. 120
Muir, L. 145–47
Munson C. 287–88, 350

N
Nansen, F. 260, 348
Napier, W. 129
Navigatio of Brendan, 3, 15, 156, 172, 257–58, 316, 327–28
Nefenhyr, 20, 138–39, 331
Nennius, 56
Nonnos, 18–19, 124, 128–29
North Wales founding legend, 87–8
Novantae, 20, 60, 138–9
Nyland, E. 348

O
Oconostota, 289–90
Ogam, 257, 260–64, 265, 267–68, 275, 298
   Ogam Letters, 260

Old Irish, 165–66, 264
O'Meara, J. 257, 327–28, 340, 348
Ortelius, 5, 145, 317
Oswald, 28, 91, 96, 183, 334
Owain Danwyn, 26, 70, 72, 101–2,
324, 329
Owain Gwynedd
  son Iowerth, 218, 220, 222, 224
  son Hywel, 222, 345
  son David, 219, 222–4, 234
  son Roderic, 222–4, 344–45
Owsley, D. 295–98

P

Padel, O. 35, 79–81, 212, 329, 333
Pa Gur, 59, 81, 333
Pa Gûr, 341
poem Pa Gur, 86
Palladius, 142, 267, 338
Pálsson, H. and Edwards, P. 259
Parry, J. 3, 94, 327, 335–36, 340
Peckham, G. 231–33, 249, 253, 345
Penda, 7, 90, 95–96, 183
Pennant, T. 50, 331
Pennar, M. 115, 117, 336
Pennington, L. 303
Pen Rhionydd, 20, 60, 83
Peredur, 108–10, 117, 187, 334
Plutarch, 153, 340
Pohl, F. 327
Prescott, W. 345
Procopius, 31, 197
Prufer, O. 161, 164
Pryderi, 49, 150, 165, 180, 207, 339,
342
Prydwen, 150–51, 153–54, 156, 165,
340
Putnam, F. 287, 350
Pwyll (father of Pryderi) 150, 165,
180, 207, 339
Pyle, R. 261–2, 267, 293–9
Pytheas, 154, 340

R

Rackham, H. 129, 337
Raffel, B. 342
Rave, H. 283–85, 349
Rechtur, 19, 59, 70
Red Book of Hergest, 8, 91, 108, 221,
226
Rees, W. 73–74, 205, 332, 344
Rex, P. 147, 339
Rheged, 89, 113, 117, 335
Rheon, 20, 59–60, 63, 67, 69, 83,
178, 180, 324
Rhinns, 64, 103, 139
Rhôs, 17, 26, 30, 39, 69–70, 82–3,
100, 102–3, 323
Rhydderch, 8, 109–10, 116, 335
Rhŷs, J. 78
Rigby, E. 200, 343
Riothamus, 70, 76–78, 324
Riryd, 220–21, 228, 233, 235–36,
246–48
Roberts, B. 86
Roberts, E. 237–38
Roberts, T. 56
Romain, W. 159
Roman coins in America, 154, 255,
301, 303, 305–9, 315
Ross, A. 330
Rowley, R. 333
Russell, P. 230, 237, 240–1, 345–6
Ruthin, 50–51, 53, 56, 179

S

Salzer, M. 138, 200
Saracens, 208–9, 211–12, 344–45
Sarris, P. 203, 344
Savory, H. 331, 334
Scherz, J. 303, 351
Scioto River, 159, 318, 340
Seaver, K. 260, 338, 348
Sekhar, A. and Asher, D. 135–37
Selyf, 91, 112–14
Severin, T. 153, 258, 327, 348
Sharkey, R. 184
Sharpe, R. 9, 327, 344, 348
Shetrone, H. 342
Sidonius, 76–77
Sigl, M. 201–3, 343
Silchester Ogam, 264
Sims-Williams, P. 8, 15–16, 40, 86,
156, 165, 168, 327–31
Sipe, C. 288, 296, 350–51
Skene, W. 1, 109, 334–35
Slover, C. 16, 328, 341
Smith, V. 202, 240, 258, 343
Snyder, C. 47, 69, 330, 332
Spence, R. 243, 346
Spoils of Annwfyn, 1–2, 13–17, 19–
20, 41, 46, 48–9, 121, 149, 153–5,
169–71, 176–7, 319–20
Squier E. and Davis, E. 160, 162,
253, 340–41, 347
Squire, C. 1, 78
Stafford, T. 295-6, 350
Stancliffe, C. 30, 329
St Christopher, 190, 195
St Edmund, 189–90, 194
Stenton, F. 96, 334
Stephens, T. 11, 215–16, 221, 229,
232, 235, 237, 243–4, 254, 269, 279
Stevens, C. 33

St Lawrence, river, 157–59, 172, 205, 281, 315, 317–18
Stoddard, A. 289
Stokes, W. 328
Stone, W. 281
Stone of Huail, 50, 331
Stothers, R. and Rampino, M. 343
St Peter, 226, 240, 248
Strabo, 122, 183, 210, 336, 342
St Teilo, 205–6
St Tyfrydog, 226
Synnott, E. 247–48

T
Talhaearn, 75, 82, 119–25
    father of inspiration, 82, 119–20, 123–25
    greatest sage, 124
    Christian bard, 20–21, 122, 131
    near Dinarth, 82, 120
Taliesin,
    historical, 112–120
    possible poems, 112
    Tale of Taliesin, 208
Taylor, E. 4, 49, 141–43
Teÿrnon (reference to Arthur), 180–81, 213, 341
Thomas, C. 273
Thomas, H. 343
Thomas, N. 335
Thompson, E. 207
Thorpe, L. 4, 51, 76, 148, 209, 226
Thule, 154–55, 340
Tierney, J. 340
Totten, N. 302, 306–7, 312, 315
Tribruit, 11, 57, 59, 342
Trusty's Hill, 62, 64
Tschan, F. 147
Tsu, W. 135
Typhon, 18–19, 128–29
Tywysogion history, 221, 224, 227–28, 245

U
Urien Rheged, 65, 75, 112–22, 183, 208
Uthr, 17, 69, 74, 83, 85–87, 97–103, 107, 250, 323, 332

V
Van Hamel, A. 78–79, 211
Vitalinus, 35, 97
Vortigern, 23, 33, 35–36, 38–39, 71, 97, 105–6, 111, 139
Vortipor, 24, 66, 100, 213
    Vortipor Stone, 25

W
Wallop, 33, 35, 97
Walweitha, 60
Walwen, 60, 63
Watson, W. 45, 59, 330–31
Watts, V. 330
Weets J. 184
Wells, D. 303
Welsh Annals, 3, 10, 12, 29, 67, 92–93, 108, 112, 173, 177
Welsh 'Bibles', 234, 279–80, 290
Welsh breastplates, 290
Welsh Indians, 232–35, 254–55, 279–80, 285–87, 301
Welsh Triads, 20–21, 29, 48, 60, 67, 83, 93, 246
Whitaker, I. 340
Willem's Madoc, 237, 242, 249–50
William of Malmesbury, 60, 63, 83, 255
Williams, G. 75, 216, 230, 235, 237, 249, 251, 253, 279, 285, 289, 301
Williams, H. 51, 329, 331
Williams, I. 58, 72, 75, 89, 94, 112–13, 119-21, 183
Williams, J. 226, 233–5, 249
Williams, J. S. 254
Williams, S. C. 308
Williams I.M. and Smith, J. 240
Williams ab Ithel, J. 269, 274
Winterbottom, M. 26, 37, 67-68
Witte, K. 285
Wonderful West Virginia, 261–62
Wood, M. 35
Woodruff, S. 281
Woods, D. 31
Woodward, S. 294–95, 297

Y
Yellow Hair, 283
Yellow Pestilence, 33, 73, 205–6, 212
Yeomans, D. 135, 337
Yrfai, 64–66
Yrth, 17, 83, 98–99, 103
    translated, 99

Z
Zhuang, T. 136
Ziegler, M. 71